ZOLAR'S
BOOK OF
ASTROLOGY
DREAMS
NUMBERS
AND
LUCKY DAYS

PRENTICE
HALL
PRESS

New York   London   Toronto   Sydney   Tokyo   Singapore

PRENTICE HALL PRESS
15 Columbus Circle
New York, NY 10023

Compilation Copyright © 1990 by Simon & Schuster, Inc.
It's All In the Stars Copyright © 1962 by The Illuminati, Inc.
Zolar's Book of Dreams, Numbers & Lucky Days Copyright © 1985 by Zolar

PRENTICE HALL PRESS and colophon are registered trademarks
of Simon & Schuster, Inc.

Library of Congress Cataloging in Publication Data

ISBN 0-13-984170-9

Manufactured in the United States of America

First Edition

This is a compilation of two previously published books, *It's All in the Stars* and *Zolar's Book of Dreams, Numbers, & Lucky Days*, by Zolar.

CONTENTS

BOOK I
IT'S ALL IN THE STARS

BOOK II
ZOLAR'S BOOK OF DREAMS, NUMBERS, AND LUCKY DAYS

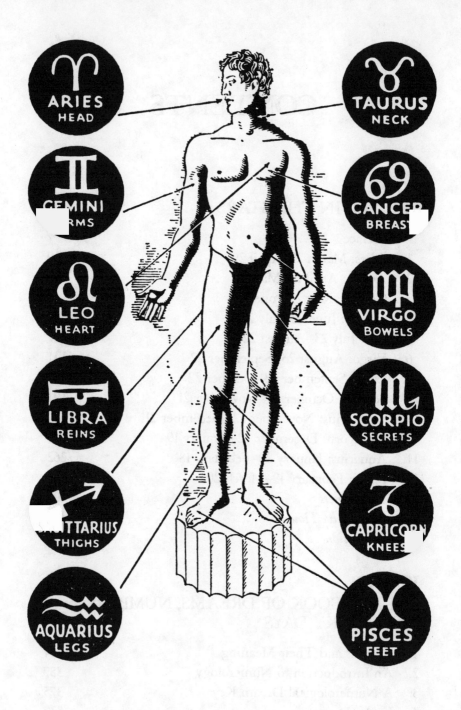

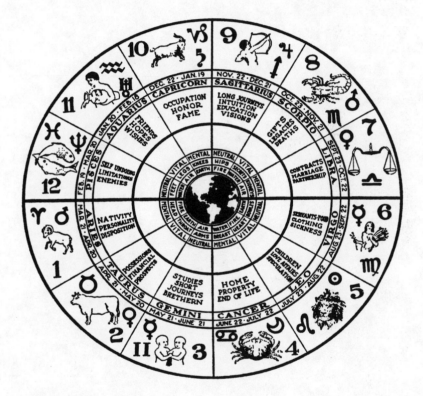

BOOK I

IT'S ALL
IN THE STARS

PREFACE

Astrology itself is a combination of two sciences: Astronomy and Correspondences. These two are related to each other as hand and glove. The former deals with Suns, Moons, Planets, and Stars, and strictly confines its researches to a knowledge of their size, distance, and motion. The latter deals with the spiritual and physical influences of the same bodies—first upon each other, then upon the earth, and, lastly, upon the organism of man. Astronomy is the external lifeless glove; Astrology the living hand within.

It was from the mystical land of Chaldea that the Egyptians derived their knowledge of Astronomy and Astrology. This knowledge was, fortunately, transplanted to fertile soil and flourished for untold ages under the fostering care of a mighty priesthood and colossal sacerdotalism.

From the fertile valley of the Nile, long ages before Abraham and his herdsmen wandered over the desert of Arabia, this sublime science of the starry heavens, with its priestly devotees, was carried by tidal emigrations over the Caucasus, across the arid steppes of Asia, through the wild mountain passes of Afghanistan and Tibet, to the burning plains of Hindustan, and thence spread by India's dusky sons among the Mongol and Tartar races of the still more remote East.

7

From the magical schools of lost Atlantis the sacred stream of learning flowed toward the rising sun into the regions of Central Africa, and from there to the coast, up the Persian Gulf to Chaldea. Then from the banks of the sacred Euphrates and the plains of Shinar the stream flowed backward (as though weary and seeking rest) toward its native home in the Western seas. It was detained upon its journey and found a temporary resting place in the wondrous valley of the Nile; but after changing its personal appearance somewhat and adopting the dress of its gifted patrons, it was again projected onward by the restless impulse of Egyptian enterprise, along the shores of the Mediterranean and Black Seas to the Caucasus, and thence eastward, as before mentioned, to the dreamy skies of India.

When we come to think of the imposing vastness and inconceivable beauty of the glittering worlds which stud, like jewels, the dark canopy of our midnight skies, we must admit that the contemplation of the shining heavens, with its myriad galaxies of starry systems and stretches of fathomless space, forms a sublime area of luminous study. There, alone, can we see something of the unbounded unity of the universe. But to the Occult student of Urania's blazing firmament, the shining constellations, with their cabalistic names and weird mythological histories, the glittering suns of these far-off astral systems, and the shining planets which belong to the same solar family as ourselves possess a deeper interest. Everything around us, save it, is in a state of transition. Besides the fleeting changes which the return of the seasons brings, the landscape around us changes its aspect every year. In fact, all around us is change.

But the gorgeous creations in the sky are still there: undimmed in brightness, unchanged in grandeur, performing, with unflagging pace and unvarying precision, their daily, annual, and mighty cyclic rounds.

Upon the same heavens, just as we see them now, bespangled with the same planets and with the same familiar stars, gazed the first parents of our race when they began and ended their pilgrimage upon this mundane sphere. The same constellations, Arcturus, Orion, and the Pleiades, sang together with the morning stars when the fiery foundations of our earth were laid, and they rolled in the fabled darkness over Calvary when the gentle Nazarene was slain. They are truly the only objects which all nations have witnessed, and all people admired. They are truly the only objects in the universe which have so far remained unpolluted by the finger of man. They presided at the Horoscope of our birth; they will sing the funeral requiem when we die, and cast their pale radiance over the cold, silent tombs beneath which we are ultimately destined to repose.

Before the aspirant can become an Astrologer he must make himself familiar with the general principles of Astronomy, and learn how to trace the external symbols of physical life, which are the phenomenal results, back into the stellar worlds of cause.

One must not expect the revelation of some divine, mysterious secret that will instantly convey the power of reading the past, realizing the influence of the present, and foreseeing the momentous events within the sphere of the future. On the contrary, one must expect nothing but a clear and concise statement of nature's immutable laws, which require both study and application to master. The principles involved and the ultimates evolved as the natural outcome of cause and effect can only be mastered and understood by devoting time and unprejudiced thought: first in learning the theory, and then in reducing that theory to practice.

Astrology does not imply fatality. On the contrary, probably two-thirds of man's so-called misfortunes are the result of his ignorance. Man, when ignorant of the laws of nature which control his existence and destiny, is somewhat like a lifeless log floating with the stream. It may be that the various currents of the river will carry him safely to the river's mouth, and launch him uninjured upon the great Ocean of Eternity. But it is far more likely that the winding course of the river of life will land him into a mud bank of trouble where he may stick fast for the remainder of his days; or, liberated by some stronger current, may again take his chances, either on future safety or on floating into some whirlpool of destruction.

When man understands the laws of his being, he is then safe on board a strong boat. He sees the whirlpools and mud banks of life ahead, and skillfully, by the use of his steering apparatus (the will), avoids collision. But it often happens that with all his knowledge and skill he cannot successfully battle against the mighty currents that oppose his way, simply because there are, in these days, too many lifeless logs of human lumber that are constantly throwing themselves with the swell of the current across his path. It must be at once apparent how infinitely superior the one is to the other, and how enormous the chances of success are upon the side of the one who has attained this wisdom—who, by study, knows himself.

"The heavenly bodies urge, predispose and influence to a great extent, but they do not compel." When we are ignorant of their power, we decide our actions to the best of our worldly knowledge, and we think we have free will in the matter. If we could only see the influences at work moulding our actions, we would realize that we are obeying the stellar powers with slave-like servility—not always wisely, but blindly and too well.

Under such a state of bondage the planetary influence would, indeed, be fatality. Knowledge alone is the great liberator of human suffering and social inharmony. Our self-control increases exactly in proportion to the extent of our knowledge. "It is the Wise Man who rules his stars, and the fool who blindly obeys them." Consequently, this Chaldean science of the stars, in order to be practically utilized, must be thoroughly realized; but when realized it will repay a hundredfold for the time and labor bestowed. It will give the student a tangible foundation whereon he may safely stand amid the wild and conflicting opinions of unbalanced mystics. In it he will find the key to the sacred sanctuary wherewith he may eventually unlock the doors of the temple and penetrate the mystic veil of Isis, there to behold the lovely form of the Goddess and to read the glowing verities of nature inscribed upon the imperishable scrolls of time and, if he have the will to seek further and deeper, the truths of eternity itself.

Astrology, in its purity, though forming a system of divination, is totally unconnected with either fortunetelling or sensitive, irresponsible mediumship. It is a divine science of Correspondences, in the study and application of which the intellect and intuition become blended in a natural, harmonious manner. They commence to vibrate in unison. When this union becomes complete, the ignorant man becomes the prophetic sage.

The Chaldean sages, when constructing their mighty system of sidereal Astrology, held to one idea throughout the whole of their philosophy. In order to penetrate the mysteries of God, they first sought out the mysteries of man, and then formulated a complete science of Correspondences. The human organism, so complex in its wonderful mechanism and so beautifully harmonious in all its parts, became their architectural design upon which they constructed the Grand Man of the Starry Heavens. The twelve Signs of the celestial Zodiac were divided into sections of the human frame, so that the entire Zodiacal belt was symbolized as a man bent round in the form of a circle, the soles of the feet placed against the back of the head. Each of the twelve Signs contains 30 degrees of space, the whole making 360° of a circle. The number 360, therefore, is the symbol of completion. When the 3 and 6 are added together they make 9, which is the highest unit we possess, and as such is held to be the sacred number of Deity. It is a triune trinity—3 times 3.

The mystical symbolism relating to the twelve Signs of the Zodiac and the human organism hold an important position in our system. In this connection, they form the body of the musical instrument, as it were, while the Sun, Moon and Planets constitute the strings. Our bodies then, when astrologically considered, are merely sounding boards for the celestial notes, struck by the starry musicians during the performance of their celestial opera. It will be noticed that the Sun and Moon, through mediumship of their Signs, Leo and Cancer, govern the two principal organs: the heart and stomach. When these are in harmony within the body the whole system is healthy.

More depends upon the position, aspect, and power of the Sun and Moon at birth than upon all the planets of our solar system combined. For this reason, the Sun and Moon are, to us, the transmitters of the stellar forces. They act in the capacity of astral mediums and cast their gathered or reflected potencies into our magnetic atmosphere, harmoniously or discordantly, according to how they are aspected by the malefic or benefic rays of the major planets.

Man has five positive points of projection and four positive centers of energy, thus making up the mystical nine, symbol of Deity. The head, hands, and feet are the five points of projection from which streams of vital force are constantly radiating. These are symbolized by the five-pointed star.

The positive centers of energy within the odylic sphere are the brain, the spleen, the heart, and the generative organs, while the great center of reception is the solar plexus.

When trouble or anxiety of mind crosses our path the first place we feel its influence is that part of the body called the pit of the stomach. This sensitive region is within the solar plexus. How many times do forebodings of coming trouble impress themselves upon this delicate center? As a rule, when we are in trouble we have no appetite. This calls forth inharmony in the various secretions of the body. Mental and psychic liberty depend, to an extent hitherto undreamed, upon the perfect freedom of the physical organism. Therefore, that which cramps, binds, and warps the body out of its natural proportion is fatal to any real spiritual progress, because it correspondingly inharmonizes the action of the odylic sphere. For this reason alone, India, Chaldea, and Egypt adopted the loose flowing robe, and the dress of all priesthoods is loose and ample to give them the very fullest measure of physical freedom.

When we regard the astral structure of man and closely examine his organism, we see that he forms a beautiful oval or egg-shaped figure, the narrow end being the feet, the broad end being the brain. This oval form constitutes the magnetic atmosphere, or the odylic sphere of the person, and consists of seven concentric rays of force, each of which has a direct affinity with the seven creative principles of nature, and therefore corresponds in color to the seven prismatic rays of the solar spectrum. Each zone or ring exercises a peculiar power of its own, and is pure or impure according to its state of luminosity. When mediumistic clairvoyants assert that such and such a particular color denotes a pure and benevolent person or one who is depraved and sinful, they assert that which is untrue, for each color has a special quality of its own—purity and impurity depending entirely upon the brightness of its tint. For this reason, the animal passions, when exercised, dull and becloud the soul sphere, while the exercise of the spiritual faculties illuminate. The brain center is represented by a Sun, the feet by a crescent Mòon, and the three secondary centers of force by stars.

From these colors are formed every conceivable shade and tint in the infinite variety of combinations found in the infinite variety of human beings; each and all depend upon the ever-changing positions of the stars, and also upon the corresponding magnetic states of our atmosphere at their respective moments of birth. The color and magnetic polarity of this odylic sphere are fixed, quick as lightning's flash, at the first moment of our separate material existence. This true moment is, generally, when the umbilical cord is severed and the child exists as a separate being, independent of its mother. Until that time the body is polarized by the soul force of its parent, and the planets can only influence it by reflex action from the mother's organism. But when the tie is severed, the lungs become inflated with the magnetic atmosphere, charged with the stellar influx, and in an instant the whole organism thrills with the vibrations of celestial power. These vibrations produce, in each of the concentric rings of the sphere, the exact tint and shade of color corresponding to the harmonious or discordant rays of the heavens at that time.

The vibrations, once in action, retain their special polarity for the whole tenor of earthly existence. They form the key note of the musical instrument which is ever sounding forth the harmony or discord of its material destiny. This key note is either high or low according to the particular influences which may be operating upon it at the time. At one time the life forces may be so low that the note will be too faint for the most sensitive to detect; at other times the throbbing pulsations of life will be so strong with the physical vitality that it will swell into the highest octave, and launch forth such potent health-giving vibrations as to affect other bodies near it, and draw from them responsive vibrations, thus giving life and health to others in harmony with, but weaker than, itself. But should the bodies with which it comes in contact be naturally antagonistic to it, in temperament and magnetic polarity, then, instead of responsive harmony, their contact will produce fierce jarring commotions of discord to the detriment of both, the weaker being the greater sufferer.

The action and interaction of planetary influx upon the human being after birth is determined upon the same lines. When a planet, by its progressive motion, reaches a point on the sphere where it forms an inharmonious angle with the angular vibrations set in motion at birth, magnetic discord is produced. When this magnetic storm awakens and sets in motion the cosmic and other elementals corresponding in their nature to the primary cause, external misfortune and trouble are the material results, and vice versa should the planets form benefic rays. This is the true secret of planetary influence as concerns good and bad luck. It is planetary harmony or discord.

It is utterly impossible for antagonistic natures to benefit each other mentally, no matter how good or pure they as individuals may be. To attempt to do this is like trying to make oil and water harmonize. This is the true secret of the Astrologer's lack of success with certain individuals.

For example, any person born under and controlled by the planet Mars, which corresponds to the element of fire, will prove antagonistic by nature to anybody and everybody who is governed by the planet Saturn. Their personalities will not blend and mingle. The most gentle and loving spirit that it is possible for the Astrologer to exercise under such circumstances will recoil from the odylic sphere of the other like a thunderbolt.

At this stage it is necessary to explain several matters of great importance in forming a true conception of astral law. One must not suppose that the planets are the sole cause of the fortunes and misfortunes which fall to the lot of mankind generally. This is by no means the case, for the primary cause has its origin within the soul sphere of the parents. The sexual relationship between man and woman has its laws, its harmonies and discords. It is man's duty to investigate and know these laws, especially when we bear in mind the fact that there is neither morality nor sentiment in the cold inflexible justice of nature.

It is equally in accordance with the same immutable laws that every species of crime is born into the world. When inflamed passions and cruel thoughts are latent within the parents, and remain uncontrolled by the higher self during the conjugal union, we must not be surprised if a child with a similar nature is conceived. When such is the case there is no benevolent God to graciously interfere and prevent a criminal from being launched upon society. Only when the matters are harmonious can that which we term good become manifest upon the earth.

The stars and planets are the magnetic instruments of the nine creative principles. They influence externally, by their attractive sympathies and repulsive antipathies, the cosmic life forces and physical organisms of precisely the same objects, which, in the realm of spirits, are controlled by their celestial progenitors. By this we mean that the various physical orbs called planets, stars, etc., act as so many magnetic centers. They are magnetic by solar induction.

The Sun itself is not magnetic but electrically positive. This mighty force acts upon the planets in precisely the way an electric current acts upon iron. When a piece of iron is charged with electricity it becomes at once a magnet, its power depending first upon its mass and secondly upon the strength of intensity of the electric current. Without this current the iron ceases to be a magnet. Remove the Sun from our system and the planets would immediately lose their peculiar physical influence.

The sum total of those powers which we term "planetary influence" is contained within the potentiality of the Solar Ray. But when so united, as primal cosmic force, the action of this Solar Ray upon the human organism and its material destiny is neither harmonious nor discordant, fortunate nor unfortunate. To become potent in special directions, it is necessary for this solar force to become refracted and resolved into its active attributes. There are nine of them, to which each is allotted a single attribute or principle, each according to its peculiar nature and affinity. While the solar orb itself retains but one active energy whose potency is embraced within the orange ray of the spectrum, these planetary bodies, having become magnetically charged with their own special energy, are powerful radiators of the same attribute which they have received from their solar parent. These energies possess a distinctive motion and potency, each peculiar to itself, which when externalized upon man's internal nature, produce a marked contrast in his mental and physical characteristics.

It is an ancient theory that the shepherds during the silent watches of the night, having no other objects to contemplate than the view which the heavens above presented, soon began to divide the firmament of stars into particular constellations, according to how they adjoined each other. They filled the heavens with symbolical objects.

By this division, the stars were easily distinguished from each other; and by the help of the celestial globe on which the constellations are delineated, any particular star could easily be found in the heavens; and the most outstanding stars were placed in such parts of the constellations as are most readily distinguished.

The heavens were thus divided into three parts:

1—The Zodiac, which is a great circle extending around the heavens, nearly sixteen degrees broad, so as to take in the different orbits of the planets, as well as that of the earth's satellite, the Moon, in the middle of which is the Ecliptic or Path of the Sun.

2—All that region of the heavens which is on the north side of the Zodiac, containing twenty-one constellations.

3—The whole region on the south side, which contains fifteen constellations.

Astrologers, however, confine their observations to only twelve, which are denominated by the twelve Signs of the Zodiac. These Signs answer to twelve periods of the year.

Astrologers further divide each Sign into three parts of ten degrees each, and for closer observation, each degree or birthdate is delineated as to character and destiny.

We shall now consider the influence of the Sun's apparent passage through the twelve Signs of the Zodiac, caused by the earth's movements around the Sun. From the Sun's position each day we may judge the contrast between those born from December to June, and those born between July and the end of November. We should find that the longest livers are born in March, April, and May, so a great majority will be found to have their natal day in these months. On the other hand, a majority of the short-lived population will be found to be born during the months of August, September, and October. This is only true on general principles and does not apply to any one individual Horoscope; in fact, the remarks in reference to the four Triplicities will also apply here. The increase of the Solar Light simply governs the vitalizing capacity of the race and not the individual.

Everything in nature, though constituting a Trinity in itself, possesses a fourfold application when viewed from the external plane. At least, we find this fourfoldness a truth so far as "the things of Earth" are concerned and, therefore, by the laws of Correspondences, the same application must hold true in regard to the celestial objects in the heavens. The Hermetic rule is a very precise rule upon this: "As on earth, so in the sky."

In the following pages I am going to delineate the twelve Signs of the Zodiac, based upon the Sun's apparent progression through the 360° of the Zodiac. These are the most comprehensive astrological readings possible when the time, day, year, and place of birth are not known.

They should not be confused with a personal Horoscope, which can only be prepared when the time, day, month, year, and place of birth is known.

The wise men of Chaldea inspected the beautiful constellations of heaven, and learned therefrom the mighty secrets of the soul's origin and destiny, as well as the material details of their physical lives. The same book of nature is open now as then, but only the pure in heart can read its pages and trace the mystical chain of life from nature through the stars.

—Zolar

ARIES

MARCH 21—APRIL 20

T<small>HE</small> <small>SIGN</small> <small>ARIES</small> in its symbolical aspect represents the sacrifice. The flocks and herds bring forth their young during the portion of the year that the Sun occupies this Sign. The symbol of the Sign is the Ram.

The Ram also symbolizes Spring, when light and love, symbolized by the Sun, are bestowed upon the sons of the Earth. The Sun once more has gained victory over the realms of winter. The Sign Aries represents the head and brains of the Grand Man of the Cosmos.

The gems of this Sign are the amethyst and diamond.

The fortunate day is Tuesday.

Fortunate numbers are seven and six.

The colors are shades of bright red.

Best locations for success are large cities.

Aries is the first and highest emanation of the fiery Triplicity, and is located in the constellation of the Planet Mars. It radiates an influence which is sharp, energetic, thoughtless, intrepid, and fierce. It is without either fear or timidity—an influence which is free with everything and everybody.

Addressing an Aries, I would say: You have an active and dynamic personality. The expression which you give to your

19

mind and emotions determines the actual degree of personal, social, and economic progress and success you will experience in life. You have natural, charming manners and good mental power; you are fond of having others look up to you. You have the happy faculty of exercising diplomacy to swing others toward interesting themselves in you or acting upon your ideas and suggestions. Courageous to the point of daring, you possess an active spirit of adventure and enterprise. By nature you are restless and fond of all sorts of activity. You will do well to cultivate an understanding of your adventuresome nature. Avoid engaging in unwise and risky or hazardous ventures. Under ordinary circumstances, you display an affectionate, courteous, and generous disposition. You are often inclined to be too generous for your own good, particularly when your personal feelings and emotions are aroused. This disposition may lead you to be quite generous to people who may not be deserving while you neglect those who should receive more consideration.

You are quite sensitive emotionally. You have a quick temper and can be easily angered at little things that could be straightened out with a few seconds of logical thinking. *It is one thing to have a quick temper and another to let it rule you.*

You are inclined to hold a grudge. By nature you are aggressive, self-willed and determined. You have the type of personality and temperament that can make or break your own destiny. Many of your personal misunderstandings and difficulties arise because you have an impulsive tendency to hurry and be impatient. *Learn to be more patient with yourself and with others.*

You love action, and you will be wise if you will apply some thought to your own interesting nature. You are an independent thinker, but this does not mean that you are always right or logical in your thinking. The most important thing for you to guard against is a tendency to judge matters according to your personal feelings and emotions, especially when you are upset. If you will adhere to the principles of sound reasoning, you will overcome intolerance and prejudiced attitudes.

You are capable of mentally grasping and understanding the minute details of a proposition before the average individual has given the matter much thought. The only drawback to such quick perception is that you are apt, at times, to become over-confident and neglect important details. Quick perception is essential to your particular type of personality. Your thought and action shows good coordination between mind and body and is essential to your progress. Your restless and aspiring mentality shows an active imagination. For you to accomplish anything, you must learn to use your imagination. You are capable of thinking up original ideas, and have the ability to carry them to practical conclusions. You have the ability to make some of your daydreams a reality. You are naturally very studious of things that interest you. Your particular type of personality is dependent upon a good memory, since your venturesome nature inclines you to face many and varying situations in life.

You are capable of acquiring and retaining a great amount of knowledge without applying much effort. This capacity is an asset and it will aid you to increase the power and influence of your personality. It helps to make you an interesting and witty conversationalist and will prove valuable in whatever line of work or business you choose to follow.

Your greatest difficulty is an inclination to act on impulse. You must carefully investigate your impulsive ideas before acting on them. Do your best to determine the logical outcome of an impulsive idea before you act. Thus, you may not act at all and so wisely save yourself from financial loss or personal disillusionment.

You have within yourself the Voice of Intuition.

It will give you foresight and help you master many difficult problems and obstacles in the course of life. Intuition can provide you with the happy faculty of divining the causes of your failures and help you eliminate them, thus enabling you to live a progressively more successful life.

You also have the Power of Inspiration within you.

There are times when you are inspired to do certain things. Your difficulty will be discriminating between ordinary impulses and an inspired idea.

Very few persons really understand the true intensity of the mental activity of those born under Aries. There are times when you may be called rash and impetuous. These charges, if you are honest with yourself, must be, at times, admitted as true. It is also true that you cannot stifle your individuality which is manifest in everything you do. You can, by an effort of will, express, direct, and apply your mental efforts and energy in a wise and progressive manner. Because of the intensity of your mental, emotional, and physical activities, give thought to your diet and your health. You are inclined to burn up more mental and physical energy than the average individual. *Fresh air, sunshine, good home surroundings, proper diet, relaxation, and rest should enable you to avoid many ailments common to persons of your temperament.*

Your Sign presides over the head and face—common head colds should be guarded against in order to avoid serious complications. The eyes should receive attention and should not be overworked. The teeth should be looked after carefully at all times. Colds are more apt to affect the sinuses and throat than the chest. Exercise moderation in drinking and eating, as the kidneys may become affected. Most of your ailments will be of an acute, rather than a chronic nature. Chronic ailments with Aries people are usually the result of sheer neglect. Avoid mental, emotional, nervous, and physical strain after the middle years of your life. *Aries are generally born with a good physical constitution and good recuperative powers.*

It appears that there will be more than one outstanding love affair in your life. *Emotionally, you are affectionate, tender, and inclined to passion.* You are unusually sensitive in love matters; you must guard against unreasonable jealousy. Avoid too great a mental and emotional domination over the object of your affections, and your love life will be much happier and more harmonious. Disappointments in love are indicated during the early twenties and at about the thirtieth year. Uncertainty and instability in your home life and domestic affairs are also indicated during the first half of your life, because of your adventuresome nature. You love and respect your relatives, but you desire that they recognize your individuality. In the later years of life you will become more settled in matters that pertain to home life and family affairs. You desire to have your home in a prominent location.

Indications point to considerable love of pleasure, which is expressed in games, sports, adventures, and travels. You have a great appreciation of the beauties of nature. You enjoy reading and the theatre.

You are aggressive, energetic, and have a determined nature with qualities that will enable you to follow several vocations. Your rise in life will be gradual and deliberate rather than spontaneous. The personality and mental make-up of the average Aries qualifies you for medicine, law, teaching, construction work, electrical engineering, aviation, mechanics, stage and screen work, accounting, merchandising—in fact, for most type of work you might desire to do, because you have natural organizing and executive ability, and can be trusted with important commissions and responsibilities. You are loyal to your work. Your independent nature does not qualify you for partnership ventures unless you have full freedom to work things out in your own way. *Enter into business for yourself.* Remember, there will be times in the beginning when you must guard against becoming discouraged too easily.

There are indications that you can be fairly successful in money matters. Your earning capacity should be good, but you are inclined to be a generous spender. You desire to have the best money can buy, and to spend money more for temporary than for permanent benefit. *Your money, like your mind, needs careful handling.* During favorable financial periods of your life you will find it to your advantage to make conservative investments. Your adventuresome nature inclines you toward speculation and gambling. You may not be aware of it, but in such matters you are inclined to "stack the cards against yourself" because of your impulsiveness. You will obtain true wisdom when you cease taking chances and spending to suit your personal whims, fancies, and impulses. Be conservative in financial matters and your money will take care of you. There is no other road to travel in order to attain financial security and success. If and when you make investments, avoid speculative issues and get-rich-quick schemes.

You are exceedingly loyal to those you consider close friends, and will stand up for them forcefully if necessary. You are inclined to be generous with close friends and associates, and will aid them in every manner possible when they are in difficulties. Your general attitude in social matters, aside from friendships, is variable. There are times when you enjoy being with a great number of people, but in the main you prefer the companionship of a few loyal friends. In society you are capable of commanding the respect and good will of many, and have the ability to lead in your own set.

You have all the essential mental, emotional, and physical faculties and qualities which should enable you to make a reasonable success of your life. Understand these faculties in order that you may apply them with wisdom. It is up to you to direct yourself and your energy for progress. Pay attention to your shortcomings. Do not be afraid of them. Learn to know them and seek to use your energy constructively, in order to be the master of your own destiny and the captain of your own soul, and you will know the true meaning of happiness, success, and security in life.

THE ARIES CHILD

The Aries infant will turn out to be aggressive and pioneering; he will not like to be ruled by other people. The parents of the

Aries child must use discretion, lest he become stubborn, and leave home at an early age. Much heartbreak can be avoided if the parents will notice this inclination, and accept the idea that he can be more easily handled if not "driven." Children of Aries often tend to impulsive action—at times rather fiery. They are ready to take the initiative in any movement that appeals to them, regardless of danger, yet they sometimes lack the necessary persistence to sustain their efforts over serious obstacles. Therefore, we must teach them consistency of purpose, so that success and happiness will be attained later in life.

Prominent leaders, explorers, and pioneers are often born under this sign. The child can grow up to become successful in government work, work connected with tools and sharp instruments, or occupations that require wearing a uniform, such as fireman, policeman, or soldier. If you watch a group of children at play, you can depend upon it that the Aries child will usually be "on top of the heap"—always telling the others what to do. This "leadership complex" may be a splendid thing but it has to be developed in a balanced manner. Otherwise, the child will grow up into a domineering individual, disliked and avoided by others. These children will be courageous, which will often take them into hazardous work. All of this should be taken into consideration in their education and upbringing. Generally speaking, children who are born between April 10 and 20 are likely to be more fortunate and successful as their life progresses than those born earlier in the sign.

THE ARIES WIFE

The Aries woman personifies one of the highest feminine developments of the Zodiac. These women make wonderful wives for ambitious men. They like to spend their spare time in constructive self-improvement. They are witty, clever conversationalists, with wonderful social presence. Either they are willing to help the husband in business or they have some lucrative side line of their own that adds to the family fortunes.

The appearance of the Aries wife is very smart, for she is usually a good-looking woman who takes great pride in the way she looks. Pride is one of her outstanding qualities. She has such a superior opinion of her own family that it shows quite plainly in her behavior and sometimes causes others to be resentful.

Jealousy and a desire for a competitive social life are two of her worst faults. She is apt to be jealous of her husband's attentions, and may have a vivid imagination when she feels she might have been wronged. She knows her worth and wants her husband to concentrate upon her with great intensity. This type of woman should marry a passionate, possessive man—one who makes her own sense of possession seem fragile by comparison. She should not have reason to seek grievances, for she is at her best when making self-sacrifices for her family.

When family life rolls along smoothly the Arien wife can become rather extravagant. She is also generous, so much so that she frequently goes overboard for family and friends. She likes people to be obligated to her and is hesitant to accept repayment for her generosity.

She loves only the man she can greatly admire; his ability to control her is an important part of her devotion to him. If his hold over her is dominant, and his constitution is virile, she is his for life.

THE ARIES HUSBAND

The Aries husband is a distinguished, desirable sort of man. He is the kind of man that all girls aspire to own, but who is by appearance and temperament a little hard to acquire. This is because he is exacting. He has a romantic mental picture of what he wants in a wife, and this image is his idea of perfection. The lady must be beautiful, clever, and most understanding.

Such men are conventional in thought and do not generally go in for Bohemian types of romance. They demand a high moral code in the women of their choice, regardless of their own leanings—usually an isolated adventurous fling. As a matter of fact, the Aries man dislikes clandestine affairs. He is outspoken to a fault, and refuses to hide or lie about his activities. He would consider it a personal affront that he might have to look outside of his home for affection. He is rather demanding sexually, and if not gratified at home, he may look elsewhere.

The Aries man is ardent and proud; all through life, he has an appeal for the woman he married. About the most difficult problem in his married life is to satisfy his romantic conception of physical love. He has a voracious appetite which he will not sublimate. No substitute devotion satisfies him, but a wife can gain his everlasting faithfulness if she harmonizes with him physically and mentally.

THE CUSPS OF ARIES

(If your birthday is not within the cusp of your Sign, the following does not apply to you.)

If your birthday is from March 21st through March 23rd.

You are an Aries with Pisces tendencies. Your ruling planets are Mars and Neptune. This gives you unusual intelligence, understanding, and originality. You are cautious, studious, amiable, and thorough in whatever you do. You are extremely ambitious and painstaking, but want to carry out your plans in your own way. You resent being forced or interfered with. You should be interested in the mechanical and electrical sciences. You like to direct the activities of others. To some extent you will disagree with general public opinion and have the urge to introduce new ideas. While many will regard these ideas as radical, others will respect them because you show courage. *To get the most out of life, curb your tendency to be impatient and irritable.* You are fond of adventure, and delight in entertaining your friends to whom you are loyal. You are destined to succeed in some outstanding way through a career quite different than the one you started to follow early in life.

If your birthday is from April 17th through April 20th.

You are an Aries with Taurus tendencies. Your ruling planets are Mars and Venus. You have all of the indications of Aries and a few of Taurus. This makes you fiery, romantic, and determined. You will succeed regardless of hazards but you will not trample the rights of others. You possess an impatient and nervous temperament. You are endowed with wonderful talents that may not at first be apparent. You attend to one thing at a time and are likely to become annoyed when things around you are disorderly. You have a high moral sense and are almost immune to unchaste thoughts. You do everything in your power to excel in whatever you may undertake. You can achieve success, while holding the respect of your relatives, friends, and business associates.

THE DECANATES OF ARIES

If the birthday is between March 21st and March 31st.

Your personal and ruling planet is Mars, which is doubly forceful in this aspect. Mars will tend to bring out the more dominant dictatorial and positive side of your nature. There is a tendency to become impatient and irritable with others because they may not have the ability to think and act as quickly as you do. It is highly important to practice tolerance, patience, and understanding. An active body and an impetuous, spirited nature is shown by the double aspect of the planet Mars in your chart. You are capable of acquiring and retaining a great amount of knowledge without much effort. Your personality will always be aggressive, independent, temperamental, and persevering. Avoid a tendency to talk too much and monopolize conversation. While you may have many original ideas, you prefer to have others execute them for you. Your best results will be obtained when you are permitted to assume leadership.

If the birthday is between April 1st and April 10th.

Your personal planet is the Sun, known as the Ruler of the Day. As the giver of life it is the center of the Solar System. The Sun stands for dignity, honor, and ambition. The Sun in this decanate causes great love of change and a desire for reform. The Sun governs pride and personal ambitions. It will confer good fortune and assist greatly in offsetting some of the negative aspects of your ruling planet Mars.

If the birthday is between April 10th and April 20th.

Your personal planet is Jupiter, which is known as the God of Fortune. It influences the intellectual, moral, and sympathetic tendencies. Jupiter will greatly aid the aspects of your ruling planet Mars, since it stands for sincerity and honesty, and inclines its subjects to become genuinely warmhearted. A noble nature, ever grateful and courteous to all, is one of the favorable aspects of this planet. It is well said that Jupiter is the most fortunate and beneficent of all planets. It brings good fortune and success.

THE DEGREES OF ARIES

March 21st.

You possess an ambitious and determined personality. You show a marked aptitude for dealing in financial matters, and should obtain a position pertaining to monetary pursuits. Intense concentration will aid you materially, providing you overcome a tendency to display your strong likes and dislikes. One aspect in this Horoscope indicates the possibility of a military career or fame in the art world. You are positive and forceful.

March 22nd.

You possess an independent personality and splendid intuitive powers. You should train your impetuous nature and overcome a rash temperament. Because of your highly practical mind, you are a good organizer. Your fertile mind will help develop your ability as a scientist and a mathematician. Persons born on this day are enterprising, practical, and charitable.

March 23rd.

You possess a good sense of humor. Your versatile mind and marked social instincts indicate that you would be successful in some form of public service. One aspect of your Horoscope shows that you may become successful in the literary field. You are ardent, refined, and ambitious. You should avoid overindulgence in both food and drink.

March 24th.

You possess a highly magnetic personality. A strong and healthy body coupled with good recuperative powers will enable you to overcome most physical dangers. Your loyal disposition will bring many sincere friendships into your life. One aspect in this Horoscope indicates a passionate nature with a good degree of vanity. You will meet with good fortune sometime during your life. Although impulsive and sensuous, you are capable of great attachments.

March 25th.

You possess great creative ability. You can become a patron of the fine arts. Keen interest in literature endows you with the qualities of an intellectual personality. You accomplish your purpose through your marked sympathies and sense of fair play.

You will attain the greatest measure of success and happiness in life by catering to the public.

March 26th.

You possess a discerning personality. Your restless nature may cause you to become involved in some unfortunate undertakings during your lifetime. A sense of purpose should be developed in order to overcome unsatisfied longings. You are fond of animals. You could be successful as a trainer or owner of race horses.

March 27th.

You possess lofty ideals and great intensity and sincerity of purpose, which tend to make you over-critical when your plans and ambitions are interrupted. You can avoid the development of this aspect by carefully analyzing inevitable difficulties and their consequences. You are fond of outdoor activities. Mother Nature will help you relax. A spiritual nature with high ideals indicates an ideal marriage.

March 28th.

You possess the qualities of an orator. You can be cutting and sarcastic in your manner of speech. A fondness for mysteries is indicated, along with a love of argument and debate. These qualities add greatly to your store of knowledge and can be prime factors in the development of your mental faculties and social background. While you may be affectionate and magnanimous to your immediate family, you show a tendency to be somewhat inconsiderate towards others. You can be turbulent and vengeful where outsiders are concerned.

March 29th.

You possess a courageous and aggressive disposition. You are independent and have the ability to carry out your objectives without much assistance from outside influences. Do not attempt to force yourself into a vocation, but permit your natural foresight to hold full sway. Your great desire to travel may be satisfied by a military career. A career in the law enforcement field should be considered.

March 30th.

You may rise to great heights of success with the aid of influential friends. Because you possess a natural, aristocratic bearing and a flair for social recognition, you may have a tendency to attach too much significance to appearances. There are times when you become quite intolerant and vindictive. Curb this tendency.

March 31st.

You possess a resourceful and capable nature. You have a scientific mind, and possess the energy and ability to understand situations and command the respect of your friends and associates. Hopes and ambitions are sometimes realized through sheer genius by many natives of this degree. Follow your hunches; they are usually right.

April 1st.

You possess great intuition. You will only succeed in life through your own merit and natural capabilities. You are clever with details and will achieve success in any position or business where intelligent application of detailed knowledge is essential. Certain aspects in your Horoscope indicate many trials and tribulations. There is also a tendency to daydream.

April 2nd.

You possess an imaginative and intuitive mind. One aspect in this Horoscope indicates the ability to achieve fame in the humanitarian fields of medicine, philosophy, and psychology. It is necessary to overcome the tendency to be lustful and destructive when you are forced to yield in your ambitions.

April 3rd.

You possess a violent temper and a brooding nature. Unless you are in congenial surroundings, your sensitive disposition can easily develop into an inferiority complex. You are markedly introspective and have an inclination to become moody and despondent at the slightest provocation. You are vehement in your desires and should temper your aspirations with logic. Fame may come through athletic prowess.

April 4th.

You possess a bright, literary mind. Great generosity and kindness of heart are also indicated. One aspect in this Horoscope shows a marked tendency toward daydreaming and timidity, yet you are always well disposed. You must learn concentration and the importance of completing one task before starting another. Great sex appeal will bring popularity in love. You have a flair for speculation.

April 5th.

You possess an appealing and persuasive personality. You have ability as an orator. One aspect in this Horoscope shows a judicial and perceptive mentality coupled with a high-strung nervous system. You are extremely fond of your family and friends. You may be more fortunate in business and vocational affairs than in personal and intimate matters. You are artistically inclined.

April 6th.

You are fond of children and will experience much happiness through them. An artistic temperament and lovable nature brings the desire for better things in life. One aspect in this Horoscope indicates a marked tendency to consult occult and mystical literary works. You have the ability to sense the thoughts and feelings of others.

April 7th.

You are emotional and romantic. You can develop an excellent literary career. One aspect in your Horoscope indicates a tendency to find fault with others. This failing is perhaps due to a highly sensitive and emotional nature. Nevertheless, many natives of this degree will devote their lives to scientific research.

April 8th.

You possess a fertile mind and a noble disposition. You display unusual prowess in outdoor sports and all physical activities. There are indications of possible fame in athletic games. Your strong will power and well-defined course of action will enable you to overcome many obstacles in life. You have the natural ability to make friends readily, because of your ardent personality and ability as a lover.

April 9th.

You possess a resourceful and shrewd mind. Executive traits and natural charm will bring many profitable friendships. You show great enterprise in acquiring the good things in life, and success will be attained mostly through your own efforts. One negative aspect is a tendency to become unscrupulous when pressed.

April 10th.

You possess an active and impressionable mind. There is a tendency to become irritable and impatient when your plans and desires are not easily fulfilled. There is a strong liking for the sea. One aspect in your Horoscope shows that you will make any sacrifice to help those you love.

April 11th.

You possess a profound but melancholy disposition. A magnanimous personality and desire to help those who are in less fortunate straits will lead you into many strange experiences during your life. Studies of a scientific nature, which can be used for the good of humanity and the alleviation of sorrow and suffering, may be your life's ambition. Just rewards in the form of honor and success will be the result of such undertakings. One aspect here shows instability under certain circumstances.

April 12th.

You possess a strong personality and a pleasing, honest disposition. You are fond of music and art, and enjoy the beautiful, refined, and aesthetic things in life. One aspect of this Horoscope indicates a tendency toward self-indulgence which should not be encouraged. You are a seeker after strange and unusual places; this curiosity leads to a desire to travel in foreign lands.

April 13th.

You possess a silent, philosophical, yet flexible nature, and a methodical, prudent, but gentle disposition. Marked capability in dealing with the masses and success through association with influential and prosperous friends are indicated. An education which will equip you for a life of public service will bring greater happiness and success. You are not receptive to any proposition that does not coincide with your own inherent sense of justice and fair play. You have great patience and forebearance, and are a born optimist.

April 14th.

You possess a restless and aspiring nature. Because you are somewhat hasty emotionally, you should practice self-discipline and restraint. Develop consistency of purpose and your natural ability, intuition, and keen foresight will assure success. One aspect in this Horoscope indicates that you should exercise caution while traveling. Foreign lands intrigue you.

April 15th.

You possess an inspirational and creative genius. You are fond of social activity. You show a marked aptitude for organization, and are always ready to accept responsibility. You possess versatility and an artistic temperament; you can best serve yourself by developing latent talents.

April 16th.

You possess a bold imagination and a keen mind. These characteristics will aid in the attainment of success in the business world. A bold nature and a decided flair for leading others assures your success as an executive in the field of your choice. At times you can be very willful and obstinate.

April 17th.

You possess a meditative and somewhat gloomy disposition. You are gentle and prudent but lack confidence. You are considerate and obedient to the wishes of your loved ones and usually bear the brunt of family responsibility. You are thoughtful but lack tenacity of purpose and are inclined to be something of a recluse.

April 18th.

You possess lofty ideals and great intuition, but also have a decided tendency to be contrary and mischievous. Good business ability and commercial foresight will greatly aid you in the attainment of success in the business world. Trouble through relatives is shown at various intervals in your life; however, children will bring much satisfaction, and possibly honor.

April 19th.

You possess a well-balanced mind, good intuition, and a kind, affectionate nature. You have a magnetic personality, and the gift of foresight. You may have a delicate constitution and should not over-exercise or go to extremes in mental or physical exertion. Enlightenment through personal efforts and past experiences is indicated.

April 20th.

You possess a profound mind alternately swayed by principle and ambition. You show a great deal of adaptability and unusual aptitude for imitation. One aspect in this Horoscope indicates a tendency to become extremely temperamental and excitable when anyone interferes with your plans and ambitions. You are a born leader and want to have your own way in all matters. Develop tact and diplomacy.

COMPATIBLE AND INCOMPATIBLE SIGNS OF ARIES

Much heartbreak and disappointment might be avoided if one takes the advice and absorbs the knowledge offered by the dependable impartial adviser—Astrology.

Aries is a rash, impetuous, and headstrong Sign. People born under this Sign tend to be impulsive in love and marriage, as in everything else. As befits a martial sign, it is passionate, but there is also a great amount of idealism. Sexual indulgence is more a matter of sudden impulse than of deliberate seeking. Aries generates a positive type which does not harmonize well with a positive partner; an Arien tends to seek someone of a weaker nature on whom he can impress his sexual qualities.

A man with Aries rising is attracted by beauty and apparent helplessness. He needs a wife who will be content to remain in the background and duly admire his prowess and ability. Normally Aries is a better Sign for a man than for a woman.

The Aries woman is apt to be too masterful, too much of a whirlwind in the house for anyone who is not of a quiet and passive type. She is capable and generous, but can easily become loud, self-opinionated, shrewish, and "bossy" under affliction; i.e., when born with adverse planetary aspects.

The Aries nature is intense, capable of sudden violence and great jealousy. With certain afflictions, especially from Mars or Uranus, a sadistic tendency can easily develop, though by itself it is a too direct, simple, and primitive Sign to lend itself readily to perversion. Aries must always strive for leadership, however, whether in man or woman, and unless the partner is content to be led, constant friction may develop. For this reason, Aries marriages are often unhappy, though other factors also contribute to cause disharmony. One of them is a tendency to physical or psychic sex weakness, which is sometimes present in the Aries man, or sometimes to sexual indifference in the Aries woman; and another is the propensity of the Aries man— and sometimes in the Aries woman also—to indulge in promiscuous flirtations and love affairs. The underlying reason for such affairs is usually that they flatter the Aries vanity, but in the man there is also the additional search for the ideal, often the cause for matrimonial infidelity.

Arien and Arien.

If one partner will permit the other "to rule the roost," there should be much compatibility between two persons born in the same Sign. Although there is a lack of contrasting personalities, there will be a sympathetic understanding on the part of both regarding the qualities and shortcomings of the other.

A note of warning, however, must be sounded here. If both Ariens have dominant and forceful aspects in their Horoscopes, much conflict will arise because of the unflinching desire of both partners to be the head of the house and family.

Arien and Taurus.

This combination should make an excellent match. The Taurean nature is ruled by Venus, the Goddess of Love, the one thing an Arien always seeks in a mate. Though the slow-moving Taurus may find the going a bit hectic, the excitement may help to stimulate the courtship. One thing the Arien must avoid is temperamental outbursts, for while Taurus is not highly emotional on the surface, he can become obstinate and ferocious as a bull when it sees red!

Arien and Gemini.

This alliance usually results in a great deal of bickering due to strong differences about sex. Gemini is a mercurial Sign where the mind plays an important part in all love-making.

The emotional Martian Arien may prove too much for the conventional nature of the Gemini.

Above all, Gemini respects the refined, intellectual approach to connubial bliss. The impatient Arien may find this frustrating, and after a time seek a less difficult companion.

Arien and Cancer.

This is usually a hard combination to match. Cancerians are ruled by the Moon and are moody, sentimental, and secretive. They have a tendency to live in the past, and rarely forget serious quarrels or family disagreements which occur early in marriage. What might be an unimportant breach to Aries could become a traumatic block to Cancer. Though the Cancerian holds on with the tenacity of a crab, he has a tendency to back away from situations which have been hurtful in the past.

Arien and Leo.

This is usually a splendid combination. While both Signs are emotional in their make-up, Leo will lionize an Aries mate. This is particularly true if Aries will allow Leo to hold the center of the floor on occasions. The impetuous Aries lover will find a welcome home in the lion's den. Leo admires the aggressive tendencies of fiery contemporaries.

Arien and Virgo.

This combination is similar to the Aries-Gemini combination. Virgo is ruled by Mercury and does not blend well astrologically with the Martian tendencies of Aries. Virgoans are usually too precise and fault-finding for the Arien personality. Virgo wants a well-ordered existence and will not be happy under Arien dictatorship. The prissy Virgo will, certainly, not condone the bossy Aries.

Arien and Libra.

An excellent combination of Mars and Venus. The warm and passionate Libran will make a welcome home for the fiery, impetuous Aries. This will be particularly true if both persons are on the same cultural and intellectual plane. Libra's refined and artistic temperament yearns for reciprocal attachments.

Arien and Scorpio.

Since there is never room for two heads in one family, this combination would not make an ideal partnership. Both Signs are strongly dominated by the planet Mars, which makes for very positive temperaments unless there are several benign natal planetary aspects.

While Scorpio may adore the Aries from a sexual standpoint, their more mundane interests would be constantly at odds.

Arien and Sagittarius.

This combination of the first and third sign of the fiery Trinity usually makes an ideal partnership. The Mars-Jupiter duo are an ideal match for each other. Both are creatures of impulse. They can both have outside interests without causing personal conflict and friction. The Sagittarian banner is "liberty, and the pursuit of happiness"; Aries is usually willing to subscribe to this theory.

Arien and Capricorn.

A doubtful combination. Saturn, represented by old Father Time, is the Capricorn standard bearer. Ariens are too impatient to cope with the slow, methodical plodding of the Capricornian nature. The Capricornian goat will butt up against the Martian will and an impasse is bound to occur.

In matters of sex there is an affinity; however, their inherent personalities clash.

Arien and Aquarius.

The unpredictable Aquarian may tax an Arien mate's patience while the instability of the Arien temperament will surely provoke the Sign of good will and self-sacrifice. Such are the bones of contention that make this partnership a gamble. The planet Uranus, which rules Aquarius, is unpredictable in its actions; therefore, Aquarians have a tendency to procrastinate too much to please the Arien "up and at 'em" characteristics.

Arien and Pisces.

The sentimental Pisces nature finds little comfort in the Arien's aggressiveness. Pisceans are romantic, but they desire the delicate approach that the Arien lacks. Neptune, the planet of the higher mind, gives Pisces an ethereal quality. Unless the Arien mate is willing to take a trip to the clouds now and then, the partnership will prove incompatible.

SOME FAMOUS PERSONS BORN IN THE SIGN
OF ARIES

Marlon Brando—Actor
John Burroughs—Author
Charles Chaplin—Actor
Joan Crawford—Actress
Thomas E. Dewey—N.Y.
 Governor
Robert Frost—Poet
Bernard F. Gimbel—Merchant

Alec Guinness—Actor
Thomas Jefferson—U.S.
 President
Nikita S. Khrushchev—Soviet
 Premier
Clare Booth Luce—Authoress
 and Ambassador
Henry R. Luce—Publisher

Shirley MacLaine—Actress
J. Pierpont Morgan—Financier
Mary Pickford—Actress
Joseph Pulitzer—Publisher
Leopold Stokowski—Musical
 Conductor

Gloria Swanson—Actress
Arturo Toscanini—Musical
 Conductor
Tennessee Williams—Author
F. W. Woolworth—Merchant
Wilbur Wright—Inventor

TAURUS

APRIL 21—MAY 20

THE TAUREAN is born under the rulership of Venus, the planet of love and beauty. This planet absorbs an energy entirely different from the energy absorbed by other planets. The internal influence is warm and impulsive. A pliable, receptive, clinging, and feminine nature results. This energy yields to a nature more positive than its own loving submission, hence the myths of friendship between Mars and Venus.

The Sign of Taurus, in its symbolical aspect, represents the procreative forces in all departments of nature. Its genius is symbolized as Aphrodite, who was generally represented as wearing two horns upon her head in imitation of the bull. Many mythologists have been deceived by this symbol and have taken it to represent a figure of the crescent Moon upon the head of Isis. Apis, the sacred bull of the Egyptians, is another conception of Taurus. Since the Sun passed through this Sign during the plowing month of the Egyptians, we find this symbol used as that of husbandry.

The Sign Taurus represents the ears, neck, and throat of the Grand Old Man of the Skies, hence it is the Sign of the silent, patient, and listening principles of humanity. It rules the lymphatic system of the organism.

43

The gem of this Sign is the sapphire, and this stone is the natural talisman for those born under Taurus.

The fortunate day is Friday.

Fortunate numbers are one and nine.

The color for this Sign is blue.

Best locations for success are quiet places.

Taurus is the highest emanation of the earthly Trinity, and is the constellation of the planet Venus.

Addressing a Taurus, I would say: You have a natural, magnetic, and attractive personality, which, if properly cultivated and expressed, will enable you to go far in life and progress beyond the circumstances of your birth. The cultured Taurus personality radiates mental and physical beauty. His other characteristics include a charming and unaffected refinement and an interesting, enjoyable wit. The uncultured Taurus personality is apt to be somewhat gruff, manifesting a peculiar self-willed, obstinate and self-important attitude, which often proves to be boring, dull, and antagonizing—the "I am for myself" type of personality.

The true and unspoiled Taurus character and temperament is just like the season of the year the Sign represents. There is beauty, culture, grace, honesty, depth of feeling, affection, and an understanding sympathy in the Taurus personality. However, behind all this lies a great power that can be abused. The power of determination, when it is wisely directed and applied, can do great good. The average Taurus individual is easy-going until crossed; but once crossed, rightly or wrongly, he or she can be the most obstinate and headstrong of people. This reaction takes place because these natives have an unusual emotional sensitivity. However, the great beauty of the Taurus nature lies in the deep sympathy and understanding manifested toward those they love. It will pay you many dividends in personal happiness to investigate thoroughly your nature and disposition and to seek to make wise corrections and adjustments if you find them necessary.

There will be much good in your life if you will but naturally allow yourself to blossom forth in all your radiant and latent potentialities of mind and character. Honesty, sincerity of purpose, and reliability are attributes of your nature. Others can depend upon you. You are inclined to be methodical in your way of doing things; whatever you do, you desire to do it well. You have courage, patience, and fortitude. There are times when you must guard against being influenced too much by the opinions, feelings, and emotions of others. It will be advisable for you to think things out alone, in the sacred freedom of your own mind. You will do well to learn to subscribe to the principles of logic and reasoning to avoid erroneous and prejudiced conclusions.

You do not investigate things hurriedly. You are inclined to be methodical and sure, and are not given to haphazard ways of doing things. You have a reflective imagination. In fact, your daydreaming often affords you great mental relaxation and private pleasure. However, do not indulge in this practice to excess as it may make you impractical. Daydreaming may cause you to lay foundations for disillusionment. *Endeavor to control your imagination; do not let it control you.* You are inclined to pay close attention to what you are studying or doing. You seldom overlook details that others forget.

In your education you pay close attention to what you study (which often makes you take longer than others do), because you want to be sure of yourself and your knowledge. Some people may think you are a little slow in learning, but do not let this alarm you in any way. You remember what you have learned much longer than others. You are determined, which enables you to learn anything in which you take an interest. You have sufficient imagination and power of original thought to improve, which will help you succeed in business, in professional life, or your chosen work. You are fond of the good things of life—rich foods and other luxuries.

You have the type of mind that receives inspired ideas from

time to time—inspired ideas which present opportunities for your welfare and progress. If you do not act upon them, the fault is yours alone. It is the exercise and application of your mental powers that determines the degree of success you will enjoy in life. Use your intuition which is the faculty that gives you instantaneous knowledge. Intuition often warns you about something that is to take place. It gives you an unusually deep insight into the character of people you meet in the course of your life.

You are apt to be sensitive in the region of the neck, throat, and ears. Do your best to avoid exposure to common colds for they have a tendency to affect the throat. Also avoid straining the voice. You are born with a fairly good constitution and are capable of withstanding the ordinary rigors of life. Learn to cultivate rational control over what you eat and drink. Avoid overeating and curb any tendency toward excess of rich foods. Be rational in your diet and you will do much to avoid the common ailments of the digestive system.

Your affectionate, sympathetic, and passionate nature requires expression. You are sincere and intense where romance is concerned. You desire the love, affection, companionship, interest, and attention of the object of your affection. You are faithful in your devotion as long as conditions remain reasonably harmonious. Once you have cared, you always care. Coolness and lack of attention or indifference from your loved one can darken your life, and it takes you a long time to forget. There are times when adverse conditions and circumstances affect your loved one, but you lack understanding because you are thinking of yourself then. It is not natural for those born under Taurus to live alone. You will love children and make a tender and affectionate parent. You are fond of a quiet and harmonious atmosphere at home. As you are somewhat fixed in nature, you want to be master or mistress in your own home; within this limit you desire a certain amount of independence. Without freedom you are inclined to become cross. You want the best that money can buy around you at home. You have a deep appreciation of the artistic and the beautiful aspects of life and nature.

People of your Sign make good executives, whether in business for themselves or in the employ of others; even the Taurus housewife will manage her home and its affairs with firmness. Taurus is the Sign of finance and favors bankers, merchants, brokers, salesmen, farmers, lawyers, as well as doctors and teachers.

The artistic qualities of the Taurus nature lead many under this Sign to the theater and screen. People born under Taurus also go into commercial art and interior decoration. When in business, they often manage department stores or specialty shops.

Experience will enable you to develop a keen insight into your work and the affairs and motives of others. In matters of partnership, it is advisable for you to use good judgment, particularly because you are, at times, stubborn, headstrong, and set in your ways. Others may try to shift more than your share of responsibility upon you. But if you are given a definite amount of work to handle and are not imposed upon in partnership affairs, you will do well. Your fondness for the good things of life makes you somewhat whimsical in your expenditures, so it is advisable that you develop a modicum of horse sense. During favorable financial periods, invest in practical propositions, such as real estate, but not in any speculative or get-rich-quick schemes. Success in gambling and speculation is not indicated for most Taurus people.

Although your Sign is known as a Fixed Sign, indications show there will be some travel in your life. You derive a certain amount of pleasure from travel as it affords you an opportunity for a change of perspective. The indications point to active social life. Your personality attracts many friends, and acquaintances. You are loyal to your friends, and enjoy extending hospitality to them. You are thoughtful of your friends, and many will rely on you in times of stress for advice, courage, hope, and consolation. You have, under ordinary circumstances, a soothing influence upon them.

Study your interesting mind and personality, but do not permit your sensitivity to rule your life. The unwise use of your remarkable determination can hinder you and cause much sorrow. It is well within your ability to curb or control a tendency to be obstinate, and you must do it if you ever wish to become a success. Because of your sensitive, emotional nature, it is advisable for you to exercise your best judgment in love and marriage. Your impulsiveness appears to be emotional rather than mental; herein lies your greatest difficulty. Understand this impulsiveness and do your best to direct both your mental and emotional energies wisely.

Success will come primarily as the result of applying your efforts in the right direction. You are a born builder and worker, so work out your own destiny. You will succeed because of patience, thoughtfulness, and determination. While you may not be as aggressive as some people, you have fortitude, and will go forward in the face of obstacles when many others would give up. The necessity for well-planned application of your mental and phsyical energies cannot be overstated. Good planning serves to eliminate enemies and obstacles and attracts to you friends, love, respect, and success.

THE TAURUS CHILD

This child will have a persistent, steadfast, self-reliant nature. He will be able to carry to a successful completion any idea that he might develop. The parents of children born under this Sign will be wise to handle them carefully because sometimes they turn out to be stubborn and unyielding. It follows that a great deal of tact is necessary to keep this child from turning against the parent. When provoked, the children of Taurus are quick to anger. Once the Taurus child has made up his mind, he will be found very difficult to influence. Taurus is known as a Fixed Sign and has a tendency to be very steady in ideas and opinions.

Taurus children have a basically amicable and kind disposition, but they resent contradiction. When one has once succeeded in showing them they are wrong, their inherent love of justice and truth will prompt them to acknowledge their mistakes. The parent should prevent the offspring from becoming obstinate, as this unhealthy quality may lead to a desire to leave home.

The Taurus vitality is naturally strong, but may be readily exhausted by a quick temper and overindulgence in rich foods. The child is prone to discomfort due to the latter. Diseases peculiar to the Taurus-born include abscesses, impure blood, and tonsillitis. The Sign is ruled by the planet Venus, and influences the throat. Care should be taken to avoid strain of the throat.

The following are a few of the natural vocational tendencies: actor, artisan, clothing dealer, dancer, designer, farmer, jeweler, miner, musician, singer, painter, maker or seller of toilet accessories. The Venus rulership influences the artistic tendencies as outlined above.

THE TAURUS WIFE

The Taurus wife is, perhaps, the most dependable wife in the whole range of Zodiacal types. She seldom resorts to divorce; she will endure extreme hardships rather than desert her mate. The Taurus wife is naturally adapted to domestic life. She is a perfect homemaker, a devoted mother, and a loving mate. She is usually quite ambitious, for Taurus women are domineering in their own quiet way. They appear to be calm, reserved, and friendly, yet underneath they are jealous, and covet the material things in life.

The Taurus wife never questions her husband's devotion because she, herself, seldom strays. She is a most affectionate, demonstrative woman, wholly engrossed in her home and family. She watches her family with a personal attention that occasionally exacts service from them. Beneath the goodness of a Taurus wife there is a streak of determination that pushes her husband to meet her demands. She covers her determination by seeming to be dependent.

The devotion of these women can best be held by a man who is important in the business world and can afford to give his wife a luxurious home where she may show off her housekeeping ability and her social charm. A positive Taurus woman with good planetary influences possesses well-directed determination; a negatively influenced woman is obstinate and stubborn. The great redeeming feature of the Taurean wife is a deep understanding and sympathy manifested toward those she loves.

THE TAURUS HUSBAND

The Taurus male has one of the finest qualities of all for attaining success as a husband. It would appear from previous descriptions of the Taurus-born that the man is rather stern. It is true there is a bullish tendency to satisfy the intense physical urge latent in him. But the Taurus man is so dependable, kind, generous, and faithful to his trust as a home builder that any violence in his emotional nature must be overlooked. He seldom neglects his home for an outside interest. Any such diversion is usually transitory and fleeting.

This type of husband adores his wife and children, and takes pains to give them the best home, education, clothes, and amusements that this world provides. These men often marry above their station in life, partly because they are so ambitious to establish themselves, and partly because their search for success leads them to high social goals.

The rulership of Venus in the Sign gives them great appreciation of beauty. In order to hold a Taurus husband throughout life, the wife must constantly look her best and behave lovingly. The husbands adore independence and like to feel they are the sole providers of their families' happiness. Domestic life, tiresome to so many of the other Zodiacal types, is never tiresome to the Taurus husband. Once married, he never regrets his lost bachelor existence nor does he even think of the liberty that others count as precious.

The negative type of Taurus husband is apt to be somewhat gruff, manifesting a peculiar, self-willed and obstinate attitude. He represents the "I am for myself" type of personality.

THE CUSPS OF TAURUS

(If your birthday is not within the cusp of your Sign, the following does not apply to you.)

If the birthday is from April 21st through April 24th.

You were born in Taurus with Aries tendencies. Your ruling planets are Venus and Mars. This denotes an impulsiveness too strong for your own good. You are broadminded, intellectual, clever, and practical. You have a dominating nature, strong powers of persuasion, self-confidence, and you are a good mixer. At times you may be headstrong, stubborn, and self-sufficient. When you have made up your mind about something, it is very difficult to make you change it, regardless of consequences. No one's judgment is infallible—consider all things well before you take a definite stand. You can be too generous for your own good; often you go to extremes to be a good fellow. You make a delightful companion and a dependable friend. You dislike criticism, but you will only harm yourself if you take a stubborn attitude to constructive criticism.

If your birthday is from May 18th through May 20th.

You were born in Taurus with Gemini tendencies. Your ruling planets are Venus and Mercury. With negative influences you may be sarcastic, self-willed, and indifferent to the feelings of others, but positive influences will make you confident, serious, and a good mixer. This Sign gives you talent and ambition, but there are times when your imagination runs away with reality. In this case, it becomes difficult for you to concentrate upon any one thing. Your firm and straightforward tendencies can bring about success in spite of any opposition. Your magnetic personality has the power to attract friends. You must not be too hasty in choosing a mate because many people born between these dates contract unhappy marriages. By exercising prudence in important matters and overcoming your impulsive nature, you can become a successful and happy person.

THE DECANATES OF TAURUS

If the birthday is between April 21st and April 30th.

You have the double aspect of the benevolent planet Venus in your chart. You possess perseverance, will power, and vitality. Your personal planet, Venus, which is the symbol of love and beauty, gives constancy to your affections and denotes a fixed nature. Both likes and dislikes will be maintained tenaciously. You share things freely and are charitable, especially to those who are near and dear. A truly magnanimous spirit is indicated by the double aspect of Venus in your Horoscope.

If the birthday is between May 1st and May 10th.

Your personal planet is Mercury, the symbol of knowledge. It rules the more rational part of the soul and mind. You are deliberate, conservative, and constructive with an unusually active mind. Mercury in its favorable aspect indicates an alert, perceptive, studious, and forceful personality. On the negative side, it inclines towards an inquisitive, meddlesome, careless, radical, forgetful, and effusive nature. This planet is the great mental ruler. Without Mercury's influence, we lack memory and the powers of speech and expression.

If the birthday is between May 11th and May 20th.

Your personal planet is Saturn, which is the symbol of Time. This planet is restrictive in its influences, governs the thoughtful and meditative tendencies which incline to make its subjects careful, patient, and considerate. Its powers lie in the realms of stability, endurance, tenacity, and perseverance. Gain through thrift and careful investment is indicated. You possess a truly magnanimous spirit and a kind, benevolent, and sympathetic nature.

THE DEGREES OF TAURUS

April 21st.

You possess a masterful, thoughtful, and persevering disposition. You display unusual ability in the arts. Your strong will power brings you into contact with many important people. You have the natural ability to make friends readily because of your pleasing personality. This is the degree of the dictator, so curb any tendency you may have in this direction.

April 22nd.

You possess a magnetic, determined, and generous nature. You will succeed in life through your own merits and natural capabilities. Your loyalty and inherent ability will help you find marked success in any profession of a scientific nature where intelligent application of detailed knowledge is essential. You should be surrounded by love, affection, and understanding, since certain aspects in this Horoscope indicate the possibility of developing a grasping, selfish, and materialistic outlook.

April 23rd.

You possess a well-balanced philosophical mind coupled with a kind and affectionate disposition. You have a generous nature, but at times may be somewhat temperamental and headstrong.

You may have a delicate constitution and should not go to extremes in mental or physical exertion.

April 24th.

You possess a refined, artistic, and charitable nature. You are gentle and prudent, but lack confidence. Learn to concentrate upon your problems in order to develop the ability to assert yourself with confidence. You are considerate and obedient to the wishes of others. Beware of people who are likely to take advantage of you and cause you to bear the brunt of responsibility.

April 25th.

You possess a practical and reserved nature. You will succeed best in a position of authority. Learn to be considerate of other people's feelings by using more tact. You show great enterprise in acquiring the good things in life; success will be attained mostly through your own efforts. You are a natural leader. One aspect in your Horoscope indicates the possibility of success as an officer of the law.

April 26th.

You possess a bold imagination and a keen mind, which will aid in the attainment of success in an academic career. An extravagant nature and a decided flair for fine clothes and expensive possessions is shown. You should curb your tendency to gamble, as it may cause you financial embarrassment.

April 27th.

You possess a diplomatic and a kind nature. You are intuitive and show unusual aptitude in the culinary arts. You are fond of good food. You also display a marked tendency to prefer your own company to that of others. You are, however, affectionate and magnanimous to your immediate family. You have a tendency to indulge yourself in both food and drink.

April 28th.

You have a keen and perceptive mind and possess the ability to learn quickly. A magnetic temperament and lovable nature bring the desire for better things in life. One aspect in this Horoscope indicates a marked wish to have your own way, and to get it with the least possible personal effort, thereby creating enemies. Do not permit yourself to become self-indulgent; try to overcome a tendency to pamper your whims and fancies.

April 29th.

You possess a stubborn nature coupled with a resourceful and a determined mind. Resolution combined with the ability to express yourself clearly are your outstanding characteristics. You show a tendency to become obstinate and reckless. A disregard for convention and an inherent desire to express radical views may cause you to become an influential person in the lunatic fringe.

April 30th.

You possess initiative, originality, and perception. You also show a decided tendency to be contrary in a mischievous manner. Good conversational ability and profound foresight will aid you in the attainment of success in the business world. Gains through relatives are shown at various intervals in your life. Careful training and a good education will materially aid in developing the more positive aspects in this Horoscope.

May 1st.

You possess a bright, cheerful, and affectionate nature. Generosity, kindness of heart, and a desire to help others are also indicated. One aspect in this Horoscope shows a great love for domestic life. You possess great powers of persuasion and can be successful in any career where master salesmanship is necessary. You gain through life at the expense of your enemies.

May 2nd.

You possess an artistic, ardent, and generous nature. A versatile mind coupled with marked social instincts will enable you to gain success and recognition in public service. One aspect in your Horoscope indicates a tendency to be too apprehensive where the welfare of your loved ones is concerned. Learn moderation of this golden virtue, as it is apt to cause unnecessary strain on the heart. Remember, it is foolish to worry about things that you cannot control.

May 3rd.

You possess a resourceful, scientific, and practical mind. You are inventive, and interested in all phases of scientific endeavor. You are painstaking and honest, and command the respect of your friends and associates. One aspect in this Horoscope indicates danger through misplaced friendships. Talent is shown for those who desire a political career.

May 4th.

You possess a refined and artistic nature. You have a tendency to be irritable and impatient when your plans and desires are not readily fulfilled. Because you possess an unusually progressive mind and a vivid imagination, you could become a good executive. You have a great deal of literary talent and could gain success as an author or politician.

May 5th.

You possess an ethereal mind, remarkable intellect, and a keen sense of judgment. Great fixity of purpose and skill in the art of salesmanship will bring success in business endeavors. Unhappiness is indicated in personal life due to misfortune in affairs of the heart. Misplaced affection may be the main source of trouble.

May 6th.

You possess a clever, subtle mind, and a sympathetic nature. Keen interest in literature, art, and writing endow you with the qualities of a successful author. Your sense of fair play will help to develop the practical side of your nature. Influential friends will be helpful throughout your life.

May 7th.

You possess an original mind; this will have great influence upon your friends and associates. You possess a natural aristocratic bearing and a flair for social recognition; this may cause you to attach too much significance to outward appearances. You desire to impress outsiders; this may cause you to neglect your family and those who are most interested in your welfare.

May 8th.

You possess a sympathetic nature and an intellectual mind. Unless you are in congenial surroundings and have the proper friends, your sensitive disposition can easily develop into an inferiority complex. A tendency to become introspective should be curbed. One aspect in this Horoscope shows a strong desire to help those in less fortunate circumstances than yourself.

May 9th.

You possess a resourceful, determined, and forceful nature. Self-discipline will prevent tantrums. One aspect in this Horoscope shows a judicial and perceptive mind coupled with a high-strung nervous system. This is the degree of a born leader, the man who pulls himself up by his bootstraps.

May 10th.

You possess a profound mind alternately swayed by principle and ambition. You show a great deal of adaptability combined with an unusual aptitude at reproducing and imitating. One aspect in this Horoscope indicates a tendency to become a great artist in the entertainment world. You will want your way in all matters. It is essential that you bear in mind that the desire to achieve personal satisfaction at all costs may bring with it the animosity of others.

May 11th.

You possess an aspiring nature and keen mental powers. You are quite versatile; however, a political career holds great charm for you. Your natural ability, intuition, and keen foresight also favor a legal career. One aspect in this Horoscope indicates that you should use caution while handling medicines. There are certain astrological influences that show danger due to carelessness or temporary depressive moods.

May 12th.

You possess an adventurous spirit and a strong desire to travel and visit strange places. You are fond of company and social activity. You show a marked aptitude for organizing and controlling others, and are always ready to accept responsibility. You have a determined nature and should gain fame in your chosen profession.

May 13th.

You possess an aspiring, passionate, and sensitive nature. You are independent and have the ability to carry out your objectives in life without much assistance from outside influences. When choosing your vocation, permit your foresight to have full sway . . . by so doing, you will decide your own course in life. You are impressionable; you will readily react to your environment.

May 14th.

You possess a humble spirit and a good sense of humor. A great love for travel upon the sea is also indicated. A magnanimous personality and a desire to help those who are in less fortunate straits will lead you into many strange experiences during your life. The alleviation of sorrow and suffering will be your great ambition. Just rewards in the form of honor and success will result from such undertakings.

May 15th.

You possess an imaginative and intuitive nature. An experimental and poetic mind coupled with a leaning toward mystic and occult sciences is also indicated. You should seek the company of understanding companions to avoid loneliness. One aspect in this Horoscope indicates the ability to achieve fame in humanitarian pursuits. Your magnetic personality will make you popular with the opposite sex.

May 16th.

You possess an ambitious and determined personality. You show a marked aptitude for dealing in financial matters, and should study and prepare for a position pertaining to monetary pursuits. Intense concentration of purpose will aid you materially, providing you overcome a tendency to display your strong likes and dislikes regardless of consequences. An aspect in this Horoscope indicates the possible development of an inferiority complex due to confusion of purpose.

May 17th.

You possess an eloquent and persuasive personality. You are fond of music and art. You enjoy the beautiful, refined, and aesthetic things in life. This Horoscope in one aspect indicates good fortune in marriage. You are well adapted to a business or a professional career, with the ability to patiently bide your time until a real opportunity presents itself.

May 18th.

You possess a steadfast and persevering personality. A strong healthy body coupled with good recuperative powers will enable you to overcome most of your physical dangers. A charming, winsome disposition will bring many sincere friendships into your life. One aspect in this Horoscope indicates much good fortune through a career. You can depend upon your good powers of organization to bring you success.

May 19th.

You possess will power and a prudent disposition. Capability in dealing with the masses and an ability to obtain the confidence of influential and prosperous friends will insure success. Financial gains from investments in land are under strong aspect. You will be unreceptive to any proposition that does not coincide with your sense of justice.

May 20th.

You possess a clever, perceptive mind, which coupled with intensity of purpose will influence others to cooperate with your plans and desires. Much talent in literary matters may bring substantial recognition in this field.

COMPATIBLE AND INCOMPATIBLE SIGNS OF TAURUS

The Sign of Taurus has a strongly physical sex nature. The Taurus man is often inclined to lust; this may frequently drive him to excesses. The tendencies toward self-indulgence are comparable to the equally strong inclinations to overeat. The Taurus possesses strong animal instincts. He is not one to search for the ideal. At heart, Taurus is faithful, good-natured, easily satisfied, and patient. As a husband, he is the "stick-in-the-mud" type who is happy and contented if his slippers are properly warmed and his dinner is plentiful and to his liking. Of course, if he has an aggressive Sign rising at birth, these virtues may be somewhat lessened.

The obstinacy of the Taurean has been stressed in the former sections for this Sign, but it is well to mention here that neither the man nor woman with Taurus rising can be driven, though he or she can be very easily led by affection. People born under this Sign are not demonstrative. They are persons possessed of deep, strong feelings; they are inclined to be possessive. Money is usually a big consideration in Taurean marriages, since Taurus is the money Sign of the Zodiac. Money need not necessarily be considered, for, by the law of polarity, the exact opposite may occur and the marriage may be one in which lack of money gives rise to critical situations.

Another Taurean characteristic of importance is a natural soothing and healing power, which makes this native a good partner for one with a high-strung nervous system. Taureans have an eminently practical nature; the limitations which this practical outlook imposes upon their otherwise passionate nature will, of course, yield observable effects. They are less impulsive than calculating, but when they have made their final selection and are resolved upon a course, they are firm in decision.

Taureans have a dominant, obstinate nature and are imbued with the idea that what they say must go. Once they have made up their minds, they leave no stone unturned until they accomplish their own desires. They are conservative in their mannerisms and habits. Strangely enough, despite this conservative trait, they often promise more than they can deliver. At times, they make such promises without having the slightest real intention of fulfilling them. This idiosyncrasy frequently makes them unpopular because people resent being let down. The Taurean will find the compatible and incompatible Signs in the following:

Taurus and Aries.

Although Aries is an impatient, energetic Sign, rather domineering, Taurus should not have any difficulty finding compatibility with this Sign. The slower-moving Taurus may find the going a bit hectic, but the excitement may help stimulate the court-ship since Taurus is a highly emotional Sign, though very ob-stinate when dictated to. The Taurean, ruled by Venus, Goddess of Love, will usually show the Mars-ruled Aries the error of his ways when they meet on a common level.

Taurus and Taurus.

This appears to be a compatible combination from a purely physi-cal standpoint. There could be trouble on the mental plane due to tendencies toward jealousy and stubbornness. Unless one or the other is willing to give way when tempers flare and accusa-tions fly, serious difficulties could arise to mar the nuptial bliss. One point in favor is that both understand the little quirks of the other, and if deeply in love, they will readily forgive in the privacy of the love nest.

Taurus and Gemini.

The Gemini personality may prove too restless for the Taurean nature. Emotionally these two Signs are at odds. The Mercurian outlook on intimate matters does not sit well with a son or daughter of Venus. The Gemini loves variety of thought, and delights in all mental pursuits, while the Taurean is mostly in-terested in the material things of life. The great sex drive of the Taurean could overpower the more docile Gemini.

Taurus and Cancer.

This usually makes a good combination. Cancer likes a good home and much affection. This is what every Taurean hopes to find when undertaking connubial responsibilities. From an emo-tional point of view, there is nothing in the stars that bars the prospect of a happy married life between these two partners. One thing the Taurean must remember is that Cancer is ex-ceedingly sensitive, and will crawl into a shell if unhappy emo-tionally.

Taurus and Leo.

Venus and the Sun make a good combination, especially when each understands his companion's shortcomings. Both have great sex appeal and excellent physical qualities. Magnanimous Leo is just what the doctor ordered for the Taurean's love of the finer things in life. If the Taurean curbs the tendency toward jealousy and gives Leo a little leeway to show off, all is fine and will go well with this combination.

Taurus and Virgo.

Taurus should avoid the attractiveness of the Virgonian if a love-at-first-sight predicament is to be avoided. Taurus will certainly not get his own way here. The Taurean does not like criticism, the sharpest weapon of Virgo. Unless you are willing to take a lot of nagging, it would be well to think twice before taking a Virgo mate.

Taurus and Libra.

This is a Venus and Venus combination. It should prove compatible, except under negative aspects from other planets. There will be common interests and a meeting of the mind and body. The Goddess of Love will continue to shine on these lovebirds until one gets out of line. If this occurs, beware, for the feathers will fly! Generally speaking, however, this is usually a good marital combination.

Taurus and Scorpio.

This combination belongs to the mutual admiration society. The strong sexual urge in both of these Signs will find much in common. Jealousy is the big bad wolf that keeps hovering at the door. Taurus must be very careful to keep faith with the Scorpio mate, or the roof will cave in without warning. Woe to the one who crosses the Scorpion's path—the sting is considered deadly.

Taurus and Sagittarius.

The possessive Taurean may find the freedom-loving Sagittarian hard to cope with. The Sagittarius natives are frank and generous; this Jupiterian trait can clash with the Taurean jealousy. The Taurus who marries a Sagittarius will find that no amount of arguing or berating is going to change the reckless Sagittarian.

Taurus and Capricorn.

With mutual understanding of each other's idiosyncrasies this can be a compatible marriage. Venus blends well with Saturn from an emotional point of view. Both need a certain amount of encouragement and flattery, but Taurus will be the one who must take the lead in this direction. While Capricorn may seem a little cold and aloof at first, the warm rays of Venus will soon melt the exterior of caution and prudence that is inherent in all Capricorns.

Taurus and Aquarius.

This combination usually runs into many difficulties. The unpredictable Aquarian may prove too much for the easygoing Taurus nature. Conversely, the conservative habits of Taurus soon get on the dynamic Aquarius' nerves, and tempers start to flash. While both love ease and comfort, their views on how to obtain them are widely divergent. Another source of irritation for the Taurus lover is the unwillingness of Aquarius to share his secrets.

Taurus and Pisces.

This is usually a very happy combination. Sentimental Pisces will find great comfort in sympathetic Taurus. Neptune, the ruler of Pisces, is the higher octave of Venus, who, in turn, rules Taurus. Pisces is impressionable, romantic, imaginative, and flexible, which is just what the Taurus native is looking for.

Both have much in common from an artistic standpoint, which helps to blend their mental inclinations.

SOME FAMOUS PERSONS BORN IN THE SIGN OF TAURUS

Fred Astaire—Dancer
Irving Berlin—Song Writer
Perry Como—Singer
Gary Cooper—Actor
Oliver Cromwell—British Statesman
Bing Crosby—Actor and Singer
Salvador Dali—Painter
Elizabeth II—Queen of England
Ulysses S. Grant—Soldier and President
Henry J. Kaiser—Industrialist

Guglielmo Marconi—Inventor
Nellie Melba—Opera Star
James Monroe—U.S. President
Henry Morgenthau—Financier
William Shakespeare—Dramatist and Poet
Bishop Fulton J. Sheen—Author
Shirley Temple—Actress
Harry Truman—U.S. President
Rudolph Valentino—Actor
Orson Welles—Actor and Director

GEMINI

MAY 21–JUNE 21

Tʜᴇ sɪɢɴ ᴏғ ɢᴇᴍɪɴɪ symbolizes unity and the strength of united action.

The two bright stars Castor and Pollux represent the twin souls.

The Sign Gemini represents the hands and arms of the Grand Man of the Universe, and, therefore, expresses the projecting and executive forces of humanity in all mechanical departments.

Upon the esoteric planisphere, the Sign is occupied by Simeon and Levi. "They are brethren," says Jacob, "and instruments of cruelty are in their habitation"—which refers in a very unmistakable manner to the fearful, potent powers of projection that lie concealed within the magnetic constitutions of all those who are dominated by this Sign. The mystical symbol of The Twins conceals the doctrine of soul-mates and other important truths connected therewith.

Gemini is the first and highest emanation of the airy Trigon; it is the constellation of the planet Mercury.

The planet Mercury absorbs an energy which appears to be a compound of all other planets of the spectrum put together; he has been well designated as "The Messenger of the Gods."

The mystical gem of this Sign is the emerald, which is the talisman-stone for those born under this Sign.

The fortunate day is Wednesday.

Fortunate numbers are three and four.

The fortunate colors for this Sign are silver and gray.

Best locations for success are high places, well above sea level.

The specific action which this orb radiates is purely intellectual and scientific. It is quick and active, intuitional, enterprising, careless, volatile, bright, changeable, and what we call "smart."

This influence is extremely inventive and is the originator of all cunning schemes and devices. It is what men term bright and witty. It is that which makes the man of commerce. It constitutes the leading influence embodied within that sharp, clever and chameleon-like individual who makes a fortune in real estate or the stock market.

Addressing a Gemini, I would say that you have what is known as an intellectual type of personality. You are attractive, active, and magnetic upon first impression. Your manners are charming and pleasing. You are fond of being looked up to and respected. Under normal conditions you will be well liked by the majority of people you meet. There are times, however, when it will be necessary for you to take stock of yourself and your personality. You are whimsical and somewhat changeable, especially in regard to people you associate with consistently. You will find it to your advantage to exercise your interesting personality in the direction of self-control.

Do your best to avoid unwise whims and fancies. You desire to have others show you consideration; in return, you should show consideration for others. Do all within your power to exercise the more charming characteristics of your personality and you will do much toward making yourself happy and be able to make your loved ones and others happy because of you.

You have a sensitive and active mind; emotionally you are quite affectionate, generous and impulsive. These qualities often cause you to be misunderstood by others. Your procrastination is brought about by the intense activity of your mind and your reactions to your own thoughts and ideas. There are times when you are unusually generous. You have a fairly quick temper, but this amounts to unpleasant peevishness more than downright anger. Most of the time you are over it quickly. Under ordinary circumstances you are not much inclined to hold a grudge for long. Your active mind disposes you to be talkative and even to take delight in personal arguments on many subjects. You often argue for the sake of arguing. Avoid unwise or excessive indulgence in this direction and you gain by it.

Indications point to originality of thought, vivid imagination, a good sense of humor, and forcefulness of expression. You have good powers of observation and perception and can be patient if you want to be. You are able to grasp the facts of a proposition quicker than the average individual. You learn things easily.

Your imagination often causes you to desire to live a picturesque and romantic life. Herein may lie the secret of some of your greatest difficulties and disillusionments in life. You are somewhat of a dreamer and idealist; when your ideals or dreams are shattered you are deeply disillusioned and hurt. Give your imagination the proper scale and you will do much toward improving its practical value. Use imagination's energy for constructive planning and visualization of the things you wish to accomplish. You are inclined to acquire all sorts of knowledge, with the result that your memory does not always furnish you with retained facts. You will, however, readily recall such things in which you have taken an unusual interest or have paid particular attention to at some time or another. For example, you will often recall an insult much quicker than you will a kind word. The former made a deeper impression upon your mind and the latter was something you took, more or less, for granted.

Your memory functions most efficiently in matters pertaining to work and business. Your active mind ravishes acquiring all sorts of ideas and theories. This makes you an exceptionally good conversationalist. Much of your impulsiveness rises from your subconscious mind. Someone of your temperament is apt to be impulsive, more from a mental than an emotional point of view. It will pay you to study and understand this part of your personality. It will help you to avoid many psychological and emotional errors which could make your life uncertain and unhappy. You should curb the tendency to act upon impulse.

A person of your temperament often has inspirational ideas. How far they advance beyond the point of your imagination depends entirely upon you. If you are content to just muse and daydream about them, they will never serve a useful or practical purpose. Your inspired ideas are usually of an artistic nature. You have an active intuition which gives you the power to separate the real from the ideal. It also serves to warn you in times of danger and gives you an unusually keen insight into the characters of others.

If you give yourself the proper mental training, you will find that your subconscious mind will furnish you with all the material you require. You have the power to think up new and original ideas. Many persons born in your Sign are excellent writers, creators of new forms of art, inventors, musical composers, etc.

You are sensitive, affectionate and refined as a lover. However, your affection, tenderness, and passion depend upon your mental moods. You are capable of warmth and tenderness in one moment and coolness and indifference in the next. If your attention is focused on mental problems, you show physical indifference and may readily be misunderstood. This capacity for detachment often helps to complicate your love affairs. When you wish, however, you can be exceedingly expressive. More than one outstanding love affair is indicated during your lifetime. Indications show that you are more likely to care for people from an intellectual, rather than from a physical, point of view. You appear to be flirtatious and flighty; in reality, you are interested in enjoying diversified mental companionship.

Your imagination plays an important part in your love life. You require a mental and physical balance in love in order to be happy and contented. You have a mind of your own and wish to exercise the independence of your own nature to a great degree; thus, it is advisable that you use exceptionally good judgment in matters of love and marriage. Your sensitive emotional nature requires an intellectual, affectionate, and refined mate. Your Sign does not give promise of many children.

Your Sign presides over the chest, lungs, hands, and arms. Always do your best to avoid exposure to common colds. It is also advisable not to overwork your body or mind, as this appears to tax your sensitive nervous system and makes you peevish and irritable. Use care in your diet and eat wholesome and nerve-building foods. Plenty of fresh air, sunshine and light exercise are essential to your physical and mental well-being. You should never confine yourself to close or stuffy quarters. Above all, endeavor to do your best to exercise rational control over a tendency to brood and worry. This habit, if you indulge in it, will upset your nervous system. Such upsets will lay the foundation for future complications in your state of health.

It appears you will be somewhat critical in matters pertaining to your home life. You desire to have things "just so," otherwise, you become a fuss-budget. You are extremely sensitive in your reactions to home surroundings. You have an aversion to monotony. Your active mind makes you bored with the sameness of things. You often become restless and nervous if you have to stay too long in one place. A certain amount of control of this tendency will go a long way to help you get along better with others. A vacation away from home surroundings will often do you much good. When this is not possible, it is up to you to curb your restlessness until conditions make it possible for you to get out and enjoy a change.

You appreciate the type of work which exercises your active mind. You possess natural qualifications for writing, merchandising, practicing law, medicine, or occupations connected with travel, printing, and aviation. Often you desire to follow several vocations at once. There may be times in life when you feel that your progress is too slow; then you become depressed. You will do well, under such circumstances, to realize that all progress is not rapid and that patience is the key to advancement. Many Gemini natures have proved to be their own stumbling block. Both men and women of this Sign have either active or latent artistic ability which can be developed. It may be in music, art, or dancing. Odd and unusual literature has proved profitable for many of your Sign.

You also have good promotional and sales ability and succeed in occupations dealing with the general public. In matters of partnership you can get along fairly well. You are apt to desire the upper hand and if you do not handle yourself wisely you will cause dissension. If you are thoughtful and cooperative you will be able to prosper in such ventures.

Your financial circumstances, like your moods, may vary considerably during the course of your life. You are apt to spend money for little things that bring you only temporary benefit. You are fond of dress and finery. It will be advisable for you to cultivate the habit of being reasonably conservative in your personal expenditures. During favorable financial periods you will do well to make practical investments in such things as properties, large industrial organizations, government bonds, and transportation lines. It will be well for you to curb impulsiveness in your financial affairs. The secret of financial success lies in the art of making your money work for you.

Indications show that you will have many very interesting friends and acquaintances. Although you will attract a great variety of people, your choice of close friends will be the intellectual type. You will derive much pleasure from such people, as they will afford an outlet for your keen mind. You will, however, be inclined to have serious arguments with some of your best and closest friends. You have a liking for an active social life and desire to mingle with many people. You have the type of personality that leads to success in social circles. With the ability to influence others, you can set a good example by your own ideals and philosophy.

Your greatest handicap in life arises from your tendency to procrastinate. You are selfish and have little regard for the feelings and thoughts of others. Independence of will is to be commended, but should not be overdone. Any individual with true wisdom knows the value of cooperation and will always work harmoniously with others for the common good of all. Many Gemini people are apt to assert an air of independence in order to cover up feelings of inferiority. Take stock of yourself and do all within your power to eliminate or control this tendency to be peevish and irritable over little things. You will also find it to your advantage to cultivate patience and fortitude. It is up to you to improve your mind and its qualities so that you will be able to attain a rational understanding of yourself. Take advantage of your natural creative abilities. Study such subjects as will enhance your prospects of gaining greater self-confidence. You must develop consistency of action in all constructive activities.

THE GEMINI CHILD

This child has an inquiring mind; he is continually asking questions with the intent of discovering the reason why. Gemini children are usually very humane and generous in disposition. These children have the ability to be clever, and often turn out to be progressive—with an inventive genius.

They will be fond of change and diversity. It is best to keep them busy, as inactivity will cause them to become impatient, and that's when mischief starts!

They like to use their talents in their own way; if given the opportunity, there are few things they cannot master. They are readily able to adapt themselves to persons and circumstances as they grow older, and usually they make many friends.

Parents often find it hard to understand their Gemini children.

These children are outwardly bold and inwardly timid. They like to use their own methods, while ignoring the suggestions or orders of others. A particular point for the parents of these children to remember is that, unless they are trained to complete each task before beginning another, they are apt to start much that they never finish.

The Gemini child's fundamental vitality is moderate; therefore, care should be taken in early life to guard his or her health. A study of the pathology of this birthsign indicates that the system may be kept under unnecessary tension by restlessness and nervousness. The Sign is ruled by the planet Mercury which has rulership over the nervous system. The child has a natural tendency to a nervous temperament and should not be frightened or left in the dark too long; neither should it listen to weird tales or see horror movies. Another point to be guarded against is the possibility of fractures of the shoulders, arms and hands. Lungs as well as diet should receive plenty of attention. Mental and bodily exercise will aid the Gemini child very much more than a lot of medicine.

The mountains, as well as upstairs rooms, are harmonious surroundings for them.

The Gemini child will possess latent conversational ability as well as creative powers. In general, the best training for this child is a liberal arts education. Their versatility will enable them to choose from a variety of occupations. The Gemini child will sometimes lack concentration, but if trained properly, the future possibilities for achievement will be greatly enhanced. There is also a tendency at times to be ungrateful, and it would be well to encourage and stimulate gratitude as well as sympathy.

THE GEMINI WIFE

The Gemini wife is first and foremost an intellectual woman. The strongest appeal to her is mental companionship. She must be made to feel that she is a partner, and not just a housekeeper.

It is natural for a woman of this type to want to maintain her outside activities after marriage. Of course, outside activities take up a lot of time, and many husbands resent this diffusion of interest. However, if there is to be harmony in the home it is better to treat this condition tactfully. Sometimes the wife, herself, discovers that two separate existences are impossible if justice is to be done to her home, and she gradually gives up her hobby or career. In many cases, the Gemini woman is so capable that her home and her work are managed smoothly.

When these natives are talented, it is usually in some well-paid line. They have been called mercenary, as they demand just compensation for their efforts. They are not the long-suffering type that works for nothing.

Gemini women are particular as to how their homes are run, even though they may not be in them as much as other wives. They are refined, meticulous women who abhor untidiness. They seldom do their own work if they can help it but direct efficiently and command obedience.

The Gemini woman shines brightly in society. She is scintillating and well informed. She is the type of woman who would make a helpful wife for a professional man.. One who builds his practice on agreeable social contacts would find this kind of woman the very partner for his interests. This nativity gives a somewhat flirtatious nature, and many a husband watches his Gemini with anxiety. He would feel much better if he knew that she was just using her sharp wits to enjoy a mental battle of the sexes.

Her common sense and protective instincts are strong; she would never sacrifice her home and husband for an extra-marital affair.

THE GEMINI HUSBAND

The Gemini husband is not the type of husband for a possessive, passionate wife. While these men are talented and interesting persons, they desire frequent changes in scenery. They make good newspapermen, writers, or scientists. Their domestic life is usually sketchy. The Gemini looks for a marriage partner who can share his mental and social interests and who is not too tied to her home. She must be willing to change her environment as often as he desires. The wives of these men must suffer their husband's interest in people and other women. He is inclined to be flirtatious, but his wandering fancy should not be taken seriously.

Actually Gemini men have a great deal of common sense, and while they love to pursue the "will o' the wisp," no other man can close a romantic chapter with more finality when the heat is on. If the Gemini husband could find a wife to vitalize his interest in family life without nagging, his marriage would be more successful. These natives are apt to assert an air of arrogance to hide an inferiority complex.

They have a somewhat critical attitude when it comes to home life. They like everything to be "just so," and can become very fussy when things are not up to their standards.

These men have an aversion to monotony and usually seek some diversion when they become bored at home. Though they possess a great amount of love for their children, they are apt to be strict with them.

THE CUSPS OF GEMINI

(If your birthday is not within the cusp of your Sign, the following does not apply to you.)

If the birthday is from May 21st through May 23rd.

You were born in Gemini with Taurus tendencies. The ruling planets are Mercury and Venus. This indicates a strong magnetic personality and many unusual talents. Music, art, literature, and the society of intellectual people appeal greatly to these natives.

They are good conversationalists and possess refined habits. They are full of life and energy. They always desire to excel as hosts and hostesses. They create good impressions wherever they go. The one fault they must overcome is their fear of public opinion. These natives are fond of travel and change. They possess determination and are not easily swerved from their course. They are alert, careful, progressive, and tactful.

They present a good appearance and have the ability to attract many friends, but need to cultivate the faculty of holding them. They will be popular with a wide circle of friends and are good entertainers.

If the birthday is from June 18th through June 21st.

You were born in Gemini with Cancer tendencies. The ruling orbs are Mercury and the Moon. This indicates that you are subject to self-pity; you may be too sensitive for your own good. You possess foresight and have an analytical type of mind. Graceful in movement and neat in appearance, you place much importance upon dress and style. You are inclined to be affectionate.

You can adjust yourself to many talents easily, and can master almost any profession you tackle, if you work with a congenial and intelligent partner.

You seem somewhat fond of speculation and the taking of chances, but the birthdays within this cusp do not promise much success along these lines. You make a good friend, and will meet any reasonable appeal for a helping hand, and do not listen to rumors or scandal.

You are precise and can be depended upon to do exactly as you promise. You are an idealist at heart and promote these ideals whenever possible, but be intelligent enough, also, to be practical.

THE DECANATES OF GEMINI

If the birthday is between May 21st and May 31st.

The personal and ruling planet is Mercury. It is known as the symbol of knowledge and rules the rational part of the mind. It imparts an alert, ingenious, perceptive, intellectual, studious, and forceful personality when in favorable aspect. In unfavorable aspect it inclines toward an inquisitive, shiftless, forgetful, and effusive nature.

This planet is said to be the great mental ruler; without Mercury's influence we would be devoid of memory and the powers of speech and expression.

If the birthday is between June 1st and June 10th.

The personal planet is Venus—symbol of love and beauty. It denotes a nature not liable to easily change. Both likes and dislikes will be maintained tenaciously. There is a tendency to be fearless, domineering, and obstinate. Personal things are shared freely; there is charity with the native's earthly possessions. A truly magnanimous spirit is indicated by this aspect of Venus in the chart.

If the birthday is between June 11th and June 21st.

The personal planets for this, the third decanate of Gemini, are Saturn and Uranus. These form an unusual combination with the ruling planet Mercury. The influence of these three planets is considered to be mostly mental. The native possesses an unusually brilliant mind that may verge on genius. The ideas and thoughts may be well in advance of the age in which the native lives.

THE DEGREES OF GEMINI

May 21st.

You of this day possess a sensitive, idealistic nature and a friendly, kindhearted disposition. Certain planetary aspects indicate generosity too extreme for your own good. Learn to recognize the true from the false. You will always work for the common good and will be popular with co-workers and associates.

Fondness of travel by water is shown. It is probable that a long sea voyage will result in a profitable business connection or a successful marriage.

May 22nd.

A practical and somewhat materialistic disposition is indicated here. There may be legal difficulties in the conversion of personal possessions to cash. You have strong convictions and ambitious goals. One aspect in this Horoscope shows excellent latent ability as a writer or orator. Your good speaking voice shows a talent for a public career.

May 23rd.

Here is shown a shrewd and alert mind. You will be deeply moved by higher sympathies and become a champion of human rights. There will be a tendency to meddle in the affairs of others; and while the intentions may be most charitable, many disappointments are indicated until it is learned that life's greatest rewards come to those who learn to mind their own business first. You are very capable in an emergency and will be an ambassador of good will.

May 24th.

You possess a magnetic and fanciful mind. You must learn the value of concentration in order to overcome a tendency to attempt too many things at one time. You are a fluent conversationalist and a prolific writer. One aspect in this Horoscope shows the possibility of making a financial success in some matter dealing with water or chemicals.

May 25th.

You possess an artistic personality with excellent literary ability. This is the degree of the politician and statesman. You will travel to foreign lands and exert influence as a master salesman.

A relative of this native may gain world-wide recognition for some outstanding accomplishment.

May 26th.

You possess a sensitive and retiring disposition coupled with deep emotions. You possess an inquiring mind but may develop a tendency to become too reserved and lonely. Try to overcome a sense of insecurity. Do not hesitate to show your friends and associates the shrewd side of your nature; they will admire you more for it.

May 27th.

You are courteous and affable with an obliging, perceptive mind. A highly magnetic personality and an enterprising disposition will bring many respected and beneficial friendships in life. There will be one great love in your life. You have the force of leadership, and will make a success through some original idea of undertaking. Do not let good fortune go to your head and upset your progress.

May 28th.

You possess an alert, impressionable, and often irritable nature. At times, you may become downright cantankerous and lose many friends thereby. Try to check this tendency as much as possible. One aspect in this Horoscope shows a marked degree of leadership with excellent talent for the five arts. This is the degree of the composer, the poet, and the artist.

May 29th.

You possess a romantic nature and may be an idealist and dreamer. You are most truthful, and are quite candid in your opinions of others. You may show a decided preference to be in the company of sophisticates and to associate with important persons. You will go far in the social world, and as your experience and character develops, you will move up the ladder of success.

May 30th.

You possess wholesome charm and great magnetism. You have an artistic temperament and show originality in your ideas and undertakings. Your lofty ideals will help you to attain considerable success in the social world. Gains through marriage and partnerships are indicated. One aspect in this Horoscope shows long journeys and many influential friends.

May 31st.

You possess a bright, cheerful disposition and a kind, generous nature. You are just and righteous in both personal and social matters. You should pursue a professional career, where your mental faculties will be demonstrated to the best advantage. A strong attachment for the home and parents is also indicated.

June 1st.

You possess a strong will and a commanding, energetic personality. Success in the art of dealing with the public will bring wide recognition. There is a tendency, however, towards extravagance, which should be curbed. You should learn to understand the value of personal possessions and to cherish them. An ardent, highly emotional nature, full of adventure and wild dreams, should be moderated.

June 2nd.

You possess an active, strong, and sometimes domineering personality. One aspect in this Horoscope indicates that you inspire others with your ideas and plans, but become restless and are inclined to worry a great deal if you run into obstacles. Practice tolerance and patience and there will be a better chance to fulfill your hopes and desires.

June 3rd.

You possess a keen mind and a calm, peaceful attitude toward life. A charming, open-minded manner, coupled with inherent humanitarian principles, will endear you to all. Gain is indicated through sentimental associations and influential friendships. One aspect in this Horoscope shows a tendency to take good fortune and successful ventures too lightly. This may result in taking things for granted.

June 4th.

You possess an ingenious, active, and alert mind. An artistic temperament will bring you many lasting and influential friendships. You are generous, kind-mannered, and are charitably inclined. One aspect in this Horoscope indicates that there may be a tendency to shirk responsibility. Remember that hard work and the diligent application of your many natural talents are necessary attributes to success and happiness.

June 5th.

You possess the ability to develop your mind along intellectual and scientific lines. You will display independence of thought and will possess a steady and forceful disposition. One aspect in this Horoscope indicates a desire to defy convention and become a bold innovator. An inheritance at some time in your life is indicated.

June 6th.

You possess an energetic and commanding personality. Because you are an excellent conversationalist, you will be in great demand at social gatherings. An able and orderly spirit coupled with a keen sense of diplomacy and tact will help you to attain public esteem. Your fine qualities will make it rather easy for you to get what you want from your parents, friends, and associates. One aspect in this Horoscope shows many artistic relatives.

June 7th.

You possess a dual personality and a very imaginative mind. Success in the business world seems to stem from lessons taught in the home. You will be fond of mimicry and will possess a liking for the stage and theater. One aspect in this Horoscope shows a strong will and an excellent ability to organize and direct. Success in a business or a vocation catering to women is influenced by this degree.

June 8th.

You possess artistic sympathies and a humane disposition. This combination of mental qualities is usually found in persons who attain success and recognition in public service. Try to curb a tendency to be impulsive, as such a characteristic, if permitted to develop, can prove detrimental.

June 9th.

You possess an intuitive mind. You are able to exert great skill in the execution of your duties. Persistence and determination, even in the face of difficulties, will bring success and financial independence. You choose your friends and associates discriminately and display considerable reserve at all times. You will overcome many disagreeable obstacles. One aspect in this Horoscope indicates a sensuous nature and a hasty temper.

June 10th.

You possess a quick mind and a love of travel. Success in a material way is indicated through the ability to make and hold influential and beneficial friendships. Marked originality and a good sense of humor will make for a position of prestige in the social world. A vivid imagination, coupled with excessive energy, may cause you to become impatient at times. Learn that "haste makes waste."

June 11th.

You possess a retiring, studious, and chaste nature. An envious streak, which may become apparent from time to time, should be curbed. You are fond of literature, music, and art. You should make the maximum use of your intellectual and commercial talents. Learn self-confidence and the ability to see the other person's point of view. Due to lack of emotional stability, you may be hard to understand at times. This degree shows public acclaim through artistic or literary endeavor.

June 12th.

You possess an imaginative mind coupled with excellent powers of observation. Avoid a tendency to trust too much to luck. You are a natural student with excellent mathematical ability. This is the degree of the inventor and the scientist. You are very sympathetic and will do well in government work.

June 13th.

You possess a serious, aspiring nature coupled with strong mental capabilities. You are profound and practical. A strong sense of independence and desire to help those in less fortunate circumstances is indicated by this degree. At times you may become too magnanimous for your own good. You should learn the value of financial conservatism. Success in life through dealing with new enterprises and large institutions catering to the public welfare is indicated.

June 14th.

You possess a studious and reserved disposition with an alert, thoughtful, and intuitive mind. You are well able to concentrate upon your goal in life and will be spurred on by a desire to achieve and fulfill most of your hopes and desires. You are industrious and self-reliant because of a highly ambitious and determined disposition.

June 15th.

You possess great compassion for your fellow man. A desire to help all those who ask assistance can result in expenditures beyond your means. You are subject to flattery and can easily become the prey of designing friends and associates. One aspect in this Horoscope indicates inspirational ideas backed by a keen insight. This will be an important asset in helping you overcome periods of so-called hard luck.

June 16th.

You possess a solemn and melancholy disposition. Marked sympathies for your friends and relatives will make you very popular as a consultant. The art of diplomacy is inherent in your make-up. You will show much compassion for those who come to you for advice and help.

June 17th.

You possess a very impressionable character. A highly magnetic personality and an enterprising disposition will bring many respected and beneficial friendships in life. Guard against a desire to make changes without considering the consequences. You may experience fluctuating financial security unless you develop consistency of purpose.

June 18th.

You possess a positive and domineering personality. Develop a sense of stability in order to check your adventurous spirit. You have good ideas and will find success in unusual undertakings. This is the degree of one who makes hay while the sun shines. Many successful inventors and scientists were born in this degree.

June 19th.

You possess a good sense of direction. A strong will coupled with a desire to have your way will not hamper your success. An inquisitive, aspiring, and perceptive mind indicates success in the professional world. You will be attracted to the study of literature and music. An ability to get along well with all types of people will aid materially in attaining success as a teacher or public official.

June 20th.

You possess an adaptable, versatile, and intuitive mind. The value of concentration should be learned. You may lack the desire to combat the realities of life. See that you complete one thing before turning your attention to another. A charming personality coupled with a good sense of humor will attract many friendships, but only diligent application of your many capabilities will aid in attaining success and happiness.

June 21st.

You possess an expansive and genial personality. You will attain much popularity in your social life. An artistic temperament coupled with an aspiring mind will make for success in a professional rather than business career. Your enthusiastic and idealistic nature will enable you to participate in some very interesting and profitable undertakings.

COMPATIBLE AND INCOMPATIBLE SIGNS OF GEMINI

The Gemini outlook is purely a mental one; sex interests are quite secondary so far as these natives are concerned. Gemini is essentially a cold-blooded Sign and lacks great sensuous passion. This native is a kind of living question mark. He is forever analyzing his own and other people's actions and reactions. Mental dissection is a particularly Geminian habit. Gemini wants to analyze everything, and is entirely unmindful of the effect this may have upon others.

It is, therefore, obvious that the normal attitude of Gemini to sex matters is not only experimental, but rather cool, calculating, and selfish. These natives are born under what is known as a fickle and changeable Sign. Actually the fickleness arises not from wandering sex desires, but from a hope of attaining theoretical ideals. Unfortunately this aim—for those of Gemini—is impossible to achieve, for their ideal varies according to the mood of the moment, and can swing from one extreme to the other.

Gemini is a difficult Sign for most people to understand, as it is both more illogical in nature and more ideological in tendency than some of the others. Gemini's analytic nature produces a suspicious effort to try and read between the lines. The Geminians imagine that other people mean much more than they say. The native's mental gymnastics brings about rapid changes of thought and desire. Slowness in others is a constant source of annoyance to Gemini. The wife or husband of a Gemini must never be mentally dull or obtuse if happiness is to be maintained. Owing to a sensitive nervous system and highly moral outlook, a Gemini person with a badly afflicted Horoscope can readily develop physical frigidity because of emotional instability.

The duality of the Sign is often evident in romantic matters. Gemini natives may often carry on two love affairs simultaneously. The great desire of Gemini's heart is to remain as free as the air, which this Sign represents. Those born under Gemini should be very careful in their choice of a lover or mate, instinctively avoiding the too-possessive or jealous type. Geminians are rather difficult to cope with because they are so unpredictable in their romantic moods. One hardly ever knows how to take them, or where one stands with them. They want someone who is capable of constantly stimulating their interest and who can offer them variety, novelty, and adulation, regardless of reciprocation. However, like many Utopian ideas, this ideal is by no means easy to attain.

A pet delusion of the Gemini-born is that they are not interested in sex, so they seek a mate who is capable of catering to their varied mental interests and activities. A very real difficulty with them lies in the fact that their romantic notions are usually based upon high moral ideas. They should try to realize that love is not always logical.

As already indicated, if you were born under this Sign, you

have definite ideas as to the type of person you are seeking for a partner. The following will serve to confirm you in your choice.

Gemini and Aries.

These partners would find it hard to meet on common ground, due to the emphatic differences in their approach to sexual matters. Above all, Gemini respects the refined, intellectual approach to connubial bliss. The Arien is an impatient and emotional native of a fiery Sign, and may find the cool, calm Geminian, whose mind plays such an important part in love-making, frustrating.

Gemini and Taurus.

These two are unsuited to each other because of their emotional outlook. The Mercurian Geminian's delight in all mental pursuits, and great love of variety is not compatible with the earthly outlook of the Venus-ruled Taurus. The fixed, slow, plodding, faithful Taurus would find it hard to adapt to the restless Gemini.

Gemini and Gemini.

This should prove a compatible combination; at least both would understand each other's changeable natures. The sex demands and needs would be mutual. The one exception would be if one or the other has Scorpio rising at the time of birth. The demands of Scorpio would prove too much for the purely Mercurial Gemini nature, since Gemini's approach to sex is spiritual while that of Scorpio is more physical. A Gemini maiden would prove too puritanical for the Gemini-Scorpio rising male. This combination makes for excellent partnerships where the principals are engaged in corresponding vocations, such as singer-composer, author-publisher, etc.

Gemini and Cancer.

The home-loving Cancer may find the club-loving Gemini too elusive for a good mate. While Gemini is constantly on the alert for change, Cancer is satisfied to become a truly domesticated mate. On the other hand, the Cancerian moodiness may become too much for Gemini to cope with. This combination does hold better possibilities for compatibility where the female is a Gemini and the male is a Cancer, especially if there are several children to occupy the Gemini mother's time.

Gemini and Leo.

This combination will soon find out that they are emotionally unsuited. While Leo loves with the heart first, Gemini loves with the mind. There is great mutual attraction for both these Signs on the surface. Both Signs are naturally attracted to glamour, flattery, and the world of good fellowship. After these two return home from the party, the carefree, passionate Leo will surely clash with an unreasonable Gemini, who will complain that the Leo love nature is too material, possessive and demanding.

Gemini and Virgo.

Not a good combination for connubial bliss. Mercury, the ruling planet of both these Signs, may prove too much over the long pull. In Gemini, Mercury is logical and calculating; in Virgo, it is demanding and critical. The realistic Virgo would be constantly at odds with Gemini's ever-present desire for change. One point of compatibility would be the desire for good clothes, cleanliness, and a mutual desire for friends and associates who are engaged in intellectual and artistic pursuits. It is through these channels that many Gemini-Virgo combinations are formed.

Gemini and Libra.

This is considered to be a good astrological influence for a long and happy life of marriage. Both Signs have much in common and enough contrast to make an ideal partnership. Venus (Libra) and Mercury (Gemini) is usually a good planetary configuration. Both favor similar changes of interests. In the case of this combination, Libra is the judge and Gemini the responsive jury in the nuptial courthouse. Their intellectual and artistic interests are compatible. Libra will readily understand both sides of the Gemini nature.

Gemini and Scorpio.

Here Gemini finds a mate that can surpass the Gemini urge for action. From a mental standpoint, Gemini is more than a match for a Scorpio mate, but from a sexual and physical viewpoint, Gemini is too innately modest to meet Scorpio's demands. The jealous and possessive Scorpion nature will soon clash with Gemini's desire for freedom of action. While some Gemini-Scorpio combinations may work out fairly well, the pure Gemini-Scorpio alliance packs as much explosive as an atomic bomb.

Gemini and Sagittarius.

Here are two Signs with one purpose—freedom of limb and action. Usually a compatible combination, both Signs are frank, outspoken, and cherish a certain amount of personal freedom. Inconstancy is mutually agreeable to these two astrological affinities. They meet on common ground, and can plan their lives with equanimity. Although there will be times when the love nest will become fairly ruffled and fur may fly, these lovebirds will battle more for the sake of diversion than blood.

Gemini and Capricorn.

Here we find the Saturnian nature of Capricorn at odds with the fleet winged messenger of the Gods—Mercury. Patience is a virtue with Capricorn, but not so with Gemini. Unless there is a willingness on Gemini's part to slow down and heed the good advice of the Capricorn mate, much dissension and unhappiness is in the stars. Capricorn's great drive to excel, regardless of opposition, will prove too much for Geminians. Unless they both are willing to trim their sails, the Goat of Capricorn will go on butting until he gains the upper hand.

Gemini and Aquarius.

The humanitarian instincts of Aquarius will find a ready haven with Gemini. Uranus, the ruling planet of Aquarius, is full of sudden surprises and changes which will suit Gemini perfectly. There will be sufficient variety to afford the stimulation that Gemini needs for its dual personality. The Gemini-born are always looking for surprises; the Aquarian will readily supply them. A note of warning to the Geminian—when the Aquarian mate wants to be alone, Gemini should not be offended. This is only a passing condition and will soon disappear—but at times the Aquarian must have these intervals of solitude.

Gemini and Pisces.

The freedom of those of Gemini is at stake if they marry a Piscean. They must be prepared to give up all outside interests and devote all of their time and thoughts to the Pisces mate. The sensitive and distrustful Piscean nature will, no doubt, prove too much for the liberty-loving Gemini to cope with. Geminians must be prepared to change their personalities almost completely if they would seek happiness with a loving, possessive, and clinging Piscean mate.

SOME FAMOUS PERSONS BORN IN THE SIGN
OF GEMINI

Jefferson Davis—Confederate
   President
Sir Arthur Conan Doyle—Author
Sir Anthony Eden—Statesman
James Montgomery Flagg—Artist
Errol Flynn—Actor
Judy Garland—Actress
Dashiell Hammett—Novelist
Bob Hope—Comedian

Al Jolson—Actor
Thomas Mann—Novelist
Marilyn Monroe—Actress
Robert Montgomery—Actor
Sir Laurence Olivier—Actor
Dr. Norman V. Peale—
   Clergyman and Author
Cole Porter—Song Writer

Jean Paul Sartre—Philosopher and Writer

Alfred P. Sloan, Jr.—Business Executive

Igor Stravinsky—Composer

Josip Broz (Tito)—Yugoslav Statesman

Queen Victoria—British Monarch

Richard Wagner—German Composer

Frank Lloyd Wright—Architect

CANCER

JUNE 22–JULY 22

THE SIGN OF CANCER symbolizes tenacity. The Crab is its symbol. The Crab, in order to move forward, is compelled to walk backwards. This illustrates the Sun's apparent motion when in this Sign when it commences to move backward toward the equator again. Cancer also represents the fruitful, sustaining essence of the life forces, hence we see the symbol of the Crab occupying a prominent position upon the breast of the Statue of Isis, the universal mother and sustainer of all. The Sign Cancer signifies the vital organs of the Grand Man of the Starry Heavens, and therefore represents the breathing and digestive functions of the human family. It also indicates the magnetic control of this constellation over the spiritual, ethereal, and vital essences.

Cancer governs the powers of inspiration and respiration of the Grand Man. The Sign Cancer upon the planisphere astrologically intimates the home of the Crab, the shore. It also expresses the varied powers of cohesion, and the paradoxical truths found in all contradictories. Cancer is the highest emanation of the watery Trigon, and is the constellation of the Moon.

Cancer signifies the equilibrium of spiritual and material life forces.

It is in the fourth House of the Zodiac and governs the breast and the stomach and represents tenacity.

Those dominated by its influx express the highest form of the reflective powers; they are timid and retiring. They are truly passive and constitute natural mediums. Cancer possesses but little of the intuitional qualities. That which appears to be intuition is direct inspiration. To the external eye, the natives of this watery trigon are incessant workers on the higher, or mental plane. This Sign expresses to us the conservation of forces. Its chief attributes are sensitivity and reflection.

The mystical gems of the Sign are the pearl and the moonstone. These gems are powerful talismans for all natives of Cancer.

The fortunate day is Friday. Fortunate numbers are eight and three.

The colors for this Sign are silver and white.

Best locations for these natives will be found near or on water.

Addressing a Cancer, I would say: You have an interesting, but somewhat enigmatic personality. You are a being of considerable reserve, but are, nevertheless, capable of joy and friendship. Though you have a great amount of personal pride, you are not egotistical or vain. You are often misunderstood and accused of being self-centered. Since you are an individualist, you have a good sense of your own worth. You will find it to your advantage to cultivate the art of self-expression in the presence of other people, because you can do so much to make others happy. You are straightforward, generous, upright, and loyal to your friends and to any cause in which you take an interest. You represent the type of personality that can be trusted with any important secret, commission, duty, or work. In fact, many of your close associates and friends rely on you at various times.

The true key to your disposition and temperament lies in your reflective memory. You have great depth of feeling and these feelings can be easily hurt, even though you keep this to yourself to a great extent. In fact, most of the time you would rather hide your feelings than express them. While you seldom hold a grudge, you never forget an unkind deed or action. You are apt to be extremely sensitive in emotional matters. You dislike anything that may be construed as a small or petty act. Your natural disposition is like the Sign under which you were born. Many people are seen by you as though they were children and in your noble, yet silent, way, you guide them to the best of your ability with your logical philosophy of life. You are sympathetic and show much understanding.

You have good perception and very keen powers of observation. You are a natural student. You are meditative and have unusual powers of concentration. Except in periods of stress and emergency, you have good coordination between mind and body. There is very little that escapes your attention.

You endeavor to analyze your own thoughts and impulses. The faculty of imagination is very active in you. Musing about things and events that have taken place in the past is enjoyable to you. The ability to construct and reconstruct things in your imagination is another of your powers. This enables you to make improvements in various ways and to advance your own ideas and methods of doing things. It also helps you to be creative. There are times, however, when you are inclined to muse or daydream too much about the past. It is advisable to curb this tendency to a reasonable extent.

You can learn most anything you make up your mind to study. You are not always inclined to express your knowledge, but you can be a very good conversationalist when you so desire.

The average individual of your Sign has a natural tendency to study and analyze most of the impulses that arise from within. Those of your Sign that do not follow this process usually learn from bitter experience that it is not advisable to act upon impulse. Your excellent intuition thus gives you good insight into human nature and serves to give you foreknowledge of impending events as well as the ability to discriminate between fact and surmise.

You will find it to your advantage to study and learn more about the interesting faculties of your mind and the art of making them work for you. Very few, if any, ever understand the depth of your mind. It is seldom that you let anyone know what you actually think. You do not care to become aggressive unless circumstances and conditions make this a necessity. Your natural will and determination enables you to face obstacles. Patience and fortitude help you accomplish things long after others have given up. It may be advisable for you to share some of your interesting ideas and philosophy. It will help bring you the love, respect, and admiration you deserve.

Your birthsign presides over the stomach and the breast. Thus it is essential that you should use judgment in matters of diet in order to avoid stomach disorders. A sensible diet will do much to help you to avoid obesity and rheumatism. The problem of diet should be taken up with your family physician. Although you have a fairly good constitution, it is advisable not to overwork your body or mind and tax your sensitive nervous system. Avoid worry, moodiness, depression, and, above all, fears and complexes pertaining to ill health. Get plenty of fresh air and sunlight when you can. After the middle years of life, take up light exercises that will help to keep your body in good physical condition. Indications show that you are fond of the great out-of-doors and that you enjoy the beauties of nature. You find peace of mind and consolation around water. You derive a great amount of pleasure in reading or studying such works as interest you.

Indications show that you have a very sensitive, affectionate, and yet reserved, love nature. You do not always show your emotions but sometimes hold yourself in subjugation. This often proves to your disadvantage and is very apt to cause misunderstanding. In affairs of the heart you are tender, considerate, and affectionate. Love to you is something to be treated seriously. You are devoted to the object of your affection and have a tendency to be jealous. It is advisable to do all you can to avoid unreasonable jealousy. Owing to your sensitivity in matters of the heart, you are easily hurt, and once your feelings are deeply wounded it is very difficult for you to get over it. Many times such hurts cause you to change from one type of affection to another. Indications point to the fact that you can be among the happiest of all married people because of your love of home and the comforts of a wholesome domestic life. You are far happier in the married state than when single. Intellectual companionship plays an important part in your married life. Your personal love has a soothing and uplifting quality and you are devoted to the object of your affection. Be more demonstrative in the expression of your affection.

You have a great love for children. Your Sign is the parental sign and gives promise of some children. Your parental love is very deep rooted, but you must guard against becoming too critical of your children. If your home life is not harmonious, you will be quite unhappy. Owing to your natural sensitivity, unpleasantness in the home is apt to upset you deeply and more than the average individual.

There are times when it would prove to be to your personal advantage to take a trip or a short vacation away from your home surroundings. Avoid becoming a recluse. You are quite fond of travel, especially in the early years of your life. During the latter half of life you do not care to travel very far from your home. Your interesting mind and its remarkable powers of deduction and analysis indicate that your road to success lies mainly along professional lines. Your individuality must have it expression. Law, medicine, surgery, dentistry, navigation, instruction, salesmanship, mechanics and engineering are the vocations that are most likely to appeal to many Cancer people. Catering, running rooming houses, hotels, and restaurants also appeal to some. Cancer people also have latent and active artistic ability. Thus, you will find them designing clothes, composing music, painting, and active on stage and screen.

You have the type of personality and mind that creates its own destiny. Although others may help you at times, your actual progress depends upon yourself. Success to people of your Sign usually comes during the middle years of life, and usually continues until death. It is in the stars that you must exercise care in partnership ventures. You are industrious and conscientious and this often causes others to try to place too much responsibility and work upon your shoulders. It is true that you are capable and will not stand for much abuse. Under reasonably harmonious circumstances, you will do well in partnership ventures.

A fair degree of success comes to the people of your Sign who enter into business for themselves. When entering into such endeavor, it is advisable that you be well prepared to carry yourself over the periods of uncertainty until you get the proper start. Under such circumstances it is best to guard against becoming discouraged easily and giving up. Bear in mind that it takes courage and fortitude to achieve success.

Indications point to a varying cycle of financial success during the course of life. Your earning capacity is usually fairly good. However, you are generous and believe in purchasing the best that your money will afford. It appears that you would do well if you were to invest in real estate, government bonds, and the stocks and bonds of large corporations. You have, at times, an urge to gamble and speculate, but success in such matters is problematical. It is advisable never to speculate or gamble in big issues or to invest in get-rich-quick schemes. It is true that some Cancer people are quite successful in speculative ventures, and that their intuition helps them determine the value of a specific proposition. You are apt to experience financial difficulties during your early twenties, the thirtieth and sixtieth years of life. However, if you apply the conservative principles of your character to a reasonable extent, you will be able to attend to the problem of your own financial security in later years.

A person of your character and temperament needs but a few loyal friends. You will attract many people to you, but this is primarily because of what you may be able to do for them. You represent the type of individual who can be trusted by others and you will, no doubt, be in the confidence of many. The quality of your affection for them is usually of a parental nature. Although you are not particularly fond of an active social life, you will be able to enjoy a good social standing in your community. You take a keen delight in entertaining your close friends and associates at home.

You are meditative, and quite often like to enjoy the sacred seclusion of your own mind and thoughts; but you should also do all you can to avoid periodical spells of moodiness and brooding. Do all within your power to cast out useless fears and apprehensions that have a tendency to tax your mind and body and you will add greatly to your own progress. Indications show that your rise in life may be slow rather than spontaneous. Many of the people of your Sign work quietly for years and do not appear to get anywhere at all, but when opportunity comes they are usually ready and well prepared.

Use your higher psychic faculties to develop foresight. Realize that success must be born in your mind before you can ever hope to be successful in reality. Think it over. Investigate your own attitude and see what changes you need to make in order to create the success you are striving for.

THE CANCER CHILD

Cancer children should never be forced to have personal contact with persons whom they do not like, as it will have an ill effect on their health. These children are usually very timid and retiring, yet they want and need friendship and sympathy, though they are very sensitive about seeking it. They sometimes have a tendency to take their friends for granted. At the same time, they are very conscientious in all things entrusted to them, and use considerable discretion in whatever they do. They are generally fond of home and parents and are easily influenced by those they love and admire. Ill health is very likely to come from the stomach. It is, therefore, essential to exercise great care with their diet. They also may suffer from bronchitis, coughs, inflammatory conditions, kidney trouble, and nervous exhaustion.

As the Cancer child is extremely receptive and imaginative, there is a possibility that at times he will become somewhat melancholy and moody. It is well to remember such possibilities when rearing the Cancer child. Also to be noted is a tendency to be lethargic. It is essential that the parent stimulate the child to action in a kindly manner. These children are versatile, and it is desirable for parents to encourage these children's ambitions in the formative years.

THE CANCER WIFE

The Cancer wife mothers everyone. She, typically, is the most motherly of all the Zodiacal wives. When at her best, she is a sympathetic, affectionate, protective woman. She is patient, devoted, adaptable, and satisfied with anything her husband provides for her. Her home is wherever her husband decides that it should be, and she gives the humblest place a permanent look. Her presence is sanctifying, and she understands how to serve. She is loved and respected in return for her devotion, and is the personification of all literature that idealizes "Mother." All of this, of course, depends upon the planetary combinations in the nativity.

Negative Cancer wives have some of these qualities, but too often they are moody, changeable, and unwilling to improve. It is very easy for a Cancer girl to marry; her natural inclinations are so sympathetic that marriageable men are drawn to her. She seeks protection, and it always comes to her. But if she is a girl without a great deal of character and background, she will need the help and guidance of her husband for strength to meet life's problems. Her husband is on a pedestal in her imagination, and if he fails her, the spiritual shock is crushing.

The wives of Cancer are passionately possessive and absorbed in the life of the family. Taken generally, their whole character is proverbially feminine, and the man who marries a Cancerian wife gets a completely feminine woman.

THE CANCER HUSBAND

The Cancer husband is not an easy person to live with, despite the Sign's reputation for easygoing good nature. The type is divided into at least two groups, one of which is dominant. The husband of this group loves his home, but he is exacting, fussy, and inclined to be critical and fault-finding.

The negative Cancer man as a husband is so passive, lazy, and self-indulgent, he often goes so far as to marry for money and position. Since this kind of man is persistent and agreeable when he chooses to be, it is often possible for him to attain his ambition.

Any Cancer husband spends more time at home than another man. He has a deep love for the traditional values of home and family, and has many of the same qualities in his nature that are significant in the Cancer woman. Moodiness, changeability, sentimentality, and effusiveness can be understood in a woman's nature, but transferred to a man, these qualities are not inspiring, especially in large domestically administered doses. The Cancer husband means to be devoted, and his whole mind is preoccupied by his wife and family, but his disposition is such that these feelings are translated into exacting demands for service. Nothing satisfies him and the most affectionate family feels the burden of this intensely possessive spirit.

Husbands born in Cancer are usually faithful enough if their desires are satisfied at home. The effort entailed in conducting outside liaisons is too much for the Cancer man. He is rather timid and abhors danger. Therefore, while his senses

might lead him astray, he is unwilling to be involved in compli
cations that require effort to sustain.

THE CUSPS OF CANCER

(If your birthday is not within the cusp of your Sign, the following does not apply to you.)

If the birthday is from June 22nd through June 25th.

You were born in Cancer with Gemini tendencies. Your ruling
orbs are the Moon and Mercury. This indicates that you are brilliant, decisive, and are usually in control of any situation that
arises. You like to deal with the general public and are most
content when you hold a position that brings you in touch with
different types of people.

You are unduly sensitive and take things too seriously. In
general, you have an analytical mind, but in some matters you
are likely to overlook important details. You are somewhat moody
but possess a good memory.

Frequently you tire of your regular routine in life and try to
hunt up new experiences and associates. When you develop
new friends, you have a tendency to neglect your old ones. You
are fond of the good things in life. You are also interested in
society, and the artistic things of life have a definite appeal to
you.

If the birthday is from July 19th through July 22nd.

You were born in Cancer with Leo tendencies. Your ruling orbs
are the Moon and the Sun. This shows that you are original,
clever, idealistic, and a good mixer. You possess a quick temper
that is derived from Leo, but your Cancer qualities will usually
keep it under good control. You seem to have difficulty in making
ends meet. When things go wrong you sink into a depressed
state of mind. If you have once made up your mind you can be

stubborn and headstrong. Regardless of what others think, you will go on being just yourself. You usually possess a wide circle of acquaintances, yet few can be considered real friends.

You do not especially care for display or show. You prefer to live a simple, comfortable life where you will be left alone whenever you are not in the mood for companionship. You do not impose upon others, but quite often they take advantage of your kindness.

THE DECANATES OF CANCER

If the birthday is between June 22nd and June 30th.

The personal orb for this decan is also the Moon, known as the ruler of the night, the great symbol of life's forces, and the natural reflector of the Sun. This planet governs the domestic, idealistic and maternal tendencies.

These natives possess a humane, kind disposition, and a dislike of dissension. By nature they are doubtful, apprehensive, and mediumistic. They may have a high temper and a tendency to pamper ill-advised impulses. Due to their critical and sensitive disposition, special care should be taken to overcome the negative tendencies which may develop in the character.

If the birthday is between July 1st and July 11th.

The personal planet is Mars, known as the symbol of War and Center of Divine Energy. It influences the energetic, courageous, active, and constructive tendencies. Mars will aid the native materially in overcoming some of the weaker and more negative aspects of the maternal orb, the Moon. It will give the necessary impetus to bring about the successful conclusion to many endeavors. Without this force it would be difficult to realize many cherished ambitions. The combination of the Moon and Mars is, indeed, a fortunate one, since Mars, being aggressive and powerful, forces its natives to attain their objectives.

If the birthday is between July 12th and July 22nd.

The personal orbs are the conflicting planets Jupiter and Neptune. Jupiter is known to be the planet of Good Fortune and Blessing, with harmonious vibrations, while Neptune is known as the Spiritual Awakener, and governs the scientific, inventive, and artistic faculties. It sometimes acts to produce an involved, chaotic and nebulous state of affairs. This would indicate that the native possesses a very changeable and unpredictable nature. The greatest battle in life for those of this sector will be with themselves. The negative and positive qualities will be marked at an early age, which should give an opportunity to help eliminate the faults.

THE DEGREES OF CANCER

Each Zodiacal Sign contains thirty degrees. The Sun transists one degree per day, each representing a birthday, and gives further influence on the native's character and destiny. The following will give the analyses of all birthdays (degrees) of Cancer.

June 22nd.

A splendid character and a sympathetic nature coupled with deep emotions is indicated for this degree. The native is instinctively intellectual and matures early in life. It is essential that there be a happy environment; associates should be those whom the native can look up to and respect. There is a liking for outdoor activity and athletic pursuits. The emotional temperament yields to patient understanding rather than harsh treatment and dictatorial methods.

June 23rd.

A serious, aspiring nature coupled with strong mental capabilities are imparted by this degree. The native is profound and practical. A strong sense of independence and a desire to help those in less fortunate circumstances is indicated. There is, too, a marked respect for superiors. Those born on this day can create their own destiny. Success in life is indicated through dealing with new enterprises and large institutions catering to the public welfare.

June 24th.

A retiring and chaste nature is shown here. An envious streak should be curbed. There is fondness of literature, music, and art. There should be an effort to use any intellectual and commercial training to the maximum. Learn self-confidence and the ability to see the other fellow's point of view.

June 25th.

Those of this degree possess an original, enterprising mind, and a harmonious, contented disposition. One aspect of this Horoscope indicates that the native will be easily satisfied. The practical methods by which success is achieved should be learned. Associates should be persons who are successful. High hopes and ambitions should be tempered with an awareness of reality.

June 26th.

This degree imbues the native with a pleasing personality and splendid intuitive powers. A highly emotional nature can develop into an uncontrollable temper unless there is a real effort made to overcome this aspect. There is a tendency to brood and daydream too much if left alone for any great length of time. Above all, a "martyr fixation" should be avoided. The native may receive a great deal of help from someone befriended in the past.

June 27th.

A flexible, happy nature and a clever, imaginative mind is bestowed upon the natives of this degree. Those of this birthday may be too generous and agreeable for their own good, and should learn that caution is the better part of valor. They are fond of mimicry and possess great liking for the stage and theater.

Losses due to extravagance and misplaced confidence may be avoided by controlling a tendency to be overly solicitous.

June 28th.

A keen, intellectual mind coupled with excellent powers of concentration is indicated for these Cancer-born. A tendency to assume a too serious outlook upon life should be avoided. A bright, cheerful atmosphere and congenial company will help to eliminate this aspect. This highly magnetic personality and independent nature will make for great success in the business world. There is fondness of music and travel, and many profitable experiences in connection with both are indicated.

June 29th.

An energetic nature and great skill in the execution of duties is shown here. Persistence and determination, even in the face of difficulties, will bring success and financial independence. Friends and associates are chosen with discrimination, and there is a display of considerable reserve at all times. Tolerance and consideration of other people's feelings should be practiced. A tendency to impulsiveness is shown by one aspect here. This may lead to financial loss as a result of poor judgment.

June 30th.

This degree imparts a gentle, kind, sympathetic disposition, and a good mind coupled with a charitable nature, which should endear this native to all. The magnetic personality and ability to attract staunch and loyal friendships may result in a dependent attitude. It is necessary to learn that independence and personal accomplishments are essential to success and happiness.

July 1st.

These Cancerians possess a sensitive, idealistic nature and a friendly, kind-hearted disposition. Certain planetary aspects denote a tendency to be too generous for personal welfare. Recognition of the true from the false must be learned. There is fondness of travel by water, and indications of a long sea voyage which may result in a profitable business connection. A successful marriage is also indicated.

July 2nd.

These natives possess a kind, sympathetic nature and a pleasant disposition. Their keen sense of independence and diplomacy should be developed in order to check an adventurous spirit. An inquisitive and perceptive mind will lead to success in the professional world. Some may be naturally attracted to the study of medicine and medical research.

July 3rd.

Shown here is an adaptable, versatile, and intuitive mind. Concentration, if learned and practiced, should be of great aid in overcoming many obstacles. One aspect shown indicates a tendency to tire easily and drift aimlessly from one thing to another. This charming personality coupled with a good sense of humor will attract many friendships.

July 4th.

The natives of this degree are romantics, idealists, and dreamers. A rather "hard-to-please" attitude is shown at times, as a consequence of a self-centered, fixed point of view. There is a decided preference for the company of superiors and successful people. Tolerance and affectionate understanding is necessary when dealing with all co-workers, employers, or associates.

July 5th.

This degree endows its natives with a pleasing, courteous disposition, and an alert, thoughtful, and intuitive mind. A tendency to dominate others and assume leadership regardless of consequences should be carefully curbed. Also indicated is great animal magnetism.

July 6th.

Those of this birthday possess a courteous, pleasing, and sociable disposition. Their magnetic personality will attract many friendships and lead to popularity. One aspect in this Horoscope indicates a tendency to look on the serious side of life. This is an attribute of a sensitive and emotional nature. Successful friends will instill confidence and aid in overcoming pessimism. Too much excitement and dissension will cause an adverse reaction by the nervous system.

July 7th.

This degree imparts an original, daring, and masterful mind. A strong will power coupled with the native's desire to have his own way should be curbed. A diversified education along commercial lines will be of great advantage. Much success is indicated in the business world. By exercising tolerance and patience, an overly energetic disposition can be subdued. There may be many ups and downs in domestic and personal affairs. Impulsive and radical changes should be avoided.

July 8th.

These natives possess an unselfish and charitable disposition. The body is strong and healthy, and great interest and skill in sports is shown. It is important to overcome a tendency to attempt too many things at one time. The native can be a fluent conversationalist and prolific writer. Education and training towards some definite goal or profession will be a great asset. Once control of the emotions is achieved, success and public recognition will be assured.

July 9th.

A resourceful mind and executive ability is indicated for those of this birthdate. Discrimination between right and wrong will help to overcome many difficulties. A diversified, liberal education will be an important factor in overcoming many of the negative qualities which may be inherent in this nature. Moderation should be practiced at all times.

July 10th.

These Cancer-born possess astute, practical, and intuitive minds. Artistic temperaments with marked humanitarian principles will bring many lasting and influential friendships. These people are generous, of good appearance, of kind manner, and charitably inclined. One aspect in this chart indicates a tendency to shirk responsibility and to get by with little personal effort.

July 11th.

A benevolent, charitable, and sympathetic nature is shown for those of this nativity. A desire to help all those who ask assistance can result in extravagant expenditures beyond their means. This birthday brings susceptibility to flattery with attendant difficulties. One aspect in this Horoscope shows a tendency to become conceited due to excessive attention.

July 12th.

This degree denotes an intellectual, scientific, and experimental mind. An independent, yet orderly spirit, coupled with a keen sense of diplomacy and tact will make it easy for those born on July 12th to get what they want in life.

July 13th.

These Cancerians possess wholesome charm and great magnetism. They have inventive minds and show originality in ideas and undertakings. They will be susceptible to colds, and it is necessary that all precautions be taken to avoid drafts and sudden changes of temperature. A desire to speculate should be curbed, as many disappointments are shown if this characteristic is permitted to become a habit.

July 14th.

Those of this degree possess a keen mind, and a calm, peaceful attitude towards life. A charming, openminded manner with humanitarian principles will endear these natives to all. Gain is indicated through sentimental associations and influential friendships. One aspect here shows a tendency to take good fortune and successful conclusions too lightly. Natural gifts must be appreciated and used constructively, rather than frivolously, all through life.

July 15th.

Unusual mental qualities, and the ability to develop the mind along intellectual and scientific pursuits is indicated here. A steady and forceful disposition, and an ability to display independent thought is also shown. One aspect in this Horoscope indicates a desire to defy convention and become eccentric. This tendency must be overcome. Ambitions can be fostered, but high temper must be curbed.

July 16th.

The natives of this birthday possess a keen, shrewd, and alert mind. They will be deeply moved by their higher sympathies and will become champions of human rights. There is a tendency to meddle in the affairs of others, and while the motives may be most charitable, many misunderstandings and disappointments are indicated until it is learned that life's greatest rewards come to those who mind their own business first.

July 17th.

Those of this degree possess a bright, cheerful disposition and a kind, generous nature. They are just and righteous in both personal and social matters. They can pursue a professional career, where their fine minds will be demonstrated to good advantage. A strong attachment for home and family is shown. One aspect of this Horoscope shows a desire to be well-dressed, in the height of fashion at all times. This urge can develop into the extravagant habit of purchasing many things of doubtful value and usefulness.

July 18th.

An impulsive and somewhat radical disposition is indicated here. A brilliant mind and excellent intuitive powers are also shown. This combination of mental qualities is usually found in persons who attain outstanding success and recognition in public work. A tendency to be impulsive and erratic should be curbed, as the development of such characteristics can prove detrimental.

July 19th.

These natives possess a bright, cheerful disposition and a splendid mind. Material success is indicated through the ability to make and hold influential and beneficial friendships. Marked originality and a good sense of humor will make for a position of prestige in the social world. A vivid imagination coupled with excess energy may cause impatience.

July 20th.

Strong will power, a commanding, energetic personality, initiative, and good business acumen should enable the native to progress rapidly in the commercial world. A tendency toward extravagance should be curbed. The value of personal possessions ought to be appreciated.

July 21st.

In this degree a versatile mind coupled with marked social capacity will be of great aid in gaining success and recognition in public service. One aspect here denotes a tendency to be too apprehensive concerning the welfare of loved ones and friends. Moderation of this golden virtue is necessary. Much affection for the parents is shown, and while this is a characteristic of most people, it is an especially marked one in this native. Cancerians of this day are liable to be deceived by their emotions.

July 22nd.

A bright, cheerful, and affectionate nature is indicated for these natives. Great generosity, kindness of heart, and a desire to help others are also shown. One aspect of this Horoscope shows a tendency toward daydreaming and a desire to do too many things at once. Concentration must be developed. A magnetic sex appeal will bring much popularity with the opposite sex. ·

COMPATIBLE AND INCOMPATIBLE SIGNS OF CANCER

Cancer is extremely imaginative and emotional, with a sex outlook that is romantic, sentimental, protective, and very largely maternal. In some ways it is a changeable Sign, still capable of great tenacity and faithfulness. There are two characteristics of great importance: One is the fear of ridicule, and the other is a hatred of criticism, both of which—especially the latter—may deeply affect the native's married life.

Cancer in the highest form imparts a domesticated nature, a love of home and possessions, strong maternal love, and a desire to cherish and protect others. It is self-sacrificing, and seeks little in return for the affection it pours out upon others. Unfortunately, the highest type of Cancer, as of any other Sign, is only too rarely encountered, and the underdeveloped specimen is much more common in everyday life, carrying a distortion of many Cancerian virtues.

The only way to get on with an afflicted Cancer type is to praise and flatter him or her on every possible occasion and to never utter a word which could be twisted into a semblance of blame or criticism. Astrology claims that Mercury is chiefly responsible for nagging, and it is true that both Gemini and Virgo can argue and scold incessantly if afflicted, but Cancer produces the real self-pitying nagger.

Even when an argument or discussion has come to an end, Cancer can usually be relied upon to revive it, and keep hammering at it. This tendency shows itself in many ways.

A chance word of criticism will entail hours of work on the part of Cancer in cajoling the unfortunate critic into a recantation. Dislike of something that Cancer likes can produce an endless spate of reasons—or what passes with Cancer as reasons—for liking that particular thing; and he or she will not rest content until agreement is given. It is often for this reason that the husband of a Cancerian wife will be heard to lavish quite unwarranted praise upon her slightest action, for only in this way is it possible to keep her in good temper. In cases of an afflicted Cancer the temper is vicious and spiteful. Bad temper is one of Cancer's chief weapons; others include tears and nagging.

Cancerians are the sentimental, romantic type of lovers, and they need reciprocal sentiments from the opposite sex. Thus, it will not do for them to go in for the logical, practical types of humanity, for their feelings are bound to be hurt by such selections.

The trouble is that when Cancerians are in love, they are temporarily blind to realities, and often fail to perceive that the one they love is not the right one for them.

Their chief desire is to build a home and furnish a love nest, and they will never be satisfied until they have realized this dream. Cancerian women enjoy housework, and their homes are ever clean and tidy.

As lovers they are passionate, and personal feelings always play a big part in their lives. Marriage is the most important event in their lives, and it is especially necessary for them to select the right life-partner.

The general comparisons are as follows:

Cancer and Aries.

This combination is not a wise one. Cancer, a Sign ruled by the Moon, will produce a temperament not compatible with the aggressive Martian (Aries) make-up. Cancerians have a tendency to live in the past, and any disagreement is not easily taken in their stride. The fiery, progressive Aries will not be likely to take time out for apologetic knee-bending after small breaches which are magnified in the Cancer-ruled mind and emotions. Cancer brings the impulse to back away from unpleasant or hurtful situations. In conditions which do not stir Cancerians emotionally they will show their native tenacity.

Cancer and Taurus.

This would be an entirely compatible combination. Both Cancer and Taurus love a good home and much affection. Emotionally they are harmonious, but one thing the Taurus must take into consideration is that the Cancer mate is exceedingly sensitive, and will crawl into a shell in an emotionally trying situation.

Cancer and Gemini.

The domesticated, home-loving Cancer will find it rather disturbing trying to keep up with the mobile Gemini. Gemini is ever seeking change, while Cancer is content in his own home. Gemini cannot be said to be as domesticated as the Cancer mate would wish. Also, Cancer's moodiness may be too much for Gemini's understanding. In those cases where the female is a Gemini and the male is a Cancer, there are fair possibilities of compatibility, especially if several children occupy the Gemini mother's time.

Cancer and Cancer.

These two can make a beautiful love story of their married life, because each will have a sympathetic understanding for the other's moods, wishes, desires, and needs. Though there may be times when they are in complete disagreement, with each clinging to the experience and teaching of early childhood, each will understand the other. Both will have the tenacity of the crab who, once he sets his claws onto something, will hang on regardless of peril. Each will give sympathetic consideration to this trait in the other, and they should have no trouble in finding connubial bliss.

Cancer and Leo.

This is usually a good combination, since the Moon (Cancer) reflects the light of the Sun (Leo). There is much to be said for this combination, especially if Cancer will be happy reflecting the admirable Leonian personality. Leo's big heart will soon forgive the moody outbursts that Cancer displays from time to time and which result from the strong influence of the Moon, Cancer's ruling planet. Cancer, more than any other Sign, responds to the Moon's aspects as it moves swiftly through the Zodiac.

Cancer and Virgo.

Virgo's demands may prove too much for Cancer's desire for peace and quiet. The full, affectionate libido of Cancer will not be completely satisfied by Virgo's direct approach to the practical matters at hand. Cancer is sentimental, reticent, and even shy about sex matters, and this can be very frustrating to the Virgo temperament. Once Cancer crawls into his shell, all the tongue lashing and nagging of Virgo will not bring him out. This could drive the Virgo mate into a state of hysteria.

Cancer and Libra.

Cancer is temperamentally unsuited to cope with the freedom-loving Libran. Once these two lovebirds get into a serious disagreement, they may go for days without so much as a nod of recognition. Libra's great desire for attention may bring on a period of sulking depression that could create a highly controversial situation. Though Libra loves justice and fair play, Cancer has a tendency to take advantage of all of these qualities for his own private use.

Cancer and Scorpio.

Masterful Scorpio should make a good mate for reticent Cancer. While that "ole debil" Jealousy may plague both from time to time, their great mutual ability to love deeply will usually limit periods of dissension. Scorpio is well equipped to cope with Cancerian moods. Excess energy which Scorpio emanates will act as strong tonic for Cancer's reticence. Yes, Scorpio and Cancer could well prove the ideal marriage combination. More should try it.

Cancer and Sagittarius.

TROUBLE may be spelled with capital letters should these two marry, unless each is willing to attempt a complete change of their star-predicted personalities. Cancer admires everything about the Sagittarian—therein lies the tender trap; but once Cancer has captured the busy-footed, roving-eyed Sagittarian, he or she will find it a "more-than-bargained-for" proposition. Cancer is not going to keep the Sagittarian partner close to the hearth. The Cancer's home is his castle, but for the Sagittarian, home is little more than a place to occasionally hang his hat. Watch out!

Cancer and Capricorn.

Capricorn is 180 degrees from Cancer, and while this is an opposition in Astrology, it need not be so in life. The natives of both Signs have much in common. The Cancer's great sympathy and understanding is honey to the Capricorn's misunderstood complaints. Both these natives have a tendency to plod along until they get what they want. Capricorn has the ability to make Cancer's dreams come true, while Cancer is happy wishing for and wanting the success and security that the Capricorn mate strives for.

Cancer and Aquarius.

The social whirl of the Aquarian may prove too much for the home-loving Cancer. Aquarians love to share their good fortune with the world while Cancer is satisfied to concentrate on personal obligations. Cancer's tastes are conservative; Aquarius' tastes are usually the opposite. The eccentricity of Uranus does not go well with the moods of Luna. The odds against a compatible marriage are really too great for this combination to overcome, unless, of course, one will become subservient to the other.

Cancer and Pisces.

The marriage of these two sentimental Signs should prove to be astrologically ideal. Though both will have their moments of gloom and doom, they will soon come out into the sunshine and forgive and forget. Lovers' quarrels may be frequent, but the aftermath will be blissful. Home, possessions, and friends are cherished by both, and there will be mutual effort to fulfill all obligations.

SOME FAMOUS PERSONS BORN IN THE SIGN
OF CANCER

Louis Armstrong—Musician
Milton Berle—Comedian
Julius Caesar—Roman Emperor
James Cagney—Actor
George M. Cohan—Actor and Writer
Ely Culbertson—Bridge Expert
Jack Dempsey—Boxer
Oscar Hammerstein II—Librettist
Nathaniel Hawthorne—Author

Ernest Hemingway—Author
Charles Laughton—Actor
Kathleen Norris—Novelist
Cecil Rhodes—British Statesman
John D. Rockefeller—Philanthropist
Nelson A. Rockefeller—Governor of New York
Red Skelton—Comedian
Barbara Stanwyck—Actress
Isaac Watts—Inventor

LEO

THE SIGN LEO symbolizes strength, courage, and fire. The hottest portion of the year in the northern hemisphere occurs when the Sun is passing through this Sign. It is the solar Lion that ripens with his own internal heat the fruits brought forth from the earth by the moisture of Isis.

The Sign Leo signifies the heart of the Grand Man and represents the life center of the fluidic circulatory system of humanity. It is also the fiery vortex of physical life. Those born under this influx are noted for the superior strength of their physical constitution and for their wonderful recuperative powers after being exhausted by sickness. The sign of Leo upon the esoteric planisphere is occupied by Judah, of whom his dying parent says, "Judah is a lion's whelp, from the prey, my son, thou art gone up. He stooped down, he crouched as a lion." This Sign reveals to us the mysteries of the ancient sacrifice and the laws of compensation.

Leo is the second emanation of the fiery Triplicity, and is the constellation of the Sun.

Leo signifies the sympathies of the heart. Those dominated by its influx are generous to excess with their friends. By nature they are deeply sympathetic, and possess that peculiar grade of

117

magnetic force which enables them to arouse into action latent sympathies in others.

The mystical gem of Leo is the ruby, and it forms the most potent disease-resisting talisman for all governed by the Leonine influx.

The fortunate day is Sunday.

The fortunate numbers are five and nine.

The colors for this Sign are gold and orange.

Best locations for success are the wide open spaces.

Their star-ordained tendency is toward leadership and as orators, their earnest, impulsive, and impressive style makes them an irresistible success. An exceedingly fine specimen of Leonine oratory is given in Genesis, 44th chapter. This simple, eloquent appeal of Judah to Joseph probably stands unequaled for its sublime tenderness. The natives of Leo are impulsive and passionate, honest and faithful. Their minds are ever striving to attain unto some higher state, hence their ideas are always in excess of their means—large, majestic, and grand.

Addressing a Leo, I would say, you possess a good sense of humor and your jovial nature attracts many to you. Under ordinary circumstances, you are courteous and considerate of others. There is very little fear in you. You present a forceful, dynamic, and commanding attitude when necessary. You also have considerable ability to influence others and have them carry out your ideas. You are somewhat of an idealist and are rather generous; therefore, you are sensitive and easily hurt. Since you have a great amount of pride, it is essential that you guard against such excess and egotism, as would hinder you.

In character, you show sincerity of purpose and are courageous to the point of daring. You have a fairly quick temper. Under ordinary conditions you are not inclined to hold a grudge long. However, when angry, you can be forceful and unpleasant.

Anger upsets your nervous system, and it is advisable that you make every effort to curb or control yourself. In the main, you have what is known as a noble character. You show lofty ideals, generosity, and sympathy. In love you are inclined to be jealous. You are independent and do not lean.

Your powers of observation and perception are good. You enjoy doing your own thinking. You have a good sense of analysis, except in love and romantic affairs. Under such circumstances, your impulses rule your actions.

You are able to grasp facts and theories rapidly. Your quick perception is vital for your particular personality. A daring and adventurous nature brings you to face a great variety of situations and conditions. You have good coordination and can usually act as quickly as you think.

One of your temperament has an active imagination. Sometimes you get a great amount of pleasure in just musing and daydreaming of romance. Your imagination can help you work out new ideas and express original thoughts. The naturally artistic nature of your Sign also gives you the power to visualize. This faculty enables many Leo people to be good artists, dancers, entertainers, musicians, actors, and actresses. You have a fairly good memory. You do not have much difficulty in retaining or recalling facts and ideas.

You take an interest in a great variety of subjects, which enables you to be an interesting conversationalist. You have good reasoning ability and judgment in business matters. As you are quite sensitive, it is advisable that you study all impulses that arise from within very carefully. Most of your impulsiveness is brought about by your sensitive reactions. You must also think over impulses relating to hazardous ventures or acts of daring. Think, analyze, and then act and you will be much more successful and happy.

You have an unusually deep insight into other people and their motives. Your intuition will provide you with the knowledge of the cause of your own failures and can give you the solution for progress.

Your birthsign endows you with a good constitution and good recuperative powers. Too many Leo people lead an active life before middle-age and then, suddenly, begin to take things easy and neglect light exercise. Your Sign rules the heart and the small of the back, and these parts are usually most easily affected. Your glands respond to your mental and emotional moods. Therefore, it is advisable that you avoid moodiness and mental strain. Learn the art of relaxing. Curb and control your emotional reactions. Endeavor to be reasonable in your diet. Enjoy good foods but avoid excess. If in doubt as to your diet, consult a doctor or an experienced dietician for the most reliable information.

Your birthsign represents the romantic and entertaining section of the Zodiac. It is evident that you possess a fondness for pleasure, recreation, adventure, entertainment, and travel. In youth, there is a temptation to engage in risky and hazardous ventures, and there is a great fondness for all kinds of excitement. You are by nature a romantic. In love, you are affectionate and passionate. Your feelings, when you let them rule you, are intense. You must bear in mind that ordinarily your judgment in romantic matters is not always reliable. Because of your emotional intensity, you permit your heart to rule your head. Remember that, unless we learn our lessons wisely, Fate will take a hand in teaching us, and Fate is not sparing in its methods of instruction.

You love children and are apt to be indulgent with them, but the general influence of your Sign does not show many children. You are fond of a good home and all the comforts thereof; you desire to have the best that your money will afford. Your nature is more or less fixed. You strive to have a specific place that you can call home. You are not, however, content to stay in one place too long. You are apt to become bored unless you have an opportunity for a change of scenery. Get away from home surroundings now and then, even for a short time. Your romantic nature has often caused you to be at odds with your parents. Better prospects for a settled home life usually come after the middle years.

You are more adapted to mental than to physical work. Under ordinary circumstances you have the patience and determination to work with a proposition until you have accomplished it. Most Leo people have the mentality, ability, and temperament that qualifies them for a business or professional life such as law or medicine; they also become proficient authors, bankers, merchants, brokers, real estate operators and salesmen. Many develop their natural, artistic qualities and become actors, musicians, and artists.

Your rise in life may not be rapid, but it is usually sure. You can hasten it only by judicious use of your wits. When Leos finally achieve success they remain quite successful for the rest of their lives. Sudden success is very apt to sway some Leo natives into a false sense of security, with the result that, in the end, they would have been better off without it. Too much pride and false self-confidence have proved the ruination of many.

You have good executive ability and are capable of assuming responsibilities. You will do well in a business for yourself. Indications point to reasonable success in any line of work or business dealing with the general public, as you have the sort of personality that is pleasing. You have good earning ability, but you are inclined to be a generous, and even lavish, spender. You believe in having a good time with your money.

During the first half of your life you are apt to be quite free with your money. You must bear in mind that in order to attain financial security, you must learn the art of making money work for you. You should begin to do this in a small way at first, and once you acquire the habit, you will be able to do it on a large scale. The easy come, easy go philosophy is not conducive to financial success and security. You should be reasonably cautious in all matters pertaining to gambling and speculation. You enjoy taking chances; it appears to be part of your nature. It is wiser to make good investments in the stocks and bonds of large industrial corporations than to engage in purely speculative ventures. Do not fall for get-rich-quick propositions that offer you wealth overnight. Cultivate the art of being reasonably conservative and you will gain financial security.

Your adventurous nature shows the urge for travel and change, and you will, no doubt, travel considerably during life. Many long and short journeys are indicated for the members of your Sign.

Your interesting and magnetic personality will attract many people to you during the course of life. You enjoy entertaining your friends in your home. True friendships will be among life's most pleasant experiences.

It is apparent that if you are not careful, your emotions may prove to be your own worst enemy. It is paradoxical that you have the courage to face and combat difficult obstacles without fear, and yet you succumb to the sensitivity of your emotions. Do all within your power to exercise rational control over your reactions or you will hinder your progress.

You have qualities that will enable you to rise above the circumstances of your birth. Your need is to understand yourself. Yours is the sort of personality that makes or breaks its own destiny. The art of looking ahead will increase your prospects for a successful and happy life.

THE LEO CHILD

Leo children are born with a noble, ambitious, and aspiring nature; they develop into good leaders but poor followers. They usually scorn mean and sordid things and do not often stoop to do a mean act even under provocation. Their affections are strong and ardent. They have strong wills and can usually beat their ways to the top despite all handicaps and obstacles. There is no halfway measure with the Child of Leo; it is all or nothing. If the lower nature happens to predominate, the above mentioned traits are reserved. When this occurs, parents with understanding should mold the child to encourage the better qualities to predominate. There will be a quick temper as well as a desire to rule over other children, and if you watch a Leo child playing with others, you will see Leo is usually the boss and the leader.

Leo children usually forgive and forget readily and are generally sympathetic, affectionate, and charitable.

The vitality of the Leo child is generally strong, and the pathology of this group shows that the members' strength may be quickly overtaxed by impulsiveness and a strong desire to accomplish results at any cost. The Leo Sign has rulership over the heart. There is a tendency to fever and a possibility of poor circulation. However, as the fundamental vitality is strong, the general health should be good; but it is the parent's duty to know the ailments to which the Leo child is subject. Frequently an illness can be avoided when the parents have accurate knowledge. They should guard the child against cuts, burns, and accidents of the side, back, and knees. The Leo child will enjoy the great outdoors, and particularly woods, mountains, rivers, and all wide open spaces.

The emotional character of the Leo child leaves a susceptibility to excessive rivalry and, sometimes, to cruelty. The mental characteristics favor the development of ambition, and a tyrannical desire for dominance if the Leo child is not trained properly. Very often a temperament develops with the urge toward the acquisition of power.

The favorable quality of the Leo child tends toward dignity; the unfavorable quality tends to dictatorship.

You may train the Leo child for any of the following occupations—executive, government official, judge, lawyer, broker, jeweler, also any position connected with public utilities. Statesmen, presidents, producers, and physicists have been children of Leo. Leo children are very magnetic, intuitive, and often inventive.

THE LEO WIFE

The Leo wife is a splendid woman for a worldly and ambitious man. She has an aristocratic point of view and all of the social graces. She is a great manager. She can run an elaborate home, take first place in local social groups, and advance her husband's business chances by enjoyable entertainment. She attracts people to her home and commands great respect. She is the sort of a wife a husband wants his boss to meet because the impression that she creates is helpful.

The love of a Leo wife is passionate, enduring, and self-sacrificing. These are the most loyal women. They give and feel and bestow and bless. Their families can never show sufficient gratitude for the wealth of attention lavished upon them and sometimes they appear to lack appreciation for such loving service. The truth is that no human being could repay the Leo wife's devotion to her home and husband. Her attitude is lush and generous in the extreme, unless the husband is a very dominant man—this type of wife will rule him and the result will be a henpecked husband.

Beauty often goes with this birth position and Leonine women are usually good to look at. They demand an active life; there is nothing of the languid about them. There is a certain amount of jealousy in their make-up though they seek a wide circle of friends of both sexes. They sometimes embarrass their husbands with open suspicions. If the Leo woman is lucky enough to marry a virile, commanding man, all of her good qualities will be elevated. She will have the opportunity to exercise her latent talents and put all of her heart and passion into her relationship with her husband. A supremely masculine man can supply her with the satisfaction that her passionate nature cries for, without requiring her to sacrifice her femininity.

THE LEO HUSBAND

The Leo man fits into the scheme of domestic life quite smoothly. Usually he is a good and generous provider. He desires his wife and family to shine in the community. He is tremendously proud of them and wants them to have the best of everything. For himself he demands the center of the stage. He expects home life to revolve around him as the planets around the sun. He is affectionate, loving, and devoted in manner, but will not tolerate disrespect or insubordination.

The Leo husband is fixed in his opinions. His love is deeply romantic and very absorbing but he considers that he is the law unto himself. His attitude toward life is so conventional that he would never tolerate a wife who was disloyal. She must be above suspicion. As Leo men are acute judges of character, they usually select wives who meet with their high standards.

The average Leo man makes a fine husband. His generosity, kindness, loving disposition, and passionate loyalty in the big issues of life combined with great generosity, make him a safe and satisfying kind of husband for a clinging woman. The positive Leo man will be unhappy with a bossy, nagging wife. While he loves to show off his spouse and will usually buy her expensive gifts, he does so with the knowledge that it makes him look good in the community and among his associates.

THE CUSPS OF LEO

(If your birthday is not within the cusp of your Sign, the following does not apply to you.)

If the birthday is from July 23rd through July 25th.

You were born in Leo with Cancer tendencies. Your ruling orbs are the Sun and the Moon. This shows that you are methodical and practical. You aspire to higher things and should rise above the average station in life. You possess individuality, intelligence, and balance. You are not stubborn, and always dig into the cause for everything. You are fond of unusual entertainment and frequently get pleasure out of things other people consider tedious. You should watch your health, especially your blood circulation, stomach, and bowels. You are fond of your friends, and feel that you are fortunate in having so many. You have the ability to master any work or occupation. A professional life appeals to you. Being somewhat impatient, you seldom train yourself diligently enough in any one line. You are a leader among your associates and are always rated as a good fellow.

If the birthday is from August 19th through August 22nd.

You were born in Leo with some Virgo tendencies. Your ruling orbs are the Sun and Mercury. This gives you self-respect and an awareness of detail in your work. You have artistic ability, and an appreciation of music and the refined things in life. You are attractive in appearance, possess excellent judgment, and are level-headed. An odd thing about you is that you can give good counsel to others, but are usually at a loss to solve your own problems. You need the companionship of a congenial person to help you over the rough spots. You often go to unhappy extremes in feelings and emotions. You have a strong physique, and possess an out-of-the-ordinary determination to succeed in spite of all hazards, even when you are discouraged. You are fond of outdoor life, and a vacation is exhilarating to you when it is not a luxury trip. You are energetic and possess much endurance; you are more capable than the average person.

THE DECANATES OF LEO

If the birthday is between July 23rd and July 31st.

Your personal and ruling orb is the Sun. This greatly stimulates your mental and physical activities. The double aspect of the Sun in your Horoscope is one of the most beneficent vibrations in the entire Zodiac. The Sun in this aspect creates a great love for change and the desire to reform. A noble and enthusiastic nature and the ability to lead others is also shown. The Sun will confer good fortune upon you, particularly if you will try to eliminate some of the negative tendencies which you may have developed.

If the birthday is between August 1st and August 10th.

Your personal planet is Jupiter. It is known as the symbol of fortune and the royal planet of Divine Wisdom. It influences the intellectual, moral, and sympathetic tendencies. A noble nature, always acting honorably and gratefully, is one of the favorable aspects of this planet. Jupiter decrees harmonious surroundings imbued with devotion and happiness. It will confer good fortune and success upon you and assist greatly in offsetting some of the negative tendencies of your Sign.

If the birthday is between August 11th and August 22nd.

Your personal planet is Mars, known as the symbol of war and the center of divine energy. It influences the energetic, courageous, and constructive tendencies. Mars will materially aid you in overcoming some of the weaker and more negative aspects of Leo. It gives you the necessary impetus to bring about a successful conclusion to some of your endeavors. Without this force, it would be difficult for you to realize many of your cherished ambitions. The combination of the Sun and Mars is indeed a fortunate one, since Mars is powerful and aggressive, and forces its natives to attain their objectives.

THE DEGREES OF LEO

July 23rd.

You possess an ambitious, forceful, and somewhat brusque disposition. You are independent and have the ability to attain objectives in life without much assistance from outside influences. You must avoid hasty decisions in business and financial matters. You may meet with success and unexpected benefits from superiors. You have a good sense of authority.

July 24th.

You possess a magnetic personality and affectionate disposition. You are fond of music and art, and enjoy the beautiful, refined, and esthetic things in life. One aspect in this Horoscope indicates a tendency to self-indulgence, which should not be encouraged. You like to be pampered but this will only add to your difficulties when you come face to face with realities. You are best suited for an artistic or professional career.

July 25th.

You possess an enterprising and trustworthy nature. You have excellent powers of expression. You are a born leader and possess the energy and ability to rule situations and command the respect of your friends and associates. One aspect of this Horoscope indicates danger through misplaced friendships. You may be more popular with men than with women. Beware the false female.

July 26th.

You possess honesty and integrity. A powerful will helps offset a sensitive disposition. Marked introspection, with an inclination to become moody and despondent at the slightest provocation, indicates a retiring manner. You are capable of intelligent research of the highest order. Travel and seek favors but avoid extravagance. The opposite sex is desperately attracted to you.

July 27th.

You are generous, courteous, obliging, and hospitable. Relatives, friends, and strangers will want to help you. Successful travel is also indicated. You will rise to the pinnacle of success. You have a prophetic inspiration and will show considerable skill in the financial world.

July 28th.

You possess a bold imagination and a keen mind, ever seeking knowledge and sensation. You are affectionate with strong passions, and will gain through musical or literary activities. You will have fame as well as monetary reward in your chosen profession.

July 29th.

You possess a magnanimous, open-handed, and free disposition. You have excellent mental faculties and many original ideas, but you are prone to hasty decisions. One aspect in this Horoscope indicates the ability to achieve fame in the fields of medicine or philosophy.

July 30th.

You are firm, steadfast, and sure of yourself. You are intuitive and show unusual aptness in commercial matters. You are fond of mystery, and display a love for argument and debate. These will add to your store of knowledge and become a prime factor in developing your intellect and improving your security. While you are affectionate and magnanimous to your immediate family, you may show a tendency to be somewhat inconsiderate of other people and their feelings.

July 31st.

You have broad views and wide sympathies. Although devoted to your friends, you may experience disappointment through them. You rely a good deal upon intuition rather than common sense. One aspect in this Horoscope indicates difficulty in getting along with your immediate family, because of a desire to impress outsiders. An outspoken and impressionable nature may mark you as an eccentric.

August 1st.

You possess a warmhearted, shy, and sensitive disposition. You show a great deal of aptitude in making money for yourself and your associates. One aspect in this Horoscope indicates that many of your troubles will turn to blessings. It also indicates inheritance from wealthy relatives. Try to curb your extravagant tendencies.

August 2nd.

You possess an optimistic and philosophical turn of mind. You have a fiery temper that may need restraint. One aspect in this Horoscope indicates disappointment due to misplaced confidence. You are restless and always on the move. You will be fortunate on the whole, and excel in some special field of endeavor.

August 3rd.

You possess an energetic and courageous personality, but are inclined to be stubborn and quick-tempered. You have a strong link with your family. You are fond of taking chances, and have an air of mystery about you. This is a degree that usually gains much public attention.

August 4th.

You possess excellent powers of perception, but are inclined to be somewhat apprehensive. You will benefit much through older people and from an inheritance. You must avoid fraudulent schemes and speculative enterprises. Your sense of superiority may create some enemies from time to time. Avoid mental and physical overexertion.

August 5th.

You are fond of learning and are artistic and studious. Care should be taken when traveling on water. You have good scientific visualization and can be successful in the field of philosophy. You are a natural teacher. You are, physically, attractive to the opposite sex.

August 6th.

You are self-inspired and capable of great undertakings. You can become impetuous when your emotions are aroused. It is advisable to curb such tendencies. Your strong will power will enable you to overcome many obstacles in life. You have the natural ability to make friends readily because you have a good sense of values.

August 7th.

You possess a good intellect with a great thirst for knowledge. You can gain success in the literary, artistic, or musical world. A magnanimous personality and the desire to help those who are in less fortunate circumstances may lead to many strange experiences during your life. You have humanitarian instincts which may lead to just rewards in the form of honor and fame.

August 8th.

You possess a sympathetic, determined, and forceful nature. Watch your temper. One aspect in this Horoscope shows a judicial and perceptive mind coupled with a high-strung nervous system. It is therefore necessary to avoid excessive mental exertion which may result in nervous disorder. Indulge in outdoor physical exercise.

August 9th.

You possess a gentle yet powerful nature, which coupled with sincerity of purpose may help to make you successful. Gains are indicated through elderly relatives, social contacts, and property. This is the degree of show business. You have latent talents as an entertainer. You are fond of ease and comfort.

August 10th.

You possess an original, bold, and dashing personality. A strong, resolute nature, with the ability to express yourself impressively both in speech and writing are also indicated. You may show a tendency to become obstinate and reckless. A disregard for convention and a star-ordained desire to express your own radical views and impose your will upon friends and associates should be curbed to avoid animosity.

August 11th.

You are a dogmatic, confident, and determined person. You have a passionate temper and at times may become obstinate and headstrong. You may have a delicate constitution and should take it easy if you can. Enlightenment through past experiences is indicated. There is some danger of losses and trouble through doubtful friendships and associations.

August 12th.

You are proud, austere, reserved, and easily offended. A more tolerant outlook should be cultivated to avoid unnecessary animosity. One aspect in this Horoscope indicates a tendency to look upon the gloomy side of life. Seek well-lighted places. Patient self-training to instill confidence will help overcome gloom also. Undue excitement and too much dissension will have an adverse reaction on your nervous system.

August 13th.

You have a generous and extravagant nature. You may have many trials and tribulations to contend with. Faith, tolerance and patience will be necessary in order to guard your health and finances. Consolation will come from the opposite sex in times of stress. You have good earning ability.

August 14th.

You are industrious and commercially minded. You have good analytical ability, but may become somewhat self-centered and dogmatic. Such egotism could lead to difficulties with your co-workers or business associates. One aspect in this Horoscope indicates that you should curb a tendency to be too free with your money.

August 15th.

You possess a certain degree of prophetic foresight. You are an originator of plans and will have many interesting and romantic affairs. A happy and interesting life is foreseen, conducted with dash and verve. It is essential that you be on constant guard against accidents due to your carelessness.

August 16th.

You possess an original and perceptive mind. You show a decided tendency to be contrary and mischievous. Artistic ability and musical talent will greatly aid you in the attainment of success in the entertainment world. Trouble with relatives is shown at various intervals in your life. Some trouble through property, documents, and journeys is foreseen. A kind, sympathetic nature with a desire to help relatives may bring disappointment because of unappreciative attachments.

August 17th.

You possess a clever, critical mind and an intuitive nature. A strong will and a fiery temper may give you some cause for concern. Keen interest in literature and art, if pursued, will endow you with an intellectual personality. Curb a tendency to become sarcastic when your plans meet with outside interference.

August 18th.

You possess an adventurous spirit and a star-prophesied desire to travel and visit strange places. You are also fond of company. You show a marked aptitude for organizing and controlling others. You are always ready to accept responsibility. You may receive considerable help from your relatives. At some time during your life you will develop a practical method for attaining success.

August 19th.

You possess an enterprising and entertaining personality. You show a marked aptitude for finance and should be successful in the commercial world. Some difficulty with, or through, relatives is indicated. Unforeseen financial success from unexpected sources comes to many persons born in this degree. You have the qualities of a good executive. Beware of hasty marriage.

August 20th.

You possess a good sense of humor and an analytical mind. You like to experiment with new and unusual ideas. Curb a tendency to become proud and overbearing in your dealings with those less fortunate than yourself. You can develop a martyr complex, which may eventually cause you to lead a retiring and lonely life.

August 21st.

You possess an original, daring, and masterful nature. A strong will coupled with the overbearing desire to have your own way should be curbed. If you use your analytical mind in an intelligent manner, much success is indicated in the business world. By exercising tolerance and patience, you can subdue a restless and overly energetic disposition. Losses through law and imposition are threatened.

August 22nd.

You possess an impulsive and somewhat radical disposition. A brilliant mind and illuminating intuitive powers are also indicated. This combination of mental qualities is usually found in persons who attain outstanding success in public service. Try to curb a tendency to be too impulsive and erratic, as such characteristics, if permitted to develop, can prove to be detrimental. This is a good degree for a politician.

COMPATIBLE AND INCOMPATIBLE SIGNS OF LEO

The Sign of Leo is intensely loyal, generous, and magnanimous, but it is not as a rule fortunate in marriage. This may be due to misplaced affection, unwise and impetuous love-making, and a too implicit faith in human nature, but there is, generally, a deeper reason.

Some peculiarity of outlook will often spoil marital happiness, and in the majority of cases, the question of children will be involved.

Leo has a deep love for children, and is frequently denied them, or loses them by death. Leo often experiences sorrow through a child. Like all the fiery Signs, Leo is idealistic and tends to set love dones upon a pedestal. This leads to disappointment and disillusion through broken engagements or unhappy marriages, in many cases. It has been noticed that the twenty-seventh degree (August 19th) appears to be particularly unfortunate in marriage. In love matters, Leo tends to adopt a protective role and likes to be looked up to and admired. Leo is often rather lordly and may be dominating on occasion, for Leo always likes to oversee the management of affairs. Leo women are good managers and excellent formal hostesses.

Extravagance due to lavish generosity and love of ostentation is a great failing.

In early life Leo men are sometimes lady-killers; Leo women seek admiration from whoever will bestow it; but the Sign is not really a fickle one and is capable of great faith and loyalty once the feelings are deeply aroused.

Leos are the romantic type of lover; they know how to provide the right blend of sentimentality and passion. Leo employs dramatic effort to achieve the right effect. There can be nothing commonplace about the Leonian way of doing things!

The basic urge to excel and to appear in a glorious guise is the manifestation of the Leo ego, which frequently develops into a superiority complex. Naturally, the degree to which this is pushed will depend upon the individual aspects in the natal chart which clearly define all tendencies.

Leo will profit, perhaps to a greater degree than many of the other Signs, by a close study of those life partners with whom there will be harmony and happiness.

The compatible and incompatible signs for Leo follow:

Leo and Aries.

As a rule, this union works out well for both. While Aries and Leo both are highly emotional in their make-up, Leo will lionize an Aries partner. If Leo can take over the stage and the audience on occasion and be the "whole show," everything will be fine. Aries, with the natal impetuosity in love-making, will find a welcome in the arms, heart, and home of Leo. Fiery Leo admires the aggressive tendencies of the equally fiery Aries.

Leo and Taurus.

The Sun-ruled Leo and the Venus-ruled Taurus will be a happy combination if each studies and understands the shortcomings of the other. The sex appeal and splendid physical qualities of each are important to these natives, and, in this case, they seem to have found just what the doctor ordered in each other. Taurus, however, will have to soft-pedal a jealous streak. Taurus should let the beloved Leo have the opportunity to "show off" and all will be well with this combination.

Leo and Gemini.

While both these Signs are attracted to the same things—glamour, flattery, and the world of good-fellowship, the combination is not a good one. Leo's love is heart-felt; Gemini's love is of the mind. After the rose-colored cellophane wrapping is removed from this romance, Gemini will find Leo's passion too bossy, possessive and demanding. The zestful love nature of Leo will not find a full love life with the unresponsive Gemini. Not an advisable combination, so beware!

Leo and Cancer.

Strange as it may seem at first glance, this can make a really good combination. The water (Cancer) would, on the surface appear to be an unwise mate for the Fire (Leo), but their real compatibility is provided by their rulers. The Moon (Cancer) reflects the light of the Sun (Leo) and if Leo loves anything, it is something which reflects his own shining glory. The big, generous heart of Leo will soon forgive the moody outbursts of Cancer. This is due to the strong influence of the Moon upon the Cancerian personality. Cancer, more than any other Sign, responds to the Moon's aspects as it swiftly moves through the Zodiac.

Leo and Leo.

This should be a compatible combination, but, regrettably, it is not always so. Leo natives are positive people, who love to hold the center of the stage. They want to be the head of their social groups. When the two marriage partners are constantly contending for leadership, unhappy results can readily be imagined. The only hope for a successful partnership here is if the female is content to rule the home and the male to shine in the business and social world.

Leo and Virgo.

There is a good chance here for a happy union. Magnanimous Leo will overlook Virgo's tendency to be critical, while Virgo will take pride in Leo's accomplishments, good humor, and lovable nature. Leo will respect Virgo's clever and alert mentality. If Virgo will permit Leo to hog the limelight and refrain from being too critical of Leo's star-predicted desire to hold the central place in the family circle, there should be no real barriers to a happy and successful partnership. This is no easy task.

Leo and Libra.

The hale and hearty Leo may prove too much for the sensitive Libra nature, although there are many exceptions that could make this a fairly good combination. The Sun (Leo) and Venus (Libra) usually form a strong and luxurious aspect. Both Signs love luxuries, are subject to flattery, and are artistically inclined.

The chief difficulty may lie in the fact that Leo demands constant adulation; Libra may get the idea that what's good for the goose is good for the gander.

Leo and Scorpio.

This combination brings together two shining personalities. They have much in common, especially where the Leo is the wife and Scorpio is the husband. The Scorpio wife may be too demanding for her Leo husband. Jealousy here plays an important role in causing many serious family quarrels. Basically, this should make for one of the most compatible combinations, but the long and happy partnership will be far better when a Leo female marries a Scorpio male.

Leo and Sagittarius.

This usually makes an excellent combination. It is said that fire should be fought with fire, and this seems applicable to marriage between these two Signs, with very few exceptions. Both love change and excitement and possess a great zest for life. The one danger lies in the fact that both are domineering; this could lead to trouble if the Leo tried to relegate the Sagittarian to the sidelines. The independent nature of Sagittarius would rebel, and this could lead to a serious rift in the partnership.

Leo and Capricorn.

The slow, plodding Capricorn may prove too much for the carefree nature of Leo. Leo forgives and forgets; Capricorn is slow to anger and seldom forgets. This combination would not form the ideal basis for mutual understanding. This is especially true in matters of sex. The Capricorn has the tendency to be suspicious of motives, while Leo will wholeheartedly enter the arena with no thought of consequences. The "hail-fellow-well-met" attitude of Leo's nature will prove too much for Capricorn to cope with over the long pull.

Leo and Aquarius.

This combination of the Sun and Uranus is usually a good one. Leo likes surprise and Aquarius will certainly supply it. Both Signs are at their best when doing things for others. Leo loves the world, and Aquarius loves humanity. This makes an excellent combination for partnership that deals with or caters to the public.

In intimate matters there is a mutual understanding of each other's needs and desires. Aquarius may hold many surprises for Leo, so there should never be a dull moment in their lives.

Leo and Pisces.

The strong and hearty temperament of Leo may prove too much for the subtle and sensitive Pisces. Pisces, with resilience, takes on the changing moods of any partnership. Impressionable Pisces is easily hurt by any trivial or imagined wrong, and becomes very difficult to cope with, and dangerous to boot. While Leo is flattered by the dependency of others, if he abuses Pisces, the just resentment of Pisces may be too much for Leo to take over a long period of time.

SOME FAMOUS PERSONS BORN IN THE SIGN OF LEO

Gracie Allen—Comedienne
Lucille Ball—Actress
Ethel Barrymore—Actress
Ingrid Bergman—Actress
Napoleon Bonaparte—French
  Statesman
Bernard Baruch—Financier
Fidel Castro—Cuban Leader
Cecil B. DeMille—Movie
  Director
Marshall Field—Merchant

Henry Ford—Industrialist
Dag Hammarskjöld—Secretary-
  General of UN
Alfred Hitchcock—Movie
  Director
Herbert G. Hoover—U.S.
  President
Aldous Huxley—Novelist
Carl G. Jung—Psychiatrist,
  Psychoanalyst
Benito Mussolini—Dictator

Madame Pandit—Indian
   Ambassador
Sir Walter Scott—British
   Writer

George Bernard Shaw—
   Playwright
Mae West—Actress
Orville Wright—Inventor

VIRGO

THE SIGN VIRGO symbolizes chastity, and forms the central idea of a great number of myths. When the Sun passes through this Sign the harvest is ready for the reaper, hence Virgo is symbolized as the gleaning maid with two ears of corn in her hand.

The Sign Virgo signifies the solar plexus of the Grand Archetypal Man, and, therefore, represents the assimilating and distributing functions of the human organism. Consequently, we find that those born under this influence possess fine discriminating powers as to the choice of food best adapted to their particular organic requirements. This constellation, as governing the bowels of humanity, is highly important since the intestines comprise a very vital section of the digestive organism.

Upon the esoteric planisphere, Virgo is occupied by Asher. "Out of Asher his bread shall be fat," says Jacob, "and he shall yield royal dainties, thus typifying the riches of the harvest." Virgo is the second emanation of the earthly Trigon, and is the constellation of Mercury.

The mystical gem of Virgo is the sardonyx, a stone possessing very important virtues.

The fortunate day is Wednesday.

Fortunate numbers are eight and four.

The fortunate color for this Sign is grey.

Best locations for success are in small cities.

The Sign Virgo signifies the realization of hopes. Those dominated by this influx are calm, confident, and contented; they are reflective, studious, and extremely fond of reading. Consequently they become the mental repositories of much wisdom and learning. These desirable qualities, combined with the penetration of Mercury, which this Sign contains, all conduce to make the native of Virgo pre-eminently fitted for the close application of scientific study. They possess large, well-balanced minds, and superior intellectual abilities, and make clever statesmen when thrown into the vortex of political life.

They are courteous, diplomatic, and present a neat and attractive appearance, as they are inclined to be critical in the matter of dress. They may appear to be rather cool and reserved, but this is because of their independence of thought and observation. Their natural bearing and demeanor will command the respect and admiration of others.

They have an intellectual and nervous temperament. They are kind and sympathetic, but generosity with them is a more practical proposition than it is with most people. Their excellent powers of observation make them critical of the most minute detail. They must learn to criticize constructively. Unwise use of this ability can lead to misunderstanding in personal and social contacts with others.

Virgoans are honest, trustworthy, sincere, and reliable, and will take their full share of responsibility in matters of importance.

Their emotional nature is to be somewhat sensitive and reserved. They derive much pleasure from ideas and observations. Most people do not realize that these natives are thinkers. They have excellent powers of analysis, with unusually quick and keen perception. They should do all within their power to develop persistence and fortitude, for if they do not develop these qualities, circumstances of life will force their development. Though Virgoans have good reasoning powers, there are times when they must guard against their conclusions being influenced by personal prejudices.

True logic is as impersonal as sunlight; false logic based on personal feelings is conducive to intolerance, selfishness, and prejudice. Virgoans are quick to recognize and absorb the facts surrounding a proposition, and are, therefore, able to learn much faster than those of many other Signs. They are good at analyzing all angles of a given issue.

By nature those of Virgo are fact-finding individuals; imagination is used to practical ends. There may be times when they daydream about personal or romantic affairs, but in other matters they are realistic and practical. They also try to visualize improvements in conditions and circumstances around them; they use their imagination in the same manner that a builder, inventor, or creative artist uses this same faculty. The memory is very good, because of the deep interest and attention given to all that they observe.

These natives also have the ability to express knowledge gathered. This faculty is valuable in business and social contact. They can help many people with their sound advice and constructive ideas. A good conversationalist is always appreciated. The one error they must be constantly aware of is becoming critical. These natives are naturally subject to impulsive action, but, fortunately, they are the type of individuals who will analyze their impulses before acting upon them. This is a good habit to acquire, as it can save much heartache and misunderstanding. Sound judgment, free from all prejudice, is essential to success and happiness.

The Sign Virgo imparts to its natives the power of inspiration. A study of the lives of many prominent Virgoans reveals that they have been inspired men and women. This inspiration is an attribute of the subconscious mind, as is the faculty of intuition. Active intuitive power gives those of this Sign a deep understanding of human nature and the motives of others. It also helps them recognize truths, and often warns of impending danger. Such intuition should not be confused with ordinary fear or apprehension. An intuitive impression is sudden and spontaneous, and has no association with any previous thought or experience.

Others may have some difficulty understanding Virgo people, but this is because they are apt to mistake the Virgoan reserve for indifference. In ordinary conversation, they keep to themselves and do not volunteer information. They are natural students and enjoy the independence of their own minds.

A good physical constitution capable of withstanding the rigors and vicissitudes of life is indicated. They, being of a mental and nervous temperament, should avoid excesses which have a tendency to weaken the resistance and irritate. Since Virgo is the Sign ruling the digestive organs and intestinal tract, judgment in the diet is advisable. A balanced diet of animal and vegetable food is the natural sustenance essential to human well-being, but many Virgoans are inclined to dietary fads and fancies. Consult your doctor before going overboard on a diet. Plenty of fresh air, sunlight, and rest will do much to maintain strength, and health and appetite.

The Virgo is fond of sports, entertainments, and travel. Much enjoyment is also derived from reading, and from lectures. Pleasure comes more from intellectual pursuits than physical pleasures, although the out-of-doors is greatly enjoyed.

Their innate reserve and sensitivity keeps these natives from showing their real feelings. They are more mental than emotional in the affections. It sometimes appears as if they are afraid of love. When subjected to love, they are apt to begin to lead an intellectual and mechanical sort of life which is devoid of emotion, sentiment, and affection.

This attitude is not normal and, in time, will react upon the body and mind in accordance to natural laws.

Hurt or disillusionment—especially in a love affair—is apt to deeply affect those born of this Sign, and they are not inclined to get over it easily. In friendships, they like individuals because of certain particular characteristics they possess, but when it comes to marriage, a mate cannot be accepted just for certain qualities. The mate must be acceptable for all qualities, and these must reasonably blend with the native's own mental, emotional, and physical make-up. If such blending does not exist, an inharmonious marriage results. This, in turn, would cause the native to become extremely critical and distorted by the disillusionment he feels. In the state of marriage, it must be borne in mind that things may happen from time to time which will cause irritation. In this event, understanding must be striven for, or else eventual separation and sorrow will result.

These natives possess a great degree of parental love and may be jealously fond of their children. Two things should be guarded against in regard to children—overindulgence and overcriticism. Indications show an unsettled state of affairs in their home life during childhood and youth.

The Virgoan ideals regarding home life are high, but there is a restless element in the nature leading to a desire for mental and physical changes in matters connected with home life and surroundings. Close and confining places tend to irritate them. The native may not be aware of this consciously.

Those of this Sign are critical of the appearance of the home and its furnishings; disorderliness is utterly foreign to their nature. Disorder irritates their finer sensitivities more quickly than anything else.

Though they are methodical, monotony is apt to upset the sensitive nervous system. It is to their advantage to get away now and then, even though it may be only for a short time. They are often misunderstood by their own relatives, and, if married, by some of the mate's relatives. This is caused primarily by their independent natures. However, the Virgoans try their best to get along with others. They are willing to cooperate with kinsmen, but the latter rarely reciprocate unless it is to their advantage.

The Virgo-born will be much happier and accomplish more when they live apart from relatives. Those of this Sign are naturally industrious, conscientious, and sincere in their work. Their quick perception enables them to make improvements in their labors. They are adapted to intellectual rather than physical labor; they represent the type of personality well adapted to professional life. Many Virgo people are found in the law, the healing arts, literature, and bookkeeping. Their particular type of mind is suitable for any line of work which requires careful analysis and judgment. Many of the world's scientific minds belong under this practical Sign. Good mechanics and machinists as well as hotel and transportation people come under Virgo. They are practical in anything they do. When choosing a job or profession, they should select the kind which will give their abilities the greatest expression. It is advisable they take advantage of the high degree of persistence in their natures.

They will get along well in partnership ventures, but they require a free hand to carry out responsibilities. Indications are that financial standing will vary considerably through the course of life. Their pecuniary outlook ranges from conservatism to free spending. Because of their natural industry earning ability is good. They seldom reach the level of dire want. They will do well to consider real estate, transportation lines, and mercantile and chemical companies as fields for investment. Success in speculative ventures appear to be very limited. Small business enterprises and backing new inventions appear to bring fairly good results. However, in the main, Virgoans financial conditions are very much under their own direction, and they will, no doubt, have many opportunities in life to better their finances.

The choice of friends runs to the intellectual and idealistic types of both sexes; though the native is loyal and solicitous, there is a disposition, at times, to be critical of friends. Much pleasure is derived from social activity. Ability to be a good host or hostess creates a good impression on guests and friends.

THE VIRGO CHILD

The children of Virgo are governed by the intellect and are seldom sympathetic. They are quick mentally, but are inclined, at times, to get into a "rut" and become overly fond of taking things easy. Sometimes they cause enmities of a lasting nature, but more generally make very good friends, treating their friends well.

They are sensitive to any suggestion of ill health and can become chronic hypochondriacs. In dealing with the Virgo child, the parents should stimulate the child's interest in health and recreation. The mind of this child should be kept busy in order to avoid an uncertain mental state. Virgo children are, at times, hard to understand, and it will be to the interest of the growing child if the parents take an interest in all the activities of their offspring. A review of the health potential for the Virgo child shows that the vitality can be termed moderate. The system will have a tendency to an acid condition. Special note should be taken when this child begins to walk, as he or she may tend to poor circulation, indigestion, and bowel disease. It is well to avoid drugs as much as possible; the best tonic is care in diet, and mental and physical exercise. Fear in the mind of this child is likely to cause illness.

In considering the best occupation for the Virgo child, great care should be taken to ascertain his or her likes and dislikes. This is of the greatest importance as it can set the stage for a career. The occupations for which the Virgo child is eminently suited are connected with the earth and its products. They make fine bankers, inventors, librarians, nurses, physicians, promoters, psychiatrists, scientists, and statisticians.

The mental characteristics of this child will tend to make him critical, with a strong tendency to worry over trifles.

Music and art will always play a big part in the life of a Virgo child, and such attributes should be given every opportunity to develop. Many times opportunity is lost because the parents do not realize until too late that certain star-ordained gifts could have been developed to enhance the possibilities of success later in life.

THE VIRGO WIFE

When the Virgo woman marries, she makes an excellent wife in most respects. Her concept of marriage is that it is a legal partnership, to be run as a business. She is usually capable and arranges her housekeeping routine perfectly. The home is spotless, and under her care everything seems to remain new. She is vigilant and efficient—she is everything that can make a home run like a well-oiled machine. There is no waste or neglect in her home.

Her disposition may not be perfect all the time. In some cases, the Virgo wife is apt to be fussy and nagging. She guards the family purse jealously and, in extreme cases, she is stingy. In all her responses to life she shows the same parsimonious attitude.

Emotionally, this woman is often way below par. She handles traditional duties well but the intimate companionship and emotional ecstasy so necessary in a wife are often entirely absent. She has in her make-up a selfish coldness that resents demands for personal warmth. The Virgo wife never recovers from her maiden beliefs that she is sinning when she accedes to her husband's purely physical attention. A very clever man who is deeply in love might alter this frame of mind, but since the Virgo woman seldom inspires great intensity of passion, her best hope is for a mate as restrained, practical, and material as herself. In such an environment she makes a successful wife. It must be remembered, of course, that other planetary influences can alter the emotional intensity of the Virgo woman.

THE VIRGO HUSBAND

The Virgo husband in search for the best kind of wife would do well to choose a Virgo woman. These men are not usually interested in love in the passionate, personal, and possessive senses of the word. Virgo husbands are conventional, traditional-minded men who accept domesticity because it is part of the social scheme. They are willing to conduct their private life on a partnership basis, as if it were a commercial enterprise. In many cases they would prefer to be bachelors; this Sign produces many of them. They are abstemious and stingy, the latter which has kept many a man from matrimony.

The Virgoan is capable, and makes comfortable provisions for his wife and family, but he is fussy, critical, peevish, and complaining (especially about health or expenses). He safeguards his home and is careful to protect it from disaster.

Unless there are other stimulating factors in his Horoscope, the Virgo husband is not virile. He has little male dominance in his make-up, and is as loath to demand surrender as he is to give of himself. He does not have a passionate urge, and his deepest approach to love is flirtation. Eroticism and flights of passion would never be attempted by him, since his opinion of passionate sexual performance is not favorable. The one great exception to the rule can be a Virgo husband with Scorpio rising in his Horoscope. This contributes to a passionate attitude by giving a physical desire for ever-fresh, stinging pleasures.

THE CUSPS OF VIRGO

(If your birthday is not within the cusp of your Sign, the following does not apply to you.)

These natives are born in Virgo with Leo tendencies. The ruling orbs are Mercury and the Sun. This cusp shows kindness, optimism, and unusual success in whatever the natives set out to do. They have a good sense of humor and should capitalize on their varied talents. They are loyal to their friends and delight in doing things for others. They are fond of diversion, travel, and novel contacts. They possess an aptitude for science, invention, and original enterprises. They never betray a confidence or trust. Should they meet with financial reverses, they will make a comeback and start again with their former courage.

Through persistency they will make some of their plans come true. While at times there may be a tendency to follow the course offering the least resistance, they soon control this and get back on energetic planes. At times they worry too much over trifles. They are clear thinkers and early in life should train themselves to see both sides of any problem.

If the birthday is from September 19th through September 22nd.

These natives are born in Virgo with Libra tendencies. The ruling planets are Mercury and Venus. This indicates that they are full of many ideas, but lack a plan to carry them out. These people are kind, thoughtful, and will go to extremes to make a good impression upon strangers, though those who are closest to them are often overlooked. They possess some literary and musical ability. In romantic matters they are sincere, and anyone fortunate enough to receive their interest may count on their loyalty.

These natives benefit from past experience and seldom make the same mistake twice. Because they always try to make sure that they are right before they go ahead, they are likely to be more successful than the average person. They have the ability to accomplish any reasonable desire. Throughout life they will be popular, and will have the good will and respect of their circle of friends.

THE DECANATES OF VIRGO

If the birthday is between August 23rd and August 31st.

Your personal and ruling planet is Mercury. It is the symbol of knowledge and the Swift-Winged Messenger of the Truth. It rules the rational part of the soul and mind, and indicates an alert, ingenious, perceptive, intellectual, studious, and forceful personality when in favorable aspect. In unfavorable aspect, it inclines toward an inquisitive, meddlesome, careless, cunning, radical, imitative, shiftless, forgetful, and effusive nature. This planet is said to be the great mental ruler, for without Mercury's influence, we would be devoid of memory and the powers of speech and expression.

If the birthday is between September 1st and September 11th.

The personal planet for this decanate is Saturn, known as the symbol of time. This planet is restrictive in its influence. It governs the thoughtful and meditative tendencies, and inclines to make its subjects careful, patient, and considerate. Saturn is chiefly concerned with lending fixity to all affairs that may be classed as concrete conditions. Its powers lie in stability, endurance, tenacity, and perseverance. Gain through thrifty methods and careful investments is indicated. These natives possess a magnanimous spirit and a kind, benevolent, and sympathetic nature.

If the birthday is between September 12th and September 22nd.

The personal planet is Venus, which is known as the symbol of Love and Beauty and gives constancy to the affections.

It denotes a sensitive, generous, harmonious, perceptive, and artistically well-balanced mind—a mind capable of taking a dispassionate view of life.

These natives possess a good sense of proportion and are able to see both sides of a subject clearly. Praise and admiration will influence them to develop the more positive tendencies of their nature. They share their earthly possessions, especially with those who are near and dear. A generous spirit is indicated by the influence of Venus in this Horoscope.

THE DEGREES OF VIRGO

August 23rd.

These natives possess a romantic nature, and may be idealists and dreamers. A rather "hard to please" attitude is shown at times, due to a fixed, self-centered viewpoint. You of this birthday may show a decided preference for the company of persons having a great deal more money than you have. When dealing with those who are less fortunate, it is necessary to use tolerance and consideration. Old friendships should not be neglected or discarded.

August 24th.

This degree imparts a resourceful mind and natural executive ability. Marked determination to succeed in all undertakings may make you work alike for good or bad. Discrimination between right and wrong should ever remain the keynotes. A diversified, liberal education is an important factor in overcoming many of the negative qualities which may be in this nature. Moderation and conservative principles will pay the best dividends in success and happiness.

August 25th.

Here is a sensitive, impressionable, and reserved nature. There is a tendency here to depend too much upon others for help and advice. Wealth by marriage often makes life easier for this degree. Obstacles in business may come from elderly persons who have put you under obligation. There is a marked interest in politics, law, and humanitarian activities. Any sacrifice made to obtain a college education will well repay you.

August 26th.

Those of this degree possess a serious, aspiring nature coupled with a strong intellectual capability. You are profound and practical. A strong sense of independence and a desire to help those in less fortunate circumstances is also indicated. At times you may become too magnanimous for your own good. Learn the value of financial conservatism. Show a respect for your superiors. You will create your own destiny.

August 27th.

These Virgo-born possess a retiring, studious, and analytic nature. An envy streak should be curbed. You are fond of literature, music, and art. Make the maximum use of your intellectual and commercial training. Learn self-confidence and the ability to see the other person's point of view. Due to lack of emotional stability, you may be hard to understand at times.

August 28th.

The Virgoans of this birthday possess unusual mental qualities. You display independence of thought and possess a steady and forceful disposition. One aspect of this Horoscope shows a desire to defy convention. This tendency should be curbed. It should be borne in mind that best chances for success and happiness come through valuable friendships that are made and held.

August 29th.

A keen mind and a calm, peaceful attitude towards life are bestowed upon the persons of this degree. Gain is indicated through sentimental associations and influential friendships. One aspect of this Horoscope shows a tendency to take good fortune for granted. Persons of this degree are possessed of great sexual potency.

August 30th.

This chart shows an adaptable, versatile, and intuitive mind. The value of concentration should be recognized. One aspect in this Horoscope indicates a tendency to tire quickly. One thing should be completed before another is started. A charming personality coupled with a good sense of humor will attract many friendships. Diligent application of the many capabilities shown for you will aid in the attainment of success once a constructive mental attitude is developed.

August 31st.

You possess a sensitive and idealistic nature. Certain planetary aspects show a tendency to be too generous for your own personal welfare. Learn to recognize the true from the false. Fondness of travel by water and a long sea voyage are indicated.

September 1st.

You are endowed with an original mind coupled with a rather sensitive and retiring nature. One aspect in this Horoscope shows that you may lack the incentive to overcome obstacles. Develop self-confidence. Be practical. Pursue success. Cheerful companions and friendly associates will do much to help attain social ambitions and make life bearable.

September 2nd.

These Virgo-born possess a bright, cheerful disposition. You are just and righteous in both business and social matters. You will probably pursue a professional career where your mind will be exercised to the best advantage. A strong desire to be well-dressed at all times is shown. This can develop into the extravagant habit of purchasing many things of doubtful use. Pull in your horns and practice parsimony.

September 3rd.

Those of this birthday possess an astute, practical, and intuitive mind. An artistic temperament with marked humanitarian principles will bring many lasting and influential friendships. You are generous, of good appearance, kind-hearted, and charitably inclined. One aspect of this chart indicates a tendency to shirk responsibility, a desire to get by with little personal effort.

September 4th.

Strong will power and an energetic, commanding personality is shown by this degree. Initiative and good business acumen will enable you to progress rapidly in the commercial world. There is a tendency, however, toward extravagance. The value of personal possessions should be learned. An ardent, highly emotional nature, desirous of adventure and full of wild dreams, should be moderated.

September 5th.

A flexible, happy nature and a clever, imaginative mind are indicated here. You may become too generous for your own good, and too agreeable to protect your own interests. There is a fondness for mimicry, the stage, and theater. One aspect of this chart shows a tendency to scatter your forces, talents, and energies in too many directions at the same time. Concentration of purpose should be exercised.

September 6th.

These natives are the possessors of sensitive, impressionable, and inquisitive natures. Love of travel to distant lands is indicated. At times, you show an erratic disposition and a cross temper. This should be checked as soon as possible. One aspect here shows a rather extravagant nature, which must be curbed so as to avoid loss of credit from time to time. A marked interest in political, legal, and humanitarian activities will aid materially in achieving success.

September 7th.

The natives of this degree possess a keen, shrewd, and alert mind. They can be deeply moved by their higher sympathies. There may be a tendency to meddle in the affairs of others. While the intentions may be most charitable, there will be misunderstandings and disappointments until it is learned that life's greatest rewards come to those who mind their own business.

September 8th.

This degree imparts to its natives an energetic nature and great skill in the execution of duties. Persistence and determination, even in the face of difficulties, will bring success and financial independence. Friends and associates should be chosen with discrimination. Other people's viewpoints should be treated with tolerance. There is a tendency here to become somewhat impulsive, especially in affairs of the heart.

September 9th.

Those of this birthday possess a keen and intellectual mind coupled with excellent powers of concentration. A tendency to regard life with too serious an outlook should be avoided. A bright, cheerful atmosphere and the company of successful friends will greatly aid in eliminating this trait. A highly magnetic personality and an independent nature will make for great success in the business world.

September 10th.

Wholesome charm and magnetism are the endowments of this degree. You have an inventive mind, and show a high degree of originality in all of your undertakings. You are susceptible to colds and it is necessary that all precautions be taken to avoid drafts and sudden changes of temperature. A rampant desire for speculation should be curbed.

September 11th.

This degree bestows a splendid character and a sympathetic nature coupled with deep emotions. These natives can really succeed in life if they will curb a tendency to become too easily satisfied. It is essential that they have a happy environment and friends who are appreciative of their fine talents. The emotional problems will yield to patient and understanding treatment.

September 12th.

An expansive and genial personality is shown here. You can attain much popularity in your social life. You have a charming personality and talk well. Love of travel is indicated. The emotional nature should be stabilized. An artistic temperament coupled with a magnetic personality will make for success in a professional rather than a business career. Public recognition through literary abilities can be insured by proper education. One aspect here warns of the tendency to become too much of a carefree dreamer.

September 13th.

You possess a bright, cheerful disposition, a splendid mind, and a magnetic personality. Success in a material way is indicated through the ability to make and hold influential and beneficial friendships. Marked originality and a good sense of humor will help toward a position of prestige in the social world. A vivid imagination coupled with excess energy may cause restlessness and carelessness at times. Some danger when traveling is shown.

September 14th.

This native possesses a pleasing personality and splendid intuitive powers. A highly emotional nature may develop into an uncontrollable temper unless you develop an ironlike self-discipline. There is a tendency to brood and daydream too much if left alone for any great length of time; this is, no doubt due to a most imaginative mind. Many persons born on this day will evince much artistic, musical, and literary skill. Avoid solitude.

September 15th.

Those of this degree possess an intellectual, scientific, and experimental mind. Being excellent conversationalists they should enjoy great popularity. An independent, yet orderly, spirit coupled with a magnetic personality is also shown. These fine qualities should make it easy for these natives to get what they want from friends.

September 16th.

You possess a kind, sympathetic nature, and a pleasing disposition. You should develop a sense of independence and a faculty for diplomacy in order to utilize a too-adventurous spirit. Due to an inquisitive, aspiring, and perceptive mind, success is indicated in the professional world. You may be naturally attracted to the study of medicine. An indicated ability to get along well with all types of people will aid materially in attaining success. Conservative financial principles should be followed.

September 17th.

A benevolent, charitable, and sympathetic nature is imparted by this degree. A desire to help all those who appeal for assistance may result in extravagance beyond your means. You are subject to flattery and can easily become the prey of designing friends and associates. One aspect in this chart shows a tendency to become conceited due to excess attention. Beware of false friends.

September 18th.

These natives possess a good mind coupled with a charitable nature, which will endear them to all. The magnetic personality and ability to attract staunch and loyal friendships may result in a dependent attitude. The early home environment may also tend to encourage the shirking of responsibility. It would be wise to concentrate on concrete personal accomplishments which are essential to your success and happiness.

September 19th.

Great ambition and a keen perceptive mind are indicated for those of this birth date. A highly magnetic personality and an enterprising, forceful disposition will attract many respected and beneficial friendships. At times it will be necessary for these natives to overcome an exaggerated sense of self-importance. A wayward spirit and a star-influenced desire to make frequent changes is shown. This aspect should be moderated by intelligent training toward a more modest and stable viewpoint.

September 20th.

You possess a pleasing, courteous disposition and alert, thoughtful, and intuitive mind. A tendency to dominate others and assume leadership, regardless of consequences, should be carefully noted, and proper education and training should be sought in order to overcome these tendencies. There is industry and self-reliance shown here, and a highly ambitious and determined nature. Help may be received from persons in superior positions. Cultivate humility.

September 21st.

A polite, agreeable, and companionable disposition is shown here. The attractive personality will draw many friends and bring much popularity. One aspect here shows a tendency to look upon the dark and gloomy side of life. This is, no doubt, due to a highly sensitive and emotional nature. Patient training to instill confidence will help overcome this pessimistic attitude. Undue excitement will cause an adverse reaction of the nervous system. Pleasant surroundings and cheerful friends are essential to you.

September 22nd.

You possess a bright, cheerful disposition and a generous nature. You are just and righteous in both financial and social matters. A professional career, where the fine mental faculties shown here may be demonstrated to the best advantage, is advisable. There is a strong attachment for the home and family. These natives are extremely clothes-conscious, and wish to appear in the height of fashion at all times. Sometimes this small vanity leads to unnecessary extravagance.

COMPATIBLE AND INCOMPATIBLE SIGNS OF VIRGO

The outstanding Virgo characteristic is self-sufficiency. The old maid of caricature, with her cat or parrot, her fussiness and faddiness, her curiosity, and her love of malicious gossip, is a typical product of Virgo.

The Sign is a discriminatory and critical one, and is not easily satisfied. Virgos are fastidious, dislike being criticized, and have a deep-rooted fear of infections and ailments. These factors all play an important part in the sex outlook of its natives.

In marriage, Virgo is dutiful, and may desire to be more affectionate than appears on the surface, for the extreme shyness of the Sign prevents outward exhibition of affection. Virgo makes a faithful partner but not necessarily a sexually exciting one. The matter-of-fact, critical, and fussy manner is not calculated to win another's heart easily.

Neatness and tidiness are usually strong Virgo characteristics, and are by no means confined to the women of the Sign. These tendencies are evinced in their style and dress, and also in the care lavished upon the home and possessions. Virgo rarely praises anything, and more often grumbles and criticizes. The general efficiency of the Sign leads its natives to assume that no one else can do anything as well, as neatly, and as methodically as they can.

Virgoans have quiet, cultured, demeanors, as a rule, and they certainly know how to interest the opposite sex. Love to them is an adventure. They believe that they are interested in the opposite sex for psychological reasons only—just the simple student of life to whom the study of the behavior of others is the supreme interest—but their interest is not by any means as detached or coldly analytical as they would have one believe. Despite their explanation, the fact remains that they provoke the amatory susceptibilities of the opposite sex. In other words they can be veritable teases!

Virgo is flirtatious and intensely curious. If their penchant for criticizing others results in a rebuff, they feel hurt, and sorry for themselves. This state will not last long before the barometer changes and they come up smiling—more provocative than ever! They are interested in so many members of the opposite sex, in each of whom they see "points" others haven't got, that they are sometimes baffled as to which one is best for them. It would be good for the Virgoan to study the following comparisons of the Signs and discover the compatible and incompatible Signs for the Virgonians.

Virgo and Aries.

This combination is certainly not the "happily-ever-after" affair. Mercury-ruled Virgo will not take kindly to bossy, dictatorial Aries (Mars), and the impulsive, fiery Aries would soon become dissatisfied with the prissy, critical Virgo. Usually a difficult combination.

Virgo and Taurus.

Taurus is apt to have a love-at-first-sight attack for Virgo, but Taurus does not like criticism, which is usually Virgo's strongest weapon. In addition, Taurus can be as stubborn and obstinate as the Bull which is the symbol of that Sign, and Virgo will be inclined to do a lot of nagging and push the Taurus mate into a fury.

Virgo and Gemini.

Though both these Signs have the same ruler—Mercury—this combination may prove too much for both over the long run. Mercury in Gemini is logical and calculating; in Virgo it is demanding and critical. Virgo would soon be out of breath trying to keep up with Gemini's constant desire for change. There are some points of compatibility between these two—the love of good clothes, a predisposition to neatness, and mutual desire for friends and associates who are in artistic and intellectual pursuits. It is through these channels that many Gemini-Virgo combinations are formed.

Virgo and Cancer.

The demanding Virgo may be very disturbing to the Cancer's desire for quiet contentment. Virgo is apt to be too realistic and direct in the approach to everyday events. Sentimental Cancer is reticent—even shy—in sex matters. This will probably frustrate the Virgo and cause him to harshly criticize and nag. Such treatment would put the Cancer native in a sulking, silent mood, and Virgo would probably become hysterical. Only those who are on the highest plane would find this a compatible union.

Virgo and Leo.

This could be a very happy combination, since each seems to have what the other needs and wants. Warm-hearted, forgiving Leo will be likely to overlook Virgo's sharp tendencies and Virgo will regard the Leo mate's accomplishments with pride. Leo's good humor and lovable traits will do much to melt any Virgo coolness. Leo's respect for Virgo's mind and cleverness will nourish the Virgonian ego. If Virgo will permit Leo to hold the center of the stage, and soft-pedal criticism, there should be few barriers to happiness in this partnership.

Virgo and Virgo.

It would be difficult indeed for these two to find anything resembling compatibility. The traits of each here would make for a battle of wits with the opponents evenly matched. Each would exaggerate the faults of the other. At best it would be a commonplace marriage, with the possibility of husband and wife talking each other to distraction.

Virgo and Libra.

This is another combination that would have trouble in finding mutual grounds for marital bliss. If there is one thing Libra cannot take it is criticism, and, of course, Virgo is a champion in that department. Virgo is very meticulous in all matters pertaining to detail, while Libra is easygoing and detests detail. The conflict of interest here will surely cause storm signals to be run up soon after the sex novelty has worn off.

Virgo and Scorpio.

This combination usually belongs to the mutual admiration society. The exploring Virgo mind is fascinated with the mysterious and intriguing Scorpio. If there is any Sign that can curb Virgo's tendency to sulk, it is Scorpio. Virgo respects Scorpio's ability to analyze all situations and thereby sidesteps controversial issues before they become a basis for disagreement. If Virgo will avoid hurting Scorpio's pride, this combination will be happy and enduring.

Virgo and Sagittarius.

The Sagittarian love of freedom and change may prove too much for the meticulous Virgo disposition. The Sagittarian male is easily attracted to the Virgo female. Her spic-and-span appearance intrigues him, but once he is married, he may soon find that he got more than he bargained for. He may find that the things he liked most before marriage may put him into a strait jacket after marriage. One thing Sagittarius cannot take is bickering—and Virgo thrives on it.

Virgo and Capricorn.

There are points of similarity and compatibility in these two Signs. They are both very exacting. This eliminates many areas of disagreement. They both have great pride in appearance and surroundings. They can cry on each other's shoulder when outside influences prove too much to cope with. This Mercury-Saturn combination should find mutual ground for an agreeable partnership.

Virgo and Aquarius.

Aquarius may hold too many surprises for the conservative Virgo nervous system to cope with. This is an elaborate combination to analyze. Much depends on the cultural and educational levels of the partners. If there is a marked difference between the two, the chances for a happy and enduring marriage are almost nil. However, if both parties happen to be college sweethearts, or do the same sort of work, chances for a happy marriage are greatly enhanced. This combination is either very good or very bad—no happy medium here.

Virgo and Pisces.

Pisces is the exact opposite of Virgo. In the Zodiac they are 180 degrees apart. While opposing Signs are considered astrologically unfavorable, opposites often find much compatibility. This may be because contrast makes for interest, and in Virgo and Pisces the contrast is very marked. It will take a great deal of patience and understanding on the part of Virgo to cope with the moody, sentimental nature of Pisces over a long period of time. A little sentimentality on the part of the Virgo mate will go a long way in making this combination happy; however, a little sentimentality is a dangerous thing.

SOME FAMOUS PERSONS BORN IN THE SIGN
OF VIRGO

Leonard Bernstein—Composer
and Conductor
Pierre Curie—Physicist and
Chemist
Theodore Dreiser—Author
Greta Garbo—Actress
Johann Goethe—German
Dramatist and Poet

Arthur Godfrey—Entertainer
Alexander the Great—Conqueror
Oliver Wendell Holmes—Poet
Sophia Loren—Actress
Grandma Moses—Painter
Friedrich Nietzsche—German
Philosopher
John J. Pershing—U.S. General

J. B. Priestley—Author
William Saroyan—Author and
  Playwright
Upton Sinclair—Novelist
William Howard Taft—U.S.
  President

Cornelius Vanderbilt—
  Industrialist
H. G. Wells—Author

LIBRA

SEPTEMBER 23–OCTOBER 22

THIS CONSTELLATION symbolizes Justice. Most of our readers, doubtless, have seen the Goddess of Justice represented by a blindfolded female holding in her hand a pair of scales. This conception is purely astrological. The Sign Libra signifies the reins and loins of the Grand Celestial Man, and therefore represents the central conservatory or store house of the reproductive fluids. It is also the magnetic vortex of procreative strength. This constellation represents, in its most interior aspect, the equinoctial point of the arc in the ascending and descending cycle of the life atom. This Sign contains the unification of the cosmic forces as the grand central point of equilibrium of the sphere.

Libra signifies external perception balanced by intuition. The union of these produces reason and foresight. Those dominated by this influence constitute the rationalist school of the world's thinkers.

Libra upon the esoteric planisphere is occupied by Dan, the patriarch, in his blessing—thus referring, to his celestial nature: "Dan shall judge his people as one of the tribes of Israel." Libra represents the interior equilibrium of nature's forces, and contains the mystery of the divine "at-one-ment" of the ancient initiations.

166

Upon the universal chart, this Sign becomes Enoch, the perfect man. Libra is the second emanation of the airy Triplicity, and is the constellation of Venus.

Its mystical gem is the chrysolite. As a magnetic talisman, this stone acts as a repulsive force, and combines with the magnetic sphere of those born under its influence to repel the emanations from foreign bodies.

The fortunate day is Friday.

The fortunate numbers are six and nine.

The fortunate color for this Sign is pastel blue.

Best locations for success are places of social activity.

Theoretically, Librans are strong supporters of such conceptions as universal brotherhood, universal equality, and the rights of man, but actually they seldom (unless it pays) put their pet theories to actual practice. The natives of Libra, though possessing a finely balanced mental and magnetic organism, are seldom elevated into very prominent positions. This is because they are too even, both mentally and physically, to become the popular leaders of any radical or sensational party.

It is one of the attributes of Libra to infuse a tendency within all born under her influence to accept and adopt the golden mean, or as it has been termed, "the happy medium." Hence, they generally command respect from both sides on questions of debate, and their intuitions are light and golden.

The true Libra personality is charming, attractive, pleasing, and graceful. Libra usually indicates beauty, and many of the world's most handsome men and lovely women are born under this Sign. Ordinarily Librans show considerable poise. They usually possess a personality that is responsible for the creation of its own destiny throughout life. This orientation gives one a good start in life, but the actual carving of destiny depends upon the strength of the mind behind the personality.

In disposition, the native is kind, sympathetic, generous, and loyal, under ordinary circumstances. They have a touchy emotional nature. Their temperamental responses vary with the particular mood at the time Librans are aroused. Sometimes they are quick to anger, and at other times they are very patient and will stand for much nonsense. They dislike pettiness and injustice, yet there will be times in their lives when it will be advisable for them to take stock of themselves and see if they, themselves, are not guilty of injustice. Though they may not show it, they are selfish and self-willed, with independent natures. They resent any intrusion upon their independence of thought or action. In their business and social life they manifest the same sort of personality, often impetuous and impulsive.

Though Librans possess good sense, there are two things they must guard against. They should not get into the habit of considering things from the viewpoint of their personal feelings and prejudices, and they should avoid jumping to conclusions because of analogies or comparisons.

Such reasoning, based on either emotions of the moment, prejudices, or erroneous comparisons, is no safer than a leap in the dark.

The perception of these natives is aided by their intense desire to learn. In their eagerness to learn, however, they must guard against glossing over—or missing—some of the minor, but important, details of a subject or proposition. They are inclined to be intelligent in any matter other than their own feelings. They should be aware of this fact and do their best to view their emotions with more caution. It is hard to regard your own feelings impersonally, but with desire and the will to do so, a few lucky, determined Librans can accomplish it.

Imagination plays an important part in the life of Librans. They are natural daydreamers. They take keen delight in going over pet ideas in their minds. Romantic ideals become quite vivid in their imaginatons. Excessive indulgence in such habits is apt to create the conditions for sad disillusionment in love, romance, and marriage. Bear in mind that good ideals are lovely things so long as they are possessable in reality as well. Imagination should be used to visualize the steps necessary for progress.

Libra gives its natives good powers of expression. Though they are somewhat self-willed and just thinkers, there are times when they lack continuity of purpose—they do not always stick with an idea or proposition to its logical conclusion. There are times when they appear to be evasive, even blind, and times when they show good ability to concentrate. Emotionally, they are impulsive. Think over and analyze impulses, just as any other idea or proposition. If Librans will do this, they may not always act in haste and repent in leisure. They may be content to dream about ideas and never carry them out. A minor setback could lead them to abandon an entire project.

Libras also have the faculty of intuition, which enables them to understand human nature. There are times when they can see through and understand the motives of others. They often take an intuitive dislike to certain people they meet, but they do not know why. Time usually proves their "hunch" was right. However, when it comes to their personal feelings and emotions, they are apt to ignore their intuition and act contrary to it. They must learn to understand this voice for it will materially aid their progress.

Libra birth brings a good physical constitution; but it is imperative that Librans exercise reasonable care in diet. They should avoid excesses. Their Sign rules the kidneys, back, and loins. They should also guard against all periodical spells of moodiness and depression by seeking gaiety and diversion. They must avoid overdoing and attendant fatigue, nervousness, and irritability.

Native Librans enjoy travel, sports, recreation, dancing, and the theater. Their artistic tastes must be satisfied and the fancies of their imagination catered to. They enjoy motion, rhythm, and the beautiful things in life and nature.

Indications show that the Libra-born are affectionate, tender, sympathetic, and warm in love. Their moods, however, vary according to their mental activity. They may appear poised and calm while hiding the intense warmth of an affectionate nature, but when conditions are ideal, they are expressive and demonstrative. Their feelings are easily hurt in love affairs, but they will endure much, and willingly sacrifice much, for those they love. They are often misunderstood by their lovers and may even be accused of being flirtatious, because they take an interest in many people. This frivolity is based on intellectual rather than physical interest. They enjoy meeting and talking with anybody whenever they get a chance. In all love and romantic ventures, it is advisable that they do not permit some of their ideals to prevent good, practical judgment. Librans must remember that, regardless of whom they love, they should accept the whole person, and not make a conquest just for certain characteristics that arouse temporary romantic interest. Until they learn this, they are apt to experience disillusionment in love affairs.

There should be reasonable, harmonious balance between natives of Libra and the objects of their affections from mental, emotional, physical, and idealistic viewpoints. If such balance does not exist, the Libra-born are inclined to lose interest. They must learn to heed the voice of their intuition, making sure to guard against all impulsiveness in romantic matters. The Libra nature, even though it is self-willed and independent, revolves around others. The ideal mate must be understanding, intellectual, sympathetic, patient, demonstrative, affectionate, and idealistic.

Indications show much love for children. This birthsign is not a barren one, but it does not give promise of many children during the course of life. Certain indications denote that the domestic life of these natives may not always be as harmonious and peaceful as they desire—or expect—it to be. This will not always be due to any particular fault of the native.

Their independent natures may cause them to be at variance with their parents. They are intensely devoted to their parents and relatives, but are not always understood by them. In the home, these natives want all comfort and beauty possible. The domestic life may, at times, be unsettled because of a desire for changes of scenery. Monotony bores them, so they should take a short trip now and then. When conditions permit, Libra-influenced people enjoy entertaining in their homes. During the last half of their lives, they are inclined to be more settled.

This chart indicates adaptability and talent. In fact, Libras may possess more active talents than they know what to do with. They may experience difficulty in discovering just what they are best equipped to do in this world. Regardless of their education, their experiences may lead them restlessly into many varying lines of diverse endeavors before they find themselves. They will lean toward the intellectual and artistic pursuits.

Libra people exceed in any capacity which may take them before the general public. Libra attorneys make good judges. The Libra-marked are also to be found in all sorts of entertainment work, for Libra is the natural Sign of beauty and imitation. Librans make good instructors, writers, doctors, architects, and aviators. Under ordinary circumstances, they are highly efficient in their work, and very ambitious, energetic, and successful.

Many Libra people are apt to get discouraged too quickly at times. They should make every effort to develop "stick-to-itiveness."

Good earning power is indicated, but there is a tendency toward being a big spender. In partnerships, success will depend upon the type of partner. It is necessary for Libra people to exercise restraint over their feelings. They are capable of accomplishing much if given a free rein; they achieve a good degree of success by entering into business ventures for themselves. They are by nature thrifty. There are times when money is spent in response to a desire or impulse; then they must start saving all over again. It will pay well to develop a certain consistence in conservatism.

The Libra-charted are inclined to be somewhat speculative and it is advisable for them to be reasonably cautious in this matter so their natural impulsiveness will not lead them. Great risks should never be taken except for great stakes. Librans are often conservative in their ideas pertaining to investments, but their adventurous nature often urges them to have a small fling at some longer chance. They will achieve far more satisfactory results if they stick to such investments as government bonds, or transportation, aviation, and chemical stocks.

An attractive personality will bring many friends and acquaintances to the Libran in the course of his life. Many will be drawn because of the natural charm. Great loyalty to friends is shown here, but there is a deplorable tendency to be too critical at times. However, the Libran's unusual understanding of human nature will bring many friends with their confidences.

These natives have every prospect of rising to the social position if they desire. They should make the most of their natural charm. Their worst faults are a fondness for daydreaming and a lack of tenacity. They must resist depression and be ever watchful of their health. Proper training will enable them to attain the full measure of their aims and ambitions. Librans have far more in their favor than against them, and it is up to the individual to apply his star-granted energy constructively for progress, success, and happiness in life.

THE LIBRA CHILD

Libra children are generally very good-looking. The complexion is usually smooth and clear, and the hands and feet well shaped. Parents will find their Libra child very ardent in almost everything he or she does. One of the principal faults is that children of Libra find it hard to settle down into steady effort. The parent must urge this child to overcome vacillation. Don't be surprised if the Libra child is cheerful and then, suddenly, without apparent reason, depressed.

These children are exceedingly fond of music and art. They must have their minds constantly engaged; otherwise pent up energy may lead them into trouble.

The vitality is moderate, and the pathology shows that the

nervous system may be depleted by jealousy and moodiness. Physical ailments from which they may suffer are indigestion, headaches, backaches, and diseases of the stomach, liver, or kidneys. Libra children are easily thrown off balance in health, but yield readily to treatment.

Generally speaking, the Libra child will achieve greatest success if trained for work of an artistic nature. Parents should be careful about the selection of a career for their Libra-born because of Libra's tendency to drop one subject and start another. The best plan is to observe the child closely in the formative years. These children will be rather imitative and somewhat fickle because of their changeability. They are extreme in feelings and somewhat subject to negative moods, so proper early training is of great importance.

THE LIBRA WIFE

The Libra wife possesses one of the most interesting love natures in the Zodiac. The Sign has a decided feminine leaning, with the highest Venus influence prevailing. These women have delicate, spiritual appeal. A Libran is an ideal wife for a wealthy, successful man who is stimulated by union with a woman who is like an orchid. The Libra wife is exotic in appearance. Actually, these women are not as fragile as they appear. The Libra wife is a fine intellectual companion, wise in the ways of partnership. One of her special gifts is a talent for harmony. She attracts an interesting social circle. At the same time, she never neglects her own family, but gives them all the loving attention of which her gracious nature is capable.

The Libra wife is a luxury. She is usually quite attractive, and always has a group of admirers seeking her favors. While she requires a varied social life, she is too well-balanced to encourage indiscriminate flirtation, but if she were to find herself emotionally involved, her response would never be underhanded.

This type of woman does not encourage scandal. Because she is so attractive, her life is sometimes more complicated than the existence of plainer women. Her passions are voluptuous, and demand a "quality setting." She is responsive, intuitive, and intellectual.

Her passionate response to married life is extremely satisfying, and in many respects she is the best suited of all of the Zodiacal types to be a wife in the strictly personal sense of the word.

THE LIBRA HUSBAND

The Libra husband is not an easy man to please. The monotony of domesticity is not to his liking, but he is a passionate man and a respecter of tradition. The Libra husband is reasonable. He is a born judge, and no other Zodiacal type can order his life with so much wisdom. His superior ability to guide the destiny of the home is one of his greatest virtues. Negative Libra characters do not have this power. They have surface smoothness, but not the high intellectual development of which the best Libra men are capable. Libras provide well for their families and they seem to feel with the same intensity as a woman the necessity of elegance and luxury in the home surroundings.

The Libra husband is a passionate man, to whom love is a high art. His passions are overwhelming, and he rises to great heights in the expression of them.

This kind of husband would be deeply disappointed if he did not meet with satisfactory response to his passions. Even when the domestic partner is very agreeable, he might be tempted to seek variety. The Libra husband does not seek divorce unless the conditions of his life are not adjustable. He has an instinctive distrust of the untried, and will strain with his judicial talents to guide domestic routine to satisfy his fastidious taste.

THE CUSPS OF LIBRA

(If your birthday is not within the cusp of your Sign, the following does not apply to you.)

These persons were born in Libra with Virgo tendencies. The ruling planets are Venus and Mercury. This indicates that these people are intuitive, impulsive, and considerate. They are, at times, jovial and at other times depressed. Moments of depression come suddenly and for no apparent cause. They are ardent and sincere, but will have many heartaches and troubles in romantic affairs. Marriages brought about through emotion rather than love are seldom happy. These Librans should not marry early in life, and when they contemplate marriage, they should take considerable care in choosing a mate. More unhappy marriages are contracted by Librans than any other Sign.

They are neat in dress and take pride in their surroundings. They are endowed with so many talents that they are apt to follow the wrong one and engage in a line of business for which they are not suited. They have the faculty of seeing both sides of any problem and their judgments can be relied upon. It is desirable for them to follow their hunches and impressions. They are well-liked by many and will make many friends throughout life. If they do not scatter their energy they will become successful and prosperous individuals.

If the birthday occurs from October 19th through October 22nd.

These persons are natives of Libra with Scorpio tendencies. The ruling planets are Venus and Mars. With their magnetic powers they could become outstanding sources of inspiration to others. They are skillful, conscientious, and original. They are of cheerful disposition and use good judgment. They are rather impatient to succeed, and are constantly devising means to improve themselves and their environment. They possess originality of thought and should be successful organizers, managers, inventors, or directors. They are rather unconventional, and the mysteries of life and nature appeal to them. They are not as punctual as they should be, are quick to anger, but easily pacified. They like to be praised and complimented openly. They enjoy popularity with their friends, who assist them. These of this cusp have ideals and ambitions which, with a little encouragement, may frequently be attained.

THE DECANATES OF LIBRA

If the birthday is between September 23rd and September 30th.

Your ruling and personal planet is Venus. It is the symbol of love and beauty, giving constancy to the affections and denotes a sensitive, generous, perceptive, and artistically well-balanced mind, capable of taking a dispassionate view of life. You possess a good sense of comparison, being able to see both sides of a subject clearly. Praise and admiration will help you develop the more positive tendencies of your nature. A magnanimous spirit is indicated by the double influence of Venus in this Horoscope.

If your birthday is between October 1st and October 11th.

Your personal planet is Saturn, which is the symbol of time. This planet is restricting in its influence, and governs the meditative tendencies. It inclines to make its subjects careful, patient, and considerate. Saturn is chiefly concerned with fixity of all affairs that may be classed as concrete conditions. Its powers lie in stability, endurance, tenacity and perseverance. Gain through thrifty methods and careful investments is indicated. You have a capacity for kindness and sympathy.

If the birthday is between October 12th and October 22nd.

Your personal planets are Uranus and Mercury. Uranus, symbol of Air, signifies originality and gives its natives the ability to become advanced thinkers. It inclines them toward the profound, mystical, and more serious problems of life. Mercury is known as the symbol of knowledge and truth, and rules the rational part of the mind. It indicates an alert, perceptive, and commanding personality.

THE DEGREES OF LIBRA

September 23rd.

You possess a forceful and progressive spirit. You are kindhearted and hospitable, and would excel in the medical profession or charity work. You can also be successful in dealing with property and insurance. An elderly relative may be particularly helpful. One aspect in this Horoscope indicates possible disappointment in a love affair.

September 24th.

You are kindhearted and artistic, but lacking in self-confidence. You have a humane and sympathetic disposition that will make you a champion of civil liberties. You will always take the side of those in less fortunate circumstances. Your intuition and inspiration are well blended.

September 25th.

You possess an active and inquiring mind. You are just, sympathetic, affable, and socially inclined. You are easygoing, fond of luxury, your home, and your relations. You have marked literary talents. You have the natural ability to make friends readily because of your pleasing personality, but you must use more than ordinary precautions when signing legal documents.

September 26th.

You possess a loving disposition and you are steadfast in your friendships and affections. You can be depended upon to fulfill your obligations. One aspect in this Horoscope indicates the ability to achieve fame in the fields of medicine, philosophy, psychology, and humanitarian pursuits.

September 27th.

You possess a critical mind. On the other hand you must beware of deception when negotiating or contracting for the purchase of anything of value. Your keen interest in the welfare of others may cause you to become careless of your own. Do not permit your highly sensitive nature to make you too faultfinding of your close associates.

September 28th.

You are idealistic and romantic, with a tendency to be self-sacrificing. You are very devoted to your loved ones. You could make a great success in the social world. You are best suited for an artistic or professional career, rather than for business or commercial pursuits.

September 29th.

You possess a quick mind and a fertile imagination. You may become too impulsive for your own good and should exercise caution. Curb a tendency to indulge yourself in food and drink. One aspect in this Horoscope shows a tendency to scatter your talents and energies in too many directions at the same time.

September 30th.

You possess a resourceful, capable, and practical mind. You are endowed with great courage, but have a somewhat fatalistic outlook on life. You are a born leader and possess the energy and ability to rule situations and command the respect of your friends and associates. One aspect in this Horoscope indicates danger through misplaced confidence. Success is assured from dealings with elderly relatives in business ventures.

October 1st.

You possess a tactful, sympathetic, and proud nature. You show a great love for fine clothing and a desire to be well-dressed at all times. You possess natural aristocratic bearing and may have a tendency to attach too much significance to outward appearances. One aspect in this Horoscope indicates the possibility of loss through treachery in love and business.

October 2nd.

You have a capable and sympathetic nature. You show a great deal of adaptability and unusual aptitude at reproducing and imitating. One aspect in this Horoscope shows that you have great love for children. You have a desire to gain wide recognition for your artistic talents.

October 3rd.

You possess a gentle and retiring nature, full of sympathy and understanding. You are an excellent judge of human nature and a loyal friend. Special care should be taken with your health. You may benefit from an inheritance. You should be on guard against financial loss through deceit.

October 4th.

You have a progressive mind. You must guard against misdirecting your energies. Difficulties in romance and marriage are indicated. A penchant for speculation must be moderated. Your fine intellect and keen understanding of life's problems would make you an excellent judge.

October 5th.

You possess a receptive nature with psychic tendencies. You are resourceful and self-reliant. You will derive many benefits from strangers. You are fond of mysteries and display a love of argument and debate. This will add greatly to your store of knowledge and become a prime factor in developing your mental faculties and social background. You are very affectionate and magnanimous to your immediate family.

October 6th.

You possess an adventurous spirit and a star-influenced desire to travel and visit strange places. You are also fond of social activity. You are very impressionable and likely to suffer through deception. You are versatile and have a quick mind; you ought to exercise concentration of purpose in order to achieve happiness.

October 7th.

You are ambitious and enterprising, with a well-balanced personality. Business associates should be chosen with care. Some danger exists which arises from attempted exploitation of others. The influence of the mother is strong in this degree. You are an excellent speaker and would do well in politics. An urge to speculate should be curbed.

October 8th.

You possess an energetic personality, with latent ability to be successful in the promotion of large industrial combinations. This powerful degree also denotes much talent for scientific endeavor. Curb a tendency to take needless risk in business and personal affairs.

October 9th.

You are capable and courageous, but may be overly critical of your friends and associates. You usually get what you go after, regardless of opposition. You may experience some trouble through servants or co-workers. Tone down a tendency to make erratic changes without good cause or reason.

October 10th.

You are somewhat self-centered, obstinate, and extravagant where your own pleasures are concerned. You should restrain a strong tendency to lavish luxuries on those you wish to impress. Be careful when signing important documents or contracts. Financial loss through carelessness is shown.

October 11th.

You are a clear thinker with an open mind and are willing to work hard to attain your goals. Through tact, perseverance, and courage you will overcome most of your obstacles. An inheritance usually comes to those born in this degree. You are attractive to the opposite sex in a rather basic manner.

October 12th.

You possess a strong character and a fine intellect. You are a progressive person with some unusually fine ideas. You will be fortunate in many different ways. Care should be taken where important documents are concerned. Possible loss through carelessness is shown.

October 13th.

You possess a well-balanced mind, great determination of character, and a kind, affectionate nature. You have a magnetic personality and, at times, may be somewhat temperamental and headstrong. You may have a delicate constitution; you should not overexercise or go to extremes in mental exertion. You have excellent artistic and musical talents. Many profitable and lasting friendships will prove useful in attaining success and happiness.

October 14th.

You possess an impulsive, alert, and generous disposition. You will take advantage of many opportunities, but self-indulgence and too many romantic alliances may adversely affect your health. Many persons born in this degree will travel far and wide. Good fortune will come from a keen intuition.

October 15th.

You are industrious, ambitious, and of keen perception, but somewhat self-seeking. You will be liable to deception in some of your business transactions. The development of musical or scientific talents will bring monetary and personal rewards. Some danger of ill health from romantic and emotional troubles is shown.

October 16th.

You possess a refined and artistic temperament. You have an active and progressive mind. Your health will need continual care. Domestic and business troubles will threaten from time to time. Many trials and tribulations are shown for persons of this degree. This is particularly true where the children of the natives are concerned.

October 17th.

You possess remarkable artistic and musical talents and will be successful in these fields providing excesses in love of pleasure are controlled. You show great enterprise in acquiring the good things in life, and success will be attained mostly through your own efforts. Avoid both mental and physical overexertion, as one aspect indicates the possibility of nervous ailments.

October 18th.

You are exceedingly clever, and possess a fine character. A versatile mind coupled with marked social instincts will enable you to gain success and recognition in public service. One aspect in this Horoscope indicates a tendency to be too apprehensive concerning the welfare of your loved ones and friends. Learn moderation of this golden virtue, as it is apt to cause misunderstanding. Much affection for your parents is indicated.

October 19th.

You are sympathetic and good-natured, thus, are likely to be imposed upon. You are financially fortunate, but sometimes too pleasure loving, which ascertains varying degrees of success and happiness. A great love of animals is shown by this degree. This may include horses, with the speculative tendency toward betting on them. Remember, lady luck is elusive.

October 20th.

You possess an adventurous, mystic nature, and a scientific trend of thought. A great love of travel and the sea is also indicated. A magnanimous personality and a desire to help those who are in less fortunate straits may lead you into many strange experiences during your life. Studies of a scientific nature which can be used for the good of humanity and the alleviation of sorrow and suffering will bring success and happiness.

October 21st.

You are frank, outspoken, and fond of travel and sports. You have a charming personality which is much admired by the opposite sex. Do not permit your fortunate qualities to make you conceited and arrogant. Your love of ease should be kept under control.

October 22nd.

You are courageous, determined, ambitious, and desirous of public acclaim. Your intellectual faculties are well-developed, but care should be exercised when dealing with legal matters. Possible trouble through writing or signing documents is also shown. Being very impressionable, you will readily react to your environment. It is, therefore, necessary to select the right type of friends and companions.

COMPATIBLE AND INCOMPATIBLE SIGNS OF LIBRA

The compatible and incompatible Signs for the Libra-born will yield a wealth of information as to just who should fit into the love-life and marriage plans of those born September 23rd to

October 22nd. Although Libra is the marriage Sign by virtue of its relation to the Seventh House of the Zodiac, the fact that Libra is rising or strongly occupied in a Horoscope by no means implies that marriage will take place. Libra has an intense desire for sympathy, love, and understanding, and is hard to satisfy. Libra has a real interest in recreation, and this characteristic is shared by both the men and women of the Sign. The women are romantic and tend to be "in love with love" rather than any particular person. They crave admiration and flattery even when they know it is merely flattery. There is no Sign quite as capable of believing what it knows to be untrue as Libra.

It is incorrect to say that Libra is an affectionate Sign. Actually Libra has an affectionate manner, tempered with selfishness. People's troubles are never quite real to Libra. It is a Sign which prefers to ignore ugliness and build a world of its own.

There is no doubt about the personal charm of Libra, which is never entirely lacking even in its negative representatives. Sometimes this charm is an unconscious one, but more often it is deliberately exerted in order to obtain help, favors, and protection. Libra women make ideal hostesses, but to be at their best they must have plenty of servants to do the actual work. Libra, though capable enough, dislikes manual labor, especially if it entails soiling the hands. Libra much prefers to snuggle back into a pile of cushions and press the bell.

The sexual side of marriage is not of primary importance to Libra women, though it sometimes appears to be so. The girls and young women of the Sign are usually surrounded by many admirers and obtain a reputation for flirting. In reality, they are seeking admiration. They are flattered at the attentions they receive but are in no hurry to give in, for that would spoil the good time. As a result, they play one admirer off against another, until finally they may lose them all. In this event, they remain unmarried or rush into marriage with the first available person. This little tragedy is played by a great many Libra women, and explains why Libra marriages are not, as a rule, really happy. In many cases the "first available person" is a man who may have been rejected by someone else or is wealthy and seeks someone to grace his home, and entertain and impress his important business acquaintances. In either event, the marriage is one of convenience for Libra, and the affection is on one side only. Usually, however, such a marriage is successful enough from a material viewpoint, for Libra women can be content with a dream world all their own. Libra men, on the other hand, are not so disposed to make the best of marriage. They find it extremely difficult to resist feminine wiles and flattery.

Librans are equable, generous, and sociable people, with quite a good deal of sentimentality. When an appeal is made to their generosity, they rarely have the heart to say "No!" They are exceptionally good mixers, and are at their best in social life. They are lovers of music and the arts, and there is nothing that pleases them so much as to be considered a connoisseur of these things.

Their intellectual qualities are often above average. They are also good conversationalists, and really delight in repartée.

As lovers they are sentimental—and susceptible! Thus, their emotions are capable of being worked upon, especially as they have somewhat passionate natures. They react badly to slights, and are often sensitive in this respect, and when they do form a bad impression of someone, it usually sticks. They are at their best when among artistic, sociable types, and they admire clever people. Thus is unconsciously shaped for them the kind of partner they should seek.

There are some types, however, with whom a happy marriage would be problematical.

The general comparisons are as follows:

Libra and Aries.

This is a combination that is tops for perfection. The warmth and passion of Libra blends perfectly with the fiery, aggressive, impetuous qualities of Aries. Their rulers, Mars and Venus, are in good accord, and each seems to have what the other needs and wants. This will be even more evident if both persons are on the same cultural and intellectual level. Libra's refined and artistic temperament will be appreciated and reciprocated by Aries.

Libra and Taurus.

These two are basically compatible so far as their positive qualities go. Both have the same or similar interests. Unfortunately, negative qualities are present in most people, too. In such instances, one marriage partner should have a good quality to offset the negative one in the other. In such case, all should go well unless both of these "Bull" partners get angry at the same time—then the tempest and the mad fury may cause an irreparable damage to the relationship, for when the Taurean gets really angry, he sees red!

Libra and Gemini.

This looks like a good partnership all the way around. Mentally and artistically these two could "make the scene," and Libra can understand Gemini. There is just enough contrast to make things interesting—with little combat expected. Mercury (Gemini) and Venus (Libra) can make a very happy home together.

Libra and Cancer.

Libra is too fond of freedom to endure the absorbing, confining tendencies of Cancer; and Cancer's interests are too concerned with home and family to understand the Libran love for social flitting. Libra would never be happy with a partner who is likely to sulk and sink into deep depression if things do not go the Cancer way. They would both pout—perhaps for days—over a routine family spat, so, perhaps, both should look for another partner more compatible with their own qualities and expectations.

Libra and Leo.

These two have qualities that blend well. The Sun (Leo) and Venus (Libra) form an impressive aspect together. This is a luxurious aspect as both love luxuries. Both are artistically inclined, and both love attention and flattery. Leo demands these things to make him happy—Libra expects them as just due. Constant adulation and the center of the stage at all times must be given to Leo; eventually Libra may get the idea that it's a bum piece of rubber that doesn't stretch both ways! If Libra is willing to always "play up" to Leo, these two could really "have a ball" in marriage.

Libra and Virgo.

This is most likely a "no go" affair in many ways. All may appear well at first, while the sex novelty still possesses its shine and curiosity still stimulates, but when both land back on earth to take up life and its cold routine, there is little chance that either of these two will change his basic qualities willingly. If there is one thing that Libra resents, it is criticism; and with a Virgo mate (who takes top prize for knowing how to dish that out) poor Libra may bear soul-marks from the tongue lashing and carping of Virgo. Virgo insists on perfection while easy-going Libra hates detail. The conflict of interests here make this alliance no more than a dalliance.

Libra and Libra.

Here is a truly "made-in-Heaven" combination, unless one had an incompatible Sign rising at birth. Both have the same basic interests and qualities, so there would be great mutual understanding between these two partners. While both like to be admired, and may cast a roving eye away from home territory, each is understanding of the other's motives. There is so much in favor of this combination and so little against it (a possible incompatible Sign rising in either birth chart) that there can really be no hesitation in advising it.

Libra and Scorpio.

There is much sympathetic magnetism between these two Signs. While Scorpio is the more dominant Sign of the two, the Libran's beauty and sense of fair play appeal to Scorpio's good judgment. In Scorpio, Libra sees all the virtues she admires, for Scorpio's sex drive is all that Libra's hopes to be. There is much to recommend this union, for they have many sympathies in common. As lovers, Librans are sentimental and susceptible. This "accepting quality" appeals to Scorpio's dominant and possessive urges. As long as the pride of Scorpio is not wounded, Librans will find what they are looking for when they marry a Scorpio.

Libra and Sagittarius.

Libra may not find it easy to cope with the free and easygoing Sagittarian philosophy of life. However, this is a good marital combination. Libras will get all the excitement they want if they marry Sagittarians. The only question is, will Libra's endurance be able to last with this partner? The Libran love of beauty, luxury, and social whirl appeals to the Sagittarian, but he will not be tied to the Libran apron-string. Sagittarius hates confinement, and will not tolerate bondage, whether it be legal or not, and will use all the means at his command to break through bonds.

Libra and Capricorn.

These two personalities seem to be opposites on the surface, but the taciturn Capricorn is very much intrigued by Libra. If Libra does not find the steady Capricorn nature too boring, there is good chance here for a successful marriage. The Capricorn mate is far more liberal in his views on sex before marriage than he will be afterward. Libra had better screen the social environment to suit Capricorn's views or there may be some embarrassing moments later on.

Libra and Aquarius.

This could be a most suitable combination for marriage. Aquarians have perfect affinities for Librans. Their mutual love of beauty, society, and people help to make this an ideal union. One of the few possible causes for a misunderstanding is that the Aquarian mate is unpredictable at times, and, for no reason at all, may seek seclusion and refuse to communicate. In that event, the best thing to do would be to let him enjoy his solitude. He will soon revert to his lovable self, and all will be well if Libra doesn't insist on explanations.

Libra and Pisces.

There is mutual attraction here, but it seldom lasts long. This is especially true under intimate circumstances. Pisces will be content with Libra's exclusive company, but Libra's love of social affairs may generate jealousy and disharmony in the intimate life. Libra can get along well with most people, but the Piscean is more discriminating, and therein lies the source of many Libra-Pisces disagreements. Nothing can make a Libran more miserable than a sulky, complaining Piscean.

SOME FAMOUS PERSONS BORN IN THE SIGN OF LIBRA

Brigitte Bardot—French Actress
David Ben-Gurion—Israeli
  Statesman
Sarah Bernhardt—French Actress
Charles Boyer—Actor
Edward W. Bok—Philanthropist
  and Editor
Dwight D. Eisenhower—
  Commander and President
William Faulkner—Novelist

Mohandas Gandhi—Indian
  Statesman
Lillian Gish—Actress
Helen Hayes—Actress
Vladimir Horowitz—Pianist
Thomas W. Lamont—Banker
Walter Lippmann—Social
  Writer
Groucho Marx—Comedian

Henry L. Mencken—Editor and
  Writer
William Penn—Statesman
Eleanor Roosevelt—U.S.
  Stateswoman

Ed Sullivan—Columnist
Gen. Paul Von Hindenburg—
  German Statesman

SCORPIO

OCTOBER 23–NOVEMBER 21

THE SIGN SCORPIO, in its symbolical aspect, symbolizes death and deceit. It is the allegorical Serpent of matter, mentioned in Genesis as tempting Eve. Hence the so-called fall of man from Libra, the point of equilibrium, to degradation and death by the deceit of Scorpio. No wonder the primitive mind, when elaborating this symbol, tried to express a spirit of retaliation.

The Sign Scorpio typifies the generative organs of the Grand Man, and consequently represents the sexual or procreative system of humanity. It is the emblem of generation and life; therefore, the natives of Scorpio excel in the fruitfulness of the seminal fluids, and this creates a corresponding increase of desire.

A distinct reference to the fruitfulness of this Sign will be found in Gen. xxx: 10–11, wherein Leah, when she beheld the birth of Zilpah's son, exclaimed, "A troop cometh."

Scorpio upon the esoteric planisphere is occupied by Gad, of whom the dying Jacob says, "Gad, a troop shall overcome him: but he shall overcome at the last" (Gen. xL: 19); intimating the fall of man from a state of innocence and purity through the multitude of sensual delights, and his final victory over the realms of matter as a spiritual entity. This Sign represents the physical plane of the attributes of procreation.

191

It contains the mystery of sex, and the secrets of the ancient phallic rites.

Scorpio is the second emanation of the watery Trigon, and is the constellation of Mars.

The mystical gem of Scorpio is the topaz, the natural talisman of those born under this influence.

The fortunate day is Tuesday.

The fortunate numbers are three and five.

Their best color is dark red.

Best locations for success are near water.

Upon the intellectual plane, the Sign Scorpio signifies the generation of ideas; hence, those dominated by this influx possess an inexhaustible resource of ideas and suggestions.

Their active, evolutionary minds are ever busy with some new concept, and their brains are full of inventions. They possess keen perception, fine intuitional powers, and a positive will. Hence they excel as medical practitioners, chemists, and surgeons. In the various departments of the surgical art, natives of this Sign have no equal. In addition to this mechanical ability, they are endowed with a powerful, fruitful, magnetic life force, which they sympathetically transmit to their patients. This is why they become such successful physicians. Sexual desire is naturally strong, hence they have the potential for excess in this direction.

Scorpio natives have an attractive, magnetic, and dynamic personality, but they are quite difficult to understand because of a tendency to be secretive. Under ordinary circumstances, they are likable, and capable of influencing and soothing others. The personality, if properly developed, will prove a strong factor in their efforts and endeavors to attain success. It may prove to their advantage to become more expressive.

Ordinarily, they are courteous, generous, loyal, sympathetic, and patient. However, if they are aroused, there is no fury like the fury of a Scorpio. They not only get angry, but become obstinate and headstrong as well. They can speak bitterly and cuttingly, losing all appreciation of the sensibilities of themselves or others. When this happens they become cynical, self-willed, and selfish. They should do all within their power to avoid this type of expression, as it may be the cause of much heartache and sorrow.

The Scorpio-born have the class of mind which will enable them, with effort, to attain the degree of self-control essential to their progress. They are, then, sincere and may be depended upon. Their friends will be inclined to rely on them, and will often appeal to the Scorpio native for help when faced with disturbing situations and personal problems.

Their powers of observation are keen. They possess the ability to meditate. They are independent thinkers, and not inclined to take the other fellow's opinion as final without investigation. They rarely advance an opinion unless it is asked for by others, except in case of emergency. Where emergency exists, Scorpio people think and act simultaneously.

The more sensitive types may lose all sense of self-composure and become incapable of constructive action. Those who react this way should make every possible effort to change their ways. It is true that they are individuals with intense feeling and emotion. Nature has a method of compensation for all things, and in their case, they are furnished with all the essential qualities of mind, which, if properly applied, will enable them to apply rational control to their emotion.

With their keenness, things seldom escape their notice. They have the ability to learn things easily. When their feelings are not aroused, they can perceive the realistic value of their own ideas and impulses. Their reflective minds cause them to daydream sometimes, but, as a rule, they use their imagination to visualize facts. Their good memory springs primarily from the fact that they consciously and unconsciously pay close attention to the details of any proposition. They have fairly good powers of self-expression and make interesting conversationalists when they so desire, but as a rule, they are apt to be quite reserved in their opinions and judgment, unless it is asked for by others. They possess the type of mind that absorbs facts quickly. They have the qualities of persistency and determination of purpose which enables them to overcome many obstacles in life.

They are not mentally impulsive, but their feelings play an important part in their life. Their personal reaction to their emotions makes it most difficult for them to judge matters impersonally once the emotional thermometer rises. Once they are aroused, they are apt to be very outspoken. Calling their attention to this fact is not fault-finding, but only an effort to help them understand themselves. The corrective measures can only be applied after they understand their faults.

They have an active faculty of inspiration. There are times when inspired ideas flash into their consciousness. Some of the world's most progressive men and women have been born under the Sign of Scorpio. They were inspired beings and they worked out their inspired ideas. The same can be learned by all Scorpios —to act upon inspirational ideas and bring them to fulfillment.

They also have a good insight into human nature. It gives them an awareness of truth, and makes them difficult individuals to deceive. Their intuition often gives them foreknowledge of impending events.

The greatest asset of these natives is their power of will and determination. It enables them to overcome many obstacles which would compel others to give up. They should endeavor to keep their reason in the face of intense emotional crises. They have the type of mind which will enable them to go far in life, if they will but learn to direct and apply mental energies wisely.

This birthsign presides over the organs of reproduction, and the various glands of the body. By reaction, the head and throat are susceptible to minor ailments, thus it is advisable to avoid exposure to common colds. These natives are fond of the good things of life. Reasonable care should be taken to avoid a fondness for too much rich food, sweets, and alcohol.

Many of the major ailments of Scorpio people could be avoided by the use of judgment in diet. Physically these natives possess a fairly rugged constitution, but it is not advisable to overtax it. If the law of moderation is applied, there will be no worry about health. Indications in this chart show a great fondness for recreational activities. There is also a deep appreciation of art and the beautiful things of life.

Travel, too, is enjoyed, though most Scorpio people get tired of too much of it.

The emotional nature is deep and intense, and the love nature is affectionate, somewhat aggressive at times, sympathetic, deep, and passionate. The Scorpio's feelings in love matters can be their best friend or their worst enemy. These people are extremely serious and intensely devoted to those they love.

They are not always sure of themselves in romantic affairs. Once their love is constructively aroused, acknowledged, and returned, they become happy, affectionate, magnetic, and they radiate a most pleasant personality. It is advisable that these natives do their utmost to avoid unreasonable and unwarranted jealousy, because they are apt to become selfish. They evince poor judgment when their feelings get the upper hand. This will, no doubt, lead to many misunderstandings and disappointments in romantic matters.

The Scorpio's affectionate, aggressive, and passionate nature requires a normal expression and outlet. Love acts as an inspiration for the progress of these natives. It helps them to take an interest in their work, and stimulates their desires and ambition for accomplishment.

When the planetary aspects blend to a reasonable degree, their friendships are lasting, and free of the misunderstandings that usually plague relationships.

It is impossible for love to live with excessive selfishness and jealousy. It is evident that the Scorpio native is far happier in the marriage state than when single. These people must guard against traits which tend to destroy the very foundation of all they care for.

This birthsign is known as a fruitful one and gives promise of children. People of this Sign usually have an intense love for them but are strongly advised not to be too indulgent with them.

It is necessary that the emotional and domestic life be as ideal and harmonious as possible for Scorpios, as domestic matters play an important part in their lives. They desire a permanent state of affairs. They get much enjoyment from the comforts of their home, and want the best they can possibly afford in its furnishings. They feel pride in their home surroundings, and endeavor to keep them attractive and artistic. They have the natural qualifications of a good host or hostess. The Scorpio person is usually active, industrious, and quite capable. They are naturally ambitious, efficient, conscientious, and sincere in their efforts. Whenever they do anything, they desire to do it well. Though they have independent natures, they are capable of efficiently executing orders. They do not, however, like to feel that they are being forced to do anything.

Scorpio is a loyal, dependable, and trustworthy employee. If in business for themselves they are capable of managing affairs with a good degree of success.

Their particular intellectual talents enable them to stick to a proposition until it proves successful. In a general analysis of this Sign, it is impossible to say just what kind of work they are particularly suited for. This information must be determined by the individual's aspects in their natal chart, and since no two people in all the world are exactly alike in every respect, the personal Horoscope, cast and analyzed for a Scorpio native, will give the truest advice.

Men and women of this Sign are found in all types of work, and nearly all of them have good business ability. In partnership matters they usually get along fairly well, especially when there is no occasion for serious domination. They will often shoulder more than their share of responsibility when handled tactfully.

This birthsign has a natural affinity for financial matters. This does not mean that all Scorpio people are financial successes, but they have good earning ability. Naturally, the more conservative type will amass the greater wealth. The weaker type of Scorpio can save to a certain extent, but is inclined to be an impulsive spender. They may save for a definite purpose and be doing all right; but when they see something they like, and want—they buy it.

It follows that this type will not be able to amass much money in the course of their life. The true art in back of all financial success and security lies in one's ability to put money to work. There are many Scorpio people who are clever in money matters and make good investments.

It must be admitted that in most Scorpio natives there is a speculative streak. Generally speaking, Scorpios have their share of financial reverses, but most of them seldom get in dire financial trouble. Investments in government bonds and the stocks and bonds of large industrial corporations usually prove quite profitable. Some of these natives make good in real estate and mining ventures.

Scorpios are capable of leading an active social life with a good degree of success. Their greatest obstacle is their own emotional nature. They must learn to understand and to control their emotions, and avoid becoming too headstrong and temperamental. Envy, jealousy, and selfishness need continual efforts to be overcome. These natives have the power of will and determination to overcome all obstacles. They can reach their desired pinnacles of success financially if they will but apply the conservative principles of their nature and avoid impulsive extravagance. It is up to them to apply themselves wisely and attain their full measure of success.

THE SCORPIO CHILD

Scorpio children will develop according to the way they are trained. They are always ready to take up an argument, either in their own behalf or for someone else. They are never content with half measures and will always go to extremes, good or bad. They are not underhanded and operate in the open and above-board. They have an uncertain temper; this should be taken in hand by the parent at an early age. Efforts should be made to instill within them a tolerant attitude. Much care should be taken to teach the Scorpio child sex hygiene, because this group is under the planetary influence that rules the generative organs. It is essential the parents see to it that their Scorpio child is physically and morally clean.

The fundamental vitality is strong, but wasting or scattering of life forces will be most detrimental to the health. This child should not partake of highly seasoned foods, and should have rest and fresh air in abundance. They are subject to ruptures, toxic diseases, hemorrhoids, and sometimes prostatic stricture. They develop diseases of the blood, fevers, and inflammation. They must be protected from the possibility of burns, scalds, and mishaps due to carelessness. Since these children are usually endowed with strong vitality, the above-mentioned ailments need not develop. Scorpio children are very temperamental, and can be quite vindictive. They are subject to emotional extremes. The parent should be watchful for, and guard against, the development of a nasty temper and suspicion. They are boldly courageous, with an inclination to be overventuresome. These children usually develop a firm, yet delicate, touch, making them very skillful with their hands. This is a necessary requirement for surgeons and dentists; they could succeed in either of these professions. These children are inclined to have an "all-or-nothing" attitude, and it will be very beneficial to train and develop the child along the lines of moderation.

THE SCORPIO WIFE

The Scorpio wife is one whose deepest feminine instincts are aroused by the functions of being a wife. She takes marriage seriously, and has an old-fashioned reverence toward domestic responsibilities as long as she is in love with her husband. Should this condition change, she follows, without thought of consequences, the dictates of her heart. Happy Scorpio wives are loyal and courageous, and need no hothouse atmosphere to keep their love in bloom.

They enjoy responsibility, and a large family is a delight to them. These women are very capable. Once they are settled into domestic life, they put all of the energy of their passionate nature into the home. They have the gift of homemaking, and frequently organize a much better home than the Cancer or Taurus women who are famous for their homemaking instincts.

The Scorpio woman loves luxury, and has considerable taste in decorating. She is blunt and fearless in character, doing everything passionately from the depths of her being. Her devotion to her husband is wholehearted, and she idolizes those she loves. Her reactions to life are intensely realistic, and she sees her man exactly as he is. Since she is neither shy nor tactful, she expresses herself with the greatest force. Her sexual appetite is large, and she requires vigorous satisfaction. The Scorpio person is inclined to excess. While the moral sense rebels against the animal appetites, satisfaction usually comes first and repentance afterward. It takes a very virile man, with a deep sympathy for sexual indulgence, to satisfy the Scorpio wife.

THE SCORPIO HUSBAND

The Scorpio husband is one of the most difficult to live with in peace and harmony. The only way this can be accomplished is for the wife of a Scorpio man to be receptive to his every wish, and follow his instructions with complete obedience. He is a typical old-fashioned "Lord-of-the-Manor" and can be just as tyrannical and overbearing in his home as he is in everyday life.

Many astrological warnings have been given about marriage

to a Scorpio man with bad aspects in the seventh house of marriage. He is too extreme in his love life.

The Scorpio man, himself, is often successful and able to support a wife and a large family, but his personal passion and the possessive attitude of his devotion can prove to be a strain on the most devoted family. No matter how much love and attention he receives, he will remain suspicious.

The depths of his affection for his wife and children are genuine, but he cannot seem to curb his inherent jealousy. Such selfish love is bound to cheat itself as the unhappy Scorpio man makes his stubborn way through life.

Sexual excesses are often a part of the negative aspects of this Sign. As in the case of the Scorpio woman, the Scorpio man has a strong moral side to his nature. He suffers deeply for his indulgences and always makes inward promises of temperance after the appetites have been satisfied.

THE CUSPS OF SCORPIO

(If your birthday is not within the cusp of your Sign, the following does not apply to you.)

If the birthday is from October 23rd through October 25th.

The native was born in Scorpio with Libra tendencies. The ruling planets are Mars and Venus. This denotes that great importance is placed upon wealth; there is much admiration for those who hold positions of authority and power. They like to be among people of culture and refinement. They are aggressive, determined, and somewhat critical. Self-assurance and a positive attitude may lead others to believe that the native is unsympathetic, but he really is not as difficult as his attitude appears. These natives are not easily convinced against their will, and frequently ignore advice. They are reasonably cautious and possess good judgment. They generally accomplish what they set out to do. Each effort spurs them on to greater achievement.

Some of their best qualities are developed in competition, as they like opposition. They are usually excellent conversationalists, but also good listeners. They are capable and can accomplish more by themselves than in a group. They are distinguished in appearance and show taste in dress. They are ingenious, active, and practical. A quick temper and a restless nature should be restrained to retain poise and good-naturedness.

If the birthday is from November 19th through November 21st.

The native was born in Scorpio with Sagittarius tendencies. The ruling planets are Mars and Jupiter. They will experience many crises in life. Theirs is a life of variety. They are positive and determined. They show a fondness for travel and will have many adventures. Their word is law, and they will adhere to it, unless they discover they were wrong. They will make sacrifices for those they love, and are usually more generous to others than to themselves. They possess occult, mediumistic tendencies and can become successful clairvoyants.

They are quick-tempered, high-strung, sensitive, and are easily hurt. Those who are fortunate to win them as friends may be assured that these natives will always be loyal companions who will stick to their friends through thick and thin.

THE DECANATES OF SCORPIO

If the birthday is between October 23rd and October 31st.

The personal and ruling planet is Mars, which is doubly forceful in this aspect and tends to bring out the more dominant, dictatorial, and positive side of the nature. It is important that these natives practice patience and understanding. An active body and a highly impetuous and spirited nature is shown by the double aspect of the planet Mars in this Horoscope. There is the determination to have their way in all matters, so it is highly advisable to practice restraint for best results.

If the birthday is between November 1st and November 11th.

The personal planets for this decanate are Jupiter and Neptune, considered somewhat conflicting. Jupiter is known to be the symbol of Good Fortune and Blessing, while Neptune is known as The Spiritual Awakener. This would indicate that these natives have dualistic tendencies and a very changeable and unpredictable nature. Their greatest battles will be with themselves. Their natural negative and positive qualities were definitely marked at an early age. This should help them to overcome and eliminate their adverse tendencies, and constructively and beneficially develop the more positive ones.

If the birthday is between November 12th and November 21st.

The personal orb for this decanate is the Moon, which is the great molder of character. She is the Queen Mother of Heaven, and has chief rule over the earth. This orb indicates a highly emotional, imaginative, changeable, and proud nature.

Marked ability in artistic and dramatic fields of endeavor is indicated. This native's personality contains a sense of romance, imagination, and mystery. Popularity and recognition will be gained through the magnetic personality and sympathetic nature. The combination of the Moon and Mars is indeed a fortunate one, since Mars, being aggressive and powerful, strives to force its natives to attain their objectives.

THE DEGREES OF SCORPIO

October 23rd.

These natives possess a determined, yet flexible nature. Capability in dealing with the masses, and success through association with influential and prosperous friends is indicated. Proper education will equip them for a life of public service. They are not receptive to any dealings that do not coincide with their own inherent sense of justice and fair play. It is necessary that they learn to rely upon their own judgment.

October 24th.

Strong will power and a commanding, energetic personality is shown here. Initiative and good business acumen will enable this native to progress rapidly in the commercial world. A tendency toward extravagance should be curbed at all times. These natives should realize and understand the value of personal possessions. An ardent, highly emotional nature, full of adventure and wild dreams, should be moderated.

October 25th.

These Scorpio-born possess a clever and perceptive mind, which coupled with great intensity and sincerity of purpose may tend to make them over-critical and intolerant when their plans and ambitions are interfered with. They can avoid the development of this aspect by carefully analyzing the inevitable reactions and consequences. Physical activities should be encouraged as much as possible in order to offset the possibility of over-taxing the mind by too much study.

October 26th.

Those of this degree possess a retiring, studious, and chaste nature. An envy streak, which may become apparent from time to time, should be curbed. These natives are fond of literature, music, and art. They should make the most of their intellectual and commercial training. Self-confidence and the ability to see the viewpoints of others must be nourished and developed. Due to lack of emotional stability, these people may be hard to understand at times.

October 27th.

You are endowed with an intellectual, scientific, and experimental mind. An excellent conversationalist, you should enjoy great popularity. An independent, orderly spirit coupled with a keen sense of diplomacy is also shown. These fine qualities will make it easy for you to get what you want from your friends and associates in life. One aspect in this Horoscope indicates the possibility of becoming self-centered and easily spoiled.

October 28th.

Those of this birthday possess a splendid character, a sympathetic nature, and deep emotions. Being instinctively intellectual, they may show a tendency to become too reserved and serious. It is essential that they have a happy environment and associate with persons they can look up to. Outdoor activities and athletics are advisable. Their emotional temperament needs patient and understanding treatment.

October 29th.

A clever, critical mind and a sympathetic nature is shown for these natives. A strong will power and fiery temper may give them some cause for concern during their life. Keen interest in literature, art, and writing will endow them with the qualities of an intellectual personality. They should develop the practical side of their nature in order to attain the greatest measure of success and happiness in life.

October 30th.

These natives possess an unselfish and charitable disposition. They have strong, healthy bodies, and show great interest and skill in sports. They should learn the value of concentration in order to overcome a tendency to attempt to do too many things at one time. They are fluent conversationalists, and could become prolific writers. A passionate sex nature is also shown.

October 31st.

These Scorpio-born possess pleasing dispositions, and alert, thoughtful, intuitive minds. A tendency to assume leadership regardless of consequences should be curbed. They are industrious and self-reliant and possess a highly ambitious and determined nature. There are some difficulties through the opposite sex indicated.

November 1st.

You possess unusual mental qualities and the ability to develop the mind along intellectual and scientific pursuits. You display independence of thought, and have a steady, forceful disposition. One aspect in this chart indicates a desire to defy convention and become a bold innovator. An inherent desire to become self-willed should be guarded against.

November 2nd.

These natives are endowed with a shrewd and alert mind. They are deeply moved by their higher sympathies, and can become champions of human rights. There may be a tendency to meddle into the affairs of other people. While this may be prompted by the most charitable intentions, many disappointments are indicated until the native learns that life's greatest rewards come to those who mind their own business first. Success is shown in the fields of art, letters, and science.

November 3rd.

You of this birthday possess an impulsive and rather radical disposition. A brilliant mind and excellent intuitive powers are also indicated. This combination of mental qualities is usually found in persons who attain outstanding success and recognition in public work. An inherent tendency to be impulsive and erratic should be controlled. These characteristics, if permitted to develop, can prove detrimental.

November 4th.

This chart shows you to be sensitive, impressionable, and inquisitive. You love travel, and long journeys to distant lands are indicated. At times, you may become hard to manage and show signs of developing a cross temper. This should be checked constantly. One aspect in this Horoscope shows an extravagant nature, which should be curbed.

November 5th.

These natives possess a keen intellectual mind coupled with excellent powers of concentration. A tendency to assume a too serious outlook upon life should be avoided. A bright, cheerful atmosphere and the company of superiors will greatly aid in eliminating this aspect. A highly magnetic personality and an independent nature will make for great success in the business world, especially if the native will strive to overcome some of the more negative tendencies shown in his Horoscope.

November 6th.

You Scorpio-born possess a keen mind, and a calm, peaceful attitude toward life. A charming, open-minded manner coupled with humanitarian principles will endear these fortunate people to all. Gain is indicated through influential friendships. One aspect in this chart shows a tendency to take good fortune too lightly. Learn to appreciate your many natural gifts, and use them constructively.

November 7th.

Those of this degree possess an astute, practical, and intuitive mind. An artistic temperament with marked humanitarian principles will bring many lasting and influential friendships in life. These natives are generous, of good appearance, kindly mannered, and charitably inclined. One aspect here indicates a tendency to shirk responsibility and get by with little personal effort. It must be remembered that diligent application of the natural talents is necessary to success.

November 8th.

A benevolent, charitable, and sympathetic nature is indicated for these natives. A desire to help all those who ask assistance can result in extravagant expenditures far beyond personal means. These natives are subject to flattery, and can easily become the prey of designing friends and associates. One aspect in this Horoscope indicates a tendency to become conceited.

November 9th.

The natives of this birthday possess an original, daring, and masterful nature. Strong will power coupled with a desire to have their own way should be curbed at all times. A diversified education along commercial lines will be of great advantage. Much success in the business world is indicated. By exercising tolerance and patience, a restless disposition can be subdued.

November 10th.

These natives possess a pleasing personality and splendid intuitive powers. A highly emotional nature can develop into an uncontrollable temper unless constant and patient efforts are made to overcome this aspect. There is a tendency to daydream and brood too much if left alone for any great length of time. They should associate with persons of their own class. Above all they should see that they do not become the victims of a martyr fixation.

November 11th.

These Scorpio-born possess an energetic nature and great skill in the execution of duties. Persistence and determination, even in the face of difficulties, will bring success and financial independence for many persons born on this day. They usually choose their friends and associates discriminately, and display considerable reserve at all times. One aspect in this chart indicates impulsiveness, which should be toned down.

November 12th.

Those of this degree possess a sensitive, idealistic nature and a friendly, kindhearted disposition. Certain planetary aspects indicate a tendency to be too generous for their own welfare. They should learn to recognize the true from the false, and remember that while charity is a great virtue, it should be given only to those truly deserving of it. Fondness of travel by water is shown, and there are indications of a long sea voyage which may result in a profitable business association.

November 13th.

Great ambition and a quick, perceptive mind are indicated. A magnetic personality will bring many respected and influential friendships in life. You should curb an exaggerated sense of self-importance. A desire to make changes frequently is indicated. Success will come through the possession of property.

November 14th.

The natives of this birthday possess a serious, aspiring nature coupled with great intellectual capability. They are profound and practical. A strong sense of independence and a desire to help those in less fortunate circumstances is also indicated. At times they may become too magnanimous for their own good, and must learn the value of financial conservatism. They show marked respect for their superiors. These natives will create their own destiny.

November 15th.

You are endowed with an expansive and genial personality. You can attain much popularity in your social life through your charm and excellent powers of conversation. The emotional nature is stable. An artistic temperament coupled with a magnetic personality will make for success in a professional rather than a business career.

November 16th.

You possess a romantic nature, and can become an idealist and dreamer. A rather "hard-to-please" complex is shown at times. This is due to a self-centered point of view. You show a decided preference to associate with persons much more prosperous than yourself. This tendency should be modified as there is grave danger of suffering severe financial loss at some time in your life due to misplaced confidence.

November 17th.

Those of this birthchart possess an adaptable, versatile, and intuitive mind. The value of concentration of purpose should be realized. One aspect here indicates a tendency to tire easily, and drift aimlessly from one thing to another. You should complete one thing at a time. Your charming personality coupled with a good sense of humor will attract many friendships.

November 18th.

A resourceful, energetic, prudent, sincere, and intuitive nature is bestowed upon these natives. Much success is foreseen for many persons born on this day, especially in law, journalism, and business. However, discrimination between right and wrong will be necessary in order to avoid serious loss. Marked determination to succeed, regardless of risk, may cause the native to work alike for good or evil.

November 19th.

Those of this degree possess an original, enterprising mind, and a harmonious, contented disposition. One aspect in this Horoscope indicates that you may be easily satisfied, and because of this trait may lack the incentive to overcome obstacles. You should learn self-confidence and practical methods of achieving success. Cheerful companions and successful friends should be acquired.

November 20th.

These natives are endowed with wholesome charm and great magnetism. They have inventive minds, and show originality in their ideas and undertakings. They may be susceptible to colds and it is necessary that all precautions be taken to avoid drafts and sudden changes of temperature. An inherent desire for speculation should be curbed. Success in the field of science is shown.

November 21st.

These Scorpio-born possess a bright, cheerful, and affectionate nature. Generosity, kindness of heart, and a desire to help others is indicated. One aspect in this Horoscope shows a marked tendency to daydream, and a desire to do too many things at one time. By scattering their forces, these natives are likely to become "Jacks-of-all-trades and masters of none." They must learn concentration of purpose, and the importance of completing one task before starting another. A magnetic love nature will bring much popularity with the opposite sex.

COMPATIBLE AND INCOMPATIBLE SIGNS OF SCORPIO

The Sign Scorpio is by far the strongest and most extreme of all. The natives of no other Sign can rise to such great heights or sink to such abysmal depths as those of Scorpio. It is a strongly sexed Sign, and the Scorpio native can stand long continued excesses which would quickly break down the constitution of most other Signs. As might be expected, the outlook is usually a markedly sexual one, though it is not invariably so, for the ability for continence and self-control is quite as great as the desire for self-indulgence.

The Scorpio native has an eye to material things, and frequently contracts a marriage that offers considerable worldly advantages. The Scorpio nature is not an intensely proud one, and marriage is often entered into in order to obtain money and position. In many cases, the Scorpio native tends to seek affection or adventure away from home, but he never allows such entanglements to disturb his domestic life.

Perhaps the chief faults of Scorpio are intense jealousy and a domineering disposition. There is nothing of the "wishy-washy" about Scorpio women. They have strong character, a keen—if sometimes peculiar—sense of justice, and the capacity for deep and lasting loves and hates.

As might be expected from the extreme nature of the Sign, marriage can be either very happy or entirely the reverse. A seriously afflicted Scorpio tends to evolve fits of gloom or depression, and a persecution mania is quite common, according to the degree of affliction.

Its rulership over the sex organs make it an important factor in cases of sexual excess.

Scorpians have great strength of character, and a large supply of energy with which to put over their personality. It is this great amount of vital energy which is the real crux of their problems. Something really has to be done about it, for this energy has to be expended. If they employ it to useful, creative ends, all will be well. If they do not—well, that is another story.

Their love nature is, as a rule, far more intense than that of the average person. It can be a transcendental love, with a devotional fervor that seems to know no limits. But they have a special requirement connected with this. They need a lover who knows how to reciprocate, for they have need of constant demonstrations of affection.

Once they are convinced they have found their true love, they are in deadly earnest in their love-making. Light flirtation is not their bent and they have no time for it. When they love, they love.

Undoubtedly natives of this sign know how to choose, for they appear unerring in their character determinations, and know the merits and demerits of those whom they contact. Their moods are complex, and not readily analyzed. It takes a clever person to assess them accurately, and frequently those who attempt to do so make grave mistakes in their judgments; for the powers and talents of the Scorpio reside below the surface. They are proud of spirit, not with the same kind of pride as the Leonian, but with the pride of self-mastery. It is this pride which makes them the great fighters that they are. Woe betide those who wound them!

They are remarkably thorough in whatever they do, and if they take up a subject they certainly can master it. They are tireless in their efforts and nothing is too much trouble if an end is in view. That is why people remark upon their diligence and patience. It is not at all a question of patience, but that inner force which makes them persevere, leveling by sheer will any obstacle in their path.

They know their assets and their limitations very well, indeed, and they take care to work within these limits.

They are critical, but their criticism lacks the carping quality of that of the Virgoan. It is those who do not know them who dub them cool and calculating. Those who do know them know the warmth of feeling and great generosity of nature that is just beneath the surface.

Being natural psychologists themselves, it is doubtful if they really need too much guidance, for they know people.

The following will be a comparison between Scorpio and the natives of those Signs which may be compatible or incompatible:

Scorpio and Aries.

One throne with two kings upon it would be quite out of order, and one house with two aggressive Mars-ruled "heads-of-the-house" would be more so. These two are only compatible from the sexual viewpoint, unless one is able to become a meek and pliable little lamb who willingly steps down and lets the other rule. This is highly improbable, as a Mars-ruled person doesn't stay meek and mild very long, even in the throes of wild young love. This combination is not advisable unless both enjoy hurricanes of turmoil in the home.

Scorpio and Taurus.

This is a compatible combination for both, as the natives of these two Signs have much in common. Mentally, physically, and emotionally these two could really make a go of it—IF—they are both able to eliminate the strong streak of possessiveness and jealousy that exists in each. If either is afflicted with a "roving eye," an "H" bomb rehearsal would be the result. However, these two are well suited, so let them look before they leap—then leap!

Scorpio and Gemini.

Gemini will love Scorpio's urge for action, and Scorpio will adore Gemini's mentality; but Scorpio would be a bit strenuous for Gemini physically, and the jealous and possessive Scorpio would certainly put a damper on Gemini's love of freedom. Some types of Scorpians may combine with Gemini, but it is still too much of a chance considering the star-predicted characteristics of both.

Scorpio and Cancer.

Here are two who love deeply, and each has much to give the other. What dissension may arise from jealousy in both natures would probably be of short duration. There would also be sympathetic understanding by Scorpio of the "gloom and doom" of the Cancerian moods, and the vigorous Scorpio energy will act as a strong, stimulating tonic for the gentler, home-loving Cancer. A GOOD combination!

Scorpio and Leo.

Here are two of the "Royalty" who are most compatible IF the Leo is female and the Scorpio male. Were this reversed, a Scorpio wife may stir Leo's anger by her demands, for they would be many. Leo MUST be the center of attention at all times, but a Scorpio woman would not permit this. Jealousy is still lurking in the corners here, and could cause many really big blows—so the best bet here is if the wife is the Leo who can, with wifely submission, make it a happy marriage.

Scorpio and Virgo.

These two admire each other in every respect. Virgo, whose mind is always searching, meets a worthy match in Scorpio. Virgo's often destructive critical tongue can be quickly silenced by the sarcastic lashing of which Scorpio is capable. Too, Scorpio's penetrating mind can see right through the motives of Virgo. In this event, Virgo will conveniently change the subject to avoid making the home a battlefield. If Virgo can be considerate of Scorpio's pride, this can be a good marriage.

Scorpio and Libra.

Libra's need for affection and to "belong" will be just what Scorpio desires. The Scorpio half of this team will be the more dominant one, but the possessiveness of this Sign will please Libra, rather than irk. Libra sees in Scorpio all the virtues ever dreamed of, and all the vices desired; for the intense Scorpian love-nature is what Libra would like to have as a personal trait. Here again it will be necessary to handle the Scorpian pride with care; but the effort will surely pay off for Libra in a happy union.

Scorpio and Scorpio.

Here is one that is baffling in its outcome. If both of these individuals have a thorough understanding of their inherent traits, they can have deep sympathy for each other. The dominant, possessive, and jealous temperaments of each are things which BOTH will have to handle with extreme consideration. They are both intense in their love nature, and can get just what they are looking for in each other. If one should forget to consider the other's tender spots, or does anything to rouse the other's jealousy, then the storm will rage. This can be a wonderful—or terrible combination.

Scorpio and Sagittarius.

The dominant Scorpio will have trouble keeping her Sagittarian partner in tow. This freedom loving Sign will surely bring out the worst in Scorpio's nature. Mutual distrust is easily developed here, and the Scorpian possessiveness will make life unbearable for Sagittarius. It is true that from the sexual viewpoint, Scorpio is intriguing to the Sagittarian appetite, but there the compatibility ends. Not an advisable combination.

Scorpio and Capricorn.

A rather difficult combination to analyze. The strength and power of the Scorpio personality may clash with the Capricorn desire for the last word when it comes to important decisions pertaining to the family welfare. Capricorn can be mighty disagreeable when frustrated, and Scorpio will have to use the sting of the Scorpian barb to move the Capricorn goat from a set course. The result usually spells emotional incompatibility that becomes unbearable for both parties.

Scorpio and Aquarius.

This combination usually winds up in a battle of nerves. Aquarius is too unpredictable for the solid Scorpio temperament. Aquarius has too many outside interests to suit a Scorpio mate. Aquarians are too reserved to meet the passionate demands of Scorpio. Scorpio admires the Aquarian's humanitarian instincts, but does not want to share them with the world.

Scorpio and Pisces.

This is a love-at-first-sight combination that seldom endures the test of time. All is well until Pisces begins to pout about the many little outside interests that are always intriguing Scorpio. The possessive qualities of Pisces are not appreciated by Scorpio, who feels that possessiveness is his own sacred domain. The clinging-vine type of Piscean has Scorpio's sympathies, but respect is soon lost for the weaker member, and the partnerhip falls apart.

SOME FAMOUS PERSONS BORN IN THE SIGN
OF SCORPIO

J. Ogden Armour—Industrialist

Adm. Richard E. Byrd—Explorer

W. Averell Harriman—Statesman

June Havoc—Actress

Katharine Hepburn—Actress

Vivien Leigh—Actress

Jawaharlal Nehru—Indian Statesman

Ignace Paderewski—Pianist and Statesman

Pablo Picasso—Painter

Auguste Rodin—French Sculptor

Will Rogers—Humorist

Theodore Roosevelt—Soldier and U.S. President

Gen. Chiang Kai-shek—Statesman

Robert Louis Stevenson—Author

Ella Wheeler Wilcox—Writer

Dr. Jonas Salk—Polio Vaccine Researcher

SAGITTARIUS

THIS CONSTELLATION, in its symbolical aspect, represents both retribution and the hunting sports. We find it depicted as a Centaur, with the bow and arrow drawn to its head ready for shooting. It is frequently used to designate the autumnal sports and the chase. The Centaur is a symbol for authority and worldly wisdom.

The Sign of Sagittarius signifies the thighs of the Grand Universal Man. It represents the muscular foundation, or the seat of locomotion in humanity. It is the emblem for stability, foundation, and physical power. This Sign also represents authority and command.

Sagittarius, upon the esoteric planisphere, is occupied by Joseph. "His bow abode in strength," says the patriarch, "and the arms of his hands were made strong." We see in Joseph, the Egyptian ruler and law-giver, a true type of real authority.

Sagittarius is the lowest emanation of the fiery Trigon, and is the constellation of the planet Jupiter.

It represents the powers of "Church and State," and symbolizes the might of civil, military, and religious codes.

It indicates to us the organizational powers of humanity.

The mystical gem of this Sign is the turquoise, a talisman of great virtue to its proper natives.

217

The fortunate day is Thursday.
Fortunate number is nine.
The fortunate color for this Sign is purple.
Best location for success is the great outdoors.

Describing those born under Sagittarius, I would say persons of this Sign are loyal, patriotic, and law abiding. Such natives are generous and free, energetic, and combative. They are hasty in temperament, ambitious of position and power, besides being charitable to the afflicted and oppressed. They possess strong conservative ideals, and their chief mental characteristics are self-control, and the ability to command others.

Sagittarians have attractive, interesting, magnetic, and dynamic personalities. They are fond of being looked up to, and they enjoy meeting a great variety of people. Under ordinary circumstances they are likable and command respect and admiration.

In character they are honest, sincere, frank, and trustworthy.

In disposition they are kind and generous to their friends, diplomatic and tactful in most matters, but have a hair-trigger temper. Although they are quick to anger, they are usually over it soon and are not likely to hold a grudge.

They are changeable, impulsive, and subject to varying moods. Their impulsiveness may either be intellectual, emotional, or both. They have considerable personal pride, but not many of this Sign are unusually egotistical. Personal pride is useful when it implies enlightened self-interest. In most matters Sagittarians display an independent nature; they usually rebel at any form of restraint.

However, they have a good sense of humor and express much joviality with sharp wit when they so desire. They have a fair degree of determination and will power, but if they are crossed they can be most obstinate and headstrong.

If you are of Sagittarius, you have good powers of observation, good perception, good reasoning ability, and show good judgment in most matters, except those which relate directly to your emotional nature. In matters pertaining to work, you show accurate judgment; yet when it comes to your own personal life, you are apt to make errors in judgment. It is advisable that you make an effort to correct this tendency.

The mental grasp of Sagittarians is very quick, and they can learn most things quite readily. Sagittarians are inclined, especially during the first half of their life, to place themselves in all sorts of conditions and circumstances where quick thinking is necessary in order to avoid unpleasant consequences.

These natives have vivid imaginations, yet are not dreamers. It is true that they have flights of fancy about love, but, in the main, Sagittarians use their imagination for practical things. That happy faculty is the progressive purpose of their imaginations. Such a faculty enables man to visualize and construct the ideas essential to progress.

Sagittarians seldom forget important details. This is because they consciously or subconsciously take an interest and pay attention to all that is going on about them. They have the ability to concentrate on either what interests them, or what they need to meditate upon. Good expressive powers make them excellent conversationalists.

Their intuition serves as a warning of impending events. It helps them to become aware of the truth in important matters and gives them an unusual insight into human motives. You of Sagittarius should study and learn more about this interesting faculty and apply it in everyday affairs.

Indications point to a good physical condition that is able to withstand much abuse; but Sagittarians have a somewhat nervous temperament, and it is essential that they take reasonably good care of their health. They require balance in their mental and physical activity; they should use judgment when eating and drinking. Health is too precious to be tampered with! This birthsign presides over the hips and thighs, and, by reaction, over the chest and lungs. It is advisable to guard against colds, as they are apt to seriously affect the respiratory system.

Indications for this birthsign show a love of sports, games, travel, motoring, the solitude of the forest, streams, mountains, and the desert. These natives have the spirit of adventure.

They enjoy social affairs, and they have a deep appreciation of art, music, and dancing. Their restless and active nature will find its expression in change; a Sagittarian will move as often as possible. Travel stimulates their minds and affords them great relaxation. Indications show that although they are highly emotional, they are capable of showing reserve. Their love nature is affectionate and passionate, but its intensity varies with the personal mood of the moment. In other words, they are ardent one moment, and indifferent the next. This may cause them to be misunderstood by their loved one. Sagittarians should learn to overcome this shortcoming and adjust their mental and emotional life so that it will not bring misunderstanding and disillusionment. If they have occasion to look back upon some of their previous disappointments in romantic matters, they will no doubt find that their own fluctuating emotions may have been the actual cause for the complicated series of events that followed. Their restless and highly-charged natures require expression. They are not sure of themselves, so they usually have more than one romantic attachment.

Nevertheless, they are of the type that finds a happier state of affairs when married than single, and are very considerate of their mates. The ideal type of mate must be intellectual, adventurous, affectionate, and have a good degree of patience and understanding. In the selection of a mate those born under this Sign must guard against emotional impulsiveness which may lead them to accept an incompatible person.

Love is the power that inspires progress and constructive living. Sagittarius is not a barren Sign, but gives promise of but few children.

Indications show that Sagittarians are not always happy and securely settled in their home lives. Their active and adventurous natures sometimes make them restless and desirous of change, and if it is at all possible, they will arrange it. Sometimes even a few days away from home will help them get over a restless period. People possessing a more fixed nature may not understand these natives.

Persons of this birthsign are industrious, studious, and progressive. They forge ahead in life, primarily due to their determination and clever intellect. The proper development of their personality will enhance the prospects of success in any business or profession they choose to follow. They require work which gives both mental and physical activity. They are the kind of individuals who are well fitted for duties which bring them into contact with the public. A great number of these natives become lawyers, teachers, doctors, and authors—both literary and journalistic. They also enter businesses, such as publishing and transportation, usually in a managerial capacity. They become mechanics, scientists, research workers, and aviators.

Many Sagittarius natives are inclined to follow more than one line of work. If prepared for a professional career they may have a hobby which proves practical and remunerative.

It is apparent from the indications that one of this temperament is so constituted that he or she could enter into partnership ventures with a good expectation of success. These natives are cooperative, efficient, and reliable. Their financial prospects in the course of life may be considered fairly good. They will succeed best when working for large corporations and industries rather than small ones. They have good earning abilities, but they are inclined to be careless spenders. They are not conservative in money matters. There are times when they impulsively buy a thing regardless of its actual worth to them.

When it comes to the planning for financial security, they should consider their spending habits. Their adventuresome natures incline them to speculate with varying degrees of success, but conservative investment usually proves more advantageous in the long run.

Indications show that you of Sagittarius will attract many

friendships. Sportsmanship and frankness and a sense of humor will go far in creating many friendships.

THE SAGITTARIUS CHILD

The Sagittarius child is likely to be rather changeable, with an inclination to become confused and uncertain. This changeability often makes them difficult to understand. They are of fiery temperament, and are very unpredictable. The molding of such a child will tax the ingenuity of the parents.

These children are born with ambition, and the formative years can be the training ground for the realization of such dreams. Their vitality is fundamentally strong and they generally enjoy good health. These children should be taught deep-breathing exercises and should be encouraged to spend as much time as possible in the wide open spaces.

The pathology of this Sign is interesting, and the parent of every Sagittarian child should bear in mind that nervous depletion can be caused by restlessness, which can result in injuries and accidents.

The children of this Sign are more subject to accidents than those of any other Sign. Indulgence of the appetite should be guarded against. Care in diet is absolutely essential.

Intellectually, Sagittarian children are ambitious, curious, and frank. Emotionally, they are daring, energetic, idealistic, impatient, and often not very domestic. They should be taught to guard against extravagance which is an adverse Sagittarian aspect.

It will be noted that they have a fondness for animals.

THE SAGITTARIUS WIFE

Here is a type of woman who takes an intelligent interest in her husband's business. She is not an intruder and has enough reserve to wait until her advice is asked for. She is not only a sympathetic listener, but a useful helpmate as well.

In the field of hobbies and sports she is a real companion. All outdoor life attracts her, and she enjoys fishing, hunting, riding, and even the competitive sports.

A man does not have to search for a companion with whom to enjoy his hobby if he is married to a Sagittarian woman. She is enthusiastic about all kinds of activity, from civic affairs and social life to sports and an occasional fling at gambling. It is easy to see that a husband would have a very full life with such a companion.

In the home, she is competent, tidy in her housekeeping, and sympathetic in the care of her children. In all of her reactions to life she is clever and well balanced—a woman to be trusted entirely, if that is possible. These wives are not, however, very tactful; they are outspoken in the extreme. Both the husband and children may expect to hear any errors frankly discussed.

Born under Sagittarius, her passions are healthy, joyous, and swift. She does not make a fetish or physical indulgence, but she is rather highly sexed and demands stimulating, adventurous excitement. Her responses are enthusiastic, and her approach to physical love is highly refined and inspiring of great efforts. She brings out the best in a man.

THE SAGITTARIUS HUSBAND

The Sagittarian husband requires a wise, tactful wife. This may be true of all husbands, but this man has much to give; and frequently his family sees the worst side of his nature rather than the best.

A Sagittarian man is not ideally fitted by the stars for domestic life. His interest in world affairs is great, and his business or profession is usually chosen from a purely monetary standpoint. He is very much of a businessman. His basic mental strength goes into his business obligations, and his personal affairs become unimportant by comparison. If his personal tastes change, he sees no reason why he must continue to express a devotion that no longer exists.

The wife of a Sagittarius must be exceedingly broad-minded and free from jealousy. She will have to be a good deal of a psychologist to hold his interest, in any case.

All Sagittarians do not stay married, but many make good husbands. They are very gifted men, with whom it is a privilege to live. It is necessary for the wife to widen her own horizons so that she may see eye to eye with him.

The passions of the Sagittarian are lusty, sportive, and adventurous. They are joyous fellows who treat love like a happy adventure. All of the emotions accompanying this birthsign are high-strung and demand satisfaction.

THE CUSPS OF SAGITTARIUS

(If your birthday is not within the cusp of your Sign, the following does not apply to you.)

If the birthday is from November 22nd through November 25th.

The native is born in Sagittarius with Scorpio tendencies. The ruling planets are Jupiter and Mars. This denotes that these people are courageous and progressive, and have unusual physical endurance. Frequently they take upon themselves too much responsibility and this tends to hold them back. They have strong inclinations which are often misunderstood, and they may be criticized because of them. They will encounter many obstacles and barriers, but they usually overcome them. They possess a good supply of reserve energy and recuperate quickly from illness. They overcome discouragement readily. They have a vivid imagination, and are painstaking in their work. While they are very sensitive, they seldom show it to others. They are not too considerate of other people's feelings, but do not intentionally offend.

If the birthday is from December 19th through December 21st.

The natives are born in Sagittarius with Capricorn tendencies; their ruling planets are Jupiter and Saturn. These Capricornian Sagittarians are very entertaining to have around as they are genial, vivacious, witty and well-informed. While they possess many talents, they are somewhat critical of the viewpoints of others and, therefore, may incur the enmity of those who disagree with them. They have a strong sense of duty and accept responsibility as a matter of course. They are dignified, honorable, and capable. They have a good imagination, and they always do their work quickly and thoroughly. They keep a promise and are quick to make decisions, and do not procrastinate. If given the opportunity to develop their inclinations along their own lines, they will succeed and prosper.

They can be depended upon to do more than their share in any collective undertaking. They have a strong, magnetic, personality which attracts many to them. They seldom violate a confidence, or interfere in matters which do not directly concern them.

THE DECANATES OF SAGITTARIUS

If the birthday is between November 22nd and November 30th.

The ruling and personal planet for this decanate is Jupiter, which influences moral and sympathetic tendencies. These natives are endowed with intellectual qualities of a high order. They have a lofty sense of justice and wisdom in all commercial and personal interests.

Because they are unusually sensitive and wise, they are attracted by tenderness, love, and trust. A truly magnanimous spirit is indicated by the double aspect of Jupiter in this Horoscope.

If the birthday is between December 1st and December 11th.

The personal planet for this decanate is Mars, the symbol of War, and the center of Divine Energy. It governs the constructive, adventurous, fearless, and aggressive tendencies, and inclines its subjects to become ambitious, forceful, and courageous. This planet endows these natives with a burning ambition to attain success in all undertakings. Men who possess marked executive ability are influenced by the planets Jupiter and Mars. This interpretation indicates great success in the business and social world.

If the birthday is between December 12th and December 21st.

The personal orb for this decanate is the Sun, known as Ruler of the Day. It is the center of the Solar System, and the giver of life and individuality. It stands for dignity, loyalty, honor, and ambition. The Sun in this aspect creates a great love for change and the desire to reform. A noble and enthusiastic nature and the ability to lead and govern others is also indicated. These natives are full of enterprise and novel ideas. The Sun governs pride and personal ambition. It confers good fortune, particularly if the native will try to overcome some of the negative tendencies of Sagittarius.

THE DEGREES OF SAGITTARIUS

November 22nd.

You possess an intuitive and prophetic nature, and are gifted with keen insight. Your constant search for knowledge will add materially to your success. You will be fortunate in a commercial or scientific career, but difficulties in romantic affairs are indicated. You also have exceptional talent for philosophy and research.

November 23rd.

You are a practical visionary and can carry your ideas to successful conclusions. You will be more successful working with others than you will be in business for yourself. You may meet with obstacles at various times, but you will eventually overcome them.

November 24th.

You are broadminded and good-natured. You are a champion of the underdog. Many persons of this degree marry a distant relative. It will be necessary to tone down a rather high-strung and erratic temperament. You may display marked artistic, musical, and psychic abilities. Success in one or more of these fields is indicated.

November 25th.

You are affectionate and demonstrative. You are very fond of your home and relatives. Success in the field of electronics is indicated. Care should be exercised when on water. Your health will need careful attention at all times. Friends may not be as reliable as they appear on the surface.

November 26th.

You possess much creative ability, artistic inspiration, and prophetic insight. You have the ability and determination to overcome all obstacles. You will not have an easy life, but you will triumph in the end. Hindrances through deception is also indicated. Deal tactfully with elders, using the utmost discretion.

November 27th.

You possess a persuasive manner and have the ability to influence others. You will be subject to varying degrees of good and bad fortune from time to time. Happiness and sorrow will curiously intertwine. Sports and travel will be your favored activities. You have a powerful sex drive.

November 28th.

You possess the ability to make friends of your opponents, due to your agreeable and harmonious nature. You are dignified and well fitted for an executive position. Although your progress may be slow, it will be sure. One aspect in this Horoscope shows that elderly relatives will contribute to your good fortune.

November 29th.

Your keen insight and great fortitude will enable you to overcome difficult business and financial obstacles. Some trouble through relatives is also shown. A strong love of pleasure and a reckless attitude must be curbed.

November 30th.

You possess a rather difficult personality. While you have good powers of concentration, you are somewhat headstrong and foolhardy in your personal activities. Many trials and tribulations are shown, but you seem to get help from some secret source. Happiness and success will largely depend upon your education and early upbringing.

December 1st.

You possess a keen ambition and good executive ability. You have great love for truth and justice. Nothing will come easy to you, but on the whole you will be fortunate and successful. This degree usually receives an inheritance at some point during life. Occasional reverses will act as a tonic to stimulate your determination.

December 2nd.

You are a profound thinker, and are aggressively assertive, generous, and good-hearted. Be on the lookout for possible errors in speculative judgment. Sudden losses through unwise investments are indicated. Care should be taken against accidents. You will lead an eventful life.

December 3rd.

You possess a sensitive and somewhat restless nature. You are frank, prudent, and dependable. Success will not be easily achieved, despite help from friends and superiors. You are endowed with tremendous energy, both mental and physical, and you will lead a full life. One aspect in this Horoscope indicates sorrow through bereavement or extreme sensitivity.

December 4th.

You will lead an active life and may experience varying degrees of success and failure due to a penchant for engaging in daring enterprises and risky ventures. This, a good-luck degree, will bring help from unexpected sources. A lucky hunch may result in considerable good fortune

December 5th.

You are sagacious, capable, efficient, and hard working. Some secret matter during your lifetime may develop into a powerful influence. Love of sensationalism may cause you to suffer depressive moods. A tendency to rebel against authority should be curbed. A successful marriage or partnership is indicated.

December 6th.

You have a well-balanced mind with an intellectual outlook upon life. Friends will play an important part in your success. One aspect in the Horoscope suggests danger of heartbreak through an unfortunate romance. Being hospitable and good-natured you must be constantly on guard against unscrupulous associates.

December 7th.

You possess an independent spirit and a great desire for freedom of action. You are able to acquire a great amount of knowledge with consummate ease. You are determined and restless and become quite despondent if required to remain in the same environment too long. One aspect in this Horoscope indicates occasional reverses due to elders and in-laws.

December 8th.

You possess a philosophical, critical, adaptable, and ingenious mind. You would make an able journalist. You are venturesome yet capable of much discretion. You are well-fitted for a life in politics. Safeguard your health by avoiding chills and colds as much as possible. This is considered a fortunate degree.

December 9th.

You possess an ingenious and approbatory nature with refined artistic tastes. Many friends among the opposite sex are indicated. Your literary and philosophical turn of mind qualifies you for a place of fame in the literary world. Both gains and losses will come through secret dealings.

December 10th.

You are aggressive, ambitious, and full of mental and physical energy. While you are normally conservative and economical, there is a tendency to make exceptions where the opposite sex is concerned. Legal troubles and excesses in diet are to be closely watched. Try to curb your extravagant and speculative urge.

December 11th.

You are exceptionally fortunate, popular, good-natured, and sincere. You have excellent foresight in business matters and will be favored by your superiors and people in high places. Do not permit success to warp your good sense of judgment, particularly where the opposite sex is concerned. Secret alliances here have a way of coming to the surface.

December 12th.

You possess many fine traits and outstanding abilities. You will be a good debater and will excel as a lawyer or politician. You must always conduct yourself so as not to arouse jealousy in others. You should also curb an erratic temperament where the opposite sex is concerned.

December 13th.

You are endowed with much strength of character and an affectionate disposition. You will experience many vicissitudes of fortune. Sudden events may completely change your life. Disappointment in love or friendships is threatened. You will have marked socialistic tendencies and are very liberal in your political outlook.

December 14th.

You possess a sympathetic disposition with a psychic temperament. You are ingenious, volatile, and versatile. You must not throw caution to the winds as there will be grave risks at some time during your life of either accident or some other misfortune. This degree warns not to take needless chances, not only when traveling, but in all financial endeavors.

December 15th.

You possess boundless vitality, are good-natured, hospitable, and reliable. You are very romantically inclined; nonetheless you have high standards of loyalty. The stage, music, literature, or art would provide a lucrative and suitable career. There may be many so-called platonic friendships among friends of the opposite sex.

December 16th.

You possess much refinement, sympathy, and goodness of heart. You are bright, gay, and full of zest for life. You have a somewhat poetic and sensuous temperament, craving physical delights. Heavy responsibility brought on by your adventurous nature may give you cause for concern. Curb your desire for constant change.

December 17th.

You possess a strong character with a great desire for fame and recognition. You will be very talented in a literary field. There are strong aspects for becoming an author, due to your keen imagination. Because you are talented you will be subject to treachery and jealousy. Close family ties are essential in order to offset disillusion caused by misplaced friendship.

December 18th.

You possess an emotional and sensitive disposition. While you are fond of home and family, much travel is indicated. You are impressionable and therefore readily imposed upon. Choose your friends and associates wisely. Do not give of yourself until you are sure of the beneficiaries' motives.

December 19th.

You will have a somewhat checkered career. Courage and faith will help offset sudden unexpected upheavals. Because you are charitable, kind, and affectionate, you are liable to imposition. You possess executive ability and some business or professional success is indicated.

December 20th.

You are good-natured and have a positive outlook upon life. Care should be taken at all times near fire, machinery, and explosives. You show great enterprise in commerce and are also well qualified for a government or political career. Guard against deception in business and love. Be circumspect when meeting or dealing with strangers.

December 21st.

You have a tendency to worry and fuss about matters over which you have no control. You possess good mental ability but will be in danger of reversals of fortune caused by emotional entanglements. Health will easily be affected through digestive weakness. Depend on your keen intuition in times of stress and strain. Do not hesitate to seek advice from true and trusted friends.

COMPATIBLE AND INCOMPATIBLE SIGNS
OF SAGITTARIUS

Sagittarius is an easygoing Sign with a friendly and attractive manner. The natives are usually fond of outdoor games and exercises, and are intense lovers of freedom. It is not a Sign which favors marriage to any great extent, for both the men and the women value their freedom highly. The Sagittarian is not orthodox or conventional enough to be concerned with what people will say if he deviates from the established custom of love, marriage, and sex.

The desire for admiration makes Sagittarians apt to carry on numerous flirtations, but, as a rule, they do not mean very much, and do not seriously interfere with married life. Natives of this Sign are usually bad liars, but good detectors, and intuitively guess the truth behind any attempt to deceive them.

As marriage partners they are kind rather than over-affectionate. They are extremely inquisitive and full of well-meaning. There is much idealism and enthusiasm in the Sign, and an eccentric mentality which sometimes leads to the choice of a marriage partner for reasons which may not prove too sound.

Perhaps the worst partner for a Sagittarian is a person of narrow and restricted views. A marriage of this sort degenerates into sarcasm, bickering, and general unhappiness, which sometimes, though by no means always, leads to separation. If Sagittarius is not too restricted, marriage is generally reasonably satisfactory, and is not characterized by extremes of any kind.

Sagittarians have a generous, extrovert nature, distinguished by their frankness and straightforwardness. Naturally these traits are immediately observable in their mode of making love, for they rarely beat about the bush and cannot be said to be bashful.

Temperamentally they are flirtatious, frank, and carefree, and make friends readily.

They have the keenest regard for personal freedom and liberty, and this is the factor which makes them loathe to compromise and let themselves be tied down.

Since wrong types do not have labels to designate them as such, perhaps it will be useful to indicate those types in which Sagittarians may best seek and avoid:

Sagittarius and Aries.

This combination should be a fairly happy one, though both the natives are of the fire Signs. Mars (Aries) and Jupiter (Sagittarius) blend very well. There will be sympathetic understanding of each other's impulsiveness, and neither will take too seriously the outside interests of the other. The Sagittarian's banner of "Liberty and the Pursuit of Happiness"—or even "the happiness of pursuit"—will be subscribed to by the Arien in most cases.

Sagittarius and Taurus.

This combination does not, as a rule, prove that love can overcome everything. Taurus loves deeply and is very selfish and possessive of the loved one. Sagittarius will refuse to be contained, and no amount of argument will change him. Taurus is too jealous, and Sagittarius too freedom loving for this combination to work out well.

Sagittarius and Gemini.

This is really a fine basic combination, since both have those qualities that do not have to blend, for they are both the same. Both love absolute freedom of limb and action; both can shrug off the inconsistency that is a common trait with them. Neither will dissolve in tears and recrimination if the other strays now and then. Truly compatible. If they battle at all it will be more for diversion than any serious difference.

Sagittarius and Cancer.

Cancer would have to go to a Temperament Tailor and be entirely made over for this combination. Though they admire everything about the Sagittarians, Cancerians will never take lightly the Sagittarian tendency to drift. Cancers "gather unto themselves" all of the body, soul, and activities of their family. This combination can mean little more than trouble. Cancer will cry, Sagittarius will flee—usually not a good combination for marriage.

Sagittarius and Leo.

These two, both fire Signs, are very compatible in most things. Both love change, excitement, and have a great zest for life. There may be occasional explosions since both are extremely domineering, but basically these two have qualities which are in sympathy. A good combination!

Sagittarius and Virgo.

With the critical and meticulous Virgo, Sagittarians are letting themselves in for a bed *not* of roses. Certainly Sagittarius admires the perfectionism of Virgo—the orderly, spic-and-span appearance, the "just-right"ness of Virgo; but these qualities may prove to be ropes of steel in marriage, for they certainly will not permit the freedom of action that Sagittarius must have. Too, Sagittarius does not take to the criticism and bickering which Virgo gives out so freely. Not a good chance to take.

Sagittarius and Libra.

The Libran sense of justice and fair play may make this combination work out—but it is going to be tough on the Librans, for they will have a hard time accepting the free and easy Sagittarian philosophy of life. Librans will get everything they're looking for—and admire—in Sagittarius, but over a long period of time the sense of justice and fair play may wear thin. Both love the same things—luxury, beauty, and social-whirling, but Libra may have a tendency to attempt the old apron-string technique on Sagittarius, which, of course, will not work. The Sagittarian hates confinement of any kind. Chances for life-long happiness are just fair here.

Sagittarius and Scorpio.

Scorpio, with the strong will to dominate, will not find Sagittarius a willing subject. The fierce Scorpio possessiveness will simply make Sagittarius look for the nearest exit, and the mutual distrust between these two will not make for sweetness and love in a marriage. They are very compatible so far as physical love goes, but there is little else that could be considered in a union here. Only a good psychologist will be able to hold this marriage together.

Sagittarius and Sagittarius.

Strangely enough, unless these two are on the same intellectual and social plane, this combination is not too promising for happiness. They will have to do everything together—or not at all. They must have the same interests in social and business matters. Both are freedom loving—but they will find that even freedom must be enjoyed TOGETHER, as neither the male or female will be willing to sit at home while the other goes out on the town. A good look before the leap is made is strongly advisable.

Sagittarius and Capricorn.

Unless Sagittarians can clip their wings a little, this combination does not get the go-ahead signal. These two are entirely different in their temperaments—one is optimistic, the other is pessimistic. Sagittarius has a devil-may-care attitude, while Capricorn has a somber and restrictive temperament. This would be a very unhappy combination for the Sagittarian, as he—or she—would have to have the type of love that "passeth all understanding" to find any joy in this combination.

Sagittarius and Aquarius.

This is generally an easy combination for success. Both temperaments have much in common. This is a purely social combination that will revel in a large group of friends and public-spirited associates. Sagittarius will readily understand the Aquarius moods and peculiarities and make the necessary allowances, as he expects and appreciates reciprocal treatment. They both love travel, change, and excitement, so this should work out well.

Sagittarius and Pisces.

Free and easygoing Sagittarius may find Pisces too heavy a load to carry. While there is much here that makes for an interesting and sincere friendship, Sagittarius may find a marriage with Pisces too confining. Love would soon be replaced by pity, and then it would be a struggle between conscience and duty. Centaur, think twice before marrying a Pisces.

SOME FAMOUS PERSONS BORN IN THE SIGN OF SAGITTARIUS

Thomas Carlyle—Author
Sir Winston Churchill—British Statesman
Noel Coward—Playwright, Actor, Director
Gen. George A. Custer—Soldier
Charles De Gaulle—French Statesman
Joe DiMaggio—Baseball Player
Walt Disney—Animated Cartoonist, Producer
Douglas Fairbanks, Jr.—Actor
Ira Gershwin—Lyricist
Mary Martin—Actress
John Milton—Poet
Robert G. Menzies—Australian Statesman
Diego Rivera—Painter
Pope John XXIII—Religious Leader
Lillian Russell—Actress
Mark Twain—Humorist

CAPRICORN

DECEMBER 22–JANUARY 19

T HIS SIGN, in its symbolical aspect, represents sin. The universal offering of a kid or young goat as an atoning sacrifice for sin is significant.

The different qualities of the sheep and the goat, from a symbolical standpoint, are used by St. John in his mystical Apocalypse.

The Redeemer of mankind, or Sun God, is always born at midnight directly when Sol enters this Sign, which is the winter solstice.

"The young child" is born in the stable and laid in the manger of the goat, in order that he may conquer the remaining signs of winter and death, and thus save mankind from destruction.

The Sign Capricorn signifies the knees of the Macrocosm and represents the first principle in the Trinity of locomotion. It represents the pliable and movable parts of the body, the joints. It is the emblem of material servitude.

Capricorn, upon the esoteric planisphere, is occupied by Naphtali, whom Jacob says, "is a hind let loose, he giveth goodly words." Here we have two distinct references; the first, to the symbol a hind, or young deer, i.e., a goat with horns (goat and

238

deer are equally significant of the earthy, mountainous nature, and are fond of high hills); the second, is the Christmas proclamation, he giveth goodly words, "Peace on earth, good will toward men."

This Sign represents regeneration, and reveals the necessity of "new dispensations."

Capricorn is the lowest emanation of the earthy Trigon, and is the constellation of the planet Saturn.

The mystical gem of this constellation is the onyx.

The fortunate day is Saturday.

The fortunate numbers are seven and three.

The fortunate color for this Sign is dark green.

Best locations for success are secluded places away from noise and excitement.

Upon the intellectual plane, Capricorn signifies external form, and those dominated by its influx are among the lowest on a scale of true spirituality. The brain of this influence is ever on the alert to seize and take advantage of circumstances. The Sign rarely denotes a purely scheming mentality, but the intellectual nature is directed to the attainment of selfish ends, and the penetrating power of the mind is great.

The natives are quick as lightning to see others' weak points, that they may work to their own advantage. They are indisposed to do any hard work unless they see some great benefit therefrom in the immediate future.

The average Capricorn personality is pleasing to meet. Capricornians present a neat and attractive appearance. They possess charming manners. They are not easily excited, and show up well in emergencies. The indications ascribed to those of this Sign are thoughtfulness, diplomacy, caution, and reserve. Their personalities become dynamic when they are able to overcome a certain timidity. Once sure of themselves, they become expressive, aggressive, and show an attractive personality. Their timidity is not due to an inferiority complex; it is the result of the serious nature of these natives. They can be trusted with responsibilities, and will carry out important missions. Ordinarily they are very sensitive. They are mild-tempered, proud, loyal, and sympathetic. When their feelings are aroused, they show a strong temper, and can become exceedingly critical. They speak their mind so fast that they are not always aware of what they are saying. Fortunately, their natural patience helps to keep them from getting temperamental too often. They may not always be right, but they have their own ideas about fair play and justice. They are more apt to get angry at little things than big things.

On the whole they have good dispositions. It is up to them to study their characteristics, and to make the necessary adjustments and improvements in themselves. All of this may not be easy at first, but they have the type of mind that will help them if they so desire. They have the ability to concentrate. Under ordinary circumstances, they possess a great degree of self-control. They must do their best to guard against reasoning only according to their personal feelings, preconceived notions, and prejudiced ideas. It is an unfortunate fact that a number of people born in this Sign fall into this habit. They have a keen perception when not influenced by their inner feelings. They have the ability to overcome their natural reserve.

Many of their impulses are merely the result of personal desires or fancies. Much unhappiness is caused by acting upon impulses without recourse to reason, analysis, and careful judgment.

They should listen to the voice of their intuition. It will enable them to have a better insight into human nature and the motives of other people. Intuition should not be confused with the apprehension and fear which these natives often feel. Intuition, like inspiration, is not based upon previous association. It will prove advantageous to learn about this interesting power and faculty. It will help them to have unusual foresight in many things.

Capricorn people have the types of minds that enable them to be efficient in ferreting out facts and knowledge in instances where others fail. They have the ability to concentrate, meditate, and work many problems to successful conclusions. Under ordinary circumstances they show reliable judgment. They should learn to do the same thing in regard to their intimate feelings.

Indications point to a fairly good physical constitution. With reasonable attention to diet, they should enjoy good health.

This Sign presides over the knees. Saturn is the ruler of the Sign, and is known to rule the bones. It is advisable to guard against broken bones. These natives are more or less susceptible to digestive and intestinal disturbances as well. They should interest themselves in some form of light exercise in order to keep their bodies in good condition. They should always do their best to avoid the common cold. If they do get a cold, they should take measures to break it up as soon as possible.

They must avoid worry and periodical moodiness. Though they are serious minded and prudent, they desire the good things of life. They enjoy pleasure and travel, as well as sports, games, and social activity. They have a fine sense of artistic appreciation.

The Capricorn-born derive a certain amount of pleasure from travel, but they are not inclined to travel extensively. They are sensitive, reserved, and somewhat timid in their amours, but they are loyal to the object of their affection. Their ideals are quite high, and this occasionally causes Capricornians secret hurt and disillusion. At times they are affectionate, but, for the most part, they appear reserved to the point of indifference. This attitude on their part is apt to lead to misunderstanding between them and their loved ones.

Since they are intellectually inclined, they tend to select their companions with an eye to purely intellectual compatibility.

The Capricorn-born possess an idealistic love nature and are inclined to be selfish as regards the object of their affection. Capricornians should curb unreasonable jealousy. They need to learn that love and life are practical matters as well as ideals, romantic dreams in a world of fantasy. There is a need for self-understanding for a Capricornian to accept the intellectual, emotional, and physical qualities of both himself and a loved one. If these above-named qualities do not blend to a reasonable degree, the union will not be harmonious.

Marriage will develop the more expressive side of the personality of these natives. They enjoy having a bright perspective on life, and marriage proves a source of inspiration for their progress.

Indications for this Sign show a great love of children, and give promise of many. These natives have a deep parental love, and may prove too indulgent in the care of children. Capricorn people also manifest this same type of love in their friendships and associations with others. Though they are patient and have considerate understanding, they should do their best to avoid becoming possessive. They have a fondness for home life, particularly if they have congenial companionship and understanding. If they live alone, home is but four walls to them. Their home life during youth was probably filled with unstable conditions. They and their parents may often have been at odds and this may have had an adverse effect on their early life. Nevertheless, they are usually devoted to their parents and family.

Capricornians should choose work that affords their minds and bodies the greatest expression. These natives possess exceptional financial and executive acumen. This shows that they can be successful in their own businesses. Capricorn nativity gives industry, conscience, and efficiency in business or profession. These natives are loyal to their employer. There are some Capricornians who become shiftless, but this is usually the result of discouragement. Once such a habit is formed, only the pressure of circumstance will change it.

They are trustworthy, and capable of doing anything easy that they set out to accomplish. They have a good degree of determination and patience, which will help them to progress.

It is true that many of this Sign do not appear to get anywhere for years, but, in time, recognition comes, and often very suddenly.

They have the type of personality that will enable them to get along fairly well in partnerships. They usually have a deep sense of appreciation and are capable of true cooperation, and they will accept their share of responsibility gracefully. The superficial Capricorns usually possess a conservative quality, which, if properly applied, will enable them to save a little money. This is truly the secret of their financial success. Money, like everything else in life, responds to the treatment given it. Many of the world's greatest fortunes have been built from small beginnings and trivial economies and the exercise of conservative principles.

Good profits will be made from investments in real estate, government bonds, and the stocks of large corporations. The Capricorn-born should endeavor to use their judgment in financial affairs and should curb their speculative impulses. Financial indications during the latter half of their life appear to be quite favorable. They will, no doubt, attract many people to them, but their actual choice of intimate friends will be limited, and those will be mainly of the social, surface type. There are times when they are socially active; at other times, they desire to be alone or with a close friend who seems to understand them. Their emotional sensitivity and intellectual moodiness are their greatest handicaps, and proceed from trivial causes.

They try to be serious thinkers, but there is no reason why they should permit this effort to preclude frivolity. This is the common error of serious-minded people who have no real understanding of life.

THE CAPRICORN CHILD

The children of Capricorn are usually bashful and timid in the presence of strangers. Among their friends, however, they have a tendency to be very bossy.

A great deal can be done by the parents in the early years of the Capricorn child to eliminate some of the adverse tendencies by training them to stop worrying over trifles and trivialities. The vitality in infancy is rather low, but once infancy is past, the persistence of this Sign makes itself felt. The principle source of danger is from falls, bruises, and sprains. Change of scenery, cheerful society, and comfortable relaxation are all excellent cures for the Capricorn child. It is important for the parents to consult a competent physician at the first sign of illness. Rheumatism, cramps, hysteria, skin disease, and broken bones are common ailments. Remember, the Capricorn child should be watched carefully in infancy as this is the most dangerous period.

Capricorn children are born leaders and organizers. They chafe under restriction and dislike taking orders from others. They are capable of attaining great heights through the ability to make the most of their opportunities. They achieve a good measure of success in occupations connected with the earth and its products—Capricorn is an earth Sign. They will do well in positions of responsibility and trust. Some of the occupations for which these children may be trained with confidence of success are: builder, farmer, miner, professor, and real estate dealer.

The characteristics of the Capricorn child tend toward conservatism. They are cautious and make good friends. Emotionally, they sometimes develop a coldness in their nature and become irritable. In this group, the head rules the heart completely, and the outside rules the inside. The disposition is usually thoughtful and dignified; they seize every opportunity to better themselves.

THE CAPRICORN WIFE

These women are usually sensitive and intuitive, but they are not at all submissive. The Capricorn woman makes an excellent hostess and housekeeper and is capable and dependable. She is also ambitious for the success of her husband and children.

Capricorn women lack that certain feminine quality that usually attracts men who are looking for the pliant and submissive type of wife. The Capricorn wife is easily misunderstood. Beneath her reserved exterior she is an admirable woman. She needs encouragement and sincere affection in order to call forth her deep sense of loyalty. Capricorn women are not swayed by their emotions. In love matters they sometimes appear to be practical, materialistic, and lacking in sentiment. The real trouble is that they have difficulty in expressing their more tender feelings. They are fond of the opposite sex and are attracted to them, but if their affections are not immediately reciprocated, they can become indifferent and resentful. They put a great deal of emphasis on worldly possessions. They love ardently, if not demonstratively, and hold a deep respect for their family.

Capricorn wives should avoid overbearance with those they love. Above all, they should not be afraid to give of themselves wholeheartedly, so that they become sparkling fountains of connubial love.

THE CAPRICORN HUSBAND

The Capricorn husband falls in readily enough with the domestic scheme but adds little to it. This type of man usually marries for selfish reasons; the basic nature of Capricorn is somewhat selfish, as Capricorn is both a superficial and connective Sign.

As husbands, these men are good providers, for they are ambitious and successful in business. They do not allow much freedom of action to their wives. Even though there is plenty of money in the home, the wife is not free to spend it. A Capricorn husband is sometimes dictatorial as well as conservative—he lays down hard and fast rules for the spending of his money. The entire household is directed by him; his wife is a lieutenant. As commanding officer, he can be exacting, obstinate, and unreasonable in his laws for family routine. These laws may be in accordance with good discipline, but they are wholly unsympathetic.

He is generally a good emotional companion for his wife, and has the ability to give a part of himself to create an atmosphere of enjoyment and add to the real pleasure of the moment. He demands that everything be given to his family, but he examines whatever he gets with caution and suspicion. He believes that some contribution from himself is always necessary to heighten his own enjoyment. His passions are strong.

Naturally the tone that this powerful birth figure casts over a personality usually is tempered by other configurations. In that case, many of the negative Capricorn qualities are tempered with softer aspects, making a most agreeable person.

THE CUSPS OF CAPRICORN

(If your birthday is not within the cusp of your Sign, the following does not apply to you.)

If the birthday is from December 22nd through December 25th.

You were born in Capricorn with Sagittarius tendencies. Your ruling planets are Saturn and Jupiter. While you are very stern in your decisions, you are of a kind and sympathetic nature. You are thorough and persistent and work hard to carry out whatever plans you make. You are destined to meet with many obstacles and hindrances. You should be strong enough to overcome them so as to use them as stepping stones to bigger and better things. The varied experiences of your past life will form a good foundation for your success. A child born at this time will be particularly susceptible to beneficial parental influences, which will make for continued success in adult life.

Pay attention to your hunches and ideas, for you are a born intuitive. You are progressive and find pleasure in self-improvement and development.

If the birthday is from January 16th through January 19th.

You are born in Capricorn with Aquarius tendencies. Your ruling planets are Saturn and Uranus. This gives you understanding of mankind and makes you clever, intuitive, patient, loving, and sympathetic. You have artistic and musical ability which should be developed. You are cultured and refined and possess judgment that may be relied upon. When you enjoy good fortune things run unusually smoothly, but during adverse periods it seems that everything under the sun has gone wrong. You are generous and considerate of others. You are a loyal friend and a delightful entertainer. While you can adapt your talents to many lines, you will be most successful in the fine arts, in humanitarian work, in dealing with the public, or in the management of a large enterprise.

THE DECANATES OF CAPRICORN

If the birthday is between December 22nd and December 31st.

You have the double aspect of Saturn in your chart. Few real friendships are shown under this aspects, but those who are privileged to make the grade will be true and lasting. Saturn is the symbol of time and is restricting in its influences. This planet is concerned chiefly with the fixity of all affairs that may be classed as concrete conditions. Its powers lie in stability, endurance, tenacity, and perseverance. Gain through thrifty methods and careful investments is indicated. You possess a firm spirit and an enduring nature.

If the birthday is between January 1st and January 10th.

Your personal planet is Venus, which makes you constant, reliable, industrious, and persevering. Venus is one of the most benevolent planets in the solar system. It indicates harmonious surroundings and favors pleasure and good cheer. It also brings out the idealistic, artistic, and musical faculties, and presides over the emotions and affections. While the planet Venus has a decided influence of her own, she is greatly affected by aspects from other planets. Since Saturn is the ruling planet of Capricorn, it will naturally act as a restraining influence on the planet Venus and cause you to withhold your true inner emotions.

If the birthday is between January 11th and January 19th.

Your personal planet is Mercury, which makes you rational and intellectual, though somewhat changeable. Your personal planet Mercury is considered a convertible planet; it is strongly affected by whatever planet it is in conjunction with. Mercury controls the brain and nerves, and makes its subjects excitable and active. This planet will play a prominent part in your life, since it controls commercial, intellectual, and family affairs. With Saturn acting as a restraining influence upon Mercury, you will tend to be practical and cautious.

THE DEGREES OF CAPRICORN

December 22nd.

You possess a resourceful, capable, and practical nature. You are commercially minded and interested in all phases of business endeavor. You are a born leader and possess the ability to command the respect of your friends and associates. Many of your difficulties can be avoided if you learn to overcome a quarrelsome and combative spirit. If you permit your negative tendencies to become habits, you may become designing in your social and business activities.

December 23rd.

You possess a profound mind alternately swayed by principle and ambition. You show a great deal of determination and ambition. You have a great deal of adaptability, and unusual aptitude at reproducing and imitating. One aspect in this Horoscope indicates a tendency to become extremely temperamental and excitable when your plans and ambitions are interfered with. As a born leader you want to have your own way in matters.

December 24th.

These Capricornians possess an ambitious and determined personality. They show a marked aptitude for dealing in financial affairs. Intense concentration of purpose will aid them materially in life, provided they can learn to overcome a tendency to display their strong likes and dislikes regardless of consequences. One aspect here indicates the possible development of an inferiority complex.

December 25th.

Those of this degree possess an adventurous spirit and a desire to travel. They are fond of social activity. They show an aptitude for organizing and controlling others. They must avoid a tendency to do too many things at one time.

December 26th.

These natives are endowed with a tactful, sympathetic, and proud nature. They show a great love for fine clothes, and have a desire to be well-dressed at all times. They attach great significance to outward appearances. One aspect in this Horoscope indicates difficulty in getting along with the immediate family because of a desire to impress outsiders.

December 27th.

A bright, cheerful, and affectionate nature is indicated for this chart. Great generosity and a desire to help others is also shown. One aspect here shows a tendency to daydream. These natives must concentrate on one task at a time, completing each before starting another. A magnetic sex appeal will bring popularity with the opposite sex.

December 28th.

Those of this birthday possess an adventurous, mystic nature, and a scientific trend of thought. A great love for travel and a fondness of the sea are also indicated. A desire to help those in less fortunate circumstances will lead this native into many strange experiences during life. Studies which can be used for the good of humanity and the alleviation of suffering may be the life ambition of this person.

December 29th.

A sensitive, highly-strung nature is indicated in this chart. These natives have a tendency to be irritable and impatient when their plans and desires are not readily fulfilled. They possess progressive minds and vivid imaginations, but may develop tendencies to procrastinate. This may be caused by a desire to avoid assuming responsibility. If this is so, they should try to buckle down more!

December 30th.

These Capricorn-born possess energetic, powerful, ambitious, and serious-minded natures. Versatile minds coupled with marked social instincts will enable them to gain success and recognition in public service. One aspect of this Horoscope indicates a tendency to be too apprehensive concerning the welfare of their loved ones and friends. Moderation of this golden virtue is advised, as it is apt to cause misunderstanding and misfortune. Much affection for the mother is indicated.

December 31st.

Those of this degree possess a progressive, determined, and generous nature. They will succeed in life through their own merits and capabilities. They are clever with details, and may find marked success in any business or profession where intelligent application of detailed knowledge is essential. They should be surrounded by love and understanding, as certain aspects in this chart indicate the possible development of a selfish and materialistic character.

January 1st.

A well-balanced mind, great determination of character, and an affectionate nature are bestowed upon the natives here. They have magnetic personalities, but, at times, may be somewhat temperamental and headstrong. They may have a delicate constitution, and should not overexercise or go to extremes in mental or physical exertion. Enlightenment will come through past experiences. They may expect many ups and downs, and are likely to suffer through deception. These natives should study the deeper side of life harder and more often.

January 2nd.

These natives possess an amiable disposition, and have the ability to learn quickly due to a perceptive mind. An artistic temperament and a lovable nature brings the desire for the better things in life. One aspect in this Horoscope indicates the desire to get by with the least possible personal effort. They must not become self-indulgent.

January 3rd.

Those of this birthday possess a highly magnetic personality. A strong, healthy body with very good recuperative powers will enable them to overcome their physical dangers. A charming, winsome disposition will bring many sincere friendships into the life. One aspect in this chart indicates disappointments due to misplaced confidence. Losses through financial schemes are shown.

January 4th.

These natives are endowed with initiative, originality, and perceptiveness. They show a tendency to be contrary in a more or less mischievous manner. Good business ability and commercial foresight will greatly aid them in the attainment of success in the business world. A kind, sympathetic nature and a desire to help humanity may bring disappointments because of unappreciative attachments. This degree is not well aspected in romantic matters.

January 5th.

An intuitive, artistic, sensitive, yet practical nature is indicated for the natives of this chart. They are also independent and have the ability to carry out their objectives in life without too much assistance from outside influences. They should never force themselves into vocations, but should permit their instinctive foresight to have full sway. By doing so, they will decide their true course in life.

January 6th.

Those of this degree possess a determined, yet flexible nature, and a methodical, prudent, but gentle disposition. Marked capability in dealing with the masses, and success through association with influential and prosperous friends are indicated. They are not receptive to training that does not concur with their sense of justice and fair play. They must learn not to rely on their snap judgment, but to wait until they have attained knowledge and practical experience.

January 7th.

These Capricornians possess a refined, artistic, and charitable nature. They are also gentle, prudent, and sensitive, but they may be lacking in confidence. A charming and affectionate disposition is indicated. They must learn to develop a greater degree of concentration in order to increase their self-confidence. While they are considerate and obedient to the wishes of their families, it would be unwise for them to bear the brunt of family responsibility, as this may eventually cause them to lead a retiring and lonely life.

January 8th.

A profound mind and a reserved nature are bestowed upon these natives. Good fortune and much natural charm will bring many lasting friendships. Effort should be made to develop consideration for the feelings of others. Tact should be exercised in speech and action. These natives show great enterprise in acquiring the good things of life, and success will be attained mostly through their own efforts. Mental and physical overexertion must be avoided, except in exercise of the love-nature.

January 9th.

The indications for those of this chart show an alert mind, remarkable intellect, and a keen sense of judgment. Much social grace and charm is evident as a result of an amiable and pleasing disposition. A fiery temper and an unyielding nature should be controlled. Great fixity of purpose and much skill in the performance of their undertakings will bring success in their endeavors. Care should be taken not to sacrifice home for social life.

January 10th.

These natives possess a bold imagination. A keen mind, ever seeking knowledge and improvement, will aid in the attainment of spontaneous success in the business world. An extravagant nature and a decided flair for fine clothes and expensive companions is shown. This should be toned down. The development of a speculative impulse must be avoided as it can cause many embarrassing situations. The sensitive nature shown here flourishes in an environment of patience, tolerance, and consideration.

January 11th.

Those of this degree possess a clever, critical mind, and a sympathetic nature. An obstinate temperament may give others some cause for concern. Keen interest in literature and art endow these people with the possibility of an intellectual personality. Their sensitive natures require an atmosphere of sympathy and fair play. They should develop the practical side of their natures in order to attain the greatest measure of success and happiness in life.

January 12th.

These Capricorn-born possess a clever, perceptive mind, which coupled with great intensity and sincerity of purpose tends to make them critical and sarcastic when their plans and ambitions are interfered with. They can avoid the overdevelopment of this aspect by realizing the consequences to such an attitude. Physical activities should be indulged in as much as possible in order to offset the possibility of overtaxing the mind by too much study. These natives must not permit themselves to become too cautious, suspicious, or cynical.

January 13th.

The indications for this chart show an imaginative, energetic, and aggressive nature. An experimental and scientific mind with a leaning toward the mystic and occult sciences is also indicated. The study of science may lead to a professional life. One aspect here shows ability to achieve fame in the humanitarian pursuits. These natives will succeed best if they choose their own vocations. They may meet with sorrow and disappointment in their domestic affairs.

January 14th.

These natives are endowed with a magnetic personality and a pleasing, affectionate disposition. They are fond of music and art and enjoy the beautiful, refined, and esthetic things in life. One aspect here indicates a tendency toward self-indulgence which should be discouraged. They must not allow themselves to be spoiled and pampered as this would only add to their difficulties. They should refuse all unnecessary indulgences and conserve their strength and resources.

January 15th.

Those born on this day possess an inspired and artistic nature. They are quick in their emotional reactions and should practice self-discipline and restraint. Their natural ability, intuition, and keen foresight suggests training for a business career where they may be assured of success. One aspect of this Horoscope indicates that they must be cautious while traveling.

January 16th.

These natives possess artistic, inspired, and intellectual minds. Unless they have the proper companions and surroundings, their sensitive psyche can easily develop an inferiority complex. Marked introspection, with an inclination to become moody and despondent at the slightest provocation, should be eliminated by pleasant, physical satisfaction. One aspect in this Horoscope indicates that a career combining both executive and artistic abilities will bring great success.

January 17th.

Those of this degree possess a determined and forceful nature. Self-discipline will be valuable in order to combat possibility of a monstrous temper. One aspect of this chart shows a level-headed, judicial, and perceptive mentality coupled with a high-strung nervous system. It is, therefore, necessary to avoid too much mental exertion as this may result in serious consequences. Because these natives are studious and ambitious, they may become moody and unruly when their progress is impeded.

January 18th.

An agreeable, thoughtful, studious, and retiring disposition is bestowed upon those of this birthday. They may display great prowess in outdoor sports and physical activities, and there are indications of possible fame in athletics. Their strong wills enable them to overcome many obstacles in life.

January 19th.

The indications for this chart show a courteous, pleasing, and sociable disposition. The magnetic personality of these natives will attract many friends. One aspect here shows a tendency to look upon the gloomy side of life. These people should train themselves to instill self-confidence, and help themselves to overcome a dark attitude. Undue excitement and too much dissension will have an adverse reaction on the nervous system.

COMPATIBLE AND INCOMPATIBLE SIGNS
OF CAPRICORN

Capricorn is not considered a very sexual Sign, but there is no doubt that it can exhibit a considerable degree of lustfulness. It is a narrow Sign, lending itself easily to excesses. Generally, personal ambition influences matrimonial affairs to a great extent, and the Capricorn native usually seeks some material advantage through marriage. At the same time, there is great sex drive, and the relations of a Capricorn native with members of the opposite sex are quite free.

The men have a strong, protective instinct, while the women, though perfectly capable of looking after themselves and their affairs, affect an appealing air to seek protection.

Capricorns are born managers and seek to manage the lives of everyone with whom they come into contact.

The women use every effort to advance the careers of their husbands and relatives, and are frequently strikingly successful in making something out of quite unpromising material. Many prominent politicians and businessmen owe their positions and successes almost entirely to their Capricorn wives.

When afflicted, Capricorn can be selfish, grasping, and miserly. At the best, it is not an affectionate Sign and makes a much more dutiful than loving partner. The rigidity of outlook and the Mosaic sense of justice (an eye for an eye, and a tooth for a tooth, and so on) makes Capricorn a vindictive Sign. Capricorn people set great store by their rights, and are usually unforgiving. An offense must be expiated by just an adequate amount of punishment.

In matrimonial life, lapses on the part of the husband or wife are rarely forgiven and never forgotten. There may be no second chance for the partner of a Capricorn native. Capricorn marriages, however, are usually lasting, perhaps because Capricorn rarely marries in haste, and is more likely to err through overcaution in choosing a partner than by careless or impulsive love affairs.

Capricornians have a certain ruthlessness about them which may, perhaps, be attributed to overambitious tendencies. They like to appear practical and business-like, and those factors combine to make them materialistic. Marriage for them may, therefore, be viewed more from the standpoint of necessity than from any romantic or sentimental reason. They can be decidedly possessive. They assume an ownership in love that resembles ownership of property.

Though they may be externally undemonstrative, they inwardly have a deep craving for love and affection. If they don't get it (which more often than not is their own fault), they feel lonely and misunderstood. Theirs is a rather complex nature where love or romance is concerned, and the situation is not made easier by their mistrustfulness. As they are realists, there is not a great deal of room for optimism in their nature. They are frequently sticklers for outward convention and appearance.

Capricorn and Aries.

The impetuous and aggressive Aries will not have the patience to fall into slow and methodical step with Capricorn. The Capricorn would not be too pleased with the Aries manner of leaping forward into whatever proposition appeals to him, for Capricorn likes to think things over. Not a good combination as the Ram

(Aries) and the Goat (Capricorn) would not make good life partners. There is a compatibility of sorts in sexual affairs, but they are not suited temperamentally or emotionally to each other.

Capricorn and Taurus.

There is a fair degree of compatibility for these two IF Taurus will give Capricorn the encouragement and flattery needed. To the warm, Venus-ruled Taurus, Capricorn may seem a little cold and aloof, but if anyone can melt the iciness of Saturn, it is Venus. With mutual understanding of the little quirks in each other's nature they could make a good "go" of a partnership.

Capricorn and Gemini.

Here we find too many opposite qualities to be overcome to regard this as a good partnership. Patience is an integral part of the Capricorn nature—it is nonexistent with Gemini. Methodical procedure is a MUST with Capricorn—Gemini would lose interest in anything that takes too long. The solidarity of Saturn would not look kindly on the changeable Gemini Mercury. If Gemini could settle into a slower gait and fall into step with Capricorn, it might work for a while. Fixity is utterly foreign to the Gemini nature, and partnership just doesn't look good for these two.

Capricorn and Cancer.

Here are two Signs that could meet on common ground since each has what the other needs. Sympathetic Cancer, with love and understanding, would be a healing balm to the somewhat cold and suspicious Capricorn. Cancer's utter absorption with home and family would also be pleasing to Capricorn. Both are fitted to plod along together until their goal is reached, for Capricorn can make Cancer's dream of security come true.

Capricorn and Leo.

These two would not see eye to eye. The outgoing Leo, with freedom of action in social activity, would keep the faucet of

Capricorn's suspicion running full blast. Leo just couldn't be long satisfied with Capricorn's plodding nature. Leo is open and carefree, and will leap first and look (maybe) later. Leo forgives and forgets, but Capricorn is slow to forgive, and never forgets. This would not be a good combination.

Capricorn and Virgo.

There are many qualities in these two Signs which would make them compatible. With Capricorn's insistence on exactitude and Virgo's demands for perfection in herself and everyone else, the two Signs should get along well. Much of Virgo's carping and criticism would be eliminated, and they could weep a duet when the world gets too tough for them. Mercury, as Virgo's ruler, is quite different as Gemini's ruler. Here he would blend well with Saturn, Capricorn's ruler. Both these Signs bestow great pride upon their natives, and Virgo and Capricorn show this in their personal appearance and in their home. This is basically a good combination.

Capricorn and Libra.

It is true that Libra can attract and intrigue Capricorn, but it is likely that Libra may become bored with the steady, non-varying Capricorn. Capricorn would have to put the damper on social activity, and it would be subject to Capricorn's dictum. Capricorn is far more liberal in sex matters before marriage than after, so Libra would have to learn to walk the tight wire of Capricorn's behavior patterns. If Libra can do this, there is a good chance for a marriage between these two.

Capricorn and Scorpio.

This does not look too rosy. Scorpio is there with a swift sting and a temper that can lash violently and effectively. Capricorn meets this with the stubbornness that is his own brand. Both are very disagreeable when frustrated. Not a good combination unless softened by other aspects.

Capricorn and Sagittarius.

Here is a study in extreme opposites. One is free, open, jolly and optimistic; the other is sober, restrictive, and suspicious. Sagittarius would go far to overcome the unpleasantness that could result from Capricorn's taciturn and cold exterior, but would probably get rather weary of agreeing, complying, and conceding all the time. Unless Sagittarius is so benumbed by love that he— or she—will give up all freedoms and stay pinned to the hearth, there is not much chance for happiness here.

Capricorn and Capricorn.

These two should have an enduring marriage, for there is much compatibility between two Capricornians. Both have the same long-range aspirations and the basic qualities to attain them. One cannot find too much fault with the other as they have much the same faults. In important things, they would both have what it takes to overcome all obstacles. Fine ingredients for a happy partnership.

Capricorn and Aquarius.

Here we have a difficult combination to analyze. The sure-footed Capricorn may not be able to keep up with the nimble water-bearer Aquarius, who aims to make the world a better place to live in. Capricorn wants all effort—and anything else Aquarius has to give—to be centered at home for their mutual good. Capricorn will not tolerate the Aquarian's interest in other people. Aquarius can't abide confinement or restriction of any kind, and may pack up and go out into the world to find bigger and better goals to conquer. A doubtful combination.

Capricorn and Pisces.

Capricorn will find a sympathetic and understanding mate in Pisces, and the steady-going temperament of Capricorn is just what Pisces needs for a sense of confidence and security. The sexual needs are compatible, and the social goals are similar.

Capricorn is more practical than Pisces, but this is one of the many things Pisces will admire. Too, Capricorn will be happy knowing that Pisces' dependence will increase each year, for Capricorn is happiest when needed.

SOME FAMOUS PERSONS BORN IN THE SIGN OF CAPRICORN

Konrad Adenauer—German Statesman

Clement Attlee—British Prime Minister

Marlene Dietrich—Actress

Benjamin Franklin—Statesman

Barry Goldwater—U.S. Senator

J. Edgar Hoover—F.B.I. Administrator

Joan of Arc—French Martyr

Danny Kaye—Comedian

Johannes Kepler—Astronomer and Astrologer

Rudyard Kipling—Author

Robert E. Lee—Confederate General

George C. Marshall—U.S. General and Statesman

Tony Martin—Actor

Ethel Merman—Actress

Gamal Abdul Nasser—U.A.R. President

Sir Isaac Newton—Physicist and Philosopher

Richard M. Nixon—U.S. Statesman

Carl Sandburg—Poet and Biographer

Albert Schweitzer—Physician and Philosopher

Maurice Utrillo—Painter

Daniel Webster—Statesman

Woodrow Wilson—U.S. President

AQUARIUS

THIS SIGN symbolizes judgment. This constellation forms the starry Urn of Minos, from which flow wrath and condemnation or blessings and rewards, according to work done in the body regardless of theological faith. The earlier baptismal urns of the primitive Christians and the elaborate stone fonts of the later churches are relics of this great astral religion.

The Sign Aquarius signifies the legs of the Grand Archetypal Man and, therefore, represents the locomotive functions of the human organism. It is the natural emblem of the movable and migratory forces of the body.

The Water-Bearer, upon the esoteric planisphere, is occupied by Reuben. "The excellency of dignity and the excellency of power," says Jacob, "unstable as water thou shalt not excel." A simple but magnificent astrological description of the Sign has, from time immemorial, been two water lines, like the ripples of running water.

The Sign not only contains the rites and mysteries of consecration, but will reveal the potency of all sacred and dedicated works.

The mystical gem is the garnet.

The fortunate day is Wednesday.

The fortunate numbers are eight and four.

The fortunate colors for this Sign are pastel shades of blue and green.

Best locations for success are around busy places and in large cities.

Aquarius is the lowest of the airy Trigon, and the constellation of Uranus.

Upon the intellectual plane, Aquarius represents the truth of material phenomena. Those dominated by its influx constitute the school of inductive philosophy—the grand basis of all science. They represent the intellectual and scientific spirit of their age and generation, and cannot advance far beyond those classes of facts which are demonstrable to the senses.

The Aquarius personality is hard to define precisely, because it is changeable. This makes a personality at one time active, expressive, interesting, and attractive, and at other times moody, indifferent, and indolent. The latter are reactions to the intense activity of an unusually serious mind.

Aquarians are remarkable people to meet. They have naturally charming manners, and though somewhat reserved or timid in some situations, they can be expressive, and create a good impression upon all they meet. Aquarians are honest and make loyal friends. Altruism is one of their chief characteristics, but this does not always mean they are absolutely right in their humanitarian views. They are self-willed and can be most obstinate and independent.

They possess a good degree of the spirit of adventure.

Emotionally, they are sensitive and easily hurt. They are apt to show a temper ranging from a simple manifestation of hurt feelings to downright anger. In the latter mood, they can speak most unpleasantly. It is fortunate that they usually get over it quickly and are not inclined to hold a grudge for long. The women of this Sign are apt to hang on to unpleasant ideas much longer than the men.

Aquarians dislike pettiness in others; they should examine

themselves and apply the same critical appraisal. They have a great deal of courage and are often daring to the point of rashness. They are ambitious, and unusually persistent in anything that interests them. They are dreamers, and have the power to make many of their dreams become realities. Few people realize it, but if others would understand and leave an Aquarian alone when he or she happens to be temperamental, they would find that such an individual will get over it quickly. If one has a tendency to argue with an Aquarian at the wrong time, that argument can continue for quite a period. There are times, however, when one cannot get an argument out of them no matter what is said. When influenced by good feelings, they are among the world's most thoughtful and gracious people.

Those who reflect the best qualities of this Sign possess an intensely active mind. They are always busy at something or other, even though it is but a daydream. Usually they show good judgment, but when they are influenced by their emotions and prejudices, their judgment is poor. They should do all within their power to avoid this form of fallacious thinking.

They have unusually keen powers of observation. They are apt to note details without apparently paying much attention. Their powers of analysis, synthesis, and classification also function rapidly. They are capable of action before many people have had an opportunity to think! This quick action is all right, except in instances where it applies to their own emotions. In such cases, they are likely to act without logical analysis. In their imagination they are free to enjoy all sorts of flights of fantasy. They are also capable of using their imaginations in practical ways when they so desire. Imagination is the only faculty that enables one to visualize the creation of new things essential to progress. In musing or daydreaming, one toys with whatever thought, idea, or fantasy is in the mind. The imagination enables these natives to review the past with clarity, and helps them construct ideas as to their future progress.

They have exceptionally good memories. The power of memory depends upon the amount of attention devoted to acquiring knowledge or information. They have the ability to learn most things easily, and they are apt to be satisfied with just being aware of what they know and letting it go at that. They may forget the name of someone to whom they were introduced, but they will remember some details of that person for many years.

These natives are inclined to classify all knowledge which comes to them from external sources. They should apply the same principle to the ideas that arise from within in order to determine their true value before acting upon these musings.

In considering inspired ideas, it must be borne in mind that such thoughts come without any apparent cause, though they may be responses to certain stimuli. An impulse, on the other hand, is a personal desire or wish, and is always connected with a recent association or activity. Aquarians should learn the art of recognizing the value of their inspired ideas, for Aquarians have remarkable intuition which gives them an unusually keen insight into the motives of others. Aquarians are individualists and no one can help them in any manner until they are willing to help themselves.

Indications for this Sign show general good health if its natives will prevent their moods from causing them to become negligent. They have good constitutions, even though they have emotion-wracked nervous systems. They must guard against carelessness in diet, and avoid excesses of any kind. They must learn what agrees with them. This Sign rules the calves and ankles, and also has much to do with the glandular and circulatory systems of the body. Persons born under it must not neglect to take exercise in order to keep their bodies in good condition. Aquarians usually possess a fondness for sports and entertainment. They find pleasure in many things that other people do not seemingly enjoy. They have an appreciation of artistic things—music and the beauties of nature. They take a keen delight in all sorts of travel, and will, no doubt, travel much in the course of their lives. Travel affords an outlet for their adventurous and enter-prising nature, and adds much to their store of knowledge.

Love plays an important part in the Aquarians' lives; their sensitivity in love and romance is proverbial. Their wooing is idealistic, devoted, considerate, and intensely affectionate. They are quite sensitive regarding the object of their affections, in fact, inclined to almost unreasonable jealousy. Fortunately, if they are among the more thoughtful Aquarians, they will get over the predisposition to jealousy in time. This attitude occurs because they are not conscious of the intensity and depth of their own emotional natures. They are apt to misinterpret their im-pulses. They are so sensitive about love that they notice the slightest inattention, even though it may be entirely inadvertent. It is their sensitivity that causes disillusionment. It is true that these natives' affections are sincere and deep, but it is also true that they react against themselves in such matters because they are oblivious to their own motives. Love proves a stimulus to them and affords a powerful source of inspiration. They have the sort of mind and personality that enables them to get along with any particular kind of person they choose. Aquarians need to take into consideration their own sensitivity, and attain a meas-ure of self-mastery. The sensitive, affectionate, and ardent nature of Aquarians requires expression—they crave love, affection, and tenderness. Try as they will to hide their feelings, desire is still there. They require devotion as well as the companionship of an active intellect that preferably has patience and understanding.

Indications for this Sign show that its natives have considerable love for children. Aquarians make devoted parents, and desire to give a child great advantages. Although these people possess an active and adventurous nature, they are fond of home life and its comforts. They enjoy having a place to which they may return from their escapades.

It is indicated that the temperament of these natives is adapted to intellectual rather than physical labor, although they are ca-pable of doing any kind of work they set out to do. They are versatile and adaptable; they often take an interest in new projects, for Aquarians enjoy the unusual. They are efficient in anything they do, and are to be found in a variety of occupations. They make good salespersons, aviators, electricians, organizers, and inventors. They are found in all sorts of uncommon pursuits such as exploring, research, and experimental work, and they usually are intensely interested in the occult. They have minds which enable them to rise and progress in life, regardless of education. This is because they are *natural* students and thinkers, and possess the courage and perseverance to succeed in anything they undertake. When it is necessary to make an actual choice of vocation, they are apt to experience difficulty in coming to a decision as to exactly what they should do. This hesitation happens because Aquarians have so many talents.

In partnerships, they can be most successful, as they have a deep sense of cooperation and are enterprising. They are more successful in partnership affairs when there is someone backing them. Though they are self-sufficient enough to be in business for themselves, they must learn to be patient with themselves and to face early discouragements. It usually takes a variety of experiences in life to make the average Aquarian see things this way, but once they do, the business usually grows and is financially successful.

According to indications, many of these natives are not as careful in their financial affairs as is prudent. They are, on occasion, too generous and are ofttimes unwise spenders. Once they are able to control this extravagance to a reasonable degree and apply a more conservative principle to their natures, they may build toward financial security. They will not have much success in speculation, and it is advisable to be extremely conservative in such ventures. Practical investments in electronics industries and aviation stocks usually prove to be advantageous. They have a liking for get-rich-quick propositions, and usually succumb to clever sales appeals.

Aquarians will attract many people, for they are loyal in their friendships and do all they can to help those whom they love. The Aquarian natives lead active and interesting social lives because they are so capable of understanding human nature. In summary, they have an extremely sensitive emotional nature. This often proves to be their only stumbling block to progress.

THE AQUARIUS CHILD

These children are of a rather shy and retiring nature. They enjoy solitude to an extreme degree, and this causes them to withdraw into themselves. They are naturally affectionate and of sweet and kind disposition. They are usually pliant to the opinion of a loved one, and will readily yield for the sake of harmony. Aquarius is an intellectual Sign, and its children usually have active minds. They are persistent and usually successful.

The principle bad habit of the Aquarian child is worry. This trait reflects on their physical well-being; it is advisable for the parents to see that they do not come into contact with inharmonious companions who might worry them.

The fundamental vitality of the Aquarian child is moderate; the pathology denotes that super-sensitivity and depressive moods may develop into an inferiority complex.

Defective circulation will contribute to illness, therefore, an orderly life is necessary. The best medicine for them is harmonious surroundings. Places outside the city on high ground would be the best location for success. Diseases peculiar to this group include anemia, blood poisoning, spastic nervous diseases, swollen ankles, and varicose veins. They are subject to psychic disturbances, and obscure diseases of a nervous origin. They should never live in an environment where they will become apprehensive, as an acute nervous condition may develop. They are naturally adapted to buying and selling, as they are born traders.

Literary ability and inventive genius are two talents which, if properly developed, can lead them to occupations connected with scientific research.

THE AQUARIAN WIFE

The Aquarian woman does not slip into matrimony with ease, although she is well-equipped in that she is capable, intellectual, discerning, adaptable, and often very talented. She has the ability to accomplish a day's work without grumbling or fatigue.

Her interests are apt to be wide, and it never occurs to her to watch her husband's actions with suspicion or to check up on how he spends his spare time. She naturally trusts him. Her own behavior is above reproach. Aquarian women are the kindest in the world, and they would rather suffer themselves than create a condition which could cause someone else grief or sorrow. Basically, however, the Aquarian woman is temperamental, and should her urge for a change of partner be sufficiently justified, she would make the change without regret. Emotionally she is responsive, but her intellect rules her, and she is most appreciated as a wife when married to a successful man whose work she can share.

THE AQUARIAN HUSBAND

The Aquarian husband is the kindest and most generous of all types. The generosity of Leo and Aries is well known, but it is nothing compared to the openhanded giving without thought of reward that is part of the character of the Aquarian husband.

Aquarian men are not ardent lovers unless some other planetary configuration stimulates this urge. They are gracious and sociable; they accept marriage as part of the domestic scheme. They are perfect gentlemen in every way, and treat their wives and family with the same consideration and courtesy that they accord to strangers.

The drawback in their marital relationship appears to be their impersonality. Women seem to prefer possessive, dominant types to the broad-minded Aquarian husband. His impersonality appears to many women as a lack of interest; as wives, they want the whole attention of their husbands.

It has been said that the Aquarian's universal interest will one day be the attitude of the entire world. Such men are happy when married to highly intellectual women whose humanitarian outlooks coincide with their own.

THE CUSPS OF AQUARIUS

(If your birthday is not within the cusp of your Sign, the following does not apply to you.)

If the birthday is from January 20th through January 23rd.

You were born in Aquarius with Capricorn tendencies. Your ruling planets are Uranus and Saturn. This denotes that you are versatile, methodical, exacting, and practical. You have a good memory and quick perception. If you develop your magnetic power, it will be possible for you to become a miracle worker. You investigate every venture and do not let criticism alter you from your course.

You are always helping someone, and are often discouraged because you are not in a position to do more. Remember, self-preservation is the first law of nature. After you have provided for your own needs, you can help others to better advantage. You like to fight your own battles and seldom bother others with your worries or problems.

If the birthday is from February 15th through February 18th.

You are an Aquarius with Pisces tendencies. Your ruling planets are Uranus and Neptune. This indicates that you are inclined to be somewhat jealous and reckless in love affairs. You can easily fit into any environment.

You are likely to be successful in any undertaking along scientific lines. Your experiences in life may make you seem petty and cynical, but in reality you will always be liberal and broad-minded. You are usually suspicious before you investigate a proposition. You have a personality that attracts many friends who respect your opinions and follow your advice. You are fond of travel and will take some long journeys. Yours will be a long, prosperous, and useful existence.

THE DECANATES OF AQUARIUS

If the birthday is between January 20th and January 31st.

The personal and ruling planet is Uranus, sometimes considered the Spiritual Awakener. It is the planet of change and energy. It may bring these natives before the public early in life and endow them with a magnetic psychic personality. The double influence of Uranus will aid them to offset some of the more negative aspects of their Sign.

If the birthday is between February 1st and February 9th.

The personal planet is Mercury. It is considered a convertible planet; it greatly affects whatever planet it is in conjunction with. Mercury controls the brain and nerves, and makes its subjects excitable and nervous.

This planet is known to be the great mental ruler. Mercury will play a prominent part in the lives of these natives, since it controls commercial and literary affairs. With Uranus and Mercury as the guiding stars, there is every indication that these natives will excel in all endeavors where concentrated intellectual application is an important factor.

If the birthday is between February 10th and February 18th.

The personal planet is Venus. Venus is one of the most benevolent planets in the solar system. This planet indicates harmonious and fortunate surroundings. It favors pleasure and cheerfulness. It also brings out the artistic, idealistic, and musical faculties. While the planet Venus has a decided influence of her own, she is greatly affected by aspects from other planets. Since Uranus is the ruler of the birth Sign, the influences of Venus will be greatly expanded by the profound mental activities which Uranus governs.

THE DEGREES OF AQUARIUS

January 20th.

You are good-natured, hospitable, and diplomatic. You have a natural affinity for the sea and could be successful in maritime affairs. Some trouble through relatives, wills, or financial documents is shown. Your somewhat sensuous and artistic nature will attract many unusual friendships throughout your life.

January 21st.

You possess a highly emotional disposition. You will gain through the experience of those who may put obstacles in your path from time to time. Although deception and troubles through friends and relatives may retard your progress, you will make some unexpected financial gains despite your difficulties.

January 22nd.

You are an idealist. Being diplomatic and versatile, you will make many important friendships throughout your life. One aspect in this Horoscope shows a tendency to fly off the handle at the least provocation. This will make you liable to accidents and sudden reverses, especially through marriage, law, and property. Since you are fond of learning, use your knowledge to overcome your inherent negative qualities.

January 23rd.

There will be many influential friendships in your life. You have an inventive turn of mind and can be successful in scientific endeavors. Some persons born in this degree will gain fame and fortune through sheer ability. You have great love of travel and will move around from one place to another.

January 24th.

You may experience much sorrow and suffer many trials and tribulations. You need a great deal of love and affection to help you fight life's battles. Your strange moods will make you somewhat eccentric and contrary in your ideas and actions. Do not try to buy your friendships but earn them through good deeds.

January 25th.

You are fond of writing, reading, change, and novelty. You can be successful through your interest in new fields of endeavor. For this reason, success may be found in some ultramodern activity. One aspect in this Horoscope indicates possible trouble with the law. Some help will come to you from an elderly relative.

January 26th.

You may earn money easily, but you will be inclined to be extravagant and squander your money on pleasure. One aspect in this Horoscope indicates the possibility of injuring your health through overwork or study. Trouble from the opposite sex may cost you a considerable sum of money. Beware of false promises and secret intrigues.

January 27th.

You are dignified, ambitious, intuitive, and generous to a fault. You seek and give much pleasure to others and may, thus, suffer imposition. Nevertheless, money should be plentiful. You are liable to suffer from inflammatory ailments from time to time. Marriage is somewhat unfavorably aspected, so look before you leap, and don't be taken in by outward appearances.

January 28th.

You have a strong character and show much talent, but you are liable to impair your health due to mental and physical over-exertion. You are clever and fond of debate and politics. You can be successful in municipal government work. Excellent judges, lawyers, and law enforcement officers are shown here.

January 29th.

You will be fortunate in most things. You are ambitious, strong-willed, argumentative, clever, and worldly-wise. You have the ability to rule and direct others. You will enjoy life in your own way. You have strong love for the home and will most surely own one during your lifetime. Honor through children and a happy married life are also indicated.

January 30th.

You are sympathetic, impulsive, yet practical and tenacious. You will have good fortune with your relatives. You will have a tendency to become brusque and irritable when your plans go astray. One aspect in the Horoscope shows the possibility of success and recognition in the artistic world.

January 31st.

You will be somewhat stubborn and abrupt at times. This attitude will cover up some of your sterling traits of character and excellent intellect, which will insure a successful career. Curb a tendency to be bold and venturesome, with a tendency toward waywardness. You will go far in the business world when you learn to control your negative emotions.

February 1st.

You are strong-willed and obstinate, courageous and venture-some, impulsive and affectionate. You are fond of music, the arts, travel, and the good things in life. Success in a maritime career or in the artistic world is shown by this degree.

February 2nd.

You possess a generous, independent, enthusiastic, and optimistic attitude. You love freedom and open-air life. Your love for the great open spaces will make for a good deal of good fellowship, and public recognition in the sporting world. You are blessed with a strong constitution and, seemingly, tireless energy.

February 3rd.

You are original and persistent and have an intellectual mind. You are fond of study and may have outstanding scientific ability. Curb a tendency to be too bold and venturesome. You are liable to suffer from overstrain and accidents. Moderation should be learned and a quick temper curbed.

February 4th.

You possess powerful emotions with the ability to sway others. You should guard against nervous tension, colds, and chills. Your health may not be too robust. Trouble through property, documents, and superiors is probable. You should be successful in the legal profession. One degree in this chart shows success in banking and insurance.

February 5th.

You possess a sensitive and responsive disposition that is highly strung and irritable at times. Unexpected changes may affect your fortunes, but secret help will be forthcoming when you least expect it. This degree shows aspirations toward travel, and success in foreign lands.

February 6th.

You possess force of character and some specialized talents. You have an ambitious disposition and are always looking for perfection. There will be a friendly relationship with relatives and a possible inheritance of a considerable amount. There is also possible success in the field of electronics and modern scientific research.

February 7th.

You possess a somewhat suspicious and distrustful nature and may be given to intrigue and eccentricities. Curb a tendency to be critical of your friends and associates. One aspect in this Horoscope shows that you are receptive to great ideas but incapable of effectively carrying them out.

February 8th.

You may have many trials to contend with in business and domestic matters. You may be changeable and vacillating, and inclined to be querulous. You are unsympathetic and not receptive to the misfortunes of others. You may lead a humdrum life, experiencing little good fortune, unless you develop the more positive side of your character.

February 9th.

You possess considerable enthusiasm and some practical ability for public work. You are the type of person who will carve out his own fortune, but is liable to sudden losses in business due to unscrupulous persons. Take care and use good judgment when signing documents. You must continually be on guard against deception both in your business and personal life.

February 10th.

You may experience many vicissitudes of fortune as you are liable to unexpected reversals through ill health, treachery, and deception in business. You are brutally frank at times, yet, by nature, you are fundamentally kind and sincere. You have what is known as a complex nature.

February 11th.

You possess a hospitable temperament with some capacity for organization. You will find great inspiration in writing. You will be liable to occasional upheavals in business. You must guard against deception, both practiced and suffered. You should continually be on the alert to successfully combat a tendency to create an argument for the sake of mental stimulation.

February 12th.

You possess broad sympathies and strong emotions. Strong love for the mother is shown by this degree. You are fond of the opposite sex and will be generally successful in both love and business. You must curb fits of depression or you will miss much of the fun in life.

February 13th.

You possess an erratic and impulsive nature. You have a vivid imagination and love novelty and change, and are easily influenced by others. However, when your temper is aroused, you can become stubborn and unforgiving. You are capable of great success in any of the intellectual vocations.

February 14th.

You are artistically, musically, and scientifically minded. You are also impulsive, quick tempered, aggressive, and high strung. You have a mystical temperament with a turn for philosophical study. You are often extravagant, but you have profound understanding and possess good business ability.

February 15th.

You must learn to not be extravagant. You are clever, but inclined to be critical of others less gifted. Ups and downs of fortune will result from your impetuous nature. Curb this tendency or ill health may retard success and happiness.

February 16th.

You possess a keen intuition and a spiritual outlook. You have a kind and generous disposition, but are liable to sudden outbursts of anger and resentment. You must overcome the habit of being too pessimistic in your point of view. You will be successful in secret matters and associations. The possibility of a wealthy marriage is indicated.

February 17th.

You will be generally successful in business and love and will gain through elderly relatives and friends, especially females. You are very witty and blessed with considerable literary ability. This degree promises much good fortune and domestic joy. You have strong socialistic tendencies and are militantly democratic.

February 18th.

You possess the power to turn adversity into triumph. You will make or break your own destiny. You will be successful in business and love despite occasional disappointments through strangers. Your intellectual faculties and abilities are outstanding and your ambitions will be realized.

THE COMPATIBLE AND INCOMPATIBLE SIGNS
OF AQUARIUS

Aquarians belong to the idealistic group of Signs and are not particularly concerned with sexual matters alone. It is a contemplative, philosophical sort of Sign, with great interest in life and humanity.

The Aquarian outlook is a friendly one, and friendship largely replaces possessive love and sexuality. In spite of a progressive outlook, Aquarius is rigid in matters of morality, and tends to have old-fashioned and Victorian ideas.

Under affliction, Aquarians can become ineffective muddlers and shiftless wastrels. On a low plane they are clumsy, blundering, and harmless. They mean well and have little backbone and less common sense. The positive Aquarian is friendly, helpful, and susceptible to praise and flattery. The idealism of the Sign, however, does not altogether favor happiness or contentment in marriage—especially in the men—and this may lead to wandering affections.

Aquarians are original in their ways, and have the pleasing habit of anticipating the likes and dislikes of those with whom they come into contact. Hence, they are invariably well liked, and for this reason can become social successes. In many ways they are eccentric. For example, they may have eccentric ideas on art in an attempt to appear original. They may become snobbish in an attempt to establish an air of social pre-eminence.

Because of this eccentricity it is often an exceptional task to please them. The exterior inevitably displays no emotion and maintains a consistently impassive front. Nevertheless, their form of temperament is very pleasing to many who admire and envy the trait.

Do not confuse "excitement" with "enthusiasm," however. Certainly Aquarians are capable of unprecedented enthusiasm. Furthermore, they do not intend to hide their light under a bushel basket if they can help it. They have special qualities, and intend to let the world know about them.

In courtship and love-making they can be quite artistic. They have the ability to turn a pretty compliment; they know how to select sentimental mementos. Those of this Sign should study well the basic qualities of those whom they select as life partners. Many heartaches and much disillusionment can be avoided by doing this.

The general comparisons are as follows:

Aquarius and Aries.

The instability of Aries and the unpredictable quality of Aquarius would be provoking to both of these persons. The whole partnership would be a gamble, and Uranus (ruling Aquarius) and Mars (ruling Aries) make a rather explosive combination. Aries is exasperated by the Aquarian's changeable qualities (Uranus is the planet of change). Aries might be somewhat chagrined at the Aquarian habit of pouring water on some of his enthusiasms. Not a good chance to take.

Aquarius and Taurus.

If these two expect sweetness and compatibility to come from this combination, they are both in for shock. The unpredictable Aquarian is too much for easygoing Taurus. The conservative Taurus habits will soon get on the high-strung nerves of dynamic Aquarius, and the battle is on. Both of these natives love ease and comfort, but there is wide divergence of views as to how to obtain them. The Taurus lover is not going to take kindly to the Aquarian's unwillingness to share secrets. Better look long and hard before taking this leap.

Aquarius and Gemini.

These two should have a satisfactory basis for compatibility. The Mercurial Gemini will love the "surprise" quality of Aquarius, and both adore change. The dual personality of Gemini can find its complement in the many faceted personality of Aquarius. Neither are overly ardent in their sexual impulses, and both are intellectual. Should a union between these two take place, Gemini must not feel shut out or offended when Aquarius wants to be alone. It is a passing mood only.

Aquarius and Cancer.

This does not look like a good chance to take. Aquarians love to keep whirling on the social scene, which will wear the quiet, home-loving Cancer to shreds. Aquarians want to share their good things with the world, while Cancer believes personal obligations should come first. Cancer is conservative in taste and Aquarius more forward looking. What with the eccentricity of Aquarius and the moods of Cancer, the odds here are too great for this combination to prove successful unless one becomes entirely subservient to the other.

Aquarius and Leo.

The Sun (Leo) and Uranus (Aquarius) make a really good combination. Leo likes surprises and Aquarius will certainly supply them. There is mutual respect for the talents of the other. Both are much interested in helping others. This combination would also be ideal for a business partnership dealing with the public. They are each aware of the other's needs in intimate matters, and this could be a happy combination for both Signs.

Aquarius and Virgo.

The Virgo nervous system is in for an increase of jittery moments with the bang, bang of the Aquarius surprises. Virgo must have a precise, well-ordered existence, while Aquarius couldn't care less for "set" systems—or order—when he doesn't want it. Aquarians will not tolerate restraint, and Virgoans seek to change things to their own way of liking by criticism. Unless these two have the same cultural background and educational level, the basic differences between them would be almost insurmountable. There may be a glimmer of hope should they be college sweethearts or if they both work in the same business—but it would be well for both to shop around a little longer before taking the leap.

Aquarius and Libra.

There can be rare perfection in this combination. Both like the same things—beauty, society, and people. Venus (Libra) and Uranus (Aquarius) will give each other all things they seek, for they are perfect affinities. One tiny shadow falls across the Libran's path. They must learn to accept Aquarius' need for solitude at times, and not question it or demand any explanation. It is a basic need of Aquarians and it soon passes—Libra must take it in stride. Otherwise, this is a wonderful combination.

Aquarius and Scorpio.

Here are two who will do much better just staying friends. Marriage would probably create a battle of nerves for both. Aquar-

ians with their flitting hither and yon would set the solid Scorpio
into a tizzy. Aquarius' reserve in love-making would not fill the
passionate demands of Scorpio. The "fixed" Scorpio could not
feel sure of his own name after a month of Aquarian unpre-
dictability. They both admire a lot about the other, but marriage
would bring out the possessiveness of Scorpio and Aquarius
would rebel. Better keep it outside the fence of marriage.

Aquarius and Sagittarius.

These two could have a pleasant life together, for there is much
in common in their basic make-up. They are both social, and go
in for large groups and public-spirited associates. They both like
the change that travel gives and they both like excitement. Sagittarius is one of the few Signs who will understand the idiosyncrasies of the Aquarian temperament and will treat them con-
siderately. He wants the same indulgence regarding his own
little quirks. Could be a happily-ever-after affair for both.

Aquarius and Capricorn.

This is an unlikely combination. These two are simply too different to resolve their divergent qualities. Aquarius' interests are
wide-spread—the home alone is not enough to keep an Aquarian
spellbound. Capricorn expects home interests to come first.
Aquarius is likely to make up new definitions for boredom after
a steady diet of the slow, plodding Capricorn, and is likely to
flee to the big wide world to conquer.

Aquarius and Aquarius.

At last we have just the right mate for an Aquarian—another
Aquarian! No one on earth could be so in harmony with either
of these as they are with each other. They can well understand
the qualities which baffle, bewilder, and madden others. This is
the type of couple one meets in the out-of-the-way places of the
world doing research together. Many of the early missionaries
were Aquarian couples or those who had strong Aquarius aspects

in their Horoscopes. Yes, here is the perfect combination of the Aquarian age, the torchbearers of human dignity.

Aquarius and Pisces.

This may not be a bad combination if Pisces will study the Aquarian Horoscope. Here are tolerance and human sympathy coupled with the need for human understanding by the Piscean partner, who is willing to go all out to find that elusive cup of human tolerance and dignity. He will surely find it in his Aquarian mate. All Pisces has to do to make the marriage a happy and lasting one is to give Aquarius the benefit of the doubt.

SOME FAMOUS PERSONS BORN IN THE SIGN
OF AQUARIUS

Marian Anderson—Singer
John Barrymore—Actor
Jack Benny—Comedian
Omar N. Bradley—U.S. General
George Burns—Comedian
Charles Darwin—Naturalist
Charles Dickens—Author
Jimmy Durante—Comedian
Thomas A. Edison—Inventor
William Randolph Hearst—
  Publisher
Jascha Heifetz—Violinist
Fritz Kreisler—Composer and
  Violinist
Charles Lindbergh—Aviator

Abraham Lincoln—U.S.
  President
Douglas MacArthur—U.S.
  General
Harold Macmillan—British
  Prime Minister
W. Somerset Maugham—
  Novelist
James A. Michener—Novelist
Franklin D. Roosevelt—U.S.
  President
Ann Sothern—Actress
Adlai Stevenson—U.S.
  Statesman

PISCES

THIS SIGN symbolizes the flood because when the Sun passes through this Sign the rainy season commences, and the snows of winter melt, flooding the valley below. This Sign is also the terminus of Apollo's journey through the twelve Signs.

The Sign Pisces signifies the feet of the Grand Cosmic Man, and, therefore, represents the basis or foundation of all external things, as well as the mechanical forces of humanity. It is the natural emblem of patient servitude and obedience. It signifies confirmation, also baptism by water. It indicates to us the divine purpose of the great cycle. This cycle commences with the disruptive, flashing, dominating fire of Aries and terminates with its polar opposite, water—the symbol of universal equilibrium.

Pisces is the last emanation of the watery Trigon, and is the constellation of Neptune. Upon the intellectual plane, Pisces represents mental indifference. It is the polar opposite of the head. Those dominated by its influx express a peculiar indifference to those things which generally interest others. They take all things as they come and pay no serious attention to any.

The mystical gem of Pisces is the bloodstone.

The fortunate day is Friday.

The fortunate numbers are five and eight.

The fortunate colors for this Sign are all shades of lavender. Best locations for success are the seashore and cities near water.

There are two distinct types of Pisces personalities. One is very charming, magnetic, attractive, and pleasant to meet. The other has all of these qualities, but possesses a great degree of reserve that borders on bashfulness, and does not give any positive expression to the personality. This reserve often causes misunderstanding. If you have the latter type of personality it is up to you to make the necessary corrections and endeavor to become more expressive and self-confident.

You must bear in mind that some very great people have been born in your Sign and that they, too, had to overcome sensitivity and timidity and instill within themselves self-confidence, determination, and courage. *Study yourself, know yourself, and then set out to bring out your personality to the best of your ability; and you will be happy.*

You have a naturally kind, generous, sympathetic, patient, and reserved disposition. From an intellectual and emotional point of view, you are quite sensitive in your reaction to the spoken word and the general attitude of people around you. By nature you are peaceful. You have an extremely sensitive, yet not necessarily quick, temper. Anger and peevishness have a tendency to upset your nervous system.

It is well within your power to overcome any timidity or unbecoming reserve. By making an effort to cultivate the positive and expressive qualities of your personality, you will make yourself attractive and interesting and greatly enhance your prospects of success in life. You are faithful to any trust or commission. You have a fine and deep sense of appreciation for any kindness shown you, whether it be in thought or action. Take stock of yourself and do all within your power to build up your self-confidence, natural courage, and power of self-expression. Master your timidity and extreme sensitivity and you will do much toward making yourself happier and more successful. It is true that your mind is the power behind your personality and its expression.

You have good powers of observation, perception, and judgment. However, it would be wise to take stock of yourself and see how great a part your emotions play in the process of reasoning along certain lines, particularly in relation to matters which affect your prejudices and pet notions. When you reason according to these, your judgment is apt to be erroneous.

It is true that each and every one of us has a mind of our own and that we have the right to use it as we desire. But personal prejudice often precludes the possibility of one arriving at an intelligent understanding of a subject. In any discussion, when all facts are considered only one side can be right. With some Pisces, however, both sides can be wrong, because of their preconceived notions. Do your best to avoid this type of reasoning and you will attain true knowledge and understanding in the course of your life.

You have a keen perception and are able to grasp many details of a proposition that some others are apt to miss. You have the ability to learn things quite easily. In most instances you retain what you learn.

You have a vivid imagination and may be fond of romantic daydreaming. You enjoy the realm of fantasy to such an extent that you may experience disillusion in some of your personal affairs and romantic ventures. This is due to the fact that through your imagination you have developed a romantic ideal which is beyond the realm of possibility. It is only natural that disillusion follows. Your imagination is given to you for practical purposes. Some of the world's memory wizards belong to this Sign. They are able to recall facts with a great degree of accuracy. The original impression on the memory depends upon interest and attention. The people of your Sign, however, are highly impressionable and apt to retain this first impression.

You have the ability to learn anything that you set out to learn. Your memory enables you to retain and recall knowledge to consciousness without difficulty. You have good reasoning power. You are inclined to consider ideas until you are sure of them.

Travel affords you much pleasure and relaxation from the routine monotony of everyday life. Many minor travels, and several rather extensive journeys, usually come into the lives of the average Pisces.

Your feelings are deep and intense. Once you have overcome your reserve, you can be very demonstrative in your affection. You are devoted to and considerate of the object of your affection. You must, however, guard against unreasonable jealousy. One of your nature desires much attention and affection, and if this is not forthcoming you are apt to be deeply hurt, and you usually show it. You are extremely sensitive in love and often try to disguise your feelings. Your romantic fantasy may often lead you to lofty, but impractical, ideals; it is likely that reality will bring you back to earth with a thud. To one of your nature, love and companionship are essential to true happiness. Love inspires you and brings you renewed courage and self-confidence. You can get along with anyone that you love.

In selecting a mate, you should guard against emotional impulsiveness. If there is not a reasonable blend between your intellectual, emotional, and physical qualities and those of your mate, the marriage will prove to be discordant. Do your best to overcome unwise emotional sensitivity and you will do much to enhance your prospects of happiness.

Your birthsign shows a great love for children. Your Sign is known as a fruitful Sign. You are a fond and somewhat indulgent parent. You possess a great love of home life. A harmonious home life is most essential to your welfare and happiness. Ordinarily, you take good care of your home and show taste in its furnishings and arrangement.

Pisces are well suited for positions in the healing arts. They also make good instructors, mechanics, designers, florists, pattern makers, machinists, naturalists, religious workers, authors, actors and actresses, agriculturists, and ranchers. The average Pisces is industrious, conscientious, and faithful to his vocation. He is attentive to details, and capable of performing exacting work, such as pattern making and designing scientific instruments. Pisces may be trusted with important commissions and responsibilities.

Those born under Pisces are capable of originality in their work, and often develop new ways of doing things more efficiently and at less cost. Pisces people are inclined to be apprehensive when in business for themselves. They create their own obstacles to economic progress. They represent the type of personality that can make a success of partnership ventures. They are naturally cooperative and the right type of associate will bring out their natural ability.

In financial matters you are occasionally conservative and occasionally an impulsive spender. You have natural conservative principles but you react against them. The true secret of financial success and security lies in your making money work for you. This can only be accomplished by saving and investing wisely. Some Pisces are inclined to delve into speculative ventures with a fair degree of success.

Your generous and sympathetic nature will bring you many friends and acquaintances. Your choice of friends will be the intellectual and spiritual types. Sometimes you are apt to be slightly jealous in matters pertaining to friendship, but you have the ability to hide this feeling from others. You are loyal to your friends and often willing to make sacrifices in order to help them. By bringing out the positive and attractive qualities of your personality you can lead an active and interesting social life.

THE PISCES CHILD

The children of Pisces are of a pronounced negative disposition and subject to varying moods. They are sensitive to their environments, and for this reason it is of the greatest importance that the parents of these children guard against the influence of evil companions. The old saying about bad company corrupting good morals applies to these children, since they absorb good or evil with equal facility. Until they have learned to choose the right path for themselves, it is important that the parents guide them. They also have a strong tendency toward hero worship and there is great danger that they may become obsessed with some undesirable ideal. It will be difficult to free them from such an influence. The children of Pisces are kind and sympathetic. They are fond of rich foods, thus great care in diet is essential.

The fundamental vitality of the Pisces child is weak. Neglect may cause throat or lung disorders, while digestive disturbances result from apprehension and restlessness. It is good medicine for the Pisces child to spend as much time as possible near water. Pisces children are liable to diseases involving mucous discharge and secretion. They are also subject to somnambulism and hypochondria.

Pisces children usually learn quickly and have the ability to specialize in almost anything they choose. Though they are capable, they sometimes lack confidence in themselves and ofttimes miss opportunities. They can be successful in any line of work connected with the sea or its products. These children have a mental capacity beyond that of the average. Emotionally, they respond to their environment, as they are so compassionate.

THE PISCES WIFE

The Pisces woman is ideally adapted for domestic life. She is not as active as many of the other types, but her spiritual qualities and emotional responses are excellent. For this reason, many men are willing to sacrifice personal advantage for the spiritual and emotional companionship provided by the Pisces woman.

This woman is competent and thoughtful of others. Her home is a restful and luxurious place of refuge. The negative Pisces woman may be self-indulgent and tend to idle away the days by seeking entertainment and personal pleasure among the so-called artistic and literary set. While a reasonable amount of socializing is good, an excess becomes a major cause of family dissension. When the health of the Pisces wife is on the wane, encouragement and considerate attention on the part of the husband and her family is essential to her recovery. The negative side of the Pisces feminine nature is not inviting, but when the Sign has favorable planetary support, these women make devoted and sympathetic wives and mothers. They are extremely responsive and very good mates in the physical sense. They are adaptable and lovable, and their concept of sex is high and beautiful. Because of her supersensitive nature, the native of this Sign should take care when choosing a mate.

THE PISCES HUSBAND

The Pisces husband brings many benefits to the home. He is loving and attentive, considerate and thoughtful. He has a strong sense of dignity with a charitable and benevolent disposition. The negative Pisces type is not always a good provider. He gives his family all that he has, but because of his uncertain and diffident nature, he is not always able to obtain much in a material way. He also has a tendency to put off until tomorrow things he should do today. He dislikes facing the hard, cold facts of life. The positive Pisces husband has more than sufficient direction to guide him to success in any undertaking he chooses. He appreciates the finer things in life and does everything to attain them. His eyes are one of his outstanding features and they have the power to instill confidence and trust. In personal appearance he is fastidiousness, refined, and magnetic. He is sensual and seeks a sympathetic response to his love-making; he is the type of man to whom sexual satisfaction is important. His greatest weakness lies in his tendency to be careless of personal welfare due to a desire to please and help others, even at a self-sacrifice.

THE CUSPS OF PISCES

(If your birthday is not within the cusp of your Sign, the following does not apply to you.)

You were born in Pisces with Aquarius tendencies. Your ruling planets are Neptune and Uranus. This indicates that you are a person of high principle. You have executive ability and capacity for accumulating money. Your experiences are different from those of the average. You are quiet, refined, and a good conversationalist. While you are not careless, you are inclined to be hasty. You have odd tastes and strong likes and dislikes. You are neat in appearance and dislike untidiness in others. Your fondness for travel will bring you many advantages and some unusual opportunities. Unless you are careful, you will contract an unhappy marriage. You have an ideal character but become bored and restless easily as the commonplace things of life do not appeal to you. Among your interests are science, philosophy, religion, and invention. You are promised a long and eventful life.

If the birthday is from March 17th through March 20th.

You were born in Pisces with Aries tendencies. Your ruling planets are Neptune and Mars; this shows that you are intelligent and enterprising. You can execute important commissions with ease and accuracy. You are a keen observer and often benefit from mistakes of others. You frequently devise ways and means to accomplish things that others have given up as impossible. In your method of work you are original, and refuse to follow the lines of least resistance or to cling to an obsolete system. You like to keep your affairs to yourself and to be secretive about your plans until you are ready to execute them. A secret is perfectly safe with you, as you regard the confidence of others as something to be respected. You will travel extensively and can achieve a prominent place in life.

THE DECANATES OF PISCES

If the birthday is between February 19th and February 29th.

The ruling and personal planets for this decanate are Neptune and Jupiter. Jupiter is known as the harmonious planet of good fortune, while chaotic Neptune, the spiritual awakener, governs the scientific, inventive, and artistic faculties. This would indicate that the native possesses dualistic tendencies and a very changeable and unpredictable nature. Negative and positive tendencies will be definitely marked. This should give those of this decanate an opportunity to overcome and eliminate their adverse qualities, and to constructively develop the more positive ones.

If the birthday is between March 1st and March 10th.

The personal orb for those of this decanate is the Moon—Ruler of Night and a symbol of life's forces. It is the natural reflector of the Sun and governs the domestic, idealistic, and home-loving tendencies. The natives of this decanate may be changeable and temperamental. They are, also, democratic and imaginative and have pronounced domestic tendencies. There are indications of a dislike for dissension and combative activities as well. These natives will be apprehensive and occult. In its aspect with the planet Neptune, the Moon will cause them to be secretive in many of their thoughts and activities.

If the birthday is between March 11th and March 20th.

The personal planet for this decanate is Mars, which is the symbol of war and the center of divine energy. It influences the energetic, active, and constructive tendencies. Mars will materially aid these natives to overcome some of the weaker and more negative aspects of the spiritual planet Neptune. It will give them the necessary impetus to bring about the successful conclusion to most of their endeavors. Without this force, it would be difficult for them to realize many of their cherished ambitions.

The combination of Neptune and Mars is indeed a fortunate one; the aggressive and powerful Mars strives to force its natives to attain their objectives.

THE DEGREES OF PISCES

February 19th.

You possess a retiring, studious, and chaste nature. An envy streak, which may become apparent from time to time, should be curbed. You are fond of literature, music, and art. Make maximum use of your intellectual and commercial training. Learn self-confidence and cultivate the ability to see the viewpoints of others. Due to a lack of emotional stability you may be hard to understand at times.

February 20th.

Great ambition and a perceptive mind is indicated here. A highly magnetic personality and an enterprising, forceful disposition will bring many respected and beneficial friendships in life. You must try to overcome an exaggerated sense of self-importance. A wayward spirit and a desire to make changes frequently indicates travel in many lands. This aspect should be moderated to attain a more modest and stable point of view.

February 21st.

You possess strong will power and a commanding, energetic personality. Initiative and good business acumen will enable you to progress rapidly in the commercial world. There is a tendency toward extravagance which should be curbed. Learn to appreciate the value of personal possessions, and to cherish them. An emotional nature full of adventure and wild dreams should be moderated. You must learn that life's greatest rewards come from well-directed personal efforts.

February 22nd.

You possess an original, daring, and masterful nature. A strong will power coupled with a desire to have your own way should be curbed. A diversified education along commercial lines will be of great advantage. Much success is indicated in the business world. By exercising tolerance and patience, you can temper an overly energetic disposition. Money troubles are likely because of a good naturedness, and unwise investments.

February 23rd.

You are endowed with a bright, cheerful disposition. Material success is indicated through the ability to make and hold influential and beneficial friendships. Marked originality and a good sense of humor will make for a position of prestige in the social world. A vivid imagination coupled with excess energy may cause you to be impatient, restless, and fretful at times.

February 24th.

You of this birthday possess a resourceful mind and natural executive ability. Marked determination to succeed in all undertakings may cause you to work alike for good or bad. Discrimination between right and wrong should be carefully exercised. A liberal education will be an important factor in overcoming many of the negative qualities of your nature. Moderation should be the keynote throughout life.

February 25th.

An impulsive and somewhat radical disposition, a brilliant mind, and excellent intuitive powers are indicated for you. This combination of mental qualities is usually found in persons who attain outstanding success and recognition in public service. Effort should be made to curb a tendency to be too impulsive and erratic. Such characteristics, if permitted to develop, can prove most detrimental.

February 26th.

You possess a keen, shrewd, and alert mind. You will be deeply moved by your sympathies and will become a champion of human rights. There may be a tendency to meddle in the affairs of other people. While the intentions are most charitable, many misunderstandings and disappointments are indicated, unless you learn to mind your own business first. Success is intimated in the fields of arts, letters, and sciences.

February 27th.

An adaptable, versatile, and intuitive mind is implied in this chart. The value of concentration should not be underestimated. One aspect of this Horoscope indicates a tendency to tire easily and drift rather aimlessly from one thing to another. A charming personality coupled with a good sense of humor will attract many friendships. Diligent application of the many fine capabilities shown here will aid you to attain success and happiness.

February 28th.

You possess a sympathetic nature and a pleasant disposition, and should develop a sense of independence and diplomacy to curb an adventurous spirit. As a result of an inquisitive, aspiring, and perceptive mind, success is apparent in the professional world. You may be attracted to the study of medicine. An ability to get along with all types of people will aid materially in attaining success.

February 29th.

Those of this degree possess a pleasing and courteous disposition, and an alert and intuitive mind. A tendency to dominate others and assume leadership regardless of consequence should be carefully checked. You are industrious and self-reliant, and possess a highly ambitious and determined nature.

March 1st.

Wholesome charm and great magnetism are bestowed upon those of this chart. You have an inventive mind, and show originality in your ideas and undertakings. Beware of colds; and it is necessary that all precautions be taken to avoid drafts and sudden changes in temperatures. A desire to speculate should be curbed, as many disappointments are shown if this characteristic is permitted to develop. This birthday does not indicate an easy passage through life.

March 2nd.

Those of this birthday possess a gentle and sympathetic disposition, and a good mind coupled with a charitable nature. Your magnetic personality and ability to attract staunch and loyal friendships may result in a dependent attitude. Excess attention on the part of the parents and relatives may develop a clinging-vine disposition.

March 3rd.

A flexible, happy nature, and a clever, imaginative mind are the indications for you. You may become too generous and agreeable for your own good, and should learn that caution is the better part of valor. You are fond of mimicry, and possess a great fondness for the stage and theater. One aspect in this Horoscope shows a tendency to take good fortune too lightly. This may result in taking things for granted.

March 4th.

You possess a calm and peaceful attitude toward life. An open-minded manner coupled with humanitarian principles will endear you to your friends and associates. Gains are indicated through influential associations. One aspect in this Horoscope shows a tendency to take good fortune as a matter of course. This attitude should be corrected.

March 5th.

You possess a benevolent, charitable, and sympathetic nature. A desire to help all those who ask assistance may result in expenditure beyond your means and cause financial embarrassment. You are subject to flattery and can easily become prey of designing friends and associates. One aspect of this Horoscope shows a tendency to become conceited.

March 6th.

This chart shows an energetic nature and great skill in the execution of duties. Persistence and determination, even in the face of difficulties, can bring you success and financial independence during the middle years of life. Tolerance and consideration for the feelings of others must be learned. One aspect in this chart indicates a tendency to be somewhat impulsive.

March 7th.

A sensitive and idealistic nature and a friendly and kindhearted disposition is your good fortune. Certain planetary aspects indicate a tendency to be too generous. Learn to recognize the true from the false; remember that charity should begin at home. Fondness of travel by water and signs of a long sea voyage that may result in a profitable business connection are evident.

March 8th.

You possess an intelligent, scientific, and experimental mind. Excellent conversationalists are found in this degree; you should enjoy great popularity. An independent, orderly spirit coupled with a magnetic personality is shown. The fine qualities that come with this birthday will make it rather easy for you to get what you want from parents, friends, and associates.

March 9th.

You are endowed with a pleasing personality and splendid intuitive powers. A highly emotional nature may develop into an uncontrollable temper unless effort is put forth to overcome this negative aspect. You have an imaginative mind, and there is a tendency to brood and daydream too much if left alone for any great length of time. Associate with persons of your own age. Above all you must resist becoming the victim of a parent fixation.

March 10th.

Those of you born on this day possess a serious and aspiring nature coupled with strong mental capabilities. You are profound and practical. A strong sense of independence and a desire to help others in less fortunate circumstances is also indicated. At times you may become too magnanimous for your own good. You show a marked respect for your elders. You will create your own destiny. Success in life is intimated through dealing with new enterprises and large institutions catering to the public welfare.

March 11th.

An original and enterprising mind, and a harmonious disposition are indicated for you. One aspect in this Horoscope foretells that you are easily satisfied and may lack the incentive to overcome obstacles. Learn self-confidence and the practical methods of achieving success. Cheerful companions of your own age rather than older persons are essential. You must learn to temper your high hopes and ambitions, and remember realities.

March 12th.

Your splendid character and sympathetic nature are coupled with deep emotions. Instinctively intellectual, you will mature early, but show a tendency to become overly reserved and studious. It is essential that you have a happy environment. Pursuit of outdoor activity and athletics is strongly advised. Your emotional temperament needs patient and understanding treatment.

March 13th.

You are endowed with an expansive and genial personality. You can attain much popularity in your social life through charming manners and interesting conversation. Love of travel is indicated. Your emotional nature is stable. An artistic temperament coupled with a magnetic personality will make for success in a professional rather than a business career. Public recognition through literary ability can be assured by proper education.

March 14th.

This chart indicates an astute, practical, and intuitive mind. An artistic temperament with marked humanitarian principles will bring many lasting and influential friendships into your life. You are generous, of good appearance, kind-mannered, and athletically inclined. One aspect in this Horoscope indicates a tendency to shirk responsibility and a desire to get by with little personal effort. The diligent application of your many natural talents is for success.

March 15th.

A keen intellectual mind is in you coupled with excellent powers of concentration. Avoid a tendency to assume a too-serious outlook upon life. A bright, cheerful atmosphere and the company of congenial friends will greatly aid in eliminating this aspect. A highly magnetic personality and an independent nature can make for great success in the business world, especially if you exert effort to overcome some of the more negative tendencies shown in this Horoscope. You are fond of music and travel.

March 16th.

You of this degree possess unusual intellectual qualities and the ability to develop your mind along scientific lines. There is an indication that you can develop a steady and forceful disposition. One aspect in this Horoscope indicates a desire to defy convention and become a bold innovator. Refrain from making radical changes in love and business; you are liable to suffer through fraud and unwise speculation.

March 17th.

A sensitive, impressionable, and inquisitive nature is indicated for you. Love of travel to distant lands is shown. At times you may become difficult because of a cross temper. One aspect in this chart shows a rather extravagant nature, which should be curbed in order to prevent serious financial embarrassment in later years. A marked interest in humanitarian activity should be encouraged by proper educational training.

March 18th.

You possess a romantic nature. A rather "hard to please" complex is due to a self-centered viewpoint. You show a decided tendency to associate with persons older than yourself; try to make friends of your own age. Tolerance and understanding should be practiced. Fondness for the good things of life, which results in depletion of health and finances, should be curbed.

March 19th.

If you were born on this date, you possess a bright and cheerful disposition, and a generous nature. You will be righteous in both personal and social matters. Pursue a career where your mental faculties will be demonstrated to the best advantage. A strong attachment for the home and parents is also indicated. One aspect in this Horoscope shows a desire to be well-dressed and in the height of fashion at all times.

March 20th.

An unselfish and charitable disposition is the endowment of this birthday. You must learn the value of concentration, to overcome a tendency to do too many things at one time. You can be a fluent conversationalist and prolific writer. Train yourself towards some definite goal or profession where your many natural talents will be an asset. Once you learn to control your emotional nature, success and public recognition will be assured. You should experience more than average good fortune.

COMPATIBLE AND INCOMPATIBLE SIGNS OF PISCES

At its best, Pisces is a well of sympathy, charity, benevolence, and hospitality. As a rule the natives of Pisces are kind, sympathetic, imaginative, and highly emotional. They are intuitive, receptive, and mediumistic, but are not generally very practical. The Sign is a sentimental one that tends to be swayed by every emotion, and puts up little resistance to temptation.

Petulant irritability, incessant chatter, and the habit of "dissolving into tears" at the slightest provocation are some of the feminine weaknesses of Pisces.

The vices of the Sign, however, are based upon weakness rather than any depravity, and much will depend upon upbringing, and choice of associates.

While the negative side of Pisces is not inviting, the more robust and positive type make the kindest, most loving, devoted, and sympathetic mates. They are extremely responsive, and this tends to make them good partners in the physical sense of the word.

They are adaptable and experimental, and their concept of sex is on a high plane.

Yes, Pisceans are sentimental souls, easy to get along with as a rule, though they are subject to moody periods during which they are difficult to understand.

They have an apparently inexhaustible fund of sympathy and good fellowship, but their variety of moods may make contentment in marriage hard for them. They are somewhat unsure as lovers, for they seem to have a need for "atmosphere" in the emotional field, even though they are inwardly full of affection. The trouble seems to be the dual nature which produces a series of psychological contradictions. Thus, while they experience a strong desire for romance, a force within seems to form a brake on their emotions. They want to say the nicest things—instead they may say just the opposite.

Pisceans, more than any other Zodiacal types, need to be careful in the selection of a matrimonial partner. They are so easily persuaded that they may find themselves married to the very partner they should be at pains to avoid!

Pisces and Aries.

Aries may prove too fiery and too aggressive for the sentimental and gentle Pisces. Though Pisces is quite romantic, he desires a more delicate and refined approach to love-making than the impatient Aries cares to take time for. Neptune, the planet of the higher mind, gives Pisces an ethereal quality. Unless Aries is willing to take a trip to the clouds now and then, he'll probably have to change his mind.

Pisces and Taurus.

This is usually a happy-ever-after combination. Both natives will find just what they are looking for in each other, and their compatibility is strengthened by the fact that Neptune, ruler of Pisces, is the higher octave of Venus, ruler of Taurus. Pisces is romantic and imaginative; Taurus will like that. Taurus is steady, strong, and loving; Pisces will adore that. Both are home-loving. This combination would be a good one, indeed.

Pisces and Gemini.

This does not look good. Gemini loves to flit in the pursuit of happiness, or in the happiness of pursuit. Pisces will not like that and will probably seek retreat in a cloud of gloom. Few people can change their basic make-up and adopt an entirely new character, but that is what Gemini will have to do if he marries a Piscean. Not good at all!

Pisces and Cancer.

These are real affinities. Both like home, possessions, and friends. Both will pull together for their mutual interests. Both are sentimental and loving, and each likes to possess and hang on to what he cherishes. Certainly there will be moments of gloom and doom when both of them will feel hurt at the same time. They may wrangle all over the house, but even with these little momentary "storms," they will have happiness together.

Pisces and Leo.

Leo likes to have someone dependent on him, but he won't like the possessiveness of Pisces, or the tears; neither will Pisces' pouting appeal. This does not look like a good match. Leo's bold and vigorous temperament may be a little too much for sensitive Pisces. Better not chance it.

Pisces and Virgo.

There is a marked contrast between these two—and while "opposites" are supposed to attract, if there is too much opposition or contrast, it may not be a combination. Virgo's criticism and bossiness may break down the sensitive spirit of Pisces. Pisces' sentimental tearfulness might be just too much for Virgo to take for any length of time. There would be too much "alteration" to make on this outfit.

Pisces and Libra.

These two can like each other very much, but marriage would prove an acid test to any affection they felt. Libra is very social and Pisces is a "togetherness" person. Libra could not tolerate jealousy and suspicion; Pisces would want Libra to be exclusively his or her own at all times. Not a good bet.

Pisces and Scorpio.

This is a "love-at-first-sight" affair; but it is not likely to stand up for any length of time. Scorpio will always have an ear and perhaps will want to rove when compliments are proffered. Pisces wants exclusive ownership. Scorpio, too, is possessive, but will not tolerate that characteristic in another for long. Pisces will pout and scold while Scorpio shouts, and another marriage becomes a has-been.

Pisces and Sagittarius.

These two can enjoy a beautiful friendship so long as Pisces doesn't presume on the other's boundaries, but it would not prove to be a good combination for marriage. Sagittarius, free and easygoing, couldn't stop to lug the clinging, possessive Pisces along the road of life. Nor could he stand the abused attitude of Pisces. No matter how much Sagittarius loved Pisces, pity would soon supplant love, and it would be duty and conscience battling within. He couldn't stand the confinement of being married to a Piscean, and Pisces couldn't take the varied interests of Sagittarius.

Pisces and Capricorn.

These two have a very good chance for happiness. Capricorn, so much misunderstood, will find sympathy and understanding in the Pisces mate. Pisces will find the practicality of Capricorn admirable, for it will increase the Piscean's feeling of security. Capricorn is never happier than when someone who needs him clings fast. They are entirely compatible sexually, and there is every chance of an enduring union between these two.

Pisces and Aquarius.

If Pisces will try to understand the Aquarian mate, there will be a good chance for happiness here. Pisces can give tolerance and sympathy, and these two qualities coupled with human understanding can be the Piscean contribution. Aquarius must learn to give Pisces the benefit of the doubt; then Aquarius will help Pisces to build up self-confidence, so that the Piscean fears, which seem to be based largely on insecurity here, will prove groundless.

Pisces and Pisces.

Since these two seem to have the same virtues and vices, they should get along well together, for at least there will be understanding and sympathy for each other. Both have the same love of home and possessions, and the same basic interests. The only drawback is a possible drifting too far from practical realities. Both at last can be anchored to each other, so that they can put their shoulders to the wheel and face the responsibilities that reality demands. They have the refinement and delicacy that each desires in love, so all in all, this should be a good union.

SOME FAMOUS PERSONS BORN IN THE SIGN
OF PISCES

Alexander Graham Bell—
  Inventor
William Jennings Bryan—
  Statesman
Luther Burbank—Naturalist
Enrico Caruso—Singer
Grover Cleveland—U.S.
  President
Albert Einstein—Physicist
Geraldine Farrar—Opera Star
Jackie Gleason—Actor and
  Musician
Rex Harrison—Actor

Ben Hecht—Novelist and
  Dramatist
Henry W. Longfellow—Poet
James Madison—U.S. President
David Sarnoff—Communications
  Executive
Dinah Shore—Singer
John Steinbeck—Novelist
Elizabeth Taylor—Actress
Ellen Terry—Actress
Earl Warren—U.S. Chief Justice
George Washington—U.S.
  President

THE PLANETS

IF THE TWELVE SIGNS constitute the innate, latent possibilities of
the organism, and, as such, represent the constitution as a whole,
the planets comprise the active forces which arouse these latent
possibilities. In this duplex action of Sign and planet, both
natures come into play and produce the varying results of external life. Man, the microcosm, is merely the sounding board,
so to say, the reacting point for their ethereal and magnetic vibrations. Furthermore, while the twelve Signs represent the human
organism as a form containing possibilities, the Sun, Moon, and
planets represent the spirit, soul, and senses of that organism.
Man consists of body, soul, and spirit. As at present manifested,
he has five physical senses. The constellations are the body; the

Moon is the soul; the Sun, the spirit; and the five planets, Saturn, Jupiter, Mars, Venus, and Mercury, represent and express the five physical senses. It is in this light that we must consider the various natures of the planetary influx.

THE SUN

Ruler of Leo, center of the solar system, and Giver of Life. It rules the Individuality.

In good aspect it influences: ambition, loyalty, faithfulness, honor, and stands for dignity.

In bad aspect it influences: vanity, egoism, arrogance, hate, and domination.

Under favorable influence: you can seek employment . . . try for a promotion . . . ask favors . . . gain through personal enterprise and increased responsibilities.

Under unfavorable influence: it is best to avoid seeking favors from persons of wealth and those in superior positions . . . not to divulge your secrets . . . overcome a tendency to be egoistic, over-ambitious, venturesome, over-confident, and domineering. You are apt to suffer financial losses if you speculate or lend money.

THE MOON

Ruler of Cancer, is known as the Force of Life and rules the Personality.

In good aspect it influences: idealism, reception, grace, adaptability, domestic and maternal instincts.

In bad aspect it influences: weakness, changeability, inconsistency, laziness, and unreliability.

Under favorable influences: seek changes, journeys by water, new friendships, increased trade, better domestic conditions, and improvement for women.

Under unfavorable influence: women should try to avoid danger of illness, losses and disappointments . . . the planet affects general health conditions, public unpopularity, and possibilities for disagreeable changes as well as sorrow through females.

MERCURY

Ruler of Gemini and Virgo, is known as the God of Knowledge and rules the Mind and Memory.

In good aspect it influences: ingenuity, intellect, versatility, and concentration.

In bad aspect it influences: carelessness, artfulness, cunningness, shiftlessness, and shrewdness.

Under favorable influence: good for publishers, editors, reporters, distributors, advertisers, bookkeepers, architects, teachers, lawyers, scientists, and young people; correspondence, writing, literary work, and all mental pursuits. The mind is keen and thoughts come clearly.

Under unfavorable influence: Be careful when signing contracts . . . watch emotional impulses . . . act with prudence . . . avoid changes or removals . . . guard against friction with relatives, neighbors, or co-workers. Tends to disturb the stomach and nervous system.

VENUS

Ruler of Taurus and Libra, is known as the Goddess of Love and Beauty.

In good aspect it influences: peace, happiness, perfection, and harmony.

In bad aspect it influences: love of ease and pleasure, immodesty, self-indulgence, and thoughtlessness.

Under favorable influence: shop for a new wardrobe, jewelry, and luxuries . . . seek opportunities for romance, marriage, entertainment, social activities, and popularity . . . cultivate new friendships with the opposite sex . . . deal with dressmakers, clothiers, artists, singers, actors, musicians . . . make collections. The feelings and emotions are easily aroused and you respond more readily to affection and sympathy.

Under unfavorable influence: use moderation in all dealings with the opposite sex . . . refrain from excesses of all kinds . . . possible liability to disappointments or disagreements in domestic affairs . . . you are more sensitive and easily hurt . . . postpone important social functions . . . do not speculate . . . do business only with those you know can be trusted.

MARS

Ruler of Aries and Scorpio, is known as the God of War and the Center of Divine Energy.

In good aspect it influences: courage, activity, adventure, fearlessness, and executive ability.

In bad aspect it influences: boldness, audaciousness, destructiveness, and selfishness.

Under favorable influence: deal with builders, engineers, machinists, soldiers, dentists, and surgeons. You are more ambitious, energetic, ardent, and resolute. The tendency is toward more success and progress in business and personal affairs. You can tackle problems that call for aggressive effort, speed, hard work, and common sense.

Under unfavorable influence: keep out of controversial matters where friends or co-workers are concerned . . . guard against carelessness that may lead to accidents . . . be patient with delays, interruptions, and restrictions . . . watch temperamental displays of indiscretions . . . be cautious when dealing in property or real estate matters.

JUPITER

Ruler of Sagittarius, is known as the God of Fortune, and is the Royal Planet, said to control the Divine Wisdom.

In good aspect it influences: generosity, benevolence, happiness, devotion, philosophy, and security.

In bad aspect it influences: wastefulness, extravagance, impatience, and lawlessness.

Under favorable influence: begin new ventures, buy and sell, speculate, ask favors, proceed with matters pertaining to lawyers, bankers, merchants, brokers, politicians, and physicians. Attend important social functions. It tends to make you more hopeful, generous, and popular.

Under unfavorable influence: shun speculative investment . . . watch out for misplaced confidence, bad judgment, and extravagant urges . . . women should be very careful of all health matters, sign no contracts, and make no promises.

SATURN

Ruler of Capricorn, is known as the God of Time.

In good aspect it influences: steadfastness, vitality, justice, prudence, and action.

In bad aspect it influences: hypocrisy, discontent, deceit, and avariciousness.

Under favorable influences: good for dealings with plumbers, shoemakers, miners, gardeners, farmers, and landlords. Seek favors from elderly people. Use tact and diplomacy instead of force. Proceed to finish all matters pertaining to real estate. You can obtain a position of trust and responsibility.

Under unfavorable influence: postpone changes, removals, and long journeys . . . do not start new ventures . . . guard your speech and delay important decisions . . . be careful with elderly people . . . caution must be exercised in buying, selling or making investments . . . unfortunate for marriage . . . watch your health.

URANUS

Ruler of Aquarius, is known as the God of Air. It is a rather eccentric planet that controls all unpredictable activities.

In good aspect it influences: originality, inventions, freedom, individualism.

In bad aspect it influences: peculiarities, unexpected and unforeseen happenings, and obstinacy.

Under favorable influence: you may make changes, investigate new, original, or unique undertakings. Travel for business, work for social reform and humanitarian principles. Deal with electricians, railroads, aeronautical firms, inventors, and scientists.

Under unfavorable influence: use caution around sharp instruments or inflammable objects . . . be careful while traveling . . . avoid changes or removals . . . do not confide in strangers or persons of the opposite sex . . . enter into no partnerships, do not join any clubs or associations . . . practice restraint and avoid unconventional association.

NEPTUNE

Ruler of Pisces, is known as the God of the Waters. It is the Spiritual Awakener and gives Inspiration and Idealism.

In good aspect it influences: inspiration and idealism. Universal intelligence.

In bad aspect it influences: indolence, deceit, disrespect, and shiftlessness.

Under favorable influence: good for business dealings in shipping chemicals or perfumes, activities related to the seas and liquids in general. Favors voyages, artistic endeavors, and matters concerned with secret orders. Conducive to mysterious romantic associations.

Under unfavorable influence: avoid dealings with hospitals, prisons, and other confining institutions . . . guard against fraud, deception, and get-rich-quick schemes . . . avoid doubtful friendships.

THE PLANET PLUTO: RULER OF THE UNKNOWN

Strange as it may seem, it is nevertheless a fact, Pluto was the missing planet. It has been allegorically expressed by Jesus as the Prodigal Son; by Moses as Abel; and by the prophets of the Scandinavian *Edda* as "Ragnarok." In our esoteric system there are ten celestial bodies somewhere: The Sun and nine planets. Until 1933 we had only nine in all. Where, then, was the lost one? The exalted adept alone can solve this problem. Suffice it to say, it symbolizes the missing soul within the human constitution. Pushed out of the line of march by disturbing forces, Pluto became, for a time, the prey of disruptive actions and ultimately lost form, and is now a mass of fragments. The ring of planetoids between the orbits of Mars and Jupiter indicates to us the empty throne of Abel, whom Cain (Mars) slew in his anger. The time ultimately came when this orb was reconstituted. Until that time the missing soul sought its physical mate in vain—except in rare cases.

The old, and now much abused, Chaldean sages were thoroughly acquainted with the planetary influences, and in order to teach these principles to their youth they elaborated beautiful imagery in the form of fables and allegories. They gave the nature and power of each group of organs in the human brain to the character of that planet which they believed controlled its activities, and then worked out the theory into a series of mythical histories of gods and divine personages who incarnated themselves for the benefit of man.

Thus Mars took the character of Vulcan, the god of War; Venus and her son, Cupid, were assigned the character of Love and the sympathetic tendencies of the human heart; while the benevolent Jupiter assumed the position of Father, the kindly, generous parent, good alike to all his offspring.

To continue, the Sun becomes the great archangel Michael, who defeats Satan and tramples upon the head of the Serpent of Matter; the Moon becomes transformed into the angel Gabriel; Mercury becomes the angelic Raphael, the genius of wisdom and art; and Saturn becomes the angel Cassiel, the genius of reflection in the astral light.

Uranus, Neptune and Pluto, of course, were not known to the Chaldeans.

THE TWELVE
HOUSES

THE MAGNETIC polarity of any given geographical point of our earth's surface is changing every moment. This continual changing in the earth is accompanied by a corresponding change in the electric and more ethereal vital currents of the atmosphere. Both these varying conditions are caused, primarily, by the diurnal motion of the earth upon its axis from west to east, which causes the whole heavens to transit the visible horizon from east to west during the space of one natural day—24 hours. The secondary causes are the various motions and aspects of the Sun, Moon and planets as they relate to the positions of the earth in her annual orbit about the sun. The primary basis, the diurnal motion of the planet, claims our attention first. We will, therefore, briefly examine its nature and philosophy.

The real motions of the earth are the only motions that have any real influence upon the physical organism of its inhabitants. These motions determine the length of the day, measure out to us the proportion of light and darkness, regulate the seasons, and fix with the hand of fate, the exact duration of the year. All these have a manifest influence upon the organism of man.

314

As our mother Earth revolves upon her axis, the whole of the heavens seem to rise, culminate and set upon every portion of her surface. Though this rising and setting is only an appearance so far as the heavens are concerned, it is absolutely real to the earth's habitants, because the influences, as they transit the earth from east to west, are exactly the same as if the earth was the stationary center of our solar system, and the heavens were revolving around it.

The varying conditions of the astral and magnetic forces are caused by the various angles at which, in their apparent motions, the stellar influx is reflected to any given point of the earth. For instance, the conditions at sunrise are quite different from the conditions prevailing at noon when the Sun is shining upon the meridian. At sunset we see another wonderful difference manifested, possessing nothing in common with either noon or sunrise. Then, again, we have the midnight state of the earth and the atmosphere in which the conditions are the polar opposite of those in force at noon. These cardinal points of the day indicate the greatest changes, but, as a matter of course, these changes from one to the other are gradual. To measure this gradual angular change the ancient astrologers divided that space of the heavens visible at any moment into six Houses or mansions, as they termed them, and the opposite or invisible arc into the same number, making twelve in all, designated as the diurnal and nocturnal Houses of the heavens. Modern Astrologers follow the same principles, because their influence can be verified in every correctly calculated Horoscope, when the time, day, month, year and place of birth occupied by the native are taken into consideration.

These twelve Houses contain, like the Signs of the Zodiac, 30° of space each, but unlike them their distance is measured by degrees of right ascension, or time, instead of celestial longitude. This is the only real relation existing between the twelve Houses and the twelve Signs. Each House comprises a department of life, or mode of expression, or type of interest distinct from the other houses.

THE FIRST HOUSE . . . Relates to your personality, natural disposition, self-interest and outlook on the world generally. Physical appearance, and constitution and how you will express yourself. The first House also represents matters in health that concern the head and face.

THE SECOND HOUSE . . . Your financial prospects, your skill and conditions that have to do with earning power. Benefits of income from personal possessions, profit or loss. The nose, throat, ears and neck are the parts of the body related to the second House.

THE THIRD HOUSE . . . The logic and memory power you have, relatives and kindred, short journeys, vehicles of travel, writings, studies, mental inclinations and ability in advertising, publicity and manual skill. The lungs, arms, hands and shoulders are controlled by the third House.

THE FOURTH HOUSE . . . Conditions at home, environment, real estate, property owned, savings, the father and automobiles. Opposition in your business or career, conditions later in life, agricultural matters and mines. This House represents your digestive system and the breast.

THE FIFTH HOUSE . . . Love affairs, amusements, personal pleasures, and children are influenced by this House. Also speculations, personal attainments, affairs of showmanship, the theatre and the arts. The outlook for the year also depends upon planetary influences in the fifth House. The parts of the body controlled by this House are the heart and back.

THE SIXTH HOUSE . . . Your health, sickness arising from worry, servants, fellow workers, service to others, employer relations, food and clothing. Occupation, hygiene, the Army and

Navy. Also small animals. The digestive organs and abdomen are represented by this House.

THE SEVENTH HOUSE . . . Your ability to see both sides of a question, the general public, the husband, the wife, contracts, legal partnerships, law suits, open opposition, unions, marriage and divorce are in this House. The kidneys and veins are controlled by the seventh House.

THE EIGHTH HOUSE . . . Legacies and all matters concerned with the dead, taxes and debts. Money and goods of others. Financial affairs of your marriage partner are placed in this House. Also spiritual regeneration and occult studies. This House rules the muscular system, sex organs and bladder.

THE NINTH HOUSE . . . This House relates to philosophical and higher education. Universities and the professions, particularly legal, scientific and literary. Long journeys by water or air and interests at a distance. This House controls the nervous system, liver, hips and thighs.

THE TENTH HOUSE . . . This House represents matters of government, politics and power, credit, the mother. Also occupational advancement; profession, career. Affects honor and reputation; relations with parents and superiors. Rules the knees.

THE ELEVENTH HOUSE . . . Relates to income from occupation. Fraternities. Influences wishes, desires, friends, as well as fears and apprehensions. Controls the legs and ankles.

THE TWELFTH HOUSE . . . The House of secrets, troubles, restrictions, sorrows, self-defeat. Secret enemies. Confidential arrangements, relations with confining institutions such as asylums, hospitals, prisons. Also has to do with large animals. Rules the feet and toes.

CONCLUSION

The poet Manilius, celebrated in the days of Caesar Augustus, set forth the Astrology of the Romans in the following beautiful description of the twelve Signs and the constellations:

"Now constellations, Muse! and signs rehearse;
In order let them sparkle in thy verse;
First Aries, glorious in his golden wool,
Looks back, and wonders at the mighty Bull,
Whose hind parts first appear, he bending lies,
With threatening head, and calls the Twins to rise;
They clasp for fear, and mutually embrace,
And next the Twins with an unsteady pace,
Bright Cancer rolls; then Leo shakes his mane
And following Virgo calms his rage again.
Then day and night are weighed in Libra's scales,
Equal awhile, at last the night prevails;
And longer grown the heavier scale inclined,
And draws bright Scorpio from the winter signs.
Him Centaur follows with an aiming eye,
His bow full drawn and ready to let fly;
Next narrow horns, the twisted Capricorn shows,
And from Aquarius' urn a flood o'er flows.
Near their lov'd waves cold Pisces takes their seat,
With Aries join, and make the round complete."

BOOK II

ZOLAR'S BOOK OF DREAMS, NUMBERS AND LUCKY DAYS

DREAMS
AND
THEIR MEANING

The study of dreams is a great realm that may be divided into two territories: that of the observation of dreams, and that of their interpretation. Plutarch and Cicero did not scorn to study it, and following them there are numerous authors from olden times to the present day, not to speak of many writers of keys to dreams, always drawn up at second hand.

Many dreams have become famous, either on account of the position of those who had them or on account of the events that are claimed to have been foretold by them.

No child who has studied his Bible will have forgotten the dream of Jacob seeing the ladder placed on his breast and rising to the sky, prediction of the high destiny of his race; the dream of Pharaoh (the seven fat kine and the seven lean kine), which Joseph interpreted as the approach of seven years of plenty followed by seven years of famine; and so many others in which Jehovah appeared to Moses and the Prophets. He will remember in the Gospels the angel who foretold to the carpenter Joseph the supernatural motherhood of Mary, the other angel who warned Joseph to fly into Egypt to escape the Massacre of the Innocents, and the wife of Pilate who was excited by dreams that drove her to beg her husband to save Christ.

It was in a dream that the mother of Virgil knew, by seeing laurels, that she would give birth to a poet. In a dream Brutus saw a threatening specter foretelling his defeat on the eve of the battle of Philippi. In a dream Calpurnia, the wife of Caesar, foresaw the murder of her husband. In a dream Catherine de' Medici foresaw the tournament in which her husband lost his life. In a dream Henri II of France heard a voice predicting the wound to his eye that would come soon. In a dream the princesse de Condé was present at the battle of Jarnac, in which her son was to perish. In dreams Madame Roland knew the death of her mother and Madame de la Bedollier saw the man she was to marry, whom she did not at that time know.

Are dreams in reality prophetic?

We have all known coincidences between dreams and future events that were at least disturbing and striking. Let us add that some scientists have believed and still believe in dreams as a warning, at least to some extent. On the other hand, there are certain cases in which the dream foreboding can easily be understood. How many wives of fishermen, for instance, see in their sleep their husbands being shipwrecked, when, alas, that same night the men are engulfed by a fate which is only too common to seafarers? But do the wives not forget these same dreams when nothing happens?

Nevertheless, let us remember that, if in some psychophysical condition (especially in hypnosis) the human being shows himself apt to foresee future events, it is not extraordinary that sleep should sometimes be accompanied by a premonitory sensitiveness in which images seen transform themselves into more or less vaguely symbolic forms.

On the other hand, Thylbus remarks in his *Realm of Dreams* that dreams are predictive barely once in a hundred times. These visions of the night are often due, as we shall see presently, to the state of the body, to a physical sensation perceived during sleep, or to a contradesire (Freud's theory). Therefore, before opening a key to dreams to the dream that disturbs you, remember that it is only in cases in which a dream seems inexplicable that it may possibly have any premonitory value.

The Egyptians called such dreams "mysterious messengers," for they took them to be sent by the goddess Isis, who, with the aid of Serapis, thus sent warnings and counsel.

But let us come to more serious explanations.

In the opinion of occultists, the separation of the being into the material self and the psychic or astral self takes place rarely in a state of wakefulness but more often during sleep. And if they see in dreams a kind of presentiment or telepathy, this is, they say, because the soul is freed from the heavy weight of the material body during sleep more often than during wakefulness and thus is more easily able to communicate with the spiritual world.

Scientists, on the other hand—at least the materialists who despise every hypothesis that does not use the scalpel—explain dreams by the rush of blood to the head, allow dreams only physiological causes, and say that they are the result of the nervous system's acting on itself without communication with the outside world. Sleep, by suspending at least in part the exercise of certain faculties (attention, willpower, judgment) releases the control of all the images and thoughts that imagination brings to mind without coordination (hence incoherence).

It cannot be denied that physiological conditions affect dreams, and the ancients were well aware of this, for before accepting signs they took into account the functioning of the organs, the position of the sleeper during his sleep (which must avoid any compression of the liver, the mirror of true dreams), the hour, the day, and the season (autumn and winter, in their opinion, being not very good times). This is why, following the Arab physician Ibn Sirin (who lived in the eighth century B.C.), Moreau de la Sarthe and Maine de Biran distinguished two classes of dreams: the intuitive, and the affective or organic (connected with special conditions, pathological or other, and caused by them, as for instance a physically cold sleeper dreaming of snow).

Let us go into some detail for each of these categories.

As we said, the intuitive dreams are the only ones that have any connection with divinatory science. Even then it is perhaps going too far to believe that the gods busy themselves with our petty affairs to the extent of giving us their advice in this manner, and it may be disturbing to see the contradictions existing between the various keys to dreams that are offered to our eagerness to know the future. And besides, we know that many thousands of dreams have never seen their predictions fulfilled!

We have said that occultists saw in dreams a kind of presentiment or telepathy, which is the faculty of seeing at a distance and without the aid of the senses. By the laws of determinism, events concerning each one of us are undoubtedly always in preparation in the vast field of the invisible world; they are in some way in a condition of germination as the seed is at the bottom of a furrow. But it happens in the spiritual world as it happens in the physical world, and all forebodings do not come true, just as all seeds cast into the furrow do not blossom. Sometimes our willpower, warned by the dream, arrests or precipitates the events in their course.

We should not consider interpretations of dreams as predictions. We must be realistic and consider dreams, rather, reminiscences or the reflection of preoccupations. We must not take keys to dreams literally. Everything we can say about man's search into the future must be based solely on hypotheses and coincidences.

The ancients claimed that it was possible—by recipes, by amulets, by prayers, and by drawings of dreams—to procure sweet and pleasant ones and to avoid unpleasant ones. For this purpose they often advised the placing of a branch of laurel near the sleeper's head. Would you like some more advice on this matter? Good dreams, according to the ancients, result from peace of mind; the righteous man who goes to sleep with pleasant thoughts will have pleasant dreams. To avoid terrifying dreams, they wrote, one should not read at night.

The slightest indispositions as well as the most serious illnesses may give rise to dreams. Unfortunately, their semiological value is very uncertain: we do not know their connections with the seat and the nature of the various affections which they accompany. All that we do know is that during sleep the pathological labor which goes on in the depths of the organism induces dreams which are more or less in direct relation with the affected organ. This is so true that dreams may sometimes arouse suspicions about an illness which are not revealed during wakefulness. To give some instances: An organic affection of the heart or of the large veins is sometimes announced before its obvious occurrence by painful dreams or nightmares followed by sorrowful presentiments. If the dreams are frequently repeated, they may be looked upon as symptoms foretelling a serious lesion already very difficult, if not impossible, to prevent. When the lesion has become actual, the dreams are very short; they usually occur during the first sleep and are quickly followed by sudden awakening. Combined with them, there is an early death in tragic circumstances. According to the observations of various doctors, spontaneous hemorrhages are foretold by red dreams or by dreams of murder. The more these dreams are accentuated and detailed, the more they must be taken into consideration. It is especially during the prodromic period of neurosis and of mental alienation that dreams are found to be of such a bizarre and extraordinary character as to arouse the suspicions of a doctor. Madness, before showing itself definitely, very often reveals itself in terrible nightmares of the worst omens.

The same phenomena accompany illness more often than they precede it. Fever-stricken persons sometimes feel the most dreadful thirst, and dream that they cannot shake it. People have been known to dream that they had a leg cut off or turned to stone and to wake up paralyzed, or become so a few days later. Cold in an organ or its prolonged compression are sometimes accompanied by the same sensations.

Hindu and Chinese medicine, for centuries, has been looking to dreams for information as to the diagnosis of illness. In their system dreams are divided into five classes which correspond to the five great viscera: the heart, the lungs, the kidneys, the spleen, and the liver. Each class is subdivided into two normal conditions of the organ. The normal conditions induce no dreams of any kind. These principles having been stated, the following gives, as an example of this Asian science, a summing up of the various dreams which denote the malfunctioning of each viscus:

1. Dreams of ghosts, monsters, terrifying figures—sign of malfunctioning of the heart (vessels choked), repletion. Dreams of fire, flames, smoke, light—sign of malfunctioning of the heart: giddiness due to weakness in the blood current, and slowing down of the heart's rhythm.

2. Dreams of fights, war, weapons, soldiers—sign of malfunctioning of lungs, repletion. Dreams of plains, sea, country, difficult roads, and journeys—sign of malfunctioning of the heart.

3. Dreams of excessive fatigue, pain in the kidneys—sign of malfunctioning of the kidneys; canals overly full. Dream that one is swimming with difficulty and is in danger of drowning—sign of malfunctioning of the kidneys.

4. Dreams of songs, festivities, music, pleasure—sign of malfunctioning of the spleen, starting repletion of the canals. Dreams of dangers, battles, disputes, meals—sign of malfunctioning of the spleen.

5. Dreams of inextricable forests, steep mountains, trees—sign of malfunctioning of the liver, repletion. Dreams of grass, lawns, bushes, fields—sign of malfunctioning of the liver.

Finally, dreaming of brooks, murmuring springs, or waterfalls is a sign of anemia, and dreaming of murderers, hanging, or strangulation is explained by asthmatic suffocation.

It will be seen that this diagnosis by dreams is very similar, in some of its inductions, to that made in similar cases by Western physicians, but it is a little more extended.

In any case, it is generally recognized today that painful nightmares—of suffocation with the sensation of imminent death—reveal a choking in the great vessels of the brain and the heart. It would be wise to remove the threats of congestion indicated, by a modification of the way of living. So, also, in the case of frequent dreams of total and partial paralysis, which indicate a defective circulation of the blood.

Here, at least, dreams offer a sure interest, and it is probable that it was this practical application of oneiromancy which formed in olden times the rightly fundamental basis of this science. We should be wrong to neglect its instructive study under the pretext that the mystics and subsequently the charlatans turned it aside from its most interesting purpose.

Here are some examples of dreams without value:

a. Dreams during the first hours of sleep during the time of digestion.

b. Dreams of a person or a thing of which we have recently heard spoken.

c. The feverish nightmares due to pain, to fright, to a book read, to something seen.

d. Dreams resulting from the manner of sleeping, from the position of the sleeper.

e. Dreams due to illness or some obvious outside cause (noise, cold, etc.).

The true oracle dream: This comes in the middle of sleep, usually between three and seven o'clock in the morning, when the digestive functions are complete, when the body is in a good state of health, when the mind has not been exposed to any excitement, and when the normal position of repose causes no trouble to any organ. According to the Arab Ibn Sirin, author of the first treatise on dreams, "the sleeper lying on the right side will have abstained from all food or of drink. He will have gone to sleep with a light heart, an easy conscience, after having obeyed the precepts of the Koran as to prayers and ablutions."

INTERPRETATION OF DREAMS

These are the general rules as to the interpretation of dreams:

a. The gravity and importance of the events predicted are in direct relation with the depth of impression produced in the dream by its omen.

b. The due date of the event predicted is in proportion: (1) in the case of an animal, to the time of its gestation, incubation, or the breaking of its egg; (2) in the case of a thing seen, to the distance at which it was, in the dream, from the dreamer; (3) in the case of a recurring event, to its recurrence, etc.

c. Apart from fairly numerous exceptions, the meaning is, in general, the opposite of the dream; thus dreaming of death means marriage or happiness; of murder, safety; of a mirror, betrayal.

d. Monstrosities, deformities, and ugliness are, however, evil.

e. The right is good (also odd numbers); the left is fatal.

f. All wild felines and all huge animals are evil.

g. All domestic animals, especially if of light color (except the cat), are of good omen.

h. Reptiles are the worst possible omens (slander, crookedness, betrayal).

i. Fishes mean abundance and wealth if they are fine and appear on the surface of the water; but, if they remain at the bottom, serious danger.

j. Interpretation relating to all birds seen in dreams: On the right or east—beneficence; on the left or west—maleficence; flying high—good luck; flying low—bad luck; singing—success; hiding the head—bad luck; turning the head away—an upset; head under wing—illness of much-loved person; coming above the dreamer—reason to beware; wounded—betrayal.

k. Fruit means abundance unless its season is past at the time of the dream.

l. Vegetables are a deplorable omen with two exceptions: mushrooms and peas.

m. The various parts of the body indicate the persons to whom ones dreams refer: A dream of a head is related, in modern interpretations, to the dreamer; a dream of teeth is related to a near relative; a dream of a right hand relates to the dreamer's brothers and sisters; a dream of a left hand relates to his children; a dream of the right foot relates to his parents or grandparents; a dream of a left foot relates to his servants.

n. In the case of a dream of illness or pain, always consult a doctor.

o. Weapons are always omens of a betrayal or break.

p. It is never lucky to dream of an animal of the same sex as the sleeper. The opposite, of course, is a good sign.

q. All dreams of efforts foretell difficulties to surmount. If, however, these efforts are weak or crowned with success, you may expect a happy ending. If, on the other hand, the task dreamed of is difficult, this is a sign of serious obstacles.

r. A light, brilliant, new, or full article is a happy omen.

s. A dark, dull, old, used, or empty article is evil.

t. Going up is always good.

u. Going down is always bad, denotes at least a decrease.

v. It is preferable not to dream of insects (worries, cares).

w. Dreaming of enemies is unlucky.

x. Dreaming of living relatives or friends with whom you are on good terms is a lucky sign.

y. For a girl to dream that she sees herself married means "break": accident, possibly death.

z. All dark or black shades are bad omens; light shades, on the other hand, have cheerful meaning. Any violent color indicates excessive passion; any color mixed with black has meaning contrary to that which it has when alone.

These are the chief color meanings:
   Bright red—strong love
   Red and black—furious hatred
   Dark red—violent passion
   Light red—affection
   Dark yellow—low desires
   Light yellow—material ease
   Dark green—evilness, a threat
   Light green—serenity, cheerfulness
   Dark blue—domination
   Light blue—purity, happiness
   Warm purple—power
   Purple and black—intrigue, treason
   Deep purple—sorrow
   Light purple—gentleness, wisdom
   Orange—happiness in love
   Indigo—beneficence
   White—family joys
   Black—mourning, death
   Chestnut—melancholia, danger
   White stones—happy omens.

DREAM ANALYSIS

The complete process of dream analysis involves the following steps:
   1. the recording of the dream;
   2. the dividing of the dream into its parts or elements;

3. the discovery, by ordinary memory, of the recent dream material;

4. the discovery, by free association, of the more remote subconscious dream material;

5. the identification of the instinctive wish or fear that is the emotional power of the buried complex and the fundamental cause of the dream.

After a little practice, you will be able to analyze simple dreams merely by a brief free association from the most significant scene or event of the dream.

But if you wish to learn any new art or process thoroughly, it is desirable in the beginning to perform each step of the operation with detailed care. Then you will become more experienced and proficient, and you will be able to omit many of the details, go at once to the heart of the matter, and get results more quickly.

A mind experienced in dream analysis can almost immediately pick the significant element of the dream and, with a few links of the chain of free association, pull up from the subconscious mind the fundamental causes and meaning of the dream.

For illustration: An acquaintance of mine who is quite expert in dream analysis recently related to me his analysis of a dream that he made in a few minutes that morning while dressing.

The dream was a complex one, but the significant element was the taking of his niece to a disreputable resort under circumstances that to others would have looked very suspicious. To a person less familiar with dream analysis, such a dream would have been rather horrifying, as it appeared to involve the dreamer's attempted seduction of his own niece. But the dreamer knew from previous analysis that he had no such subconscious attitude toward the girl, who is rather plain and not in the least the type that would arouse his sexual instinct, even if she were not a relative of his.

The process of free association quickly solved this dream riddle. He had recently been urging his nephew, brother of the niece in the dream, to come to New York City. This invitation of his had the boy's parents, who lived in a small town and considered New York a very wicked place, worried. The dreamer had written to his sister saying, "If he [the nephew] were a girl you might have cause to worry." The nephew is as handsome as his niece is plain, and the subconscious thought of the dreamer had been "My kinfolks are worried for fear that this wicked old New York will ruin their boy. If he were a girl I wouldn't dare ask her to come here, for they think I am a wicked sinner because I live in New York and might even suspect me of having designs on the girl."

This thought becomes the idea which is dramatized in the dream. Without analysis the dream seems to be quite shocking, but analysis reveals the cause to be nothing more offensive than the dreamer's wish that his relatives would quit worrying over the wicked city corrupting his nephew.

Such short cut analyses are safe enough after you have considerable practice; but in the beginning you will do well to give attention to the five steps as outlined. I will therefore discuss these steps in more detail.

There is a very humorous line in an old English cookbook. The recipe is entitled, "How To Bake a Hare," and the instructions begin with this important item: "First you must catch the hare." Presumably one might buy a hare in the market, but I take it the cookbook writer considered it better to go out and catch it so as to be sure to have it fresh.

The same advice is good in our recipe for dream analysis, for a fresh dream is better than a stale one. By stale dreams I mean dreams that you remember having had some time ago, and which you thought peculiar or clever and so remembered. Likely you have told such dreams several times; and dreams, like gossip, frequently get changed in the telling. Dreams that have been written down at the time you dreamed them will be free from fault.

But there is another reason why the dreams should be fairly fresh when analyzed, and that is that in the analysis you are going to delve into the subconscious by free association, in order to find what is back of the dreams. Therefore, the more recently the dream has occurred the more readily you can discover the things that prompted the dream.

It might seem, because of the above consideration, that one ought to analyze the dream immediately. In practice I find this does not always work well, especially when one wakes up in the night and tries to analyze a dream he has just had. The mind is still too sleepy, or in case of a dream of strong emotions, too emotionally wrought up. The same thing applies to a dream one remembers on awakening in the morning if one tries to analyze it while lying in bed. It is better to go over the dream in your conscious memory and get it more safely recorded. Better still is to have a pad handy and write it out, then to go to sleep again if it is in the middle of the night or get up and dress if it is in the morning.

Then, any time during the day (that is before you go to sleep the next night) when you have the leisure for it in undisturbed circumstances, recall or reread the dream and analyze it. The one exception I would make wherein you might analyze the dream more promptly is that of a dream you have while napping in the daytime. Such dreams may be properly analyzed as soon as you have stirred about a bit to be sure you are thoroughly awake.

Ordinarily you will probably analyze in the evening the dreams you had the night before. If you wait the passing of a second night, there is some danger of the analysis being more difficult because of interdream memories from one night to the next. During the single day some minor details may be lost; but not essentials, for they are important to the subconscious mind and will be retained. In fact, they may be retained for years or a whole lifetime, as dream analysis itself will show. I have made these suggestions regarding the best time only because I want you to have everything favorable. Stale dreams can be analyzed, but the fresh dreams of the night before will be easier.

The suggestion for dividing the dream up into its elements is needed chiefly to avoid the danger of overlooking some part which may not seem particularly important in the dream but which may prove to be of importance in the analysis.

No hard and fast rules can be laid down as to this division. The elements of the dream are essentially the same as those of a story. They involve the setting, the characters, and the action or incidents.

The setting simply means the place where the dream story seemed to be happening. It may be a familiar place which you can indicate with a few words, as "I seemed to be in a living room in my uncle's house." Later on the dream scene may change: "And then we seemed to be on the shore of a lake, and there was a sailboat coming toward us." These places or prominent objects are elements of the dream. They may be either familiar places or objects that need only to be named in order to be pictured, or they may be strange places and objects that you will have to describe.

The second type of dream element is the dream character. This means the people of the dream, and animals and sometimes objects also assume characteristics of humans, as they often do in fairy stories. "My uncle was in a room, and he wore a full beard as he used to do when I was a child." The character in this is the uncle, but he should be considered with the distinctive feature that at once suggests that the events of the dream are related to some childish experience of the dreamer. "We were fishing and I caught a fish, and when I tried to take it off the hook, it seemed to have changed into some kind of furry animal." The fish and the furry animal are true dream characters, and likely to prove significant as elements of the dream. "And then the boat came up to the shore and a beautiful girl with long golden curls stepped out of the boat; I did not know her and am sure it was no one I have ever known." Here we have a dream character, and the description of her should prove important; perhaps in the analysis her identity may be revealed.

The action, or incidents, of the dream is of course closely related to the settings and characters and often can hardly be separately stated. "I caught the fish," as given above, is action; so is "The fish seemed to change into a furry animal." "A beautiful girl stepped out of the boat. . . . Then she came up to me and jerked the rod out of my hand and threw it into the lake." These items will sufficiently illustrate action or incident.

It is not necessary in dividing your dream into its

elements to rearrange the dream material, as I have done, into three groups of setting, characters, and action. But it will help you to divide it up more completely if you remember these three kinds of elements of the dream story. You can simply go through the dream as it is told in the story form and note these elements without disturbing them from their natural order in the dream. If you are working with a written copy of the dream story, you can simply underline the significant word or phrases.

You are merely one of the dream elements, but your own characterization in the dream is so important that I want to call special attention to it. So note carefully whether you are in the dream yourself and whether or not you are an actor in the dream drama or an observer. Nine times out of ten you will be in the dream scenes. But you may be as you are now, or you may seem to be in some past period of your life or experience. More rarely it will be you in a condition or state in which you have never lived but in which you have in past thought of being. Women, I find, frequently dream "I was married to so and so, or such a kind of man." Men are more likely to dream of love or sex relations without dreaming about marriage.

Occasionally you may be the actor in the dream but living, as it were, in the body of someone else. The transference of your personality comes from the thought, "I wish I were so and so," or "If I were so and so . . ."

There is no sharp distinction between the recent and the more remote dream material. We make the distinction because it helps us, in the analysis, to do so. As you have learned, most, perhaps all, dreams are set off or released by the action of some memory of what has been experienced or thought of during the previous day, or at least very recently.

This material may be discovered merely by going over the dream elements one at a time and asking yourself what recent event or thought could have caused that element of a dream.

Not all dream elements will have such recent events as causes; sometimes only the elements representing events that trigger the dream will be so easily explainable. But strange to say, significant elements do not always appear at the beginning of the dream tale as it is related. In the case of the man who dreamed he was guillotined by the board falling from his bedstead, it seemed that a very recent event started the dream but that the element did not appear in the dream until its end.

This was an exceptional case, but you will often find that the recent event that set off the dream will appear fairly late in the completed dream tale. Hence, if you wish to make a thorough analysis, it will be wise for you to go over each element in the dream and see what recent event or idea might explain that element. This analysis is proper, for which the other steps are only preparatory, and is accomplished by free association.

Take up each element of your dream, and from that scene, character, or action let your mind freely associate back into your subconscious store of memories and experiences. You will be surprised how quickly you will get results and how very clear it will be that the dream was motivated, or its driving energy supplied, from these deeper subconscious sources.

You will usually find a similarity in kind between the more important recent events that have set off or released the dream, and these may have a surprising resemblance to events that have happened many years in the past, even going back a whole life span.

It does not always follow that you will unearth very old memories in this step of the dream analysis, for some dreams, which seem wholly caused by fairly recent events, include some long-existing subconscious elements, which will explain why recent events, represented in the dream, were significant to your subconscious mind.

I will not give illustrations of this step of the operation here, because I am presently going to give you the complete analysis.

Frequently, this instinctive emotional wish or fear will be recognized at once from the recalling of experiences and thoughts back of the dream. At other times this will not be so obvious. The point I wish to make is that the mere recognition of the intellectual elements of dream memories does not in itself constitute the scientific analysis of a dream. Until the more fundamental wish-fear emotion that binds the dream material together and forms the complex of the subconscious is unearthed and comprehended, we have not fully analyzed the dream. When this core of the dream structure has been discovered, the whole dream at once becomes clear and meaningful, and your analysis is complete.

Those dreams which go, for their material, back into your past and which reveal purely subconscious wishes or fears are the ones that will prove of the greater importance in the psychoanalysis of yourself. But it does not follow that all dreams are of this order. It is true that all dreams are wish or fear dreams, but some of them may take all the dream material from your recent life and the wishes and fears that prompt them may also have been recently conscious wishes or fears.

None of these dreams are to be disregarded as unimportant, for they all help you to understand yourself. But the wishes or fears that are the oldest are most fundamental in your nature, and because you are less aware of them, they are the most likely sources of conflict with your conscious thoughts and actions.

I have detailed these five steps of dream analysis as if they were all to be performed separately. But in practice you will combine them to a greater extent, and you will be able to do this even more as you become more expert and experienced in the analysis of your dreams.

As you recall or write down the dream, you can note or mark the elements, and as you note these elements you will often, without effort, recall the recent dream material. Sometimes you will also associate and so discover the more remote subconscious material at the same time, and that usually reveals the instinctive wish or fear. In the following related dream analysis, I give the thought processes approximately as they occur in experienced practice. As I get further on with these examples, I will condense more and omit some of the intermediary details.

The dream: I dream that I meet a man on the street whom I do not recognize. He catches my arm as I pass and calls me by name, and then I realize that it is my old friend Orvis, whom I have not seen for several years. He looks strange, seems younger and more energetic than I would have expected him to be. He asks me to come with him into his office. I do and find that it is a lively place with evidence of his busy prosperity. When my friend removes his hat, I see that his head is covered with a heavy growth of black hair. This seems strange, as he was, when I last saw him, almost wholly bald, and the little fringe of hair he had was turning gray.

Recent dream material: Davis called on me a couple of days before the dream, and we spoke of Orvis and wondered how he was getting along. We remarked that he was getting old, and we feared he wasn't doing well.

Analysis by free association: I didn't recognize Orvis, he looked younger, he had a heavy growth of black hair; but he is bald, he is the baldest man I know. I suppose I will get bald too, as I grow older (wish-fear element suggested). Only a week or so ago I happened to look into a mirror while a beam of sunlight fell on my head, and it revealed that my hair is getting decidedly thinner than it was. (Recent dream material by association and wishful fear element becoming rather obvious.) Orvis's bald head not only had a growth of heavy hair, but his hair, which was really gray, had become black—my wife pulled a gray hair out of my head the other day (more recent dream material and a secondary wish-fear element suggested). Orvis was doing nicely in business, was younger and more energetic looking than I had expected to find him.

It is not necessary to follow the detailed analysis further, for the whole dream is now apparent and its analysis obvious. The fundamental fear of the dream is my fear of growing old. And this fear of the general decay of age is the emotional element of the complex which draws to it the specific ideas of baldness, grayness, loss of youthful energy, and failure in business.

More specifically, the cause of this dream is my fear of becoming bald. Yet I did not see myself as bald in the dream, but saw instead my baldest friend with an astonishing growth of black hair. Hence, the wish element (which is merely the reversal of the fear) is that baldness can be prevented or cured when it comes. There are minor wishes in the dream, one of which I had never been conscious because of its futility: it is that I might have black hair. Evidently, this has been a subconscious wish all my life, for I have always remarked on the handsomeness of black-haired men, my own hair being an indifferent brown.

This dream was simple and very easily analyzed because its material was recent and therefore readily available to the conscious mind. Yet it did require some analysis, for the dream itself, instead of picturing me as bald, showed my bald acquaintance as having hair. The direct meaning of the dream was that Orvis had grown a new crop of hair and was young looking and prosperous. I had consciously wished, when talking to Davis, that Orvis was doing well in business; but I had not thought or cared consciously about his looks or his baldness. My subconscious thoughts were about the danger of becoming bald myself, as revealed by the association of the discovery of how visible my scalp was getting when the sun shone into my hair. The speed with which this memory came into my mind is pretty good evidence that it is my baldness, not my friend's, that my subconscious was concerned with. Yet it is Orvis that gets the new hair in the dream. This is the element of dramatization or symbolism of the dream. My subconscious wished to express itself on the subject of baldness and picked out Orvis as the man who could best play the role. To put heavy black hair on his bald head was good dramatic or symbolic expression of the wish that I would not become bald myself.

Though simple, obvious, and not of great importance, the dream illustrates very nicely the typical dreaming mechanism and the method of dream analysis.

Several writers on psychoanalysis, following in the footsteps of Freud, have made it a business to collect numerous cases of dream symbolism. From these cases they have worked out and published fascinating lists of dream symbols. While it is no doubt true that many symbols have been in the same dreams of different people, there is no reason to believe they will always mean the same thing. Your dream and its analysis will reveal the symbols that you use.

Here is a case in point. The mere statement of dream and its analysis seems a farfetched case of symbolism, yet when all the facts are available, including that of a previous dream, the symbolism ceases to be mysterious.

The dreamer, whom we shall call Smith, dreams he is in a canoe with a man we shall call Jones. Smith and Jones are paddling the canoe, and another, empty canoe is tied on behind.

Now, when I tell you that the canoe the men are paddling is a certain young lady, whom we will call Miss Brown, and that the empty canoe behind is Mrs. Smith, the dreamer's wife, you may say "Bosh!" Yet that is correct, and here is the analysis as Smith worked it out.

"I dreamed that Jones and I were paddling a canoe, and that an empty canoe was tied on behind. This is the only dream, or rather all of the dream, that I recalled on awakening. When I come to analyze it I do not connect Jones with any experiences of canoeing or recall that I ever wished to go canoeing with him. I only know that he is with Miss Brown. But I am rather fond of Miss Brown myself, and I recall that on my vacation last summer I wished she were there and that I could be paddling up the lake, with just her in the canoe. At this point I suddenly remembered another dream, which I must have dreamed earlier in the night, and forgotten when I woke up. In this dream I was in a canoe with Miss Brown, and Jones was in the other end of it, we men paddling.

"I would like to share Miss Brown's love with Jones; that is, I want her for myself, but I recognize him as a fine fellow whom I have no right to cut out. It would be nice if we could both have her. But I am married, and my wife would make trouble. If I had Miss Brown, my wife wouldn't have anyone. She wouldn't stand for that and she wouldn't give me up, she would come along too. The empty canoe tied on behind is my wife.

"The wish of this dream is that I would have Miss Brown, but I would have to share her with Jones, and my wife would have to tag along without anyone. The women were evidently in the canoes to start with but got lost out some way, or rather the canoes came to represent the women. Evidently my subconscious desire to possess Miss Brown is rather ridiculous, considering the circumstances under which I would have to accept her . . ."

The analysis of this dream was rendered easy by the memory, recalled in analyzing the first one, of the earlier dream in which Miss Brown was in the canoe. The second dream gives us positive evidence of the symbolism of the canoes as the women, and shows how easily this came about by the continuance of the dream after the women which caused it faded from the picture or were fused into and symbolized by the canoes. In neither dream memory does the dreamer's wife herself appear, and yet her part is obvious enough when the rest of the dream is analyzed.

The psychoanalytical value of this dream analysis is apparent. Smith would probably not have consciously admitted that he was in love with Miss Brown and would have insisted that such a love was ridiculous, as he was married and she had another lover whom he admired and would not wish to cut out. The dreamer was still in love with his wife, yet subconsciously he had developed a secondary love complex. He was splitting his love impulse, and some of his instinctive sex energy was going to the other woman and subtracting that much from the love for his wife. Bringing this subconscious fact into consciousness will naturally have the effect of diverting all his love to his wife, because it is so evident to common sense and reason that his love is wasted on the other woman.

THE DREAM OF THE NIGHT BEFORE THE WEDDING

This dream may not prove to be what you expect from the title. It was dreamed by a girl the night before her intended marriage, and its analysis and what it let to read like a movie thriller. The dream itself was simple, but the way its analysis revealed her subconscious life was important.

She dreamed that a cat and a dog, which she used to have at home when she was a little girl, were having a fight. The cat licked the dog and was chasing him, and the dog was howling dreadfully. She thought how ridiculous it was for the dog to be whipped by the cat and felt that he wasn't much of a dog.

She was to be married the next afternoon to a man whom we shall call Henry, whom she had met only a few months before. She wasn't sure that she loved Henry a great deal, but she was sure that she was doing a wise thing in marrying him. The reason she gave herself was that he was prosperous and very much a gentleman, refined and quiet. He thought the world of her, and she felt sure he would always be very tender and kind. But Henry was a little man, an inch shorter than she was; she had taken to wearing low-heeled shoes since she had met him. How different from Albert, the man she had gone with before she met Henry. Albert was so big and rough and a little uncouth; she loved him, but they had quarreled and she was afraid of him, afraid to marry him.

Then she thought of the dream of the cat and dog fighting. And the cat had licked the dog. She could see them now as she used to play with them when she was a little girl. She had called the cat Mama and the dog Papa before she understood sex; and she remembered how embarrassed her mother had been when she had announced in the presence of callers that the dog was the papa of the cat's little kittens. . . . She remembered how her mother and father had quarreled and how small and frightened her mother had seemed.

Now she saw the meaning of the dream. She had wanted her mother to win those "fights," and yet how ridiculous the dog in the dream had looked running and howling in fear of the cat. . . . And how ridiculous a man would look who was afraid of a woman. It was evident that she had refused to marry Albert because she was afraid of him, for he was a big rough man, like her own father. But was it possible that she had decided to marry Henry instead because he was little and gentle and meek and she could "manage" him? In that moment she felt that she would be a fool to marry a man she could not respect because he was afraid of her.

It was all very clear now. She had never before admitted it to herself, but she had refused her big manly lover and come so near to marrying the little man just because in her childhood she had resented seeing her mother bulldozed and browbeaten by a big man. The complex so formed in childhood had prejudiced her against the big man, and this complex was in conflict with her natural instinct of love, which was naturally directed toward that type of man.

These subconscious truths being revealed made it evident that she could not go on with the marriage to the little man, even if he was more wealthy and refined than the man she now realized she really loved more. So she rose and sent a message to Henry breaking off the engagement that had come so near to being a wedding; and when she had removed to another part of the city, away from prying eyes, she sent a note to Albert and asked him to call.

A WIFE'S GUILTY CONSCIENCE

The dream: "It seemed as I was married to my husband and Mary X was also. We were all three of us at home [the dreamer's home on the old farm]. He was painting and I was holding the paints for him, but Mary X was making suggestions on the painting. I wanted to help, but she knew more about his art and he didn't pay any attention to me. So I told Mary X to go out and drive the cows from the pasture. And when she was gone, I said to him, 'Now let's run away before she comes back.' "

The analysis: The dream shows a clear case of substitution of one person for another. Mary X was an art student whom the dreamer and her artist husband had met only a few days before the dream. The wife was slightly jealous, as she was likely to be of any woman artist. There was no real ground for this, as the husband was much in love with his wife and did not care for the women artists he knew but said they were "a silly bunch." The wife had no real occasion to be jealous of Mary X.

The key to the deeper significance of the dream lay in its location at the old home and in the seemingly polygamous relationship. Mary X was a substitute character for the dreamer's own sister. The action of the dream was a dramatic condensation of what had really happened. The two sisters had lived on the old farm, both bright, pretty girls deserving more intelligent husbands than the rural community afforded.

A young man, raised in the neighborhood had gone away to a large city and become an illustrator. He came back to visit the old home community, and his interest in the two sisters was at once apparent. The older girl (the dreamer) had realized that he was really hunting for a wife and that she felt that her younger sister ought to have him, for she was the more artistic.

But she, the dreamer, wanted him for herself. He was handsome and clever and to marry him meant an opportunity to get away from the drudgery of the old farm. So she managed the affair to her own ends and married him, but with the feeling deep down in her heart that she had cheated her sister out of an opportunity that was rightfully hers.

The younger sister had later married very well and was perfectly happy. There was no occasion for a feeling of regret. The artist's wife now realized from his scornful treatment of women artists that, had he married her sister, the latter's slight artistic ability, instead of being an element of happiness, would have made trouble. Consciously she had nothing to regret, as affairs turned out nicely all around, but subconsciously she still suffered from the complex of guilt based on the feeling that she had taken the man that her sister had won. The feeling had lived on in the depths of her mind and had become the source of her own unreasoning fears and jealousies.

Such a dream rightly understood and interpreted should (and presumably did) do much to free her of the inner sense of guilt and make her own married life more wholesome and happy.

THE DREAM OF A BASHFUL YOUNG MAN

A young man relates this dream and its analysis.

The dream: He seemed to be in a pen with a lot of white rabbits. He was eating with them, drinking milk out of a saucer and eating lettuce. He didn't seem to be one of the rabbits but was another kind of animal, a "kitten or puppy, or something." Then the pen seemed to be surrounded by a lot of dogs, which were all barking and laughing at him.

The association: (Recall of some childish feeling): When he was small, the young man had some white rabbits which had to be kept shut up in a pen to keep the dogs from hurting them. Dogs were rough and cruel animals; rabbits were pretty and tame. Nobody ought hurt white rabbits. Boys were rough and mean like dogs, and little girls were nice and tame like the white rabbits. The little girls' mothers were afraid to have them play with the mean and rough boys. But no mother objected to his playing with the girls, he was such a nice little boy. The other boys ridiculed his playing with the girls. They called him "fraidy cat" and "sissy."

When he grew older he moved to a new town and here refused to have anything to do with girls. He grew to be mortally afraid to be seen with them. Lately he had taken lessons in dancing. He could dance fine with the instructors, but the moment he went to a social dance and offered to dance with a girl, the old terror came back to him and he danced so badly the girl wouldn't have him for a partner.

The analysis, now apparent, reveals the retention in young manhood of a subconscious complex of childish fear of ridicule. He was still afraid to be seen playing with girls though he was a fine, handsome fellow with nothing that was sissy about him, in looks or manner. He had overcome his childish sissiness but had retained subconsciously the fear of ridicule.

A DREAM OF DANCING ON A GRAVE

The following dream of a girl stenographer has a double substitution of personalities and the blurring of a name that would seem a pretty clear case of the work of the dream censor. The dreamer is too fearful and ashamed of the real thought back of the dream to permit its more direct expression. Although I do not believe in the universal working of the dream censor or of dream symbolism, I admit the evidence of such an explanation of dreams is very good in certain cases. I can only say that the analysis must determine whether the real thoughts back of the dream are the more evident ones or the more obscure ones that are clarified only when interpreted as symbols.

The dream: "I was in a cemetery with my father, and we were putting flowers on a newly made grave. There was a tombstone freshly put up, and I started to read the name on it. The first name was Elizabeth, but the last name was blurred so I could not read it. I turned to my father; he was smiling and holding out his arms to me. He said, 'There, that's done, little girl, now let's dance.' We began dancing on the grave; but the scene soon changed and I was dancing in a hall with George D."

Recent dream material: She had walked through the cemetery the Sunday before with a girlfriend. There were people putting flowers on fresh graves, but she paid no particular attention to anyone. There was no man with them on that trip. She had never walked with her father in a graveyard. No one had died in her family. Her father and mother got on all right. She had never wished or feared particularly about her mother's death—and her mother's name was not Elizabeth. She did not know anyone by that name to whom the dream might refer. George D. was her friend, and she often danced with him as she was doing at the end of the dream. Dancing with her father was quite unthinkable, and dancing on the grave was "awful."

The search for dream material in the recent experiences does not seem to solve this dream; on the other hand, the dream suggests no particular childhood experiences. Under these circumstances, we have reason to believe that the dreamer's mind is holding back, and that tendency would lead us to suspect that the obvious characters of the dream are substitutes for someone else. Further associations reveal nothing that would help toward a solution. But about George D. we get these comments: "I don't care much for him, he is just a silly kid." This gives us our cue, that the dreamer does care for some other man, an older man, for whom her father is substituted in the dream. To the question whether her father called her "little girl," we get a negative answer. To the next question, "What man old enough to be your father does call you 'little girl'?" we get the revealing answer, "My boss does sometimes; but he doesn't mean anything by it."

Obviously, we have hit upon the clue to the real analysis of the dream. Elizabeth was the name of her employer's wife; the girl at first denied knowing this fact, and yet she recalled that when the wife had been away on vacation the summer before she (stenographer) had taken dictation of her employer's letter to his wife. Consciously the girl may not have known the wife's name, but subconsciously she did, and she blurred the surname in the dream.

This whole dream, put badly, means, "I wish my employer's wife would die, so then he and I could dance on her grave."

As you have seen by the way I have told it, the dreamer had help on this analysis. Without help she might not have been able to analyze the dreams; but on the other hand, we suspect her of holding back in the analysis and of lying because she did not want to admit the truth. The dreamer lied to herself in her dream, and she lied to herself and me a little, I think, in the analysis. If she had really wanted this analysis to come out, I think she could have analyzed the dream more quickly by herself than she did with my help.

I am quite willing to admit that some of you may have a little trouble with dreams of this sort—if you have them— but I insist that if you get over the foolish tendency to be afraid of your own thoughts you will be able to analyze such dreams better by yourself than you could with help. The practical point is that there is nothing of which to be afraid. The young lady in this case did not wish to admit to herself that she was in love with her employer; she wouldn't admit it openly in her dream. But with the analysis before her she is better off than with the love hidden in her subconscious mind; she is more likely to get over it. If she can't, she can change her job; or if she wants to do it with her eyes open, she can go on and have an affair with her employer.

If some of you object to my mention of this latter possibility, I can simply say that there is actually less danger of such an ending with the thing out in the open than there was by her going ahead and lying to herself.

The boss was calling her "little girl" and had dictated letters to his wife to her, evidently not minding revealing to her that there was no great love for him in his home. From such a situation it would be very easy for the girl to drift on, pretending that "he didn't mean anything by it" until the subconscious passion grew to a stage where it would take control regardless of further efforts of conscious suppression. I am holding no brief for illicit love but merely stating that I consider it safer to know what our feelings are than to go on lying to ourselves about them until they rebel and overpower our rational conscious minds.

A DREAM OF LOVE WITH A BROADER SIGNIFICANCE

A middle-aged and happily married friend had told me many of his dreams relating to various subjects, most of which we had been able to analyze with benefit and profit to him. There was one dream, however, or rather a series of dreams, relating to the same person, that for a long time seemed to both of us to be merely memories of puppy love affairs of his childhood and without significance to his present life.

These dreams were of a girl he had known in his early teens back in his home village. They seemed to indicate that he had worshiped from afar and never been able to make much headway with his youthful love affairs.

At my suggestion that these dreams might have some significance with his present love life, the dreamer always scoffed, declaring that he was very much in love with his young, beautiful, and cultured wife and that the other girl was probably married to some farmer or grocer and had a dozen kids.

Then one day he brought me another dream of his first love. "We were having the time of our lives," he said, "and what do you think we were doing? We were running around with torches setting fire to all the churches in town."

The pleasure he took in telling this dream I easily understood, for I well knew that the man was a hater of

348

churches and religion and that this animosity greatly distressed his wife. This was in fact the one sore spot in their otherwise happy married life.

A little questioning brought out these facts. In the strict village life of his boyhood everybody went to church; and the old standby phrase "May I see you home?" at the church door was the accepted, and practically the only way, in which a lad ever got himself a girl. Now the boy had been obliged to go to one church and the girl he was smitten with to another, stern parental authority forbidding even temporary absence from the family place of worship. And so he had come to hate churches, not because, as he had later come to believe, of any genuine lack of religion in his nature, but merely because the rigid church system of the little town had kept him from the girl he loved.

"Well," he admitted, when I offered this explanation, "I guess you have pretty near hit it. I don't know that I have any grudge against churches if they would let people be natural and happy." Needless to say, this discovery to his conscious mind of the complex against churches based on the thwarting of a boyish love led to a happier state of affairs in his own home.

A DREAM THAT FURNISHES PROOF OF SUBCONSCIOUS REASONING

The following dream furnishes a curious example of subconsciousness reasoning:

A New York woman dreamed that she was in a subway station. In the space where the trains come through, there appeared a series of long platforms somewhat like a train of flatcars. People were stepping across from the main platform and crowding on these flatcarlike platforms. A gong sounded. People stopped stepping across the platforms, and little protective rails rose from the edges of the main platform, which kept the crowd back. Then a full-length subway train came rushing down the tunnel, its front end open. It ran right on without slacking speed, telescoping over the crowded flatcars and carrying them on with it.

Now another train of empty platforms rolled into place, and the dreamer stepped on with the crowd. As before, the train came through at full speed, running right over them, or rather, the shell of the train running around them; and the dreamer found herself in the full, moving train, which had thus picked up the crowd without stopping speed.

She marveled a little over this new system. She couldn't seem to understand how it worked, but it evidently did work, and she thought it fine.

Before giving the analysis of this dream, I want to call your attention to the evidence it furnishes of subconscious reasoning powers. Fortunately, the dreamer first told me of the dream while the causes that led up to it were still fresh in her memory. Thus I was able to sound her thoroughly on the subject and secure one of the finest proofs I have come across of the power of the subconscious to reason.

First, the dreamer assured me that she had (at the time of the dream and as far back as she could then remember) very little interest in mechanical and engineering problems. She was not in the habit of reasoning consciously on such subjects or of attempting to solve such problems. Her reasons for not doing so were, as you shall see later, subconscious ones. But consciously, that is, so far as she was aware, she had no such ability and no such interest. On the contrary, she distinctly lacked such ability and was bored and annoyed by such reasoning and by all consideration or discussion of such problems.

More specifically, she had positively not taken any interest in the problem of subway congestion; that is, with an inclination to think out a remedy. "I knew that the subways were congested," she said, "because it delayed me, because I had to be packed in with a lot of crude people while the subways often stalled and that made me late for my appointments. But that is all I have ever thought about it. As far as trying to figure out a solution, I never did, and I know I never could and would never try to."

Now, from such a conscious attitude toward the problem, we jump to the dream in which a finished scheme of an effort to solve subway delays and congestion is all

350

figured out. The dreamer does not figure it out in the dream but finds it in complete operation. She marvels at it, wonders how it works, and thinks it rather clever. Certainly she is not in the least aware that it is her own invention.

The fact that the invention in subway operation that she saw working in the dream is a ridiculous and impossible one by no means proves that she did not subconsciously reason, though it does prove that she reasoned rather badly. The very impossibility of a train at full speed picking up the waiting platforms of people further proves that it was not a remembered idea she had heard someone describe or had read about or seen pictured in a newspaper. But impossible as it was, her scheme was rather complicated and ingenious. Not only did she reason subconsciously, but she reasoned upon a mechanical problem and worked out mechanical details, all of which she could not and would not have done in her conscious mind.

Here is the interpretation of the subway dream: In the first place, the recent dream material is quite obvious. Her attention had been turned to subway congestion by the new turnstile, and she was annoyed by the crowded and slow subways and wished they could be improved.

That is interesting but of no great importance to her life. Yet the fuller analysis of the dream by free association unfolded a tragic life story and saved the threatened happiness of a home. This analysis revealed that the real deep-lying wish motive of her dream was sexual in a broad sense and that she wished for more peace, love, and happiness in her married life. This was a conscious as well as a subconscious wish.

A more specific wish, closely related to the dream, was strictly subconscious; she wished that she could be interested in, understand, and reason out engineering problems. Her reason for so wishing was that her husband was an engineer, and such interest and capacity on her part would have enabled her to understand his work and, by so doing, make him more happy and more efficient and prevent his attention to a woman scientist who did understand his work and to whom he went for sympathy and admiration. Now, it would seem that this wish would be conscious, but it was not, for it had been repressed; and she consciously maintained that she was disinterested in and bored by his engineering. She believed that she was sorry she had married the engineer and that he was narrow, mechanical, and uncultured; that she should have married an artist or musician.

Now the dream analysis takes us back to her childhood, and we find the little girl in a refined home with a rather silly old-fashioned mother. The girl is a normal bright child and well endowed with all human instincts of construction: the instincts that lead boys to build things and be interested in machines. The nice little girl with the nice mama, who is trying very hard to make a lady out of her, has a playmate, in the shape of a boy in overalls, who has a good mechanical bent. He is building things in the barn. The girl becomes interested and wants to help. She does help and does so very cleverly.

After a happy afternoon so spent, she comes home with a dainty dress torn and smudged in the boy's machine shop while her mother thought she was over at a nice neighbor's playing with a wax doll. Her mother scolds her and tells her she is unladylike. The mother gossips to a neighbor woman and worries over the tomboy tendencies of her child and the degradation of playing with boys in the barn. The gossip gets to the children, the little girl is called a tomboy, and there are vague, naughty, childish suggestions about being with boys in barns. So by social disapproval and childish ridicule the instinct of mechanical construction is suppressed in this girl child, as it is in practically all girl children, because that is an instinct society has seen fit to assign to men.

Now we skip a dozen years and find a typically well-bred and rather narrowly educated young lady, ignorant of science and mechanics and with little ability to think along those lines but with the native instinct to do so still alive and buried under a heap of acquired ladylike culture.

She meets a young man, and he is an engineer. He is too well bred to "talk shop" while in society (one of the silly restrictions of so-called good breeding). Moreover, he is not yet taking his profession very seriously and is interested in dancing and social life.

So they fall in love. Little is said about his engineering

and his chance to rise in the world. Yet the fact that he is an engineer revives for a time this suppressed constructive instinct, and she hopes to take an interest in and help him with his work.

So they marry. One evening the young husband comes home full of enthusiasm for a problem in engineering he is working on. The wife is interested and talks about it, but she is ignorant and unskilled in this sort of mind work, and the husband laughs at her lack of knowledge and understanding. He says "Of course, I couldn't expect you to understand this, pardon me for mentioning it."

So again the instinct is snubbed and suppressed and forced back into the subconscious. This time the suppression, with the resentment of wounded pride to aid it, creates a direct conscious antagonism to the subject. The wife actually cultivates a disinterest and inability to think along mechanical lines. But the husband grows more engrossed in his profession and ignores his wife and her social life. They begin to drift apart in sympathies and interests; she seeks compensation by following artistic lines of thought and culture, and he seeks womanly admiration elsewhere.

Such is the state of affairs when the subway dream occurs. Its analysis reveals to the wife her original instinctive interest in this broadly human passion of devising mechanical things, and she sees how that instinct was twice suppressed and how foolish and unfortunate that suppression was. The analysis of this dream, explained to the husband, shows what an unfair brute he was to kill his own joy in life by snubbing his young wife's first efforts to understand his work. He sees, too, the humor and cleverness of this dainty wife as a tomboy building things in an old barn, and also her remarkable feat of attempting to solve the subway congestion by subconscious reasoning. They laugh at that and laugh, too, at many of her other impossible inventions and impractical solutions, but he is now laughing with her, not at her. And they are going to live happily ever after.

HOW ARE YOU TO KNOW WHEN YOUR ANALYSIS IS RIGHT?

This is a natural question for you to ask when first getting acquainted with the subject. After you have had considerable experience in the analysis of your own dreams, you probably will not ask that question, though someone else to whom you might explain your work or tell one of your analyses would be very likely to ask it.

In the first place, you have the same advantage that you would have in thinking out any other kind of problem. That is, if you follow the methods that have been tested and proven by others and reach certain conclusions, the chances are that you will be correct.

But in the analysis of your own dreams you have a very much more important fact to help you. The answer you are looking for is already in your subconscious mind, so when you work back toward it and find it there is a distinct sense of recognition. You think, "Oh, that's it," and there is a feeling of relief, a feeling that the search is ended. After you have become reasonably practiced in the work this recognition will be sufficiently convincing.

To explain by an example, suppose you are trying to think of some forgotten name that has slipped from your mind, that is deeply buried in the subconscious vaults of memory. You may try rather desperately to remember it and to no avail, but if someone suggests the correct name to you, ninety-nine times out of a hundred you will say, "Oh yes, that's it." The name suggestion immediately reaches the buried memory and is identified.

The correct analysis of the dream reaches the subconscious wish or fear, and is likewise identified.

Here we see another advantage of self-analysis. The professional analyzing another's dreams does not have this advantage except as his patient chooses to give it to him. Psychoanalysis is one of the few instances in which the patient or client knows more than the doctor or expert.

CAN ALL DREAMS BE INTERPRETED?

Yes, if they are completely remembered and you have had sufficient experience in interpreting your dreams. But do not worry, especially at first, if you cannot find a satisfactory interpretation of all your dreams.

If after reasonable effort you do not get on the track of a revealing interpretation, lay the dream aside. Later, after you have interpreted other dreams, you can probably come back to the one that gave you trouble and find that it now has revealing associations. If not, it is probably that you have lost some essential part of the dream in transferring it to the subconscious mind. Hence, to force the interpretation of the fragment that is left would mean to get an inaccurate interpretation.

You can rest assured that you will have plenty of dreams to interpret, for the more interested you get in this work the better you will remember your dreams—and you do dream them, plenty of them, for you dream all the time you are asleep.

Neither should you worry lest you lose some essential messages from the subconscious because of the dream you lose or fail to interpret. If we had to depend on any particular dream our chance of success would be small; for even though we remembered so many dreams that it would keep us busy all day long interpreting them, we would still be getting but a small fraction of the total number of the dreams we dream.

But the subconscious will repeat its fundamental wishes in dreams again and again.

MAKING USE OF YOUR DREAM ANALYSIS

We interpret our dreams to find out what is going on in our subconscious mind, but the purpose of psychoanalysis is not merely to find out what is going on in the subconscious mind but to make use of the subconscious forces to gain our conscious aims and ideals in life.

When you have analyzed your dream and have determined the subconscious wish that prompted it, here are some questions you might ask yourself:

1. How does this wish apply to my present life?

2. Is the subconscious wish also a conscious wish?

3. If so, what forces within my own nature, or in the world outside, stand in the way of realization of that wish?

4. If the subconscious wish is one I cannot consciously approve, what conscious wish can I offer to my subconscious which would serve as a substitute for this wish that cannot be realized?

NEW KEY TO DREAMS

After having given these general rules, there remains for me only to draw up my own key to dreams at once synthetic and reasonable (as far as this is possible)—only by way of information, of course, as my very skepticism does not prevent my being conscientious.

For this task I have consulted the best ancient and modern sources. I have adopted the triple rule:

1. not to waste too much time on dreams which are too vague, too rare, or too bizarre;

2. to broaden the meaning of these images, for here, more than in any other divinatory art, would detail run the risk of landing in a very morass of charlatanism;

3. to neglect explanations which are silly for the very reason that they seem plain, or which have an unpleasant aftertaste, such as that threading pearls in a dream means a love affair.

I shall in the main give those meanings which have unanimous opinion in their favor, this being a sign of tradition and moral value.

AN INTRODUCTION TO NUMEROLOGY

There are many systems and methods of making predictions but none perhaps as interesting as numerology, since anyone may work it out. No long hours of tedious study are required. There are only a few simple rules to follow.

The Egyptians, the Greeks, the Romans, and the Arabians had systems of arriving at number vibrations, which are remarkably accurate. The teachings of the adepts in numerology have come down to us from the most remote antiquity.

All letters have numerical equations; therefore, all combinations of letters in names respond to certain numerical values. When a name is given to a person, city, book, or *anything*, it immediately lets loose a certain occult force expressed in numbers. Nature in its most primitive form responds to numbers. Note the geometric formation of snowflakes, of growing plant cells, the mathematical precision of the sunrise, the movements of the heavenly bodies, the procession of the seasons, etc. These, and other geometric or mathematical formulas, respond to various numerical values. In everyday life we answer to the numbers of our names, our births, and our locations by our reactions to certain things. Some names appeal to us immediately; others, we pass by unnoticed. It is our reaction to the numerical magnetism which causes us either to ignore or notice them. The universe is operated with exact mathematical precision calculated to a fraction of a second.

Every expression of rhythm responds to a numerical measure of time. When you listen to music that thrills you, you are unconsciously harmonizing with a certain number of influences in the notes of the music; or when you dislike certain types of music, it is because the numerical value of such music is not in sympathy with your own name and birth numbers. Everyday life brings some good or adverse reaction to the magnetic influence of the numbers around. They are in everything you see, hear, or feel. It is impossible to escape them. The sooner you learn the value of these numbers, the better you will be able to harmonize with life and the people around you.

On the following pages I give a very simple system of number calculation so that you may become familiar with their influence in your daily life and get the best out of your newly acquired knowledge.

To find out your fortunate dream number, reduce the key to your dream to a single digit. For example, if you dream of a baby:

$$B = 2$$
$$A = 1$$
$$B = 2$$
$$Y = 7$$

12 = 1 + 2 = 3, which would be the lucky number for baby. If you want three numbers you can use any three numbers that reduce to 3. For example, 9-1-2 = 3.

You will note that all numbers appearing before and after each dream in this book have been obtained in this manner.

THE ALPHABET

In any system of numerology the letters of the alphabet respond to the nine digits, or single numbers. Numbers of two figures are not retained except in the cases of 11 or 22, which will be explained later. The letters of the alphabet must be reduced to single numbers; consequently, more than one letter responds to the same number, as shown below:

```
1 2 3 4 5 6 7 8 9
A B C D E F G H I
J K L M N O P Q R
S T U V W X Y Z
```

You will notice that the letters A, J, and S have the numerical value of the number 1, while B, K, and T have the value of 2, etc. Whatever number a letter is under, that is its numerical power or number vibration.

EXAMPLE OF NUMERIZING A NAME

We are now ready to begin transfering names into numbers. We will choose a simple name as an example. Preferably, the first name and last name of a person should be written vertically, as it is easier to add this way than horizontally. We choose the name of Mary Smith:

M	=	4	S	=	1
A	=	1	M	=	4
R	=	9	I	=	9
Y	=	7	T	=	2
		21	H	=	8
					24

The name Mary adds up to 21, and the name Smith results in 24. To secure the full name vibration it is necessary to add 21 to 24, which equals 45. This is a double number, so we will add 4 and 5, which equal 9. This young lady then responds to the name number 9. You may now refer to the indications of the numbers in the following pages and find out what number 9 denotes.

We will now suppose that Mary Smith's birth date is June 8, 1912. To transfer this into numerical value, we would write it thus: 6, 8, 1912, because June is the sixth month. Now we add these numbers together: 6 plus 8 plus 1 plus 9 plus 1 plus 2 equals 27. This total is a double number, so we add 2 plus 7, which equals 9. We find that Mary Smith's birth date is 9, the same as her name number. Any number derived from the birth date is called the birth path. Now we wish to find her destiny number. We will add the name number and the birth date number thus: 9 plus 9 equals 18. This is a double number, so we have to add 1 plus 8, which is also 9. Thus, Mary Smith's destiny number is 9. Refer to 9 in the destiny column on the following pages and read her indications.

Certain numbers have an affinity for each other, while others clash seriously. Even numbers harmonize with other even numbers, and odd numbers harmonize with other odd numbers; but even numbers seldom harmonize with odd numbers except in the cases of 11 and 22. These two numbers are apt to be the exception and will harmonize with almost any other number. 11 is a higher octave of 2, because 1 and 1 equal 2, while 22 is a higher octave of 4, as 2 plus 2 equals 4. However, these two numbers are seldom reduced a digit because of their very strong individual powers. Therefore, when you have arrived at an 11 or a 22, you need not reduce it further but look in the indications that follow these pages for those two numbers.

We now propose to find out whether Mary Smith, with a destiny number of 9, would be successful as a typist. Secure the number vibration of the word typist. We find it gives us 2 plus 7 plus 7 plus 9 plus 1 plus 2, which equals 28. This is a double number, so we add: 2 plus 8 equals 10; this, likewise, is a double number; therefore, 1 is added to 0, which equals 1. Since the word typist responds to 1, which is an odd number as is 9, Mary Smith would be a successful typist.

In the same way we can discover whether she would be successful in Chicago, New York, Los Angeles, or any other place by working out the numerical values of such places. We can also find out if a certain street and number is favorable or not; if she should marry her lover or not; if travel by land or water or air is best for her, etc., by securing the numbers of those things the same way we worked out her name number. Many other things will suggest themselves to you that you can work out for yourself or for your friends, such as the proper hotel to select, proper room number to engage, etc.

In figuring the numerical values of names, use the one by which the person is known. If the name James has been given a boy at birth but he always has been called Jim, use the name Jim. If you find the name James produces better influences, he should immediately change his name to James and sign it so at all times, insisting too that his friends call him James instead of Jim. The name by which a person has been called all his life is the name vibration he responds to best, since the constant repetition has stamped upon his destiny the influence of the name even though it is a nickname by which he has been called since childhood. Therefore, when you are numerizing a name, the one by which the person is known is the one to be selected. Changing it, adding certain letters, or spelling it differently produces a new vibration that will bring different results and a different personality if continued for a long enough time. Many famous people change the spelling of their names when they understand numerology, so as to create better harmony.

It is sometimes best, when a woman marries, for her to retain her given name in addition to her new surname. Sometimes it is best to drop the given name and use her husband's full name, placing Mrs. before it. By working out the different combinations according to numerology the best combination can be found quickly and easily. Once the person decides to change his name, the old one must be forgotten entirely and never again used in any future dealings, introductions, or letters.

Remember: Names, articles, places, and things must harmonize—odd numbers with odd numbers, even numbers with even numbers—to be fortunate.

MISCELLANEOUS OPERATIONS WITH NUMEROLOGY

There are various ways in which numerology may be employed to amuse or benefit the many who enjoy working out their numbers. The ideas presented here are just a few suggestions. Others will come to mind as you work with the science of numbers.

SECURING FORTUNATE NUMBERS WITH CARDS

Take a deck of ordinary playing cards and remove the 10 spots. Previous to this you will have worked out your destiny number as directed on the preceding pages. We will take the destiny number of Mary Smith, which we found was 9. After removing the 10 spots and placing them aside, Mary Smith should shuffle the cards, give them one cut, then shuffle them again. She should go through the operation of shuffling and cutting nine times.

She should then deal off nine cards from the top of the pack and put them on one side. The very next card should be turned up and placed face up on the table. If the card should be a 5, her fortunate number would be 5. If she is seeking a number with two figures, she should deal off nine more cards, place them aside, and use the very next card, putting it face up alongside the first one. If she desires a number of three figures, she will deal off nine more cards and place the next one alongside the other two. Now suppose she has laid down the 5 of diamonds, the 2 of clubs, and the 8 of spades; her fortunate number is 528. Face cards are to be considered as 0. Therefore, if the last card had been the king of spades instead of an 8, the number will be 520.

Remember always to shuffle and cut the cards as many times as your destiny number. If you have a destiny number of 4, you should shuffle and cut four times and deal off four cards from the top instead of nine. Your destiny number is the index to use. This process should not be repeated for the same person more than once in twenty four hours, because to repeat it destroys the vibration of the first fortunate number and weakens the one found the second time. Note: The reason the 10 spots are removed is that 10 is a double number, and in numerology you are concerned with single numbers only.

TO FIND YOUR FORTUNATE YEARS

We wish to know if 1934 is a fortunate year for Mary Smith. Add 1934: 1 plus 9 plus 3 plus 4 equals 17. Now add the 1 and 7, which is 8. This results in an even number, so it does not harmonize with Mary Smith's destiny number of 9; consequently, 1934 is not as fortunate for her as odd years would be. The digit of the year must be the same or must be in harmony with your destiny number to be a fortunate year for you.

TO FIND YOUR FORTUNATE MONTHS

It is not necessary to work out the names of months. Merely consider the number of the month; January is the first month of the year, therefore number 1; February is the second month, therefore number 2; etc. October is the tenth month, therefore (1 plus 0) is 1. November is the eleventh month, and you always leave 11 as it is. December is the twelfth month, therefore (1 plus 2) is to 3. Mary Smith's best month is the ninth month, which is September.

TO FIND YOUR GOOD DAYS BY NUMEROLOGY

Any day which adds up to your destiny number is best for you. Mary Smith's lucky days in any month are the ninth, eighteenth, and twenty-seventh. Her fairly good days are those which add to other odd numbers. The days that are neutral or slightly adverse are those which add up to even numbers. Work this out with your own destiny number and check off your good and adverse days on your calendar, to guide you.

TO FIND YOUR BEST HOURS OF THE DAY

Find the time of sunrise from your local daily paper or almanac. For example, suppose the sun rises at 6:15 A.M. The first hour after sunrise will be from 6:15 to 7:15. Mary Smith's best hours are the ninth hour after sunrise and any other hour which adds to 9, which would be the eighteenth hour after sunrise. These hours will vary a few minutes each day as the sun varies in rising time. Always use the hours after sunrise which equal your destiny number.

HOW TO CHOOSE PARTNERS OR FRIENDS

For best results in partnerships or friendships, the destiny numbers should be the same as yours. Those who have corresponding destiny numbers will make fairly good friends, companions, and partners. Those who have destiny numbers which clash will not make satisfactory associates, and relations with them will not be permanent nor very congenial.

HOW TO MAKE MONTHLY PREDICTIONS

Secure the monthly number of any month and year (by month number is meant the number figure for any month reduced to a single digit). Add it and your destiny number together, which is your monthly number for that month. Then refer to the gallery of numbers in the pages which follow for the general indications for that month. As an example, we will see what the indications for Mary Smith are for the month of June 1934:

June 6
1934 added together 17
Destiny number of Mary Smith 9
                            Total...... 32

Three plus 2 equals 5, which is her monthly number for June 1934.

To find Mary Smith's indications for June 1934, refer to the gallery of monthly numbers. Secure your own monthly number in the same way, using your destiny number instead of that of Mary Smith. It will frequently happen that several months will respond to the same monthly number, but they will change from year to year.

GALLERY OF NAME NUMBERS

1: The number of creation, of beginning of first impulses, or of the source of energy. Persons whose name vibrates to this number are trailblazers. Most of their lives they have been leaders and thinkers along pioneer lines, and they are usually popular in whatever sphere of society they choose to move in. They are constructive in thought and like to be doing something new and out of the ordinary. They do not follow in the path of others and generally have the courage of their convictions. There is a lower level to this number also. Those who respond to this lower level are eccentric, egotistical, haughty, dominating, and self-conscious. If your name responds to this number, make every effort to overcome any weak tendencies that might show up in your character.

2: The number of beauty, culture, truth, perception, and consciousness. It is a decidedly feminine number and causes the person to respect and appreciate the refined and intellectual things in life. It is the number of cooperation, attraction, affection, emotion, and enthusiasm. Those whose name responds to this number are warm friends, congenial companions, interesting entertainers, and good judges of human nature. The lower plane of this number causes the person to be hasty, sensitive, and inclined to be too particular. If your name responds to this number, strive to overcome any undignified tendencies that might show up in your character.

3: The number of enlightenment, thoroughness, and refinement. This number causes a person to be tender, affectionate, sympathetic, very cautious about details, prone to self-sacrifice for some idealistic principle, and often willing to do without things to assist friends. It is the number of the Holy Trinity and causes the person to be highly religious, impressionable, intuitive, and magnetic.

4: The number of realization, security, protection, stability, and ambition. Those whose names respond to this vibration are true friends and good company. They possess brilliant and inventive minds and are inclined to reach the goal of their ambitions regardless of obstacles. They usually like a life of activity and variety and have many interesting experiences from which they learn much of the usefulness of life.

5: The number of uncertainty, hesitancy, doubt, and discouragement. Those whose names respond to this number will often become confused, restless, irritable, impatient, and moody. They find it hard to form congenial companionships and frequently disagree with the opinions of others. They sometimes feel that life has been unkind to them, as though they were living an existence against which their nature rebels. If this is your name number and you feel that you do not want to fight against the influences any longer, it might be a good idea to change your name slightly so that it will respond to some other number.

6: The number of dual personality, indecision, temptation, and excess. Those whose name responds to this number have a peculiar nature. They are not always understood and very often cause their own failures. If they will learn to gain from their experiences, they will make this a fortunate number, but drifting through life will never get them anywhere. They like to follow the lines of least resistance, and should overcome a tendency to indiscreet actions. Determination will help them conquer the uncertainties of this number.

7: The number of spirituality, mysticism, wisdom, and success. Those whose names responds to this number are receptive, studious, creative, and intellectual. They possess a deep understanding and desire for the finer things of life. If there are no conflicting influences in their numbers, they make warm friends, valuable employees, and ideal companions or partners. They have magnetic personalities, are very unselfish, and possess rare outlooks on life.

8: The number of justice, evolution, strength, inspiration, and genius. Those whose names respond to this number have strong personalities. They are very magnetic, self-willed, independent, progressive, intuitive, and honest, candid, and straightforward in dealings. The number 8 vibration is an extremely strong one, difficult to overcome. It causes a person to be very active, seldom contented for a great length of time, and eager for changes of events and scenery.

9: The number of dominance, efficiency, psychic powers, humanitarianism, and renewed energy. Those whose names respond to this number are clever, active, philosophical, and intuitive. They have fertile imaginations and high ideals, and are endowed with poetic or artistic ability. They are usually very dignified and pleasant but odd and whimsical. They are refined, gentle, sympathetic, and

even tempered. They make friends easily and are quick to
solve others' problems.

11: The number of power, courage, success, adventure,
impulse, and energy. Those whose names respond to this
number are an octave higher than those who respond to 2.
They are deep thinkers and fond of exciting adventures.
At times they are vague in their statements. Their minds
grasp the general outcome of things, but they usually skip
details. The number has such a powerful influence that
they often find themselves confused by many contradictions, likes, and dislikes. Clear thinking, determination,
and concentration are qualities of mind necessary to develop in order to control the restlessness this number
creates.

22: The number of rashness, errors, haste and changeability. Those whose names respond to this number should
overcome a tendency to be critical and restless. They often
do not understand their own peculiarities. They say and
do things on the spur of the moment and then wonder
why they did them. They usually do not look before they
leap. They are inclined to go to the extremes, even against
their own better judgments. They have hard struggles with
themselves.

GALLERY OF BIRTH PATH NUMBERS
(secured from year, month, and day of birth)

1: If this is your birth, you will have many strange
experiences. You will go through life making your own
conditions and carrying out your own ideas. You will lead
a constructive life.

2: If this is your birth path, you will seem to go around
in circles and have repetitions of certain experiences at
regular intervals. If you cultivate self-control, you will
have an interesting, useful life.

3: If this is your birth path, you will have many of the
better things in life. You will travel much and gain from

the experiences of others. Yours will be a fortunate, contented life.

4: If this is your birth path, you will have many loyal friends. You will gain some prominence in the business and professional worlds. Yours will be a successful, pleasant life.

5: If this is your birth path, you will have strange experiences, at times difficult to overcome; yet with your strong personality you will win out. Yours will be a long, contented life.

6: If this is your birth path, you are apt to be too careless of your actions and general health and welfare. Success will be attained only through firmness of purpose and stability. Yours is a changeable but useful life.

7: If this is your birth path, you will undertake and usually accomplish big things. New and interesting experiences will present themselves. You will be the master of your own destiny. Yours will be an unusually successful life.

8: If this is your birth path, you will lead an active life but not necessarily a peaceful one. New ambitions will always spur you onward. Frequent outbursts of temper will alter your course of life. Yours will be an adventurous career.

9: If this is your birth path, you will travel extensively and engage in unusual affairs and odd professions. Literature, art, music, and the stage will attract you. Yours will be an adventurous career and an interesting life.

11: If this is your birth path, you will engage in many risky adventures. You will overcome obstacles by sheer force of willpower. You are captain of your soul and master of your own destiny. Yours will be a progressive life.

22: If this is your birth path, you will create many of your own difficulties. Losses may occur through bad judgement and unreliable associates. Learn to think constructively and act with discretion. Cultivate self-control, and you will succeed.

GALLERY OF DESTINY NUMBERS
(secured by adding name number and birth path number)

1: If this is your destiny number, you will achieve great success through your constructive efforts. Some help will be given you, but in the main you will be self-made.

2: If this is your destiny number, you will have many ups and downs in life, but through the aid of friends and relatives you eventually will be successful. You will have wealth if you utilize all your productive faculties.

3: If this is your destiny number, you will experience many successful ventures. The better things of life will assist you to the goal of your ambitions.

4: If this is your destiny number, you will have a life of usefulness, financial success, and honor. Choose your profession carefully and forge ahead. Nothing can stop you if you persist. You will likely acquire much property.

5: If this is your destiny number, you will stand in your own way many times. Guard against accidents and do not trust strangers. Your life is one of varied experiences, some pleasant, others discouraging.

6: If this is your destiny number, do not permit yourself to drift. Control your emotions and make the best of your opportunities. You are apt to overlook them. Success will come to you if you are alert and industrious.

7: If this is your destiny number, you may expect to attain prominence in life. Your light will shine far and you will travel extensively. Friends will be attracted to you.

8: If this is your destiny number, you will encounter financial difficulties often but usually will overcome them with experience and shrewdness. Your life will be very active.

9: If this is your destiny number, you will live a very useful, contented life. You possess many talents, are admired by friends, and enjoy an excellent reputation.

11: If this is your destiny number, you will lead a very active life, will succeed in big undertakings, and be prominent in your sphere of life. You will be the master of your destiny and creator of your fortune.

22: If this is your destiny number, the lower qualities of your nature may control your life unless you strive to change them. Avoid schemes and questionable enterprises. Be deliberate in all productiveness.

GALLERY OF MONTHLY NUMBERS
(secured by adding the destiny number to number of month and year)

1: Any month that responds to this number for you is a month of new happenings. It is a good month to make and start things, take trips, ask favors, start new business ventures, write letters, etc. Anything you can manage to carry on without aid from others should succeed this month. It is a good time to buy, advertise, hire new help, look for new work, and make changes.

2: Any month that responds to this number for you is a month of varied experiences and unexpected turns of events: if unmarried, possible wedlock; slight restlessness; and danger through carelessness. This month holds many arguments, broken friendships, etc., unless you make an effort to control things. Think much but say little. Guard your health and avoid conflicts.

3: Any month that responds to this number for you is ideal for carrying out plans, making changes, taking trips, handling financial matters, dealing with business and professional people. Important, beneficial changes are apt to occur in your domestic and personal life. Make the most of your opportunities.

4: Any month that responds to this number for you is a good month to try and complete unfinished tasks, to make an effort to realize your ambitions, secure the good will of others, deal in lands, property, and legal affairs. If you exercise a reasonable amount of determination and good judgment, you should succeed at this time. You should be able to build a foundation for future activities.

5: Any month that responds to this number is a month in which you should use caution in all you undertake. Guard against fires, accidents, losses, slander, scandal, extravagance, and outbursts of temper. Guard your health and take no risks or chances on anything. Distressing bits of news may come to you this month, but refuse to be alarmed. Avoid litagation, general unrest, and loss of friends.

6: Any month that responds to this number for you is a month which depends upon your own initiative; you can make it either a profitable or an unprofitable month. You may experience some trouble in your domestic affairs and minor delays in carrying out your plans, but if you retain poise you will be able to straighten out everything satisfactorily. Guard your health and control your temper.

7: Any month that responds to this number for you is a month of good results. Follow your hunches and impressions. A good time to read, study, and investigate, it is also favorable for visiting, planning, traveling, starting new enterprises, seeking new work, buying and selling, and investing. New friends and pleasant experiences should enrich your life.

8: Any month that responds to this number for you is a month of radical changes, new ambitions, and much progress. During this month's influence you will be enthusiastic and courageous. Deal with prominent people, develop new propositions, advertise, travel, attend to important financial matters, and push all things of material importance. Avoid undue haste and too much force. Guard against accidents, fires, and minor injuries.

9: Any month that responds to this number for you is a very important month. You will have opportunities to complete tasks that have been pending for a long time, things that you start now rather than having started before. You will have renewed hopes and ambitions and new ideals. Ideas should be carried out carefully. Develop your personality and energy.

11: Any month that responds to this number for you is a month of intense activity. You will be busy yet seem to lack time to finish your plans. However, the headway you gain will be permanent. You will discover that you have a stronger willpower than you realized and that you can conquer obstacles more easily at this time. It is a month of a rise in power, new adventures, and a realization of ambitions, partial or complete.

22: Any month that responds to this number is a month in which you should be careful. You are apt to be influenced by others, to your detriment. Avoid extravagance, rashness, temptations, losses, and controversy over legal matters. Control your emotions and temper. Guard your health and take no risks or chances. You are likely to be impulsive and hasty.

DEFINITIONS

NAME NUMBER—The number secured by transfering the letters in a person's name to numbers. This shows the general characteristics the person has developed from the use of his name throughout his life.

BIRTH PATH NUMBER—The number secured by transforming the month, date, and year of the person's birth and the outstanding events to be experienced.

DESTINY NUMBER—The number secured by adding the name number and birth path number together. This shows whether the name adds or subtracts to the birth path indications. If it subtracts, the name should be changed for the future.

MONTHLY NUMBERS—The number secured by adding the destiny number to the number of any month and year. This shows the general indications for that month and year. Monthly numbers change from year to year. Name numbers remain the same always, unless the spelling of the name is changed. Birth path numbers never change; they always remain the same. Destiny numbers remain the same unless the spelling of the name is changed.

A NUMEROLOGICAL DREAM KEY

A

6 Abandon—This is an unfavorable dream and indicates the loss of friends or the failure of some fortunate expectation. Trouble is indicated, whether you abandon some other person, or whether he abandons you. Abandoning your lover: Will be guilty of foolish actions. 132

8 Abbey—Anything connected with a church shows peace of mind and freedom from anxiety. The more important the structure, the better the prospect. 215

9 Abdomen—It is an omen of contrary meaning. When you are in pain in your dream, your health will be good and your affairs will prosper because of your physical vigor. But if you dream of your unclothed abdomen, then it is an unfortunate omen, especially if you have a lover or are married, for you may expect unfaithfulness or even treachery on the part of some loved person. Do not rashly give your confidence after such a dream. 234

5 Abhor—To dream that you dislike anything or any person is an omen that depends upon the circumstances. If your feeling of distaste disturbs you seriously, then it foretells difficulties in your path; but if you merely dislike any article and can get rid of it, then you will overcome your worries. 931

4 Abortion—A warning as regards the health or the happiness of your partner in marriage; be on your guard as to both. 103

9 Above (hanging and about to fall)—Some danger awaits you, but it may be avoided if the object does not fail. 234

5 Abroad—A change of work is probable. This dream shows that you are in an unsettled state of mind. Others going abroad: Triumph over enemies. 932

5 Abscess—A dream of illness is one of contrary meaning and signifies that you will enjoy good health, or a speedy recovery if you are already ill. An abscess being operated on: A mystery will be solved. 293

4 Abscond—To dream that some person, whether stranger or acquaintances, has absconded with his employer's money or otherwise done some serious wrong is a warning to you of treachery among those around you. If you yourself are the person in question, the injury will be slight and you will recover from your losses. 319

4 Absence—This is usually a dream of contrary meaning. If you dream of the death of an absent friend, it foretells a wedding. A loved one being absent: Danger in love matters. 832

6 Absinthe—Drinking spirits or cocktails in your dream is a warning of coming trouble; the more you drink, the more serious the disaster will be. 357

2 Abstinence—To dream that you refuse to drink is a sign of good fortune coming, but it may not be lasting in its effects. 902

2 Abundance—To dream of plenty is always a good sign and indicates success in your plans. Relatives having an abundance of everything: Approaching money. 353

3 Abuse—To dream that someone is abusing you is a bad sign, but it applies to your business affairs only. To dream that you are abusing others foretells success after hard work. 831

2 Abyss—To dream of any hollow space is a sign of difficulties ahead; it is an obstacle dream. If you escape from the abyss, you will overcome your troubles; but if you fall therein, then be careful in your business affairs. Do not lend money, for it will not be returned to you. 192

7 Academy—To dream that you are master or mistress of an academy indicates that you will be reduced in your circumstances; if you are single, that your intended marriage will be characterized by adversity. 243

3 Accept—To dream that you have been accepted by your lover or, if you are a woman, that your lover has proposed to you and that you have accepted him, is generally considered a dream of contrary meaning. It is

a warning that your love affair will not prosper or at least that it will be a long time coming right. In some localities, however, it is looked upon as a fortunate omen. 687

5 Accident—This dream depends entirely upon the surroundings. If the accident occurs at sea, it means disappointment in your love affairs. But if it happens on land, it concerns your personal and business ventures. Being in an accident: Your life is threatened. An accident in an automobile: Approaching money. 329

6 Accounts—To dream that you are engaged in adding up accounts or checking business figures is a warning to you to be careful or you will lose money by giving credit too freely. 312

7 Accuse—Obviously, there is not much difference between this and abuse, except that the nature of the trouble is more clearly defined. It is a sign of approaching trouble in business, but in this case, if you can prove your innocence, it shows that you will overcome your difficulties. Vague abuse will show undefined troubles or worries, a definite accusation, more serious trouble. 457

8 Ache—This depends entirely upon the circumstances, but it is usually found to be a case of contrary meaning. If it is a trivial ache, it is probably due to some physical cause and is a sign of ill health. But if the pain is severe and obviously imaginary, it denotes some important event that will prove to be beneficial to you. To the business man it foretells good trade and a fortunate season's business. To the lover it indicates a favorable time for him to push his suit. To the farmer it promises a good and profitable harvest, with high prices. To the sailor it shows a successful voyage. 359

8 Acid—to dream of handling acids foretells danger concerning a promise. Fulfill your own promises and do not trust blindly in those of others. Others handling acid: death of an enemy. 953

4 Acorn—As a rule, any indication of Nature's good will is a favorable sign. To the lover it is a sign of future happiness; to those in difficulties, a proof of speedy relief. If you gather the acorns in your dream, it is

supposed to indicate a legacy or some good fortune from outside your own life. 652

1 Acquaintance—To dream of some person whom you know is a good sign, but it depends upon the degree of friendship and also upon what happens in your dream. If you quarrel it is a bad sign and often applies to the health of the dreamer. Making new acquaintances: A change in life will soon come. 739

7 Acquitted—To dream of being accused before a court and acquitted foretells prosperity to yourself and failure to your enemies. Others being acquitted will have prosperous business. 124

6 Acrobat—To watch other people performing clever gymnastic feats is a dream of contrary meaning; be careful, or an accident will befall you. Do not take long journeys for seven days after such a dream. If the acrobat in your dream has an accident or is unable to perform the attempted feat, then you will escape the full results of the peril that is hanging over you. 258

9 Acting—To dream that you are acting or taking part in some entertainment is a warning that some slight difficulty will delay the consummation of your plans. Persevere, however, for all will come right. Others acting: Will take a short trip. 216

3 Actor or Actress—To dream that you meet an actor or actress is an indication of trouble of a domestic character. Keep your temper and do not allow yourself to be disturbed if anything goes wrong in the home. A comedian actor or actress: Good success in present business. A tragic actor or actress: Unhappiness. 498

6 Adam—It is claimed to be a fortunate omen if you dream of Adam and Eve and if you see either of our first parents. If you speak to them or if they speak to you, it indicates some delay in the realization of your wishes, but you must be patient. To see both Adam and Eve at once is the most fortunate dream you can have. 384

7 Address—If you dream of writing an address, be careful of your financial affairs and do not enter into risky speculations. Others writing an address: Misfortune in business. 628

4 Adieu—To dream that you are saying good-bye to anyone is an indication of misfortune due to ill health. Take no risks, such as chills. Others bidding adieu to you: Will take a tedious journey. 382

4 Admiral—To dream of a naval officer of high rank foretells events of importance to yourself. Being an admiral: Danger in love matters. Being the wife of an admiral: Insurmountable obstacles confront you. 193

5 Admire—If you dream that you yourself are admired, it indicates useful friendships with people whom you like. It is, in that sense, a dream of contrary meaning. If, however, you find yourself admiring some other person, it shows the friendly feeling of some other person for you, but he may not be the person about whom you are dreaming. This point should be borne in mind, as it is very apt to mislead. 590

3 Adopted or Adoption—This is a dream of contrary meaning. If you dream that you have been adopted by someone or that you have adopted some child, it shows that some relative or close friend will appeal to you for help in some crisis. 471

7 Adornment—To dream that you have received a present of some article of clothing such as a frock or a hat is a dream of contrary meaning. Expect some misfortune shortly. The more elaborate or costly the gift, the greater the coming trouble. But if, in your dream, you refuse the present, then you will overcome your trouble. If you accept but do not actually wear the gift, then expect difficulties that will require great care and patience on your part. 853

4 Adrift—To dream that you are adrift in a boat is a warning of difficulty ahead; it is an obstacle dream. If you reach land safely, you will overcome your troubles, but if you fall out of the boat or if the boat should be upset by rough waves, then expect very serious difficulties. Even then you may swim to land or be rescued, which would indicate ultimate success. 292

7 Adultery—To dream of temptation to crime means a virtuous life and success to your plans; to dream of guilt forebodes failure. Committing adultery: Your morals are excellent. 862

3 Advancement—This is a most favorable sign and indicates success in some important undertaking. You may be in some employment and advanced; your success is certain. This dream often occurs in connection with legal matters. But if you dream of a lawsuit, you will lose. 174

3 Adventures—To meet with exciting adventures in a dream predicts a surprising alteration in your fortune. Going on an adventure with a man: New interest and surroundings. Going on an adventure with a woman: Someone is watching you. 507

5 Adversity—This omen has much the same meaning as adversary; it is a favorable dream and indicates prosperity. Fight with an adversary: Doomed for disappointment. Having adversity in business: Will realize high ambition. Having an adversity in love: Be on guard against spiteful gossip. 158

2 Advertisement—To dream that you are advertising in the papers is a sign of difficulties ahead of you. It is a good sign, on the other hand, to read an advertisement inserted by someone else. 893

8 Advice—An indication of useful friendships whether you are being advised or are giving advice to some other person. In this case the dream person concerned is seldom the same as the actual friend; you must seek elsewhere for the real name. 719

6 Airplane—A sign that money is coming to you but that your methods may not be above suspicion. Study your plans carefully. 312

7 Affection—To dream that there is great affection shown between you and some other person is a dream of contrary meaning. It shows that you are not quite straight in some of your plans. Affection between two loved ones: Inheritance. Having the affection of children: Will receive unexpected money. 583

5 Affliction—A dream of contrary meaning. The greater your trouble and difficulty in your dream, the more certain is your success in life. 581

1 Affluence—The greater your appearance of show and wealth in a dream, the heavier will be your loss in business, for this is an omen of contrary meaning.

Others having an affluence of property and everything: avoid rivals. 163

8 Affront—To dream that you feel offended by the conduct of some person is a dream of contrary meaning, unless you quarrel violently and part in anger. To dream that you annoy someone else is a sign of trouble in the near future. 062

1 Afloat—On smooth water a happy destiny is in view; on rough sea, trouble nets of your own making. Seeing someone afloat: Will have troubles caused by others. 613

3 Afraid—Another dream of contrary meaning, since it shows that you realize your difficulties and are likely to overcome them. To the timid lover it foretells success. 786

2 Africa—An unexpected advancement in your fortune will soon take place. Taking a trip to Africa alone: Will make new friends. 183

9 Afternoon—A fine afternoon warns the dreamer to act cautiously in personal affairs. Fortune favors you if you beware of knavery from those around you. 432

4 Age—To worry about your own age when dreaming is a bad sign, and indicates an approaching illness. In a sense it can be looked upon as resulting from physical causes rather than as a dream warning. The more you worry, the more serious that coming illness will be. 238

8 Agony—Authorities differ over this dream, and it might be wise to treat it as an obstacle dream. Some people claim that to feel pain in your dream is a very fortunate sign for business affairs. Others say that it shows domestic troubles. Sometimes both versions might prove true, for example if a married man or an affianced lover gave much too much time to business and neglected his wife and family. 719

9 Agree—This dream is always held to be a warning of some flaw in your plans, some oversight that will upset your calculations and hopes. If you do not actually sign the agreement but only read it, you will get through all right. Canceling an agreement: Will have uncertain profits. 216

1 Air—A dream about the open air depends entirely upon

the circumstances. If the air is clear and the sky blue, then it indicates success. But if the air is misty or foggy or if there are clouds about, then trouble is foretold. You should postpone or reconsider any proposed change. 901

8 Airship—A sign of money making, but watch your speculations or you may be caught and lose instead of gaining. Being in an airship with loved ones: Will be guilty of foolish actions. Being in an airship disaster but not killed: Financial gains. 539

2 Aisle—The inside of a church, when forming part of a dream, is considered unfortunate. 398

5 Alligator or Crocodile—To dream of any unusual animal denotes an enemy, and you should be cautious in speculations or in making new business ventures. 761

5 Almonds—This is one of the unreliable omens, since it is looked upon as favorable in the East, whereas in the West the authorities differ. If you are eating an almond and enjoying it, you can look upon it as a good sign, but if the nuts are bitter to the taste, then you should be careful, for your ventures are liable to fail. Should you dream of an almond tree and not of the fruit, it is a good sign, both in your home and in your business. 437

9 Alms—This dream depends upon the circumstances. If, in your dream, someone begs and you refuse him, it is a sign of misfortune for you; but if you give and give freely, then it is a sign of great happiness, either to yourself or to some intimate friend. 378

9 Almanac—To dream you are reading one: A light quarrel with someone dear to you. 036

3 Amber—To see amber is a warning against pride, which may be a barrier between you and someone you love. 706

9 Ambulance—This means speedy realization of your desire. 297

6 Alter—To dream you are inside a church is not considered fortunate; it does not carry the same fortunate meaning as a view of the outside of the sacred building. 159

5 America—A good fortune is coming to you through your own efforts. 293

8 Ammonia—Danger through illness or accidents; take no risks for a time. Using ammonia: Quarrels with a friend. 602

3 Amorous—If you dream you are of an amorous disposition, it is a sign that you are likely to be a victim of scandal. Others being amorous toward you: Be careful in love affairs. Young girls being amorous: Will make a wrong marriage. 723

9 Amulet—To dream you are wearing one means that you have an important decision to make shortly. Think well before choosing. Receiving the gift of an amulet: Will experience the loss of a lover. 198

6 Ancestors—To dream of your ancestors preceding your father or mother is considered a warning of illness. Grandparents: Speedy recovery from an illness. 483

5 Anchor—If seen clearly, this is a fortunate sight, but the whole of the anchor should be visible to the dreamer. If it is actually in the water, it indicates disappointment. Raising an anchor from the water: Will have good earnings. 356

4 Angels—Another fortunate dream, but it refers to love affairs, partnerships, and friendships. Several angels: Will receive an inheritance. An angel being close to you: will enjoy peace and well-being. An angel coming into your home: Prosperity. 832

9 Anger—A dream of contrary meaning. If you are angry in your dream with some person whom you know, it shows that you will benefit in some manner through that person. If it is a stranger, then some unexpected good news will reach you. Becoming angry with strangers: Will receive unexpected good news. Becoming angry with children: Will get invitation from a prominent person. 216

5 Angling—As with an anchor when seen in the water, this dream indicates disappointment in some cherished project. Angling and catching fish: Good news will follow. Angling but not catching fish: Evil will come to you. 464

6 Animals—To see wild animals in a dream is generally a

dream of contrary meaning; but there are a few special animals, such as the lion, the leopard, and the tiger, which carry distinct meanings. Any very unusual creature such as a crocodile is a bad sign. Domestic animals have separate meanings, and the cat and dog are not considered good dream omens. Cows and bulls depend upon their attitudes: if they are peaceful, they are a good omen; but if they attack you, then expect difficulties in your business ventures. 258

6 Ankle—An injury to your foot or ankle in a dream is a fortunate omen, but you will have to face difficulties for some time first. A woman showing her ankles: Realization of her desires. Having beautiful ankles: Will have plenty of money in old age. 519

6 Annoy—To dream that you are annoyed about something is a dream of contrary meaning. Good fortune awaits your plans. 348

7 Anthem—Church music is naturally associated with the interior of the building and is not therefore very favorable. But the combination of pleasant musical sounds with an unfavorable omen will indicate illness in your family circle. Singing the national anthem: Temptation will come to you. Hearing an anthem at an official ceremony: Will receive good news. 176

9 Ants—To dream of these industrious little creatures shows business activity, but in some fresh district or surroundings. Having ants in the home: Illness within the family. Ants on food: Happiness is assured. 657

7 Antelope—To dream you see one means that someone dear to you has placed faith and affection upon you. 421

4 Anvil—This is generally considered to be a good omen, but there should not be much noise connected with the dream. Other people using an anvil: Good times ahead. 931

8 Anxiety—A dream of contrary meaning which shows that some worry will be relieved very shortly. Having anxiety over others or your children: Will have good health. Having anxiety about your mate: Troubles are ahead. 314

4 Ape—As in the case of all unusual animals seen in dreams, this is a warning of coming trouble. 193

1 Apology—A change of companionship, possibly a return to a former friendship. Receiving an apology: Happiness in love. Apologizing to friends: Return of a former friend. 793

6 Apparel—It is a dream of contrary meaning to be concerned about your clothes. The newer and more up-to-date your attire, the greater the trouble coming across your path. To see yourself in rags is therefore a very fortunate sign. But the true meaning of a dream concerning clothes often depends upon the color, which you should consult. If you see yourself or other people in a dream without clothes, it is a sign of some unexpected good fortune. 861

2 Apparition—No harm is foretold by a dream of ghosts or other apparations, unless their presence or sudden appearance frightens you or makes you ill. In that case, you must expect financial difficulties or perhaps ill health. 254

8 Appetite—It is not a good sign when you appear to be hungry in your dream; it is Nature's warning of some health trouble. Feasting is also a bad sign but refers to money matters. 872

1 Applause—To dream that you receive the open approval of your friends and neighbors is an omen of contrary meaning. Beware of family quarrels or separation from some friend due to ill feeling. Giving applause: Are unselfish and envious of others. 289

6 Apples—Fruit is generally a good omen in a dream, as with all products of Nature; but if you eat the fruit you will yourself be responsible for some misfortune. To dream of an apple tree is also fortunate. Eating sweet apples means a good and favorable event. 123

1 Apricot—to dream of this popular fruit is a sign of coming prosperity, both in business and in love affairs. 163

1 Apron—It is an omen of contrary meaning when you dream of any mishap to your clothes. If you tear your apron, it means some small benefit, as the garment is not an important one. 982

5 April Fool—To dream that you are made one means that you will soon be given power over another. Be careful to use it well. Fooling others on April Fool's Day: Means a loss of a friend. Fooling childrer. on April Fool's Day: Happiness in the family. Being born in April: Will be happy in love affairs. 131

1 Aquamarine—To dream of this jewel assures you of the affection of a very youthful relative or friend. Buying an aquamarine stone: Happiness is assured. Losing an aquamarine stone: Disappointment in love matters. 208

4 Arab—To dream of a foreign person concerns your love affairs or some important transaction with someone quite outside your family and usual business circle. Many Arabs: Will have a love affair. Going with an Arab: Will have an important and good transaction. 283

3 Arch—It is not a good sign to dream of passing under an arch, since it foretells interference in your love affairs. It is, in reality, a mild form of obstacle dream that concerns your personal affairs, rather than financial. 381

8 Archer—To the single, a speedy engagement; if already married, be true. Danger is near you. 503

3 Arena—A warning of danger. Avoid crowds. If you are not alone in your dream, the danger is lessened. Fighting in an arena: Will realize high ambitions. 381

5 Arm—To dream of an accident to your arm is a sign of ill health in the family circle. To lose one arm generally foretells death or a long and serious illness. To dream of a still arm is usually a sign of some money loss due to ill health. Having arms covered with hairs: Will be very rich. Having an arm cut off: Loss of a relative. Having an accident with the arms: Ill health within the family. 410

3 Army—An obstacle dream, but it only foretells difficulty or a journey followed by a successful issue of your venture. If the men are fighting, it becomes a serious matter. Several armies of different countries: Fortune and joy. 696

8 Armchair—Hasty news. 215

9 Arrest—A sudden and unexpected success will come to

you, but you must choose your friends carefully. Being arrested: Will have misery followed by joy. Others being arrested: Will receive an unexpected gift. 369

4 Arson—Not a fortunate dream. News of accidents at sea, possibly to yourself. 427

2 Arrow—To dream that you have been struck by an arrow is a sign of misfortune from some unexpected source. Some person who appears to be friendly is really working against your interests. Throwing an arrow: Unhappiness. Having many arrows: Are surrounded by enemies. A broken arrow: Failure in business. 983.

6 Artist—To dream that you are acting as model for your portrait is a warning of treachery on the part of some acquaintance. If, however, you dream that you are painting a portrait of someone, then your plans should be revised carefully, for you will risk failure by striving to take unfair advantage. 789

9 Artichoke—Vexatious troubles, which, however, you will surmount. Eating artichokes: Dissension within the family. 306

1 Ascent—Any form of progress upward is a sign of success, and if you appear to reach the top of a hill, it shows that you will have great success. 091

7 Ashes—Something lost through your own carelessness. Having ashes in own fireplace: Loss of money. Cremated ashes: Will live a long life. 538

4 Asparagus—Another valuable gift from Mother Nature, a favorable sign. Push on with your plans, and you will be successful. Raw asparagus: Success in own enterprises. Cooking asparagus: Own plans will be successful. 391

3 Assault—False information will be given to you. Be on your guard and prove the facts. Assaulting others: Monetary gain. 858

8 Asthma—A warning to you that some favorite scheme will not prove as profitable as you expect. Revise your plans and avoid all speculation or risk. Having asthma: Will recover soon by change of residence to another state. 629

1 Asters—A warning to you that some favorite scheme

will not prove profitable, as you expect. Revise your plans and avoid all speculation or risk. Picking asters: Will receive a letter with good news. Receiving a gift of asters: Abundance. 802

1 Asylum—This suggestive omen depends for its correct interpretation upon the circumstances of the dream. If you remain outside the building, you should take advantage of every chance you have to help someone in trouble, when you may expect good fortune for yourself. But if you find yourself inside, then look out for trouble of a serious nature. Avoiding being put into an asylum: Take care of your health. A young girl dreaming of an asylum: Will marry soon. 613

8 Athlete—Not a good dream to any but the very strong; beware of overstrain. Being in the company of an athlete: Avoid rivals. 341

9 Atlas—To dream that you are consulting a map or an atlas is considered a sign of business ventures at a distance; in the case of the atlas, it probably indicates a visit abroad. 153

8 Attic—A premonition of an engagement to the single. If married, avoid flirtation. The attic of others' homes: Are confronted with insurmountable obstacles. 269

1 Attorney—Business worries are in front of you. Be careful of your plans and avoid all speculation in stocks and shares. Being in court with an attorney: Avoid speculation in stocks. Dealing with an opposing attorney: Big catastrophe ahead. Having conferences with several attorneys: Troubles ahead. 901

2 Auction—An unfavorable sign, somewhat similar in meaning to attorney or lawyer. Be careful, or some acquaintance will take advantage of you. 672

7 Audience—To dream of having an audience with a prominent person: Will have good earnings. Having an audience with a priest: Will soon be in trouble. To dream of an audience in general: Social pleasures and distinctions to come. 431

8 August—To dream of summer in winter time foretells unexpected news. Being born in August: All will go well in life. Children being born in August: Big fortune. 152

2 Aunt—To dream of close relatives is a fortunate sign

and shows success in money matters. Being an aunt: A successful matrimony is being planned. Visiting with an Aunt: Will receive a legacy. 452

2 Author—To dream of a great author brings unexpected pleasures to the single. To the married: Good fortune in the family. Dealing with an author: Good times are coming. 389

8 Autumn—There are unfortunate and hostile influences around you. Walk warily, and you may avoid them. Autumn in the spring: Unfriendly influences are nearby. Autumn in winter: Good fortune is coming. 458

4 Avalanche—Good fortune of an astonishing nature will soon befall you. Being buried under an avalanche of snow: Good profit. Others being buried under an avalanche: Change of surroundings. 364

1 Awaken—It is a good omen if you awaken some person in the course of your dream, and it will go far to soften any unfavorable omen that may be present. This is especially the case if the sleeper is in bed, as the color white helps good fortune and serves to confirm the fortunate issue of events. Being awakened: Be on guard against coming troubles. 316

B

3 Baby—It is a curious fact that it is fortunate to see children in a dream if they are old enough to be independent but that a helpless baby is a bad sign. It usually shows some disappointment in love, or if the baby is unwell, a serious illness, or even a death, in the family. A married pregnant woman dreaming of a baby: Big success in love. A single woman dreaming of having a baby: Sorrow. A baby sucking milk from mother's breast: Success in everything. A baby taking its first steps: Difficulties in business. A baby being sick: Serious illness within the family. 183

1 Bachelor—If the man is young it is a good sign, but if he is old the dream foreshadows loneliness or the loss of a friend. Being a bachelor: A change in life will soon come. Becoming a bachelor after an annulled marriage: Financial gains. A bachelor getting married: Will find a rich woman to marry. 109

8 Back—If in your dreams some person turns his or her back upon you, it shows opposition and difficulty, though this may not be very serious or persistent. If the person turns around and faces you, it is a sign that all will come well before long. To dream of your own back is a favorable sign, though this is not met so often as dreams of your arms, legs, or body. 728

6 Back Door—To dream that you are making use of the back door instead of the front entrance of your house is a warning of some coming change in your fortune. This may be for good or for evil, according to other circumstances. Friends entering the back door: Caution must be used in business ventures. Robbers breaking down the back door: Approaching money. 060

8 Bacon—An unfortunate omen whatever else happens in the dream, whether you are eating it or merely buying it. Generally, it concerns the health. 278

4 Backgammon—To dream of taking part in it: Test of your character is soon to be made. 427

1 Badge—You are under observation and will shortly be promoted. A badge on others: Warning of troubles. Pinning a badge on a policeman: Family reunion. 352

1 Badger—A typical dream showing that hard work is in front of you. Killing a badger: Will fall in love. Catching a badger: Good luck attends you. 415

1 Bag—A sign of better times, especially if a heavy one. Carrying only one bag: Will incur plenty of debts. Carrying several bags: Treachery from a friend. Bags being in a car: Unexpected money will arrive. 820

5 Bagpipes—As with the most unusual things when seen in a dream, this musical instrument is not a favorable sign, and in particular it indicates matrimonial worry and difficulty. 914

9 Bailiff—To dream that you have trouble with this officer of the court is an omen of contrary meaning. Some

unexpected legacy will come your way before long. 126

5 Bait—Do not trust blindly in those who seek to please you. Putting bait on a fishhook: Will have a great joy. Others attempting to please by baiting you: Don't trust them blindly. 536

8 Baking and Baker—To dream of some person baking is a good sign in every way; you will not have to wait long for some favorable turn of events. But if you yourself are baking, it indicates the serious illness of some one dear to you, either a member of your family or your betrothed, if you happen to be engaged. 296

5 Balcony—A dream of a balcony should be classed among the obstacle omens, though the difficulty to be faced will not be a serious one. If you leave the balcony, all will be well. It is slightly more serious if you are seated than if you are standing, as your quick recovery is delayed. 824

1 Bald—A dream concerning your health. The less hair you appear to have, the more serious will be the coming illness. In the case of a woman, it indicates money troubles or some difficult love affair. 316

2 Bale—Good fortune, more or less, according to whether it is cotton or wool. Owning bales of wool: Will have many troubles. Buying bales of cotton: Will overcome enemies. 641

5 Ballad—To hear one: Beware of false judgements. To sing one: Someone you care for thinks you unkind. 968

9 Ball—This dream depends upon the circumstances. If you see yourself among the dancers, some favorable news will reach you. But to watch other people dancing and enjoying themselves shows that some cherished wish will fail to realize. Attending a masquerade ball: Beware of a trap. Playing ball games: Will have many good friends. Playing with a billiard ball: Good news. Football: Uneasiness. Tennis or rubber balls: Certain birth of a child. 729

7 Ballet—To dream of a stage Ballet or other professional dancing is a warning concerning your health. Take no risks if the weather is wet or stormy. 142

8 Balloon—Another unusual omen, and therefore an unfavorable sign for the dreamer. Ascending in a balloon:

Will have misfortune during a journey. Descending in a balloon: Will make unfavorable money ventures. 458

8 Ballot—A difference in position and surroundings, possibly for the better. Casting a ballot: Will have a change of companionship. 214

6 Banana—A fortunate omen, though the dream may concern some small affair only. Eating bananas: Will be imposed upon to fulfill some duty. 429

7 Bandage—Fresh influences will surround you. Wearing a bandage: Expect good news. Putting bandages on others: Abundant means. Others wearing bandages: Will receive bad news. 295

5 Banishment—If in your dream you are forced to leave your abode, it is a fortunate sign. The more serious the disturbance appears to be, the greater your future prosperity. Other people being banished: Will soon receive plenty of money. 581

1 Bank or Banking—To dream that you have dealings with a bank is a bad sign. It indicates some sudden loss of money. Owning a bank: Friends are making fun of you. Receiving money from a bank: Bankruptcy is near. 316

3 Bankruptcy—To dream that you have lost money and are now bankrupt should be taken as a warning. Some plan is not very creditable to you and should be abandoned at once, as trouble will follow. Be cautious in your transactions and seek the advice of friends older than yourself. 651

9 Banner or Flag—A good omen, but it concerns your personal position rather than your business affairs. A red banner: Will receive help from friends abroad. A banner on a house: Failure of enemies. Receiving a banner: A promised gift will not be given. 306

8 Banquet—This is usually considered a fortunate omen if the dreamer is young, but not if he or she is old. Being in attendance at a banquet: Pleasures will be costly. Attending a political banquet: Disappointments. 926

8 Baptism—This foretells disappointment through unforeseen circumstances. 314

3 Bar—Your friends esteem you more highly than you know. Having a drink alone in a bar: A false friend is

nearby. Drinking with company in a bar: Must control passions. Single woman drinking in a bar: Financial gains. 219

1 Barber—To dream that you are in a barber's shop foretells some difficulty in your business affairs. Being a barber: Will have big success. Having a shave at the barber's: Loss of money. 856

7 Bargain—A warning to be steadfast and trust your own opinions. Being cheated out of a bargain: Own home will be robbed. Having made a good bargain: Advancement within position. 781

6 Barge—You are about to travel some distance. A loaded barge: Triumph over enemies. An empty barge: Troubles will arise from prying into the affairs of others. 852

8 Bare Feet—It is considered fortunate to dream that you are naked. If only the feet are bare, then you may expect some trouble or difficulty, but by perseverance and hard work you will prove successful. Children going barefooted: Shame and sorrow. Feet and legs to knees being bare: Dishonor in social life. 512

9 Barley—A good omen, as with most things connected with nature. 036

3 Barmaid—To dream of a barmaid is a sign of difficulty probably due to your own carelessness. Being a barmaid: Difficulties due to own carelessness, will improve slowly. Dating a barmaid: Beware of jealous friends. Being married to a barmaid:Will soon experience troubles. 543

8 Barn—This is a favorable dream if the barn is full or nearly so; but it is unfortunate to see an empty Barn with open doors. Being in a barn: Will win a lawsuit. Handling grain in a barn: Will live a happy life. 953

1 Barracks—Your difficulties will soon be lessened. Many soldiers living in barracks: Warning of troubles ahead. 721

2 Barrel—An upright and full barrel: Prosperity. Rolling and empty barrel: Hard times to come. An upright and full barrel of wine: Better times ahead. Owning a barrel: Will receive an unexpected gift. 245

6 Bashful—A happy time at large party. Having bashful

children: Joy. Having bashful friends: Warning of troubles ahead. 312

9 Basin—To dream of eating or drinking from a basin is an unnatural dream. If you are in love, you must expect difficulties and may not marry the first object of your affections. Using a full basin of water: Will have plenty money. An empty basin: Will have or incur many debts. 135

4 Basket—An obstacle dream, since it is so easy to upset the contents. Be careful of your business ventures, or you will lose money. 247

4 Bat—Treachery is clearly shown when you dream about these curious nocturnal creatures. Beware of discussing your plans. Don't lend money, and avoid all speculation. 634

7 Bathing—The meaning of this dream depends upon what is happening. If it is in the open and the water is clear, then it shows success in business. But if the water is dirty, muddy, or choked with weeds, then you may expect difficulty and trouble in your work or profession. If you yourself are taking a bath indoors, it is not a good sign. If the water is cold, it shows sorrow; if hot, a separation from a friend or loved one, perhaps a quarrel if steam is seen. To see yourself naked is a good sign in itself, but you must not be in water. 925

6 Battle—This is another unusual event and foretells trouble, a serious quarrel with neighbors or a lover. But if you are on the winning side, whether fighting alone or with others, then things will come right in the end. A naval battle: Will be triumphant. A battle on land: Will live a long life. A battle with fire: Double cross in love affairs. 195

4 Bayonet—A quarrel soon to be made up. Carrying a bayonet: Success in own enterprise. Others holding a bayonet: Will be under the power of enemies. A soldier having a bayonet: Worries will be smoothed away. 109

4 Bazaar—To dream that you are assisting at a bazaar, or any other cause devoted to charity, is a fortunate omen for your love affairs. Buying things at a charity: Will

realize high ambitions. People selling things at a charity: will receive a proposal. 175

5 Beans—Difficulties lie ahead of you, so be careful. 374

8 Bear—An indication of the difficulties ahead of you but that they are within your power if you work earnestly. If you succeed in killing the bear or in driving it away, you may expect success eventually. A bear dancing: Will be tempted into speculation. A bear in a cage: Success in the future. Being attacked by a bear: Will be persecuted. Killing a bear: Will have victories over enemies. 143

3 Beard—If you see in your dream some person with a full beard, you may expect some unexpected success; the fuller the beard, the better for the dreamer. A married woman dreaming of a man with a beard: Will soon leave her husband. A pregnant woman dreaming of a man with a beard: Will give birth to a son. A white beard: Very big prosperity. 732

3 Beasts—Most animals represent difficulties and trouble when seen in a dream, unless in some manner you drive them away. Even our domestic pets, cats and dogs, are not fortunate, but birds, as a rule, are a good omen. Beasts fighting: Sickness. Being pursued by a beast: Vexation caused by enemies. 759

4 Beacon—Avoid misunderstandings, but should you unavoidably quarrel, take the first step toward reconciliation, or you will regret it. 382

4 Beads—False friends or dissatisfaction. 526

3 Beam—If of wood, a burden to be borne; if of light, a well-merited reward. 462

4 Beating—If a married man dreams he is beating his wife, it is a very fortunate sign and denotes married happiness and a comfortable home. But for lovers, it is considered a bad dream. It is also fortunate if a man dreams that he is beating some woman who is not his wife. In the same way, if a father or mother dreams that he is punishing one of his own children, it is a fortunate sign; but it is not if the child is a stranger. 193

2 Beauty—A dream of contrary meaning. If you see

yourself as beautiful, it indicates an illness; if some other person, then he will be the invalid. 524

2 Bed—To dream that you are in a strange bed shows some unexpected good turn in your business affairs. If you are in your own bed, it concerns your love affairs. To dream of making a bed is a sign of a change of residence. To sit on a bed is considered a sign of an early marriage. Having clean white sheets on a bed: Will have cause to worry. An empty bed: Death of a friend. Being in a strange bed: Good turn of events in own affairs. A stranger being in your bed: Matrimonial unfaithfulness. 821

9 Bedroom—If the bedroom in your dream is more sumptuous than your own, it shows a change in your circumstances that will eventually prove favorable for you. But you must be prepared for some delay in plans if your dream concerns the earlier hours of the night, whereas the change will come soon if your dream is of the dawn or of the early morning hours. 396

9 Beef—To dream that you are eating beef or mutton, shows that you will remain comfortably well off but never be rich. If you appear to have plenty of food but are unable to eat it, then you will have to spend time to appeal to others to help you. Purchasing beef to cook: Winnings at gambling. Eating raw beef: Long-lasting happiness. 729

3 Beer—If you dream that you are drinking beer or ale, it is a sign of some loss of money in connection with speculation. If you only see the ale or beer or if other people are drinking it, but not yourself, the loss will be small. For all that, you should be careful in betting or speculation. 165

4 Bees—This is a good omen unless they sting you in your dream. They concern business matters, however, not love or friendship. Moving bees in swarms: Will have a fire in your own house. Bees coming into your house: Will be damaged by enemies. Bees flying around their beehive: Will have productive business. Killing bees: Will have a big loss and ruin. 328

5 Beetles—To dream of these unpleasant little creatures is a sign of quarreling with your friends or some difficulty

in your affairs due to malice. If you kill the insects, you will put matters right quickly. 923

5 Beets—Some interference with your love affairs is indicated when you dream of beets, but all will go well if you eat them. Buying beets: Will receive an expensive gift. 753

4 Beggar—A sign that you will receive unexpected help, a dream of contrary meaning. Aged beggars: Exercise economy. Many beggars: Will have fortune and happiness. A crippled beggar: Disputes within the family. Giving money to a beggar: Love will be reciprocated. A beggar coming into the house: Troubles and worries will come. 319

9 Belle of the Ball—To dream that you are dancing with the prettiest woman in the room is an omen of contrary meaning. You may expect trouble in your family affairs or from some woman acquaintance. If a woman dreams that she is the belle of the ball, it has a similar meaning, provided she is dancing. But if she finds herself neglected, then the trouble will be short lived, and all will end happily. 828

5 Bells—To dream that you hear the ringing of bells is a sign of coming news, but it may not be favorable. Hearing church bells ringing: Be on guard against enemies. 356

3 Belt—To dream of putting one on is a good omen of a happy future. An old belt: Will have to work harder: A new belt: Honor. A blue belt: Happiness. A black belt: Death. A brown belt: Illness. A green belt: Good wishes. A gold belt: Big earnings. A silver belt: Profit. A yellow belt: Treason. 904

5 Bench—An unfortunate dream. Attend carefully to work, or you may lose it. Sitting on a bench: Will have a comfortable life. Children sitting on a park bench: Good times are coming. 941

8 Bequest—To dream that you are bequeathing money or property to other people is an omen of contrary meaning. You will receive money from an unexpected source. Canceling a bequest: Fights within the family. 602

2 Bereavement—News of a friend's marriage soon to take

place. Suffering bereavement: Someone else will benefit from your actions. 524

4 Berries—Social activities of a happy nature. If you dream you are picking many blackberries, financial gains. Eating berries: Abundant gains. Buying berries: Important and very beneficial events to come. 814

1 Best Man—To dream you are acting as best man denotes the failure of a plan of yours through a false friend. A woman dreaming of a best man: Confidence and security. 172

9 Bet—To dream that you are betting is a warning not to allow other people's opinions to interfere with you. Winning a bet: Will have a change for the better. Losing a bet: An enemy is seeking your ruin. 315

7 Betrothed—It is not a favorable sign to dream that you have just become engaged to be married. Expect trouble among your family circle or with your lover, if you are really engaged. Relatives becoming betrothed: Will have family arguments. Friends becoming betrothed: Will realize high ambitions. 628

3 Bible—Reading a bible, family troubles will come soon. Taking a Bible to church: Happiness. Believing in the Bible: With perseverance, will overcome enemies. Children reading the Bible: Joy without profit. 642

5 Bicycle—To dream that you are riding one means that you will have to make a decision. Think well, and then act as you think best. Selling a bicycle: Good wishes. Buying a bicycle for children: Advancement in own affairs. 365

7 Bier—If you are lying upon it, it signifies a triumphant ending to your hopes. Relatives lying upon it: Will receive a legacy. A friend lying in a bier: Advancement in own position. 214

3 Bigamy—Unfortunately, it is considered a fortunate omen to commit bigamy in your dreams. You are assured of a happy and prosperous married life. 723

5 Billiards—Another dream of unusual occurrence, unless you play regularly, when the omen loses all significance. It indicates some difficulty; if you are in love or engaged, it means that you will be opposed by your betrothed's family. Married people playing billiards: Love of mate

sincere. Single people playing billiards: Will soon be married. 239

9 Bills—To dream that you are paying them denotes speedy financial gains; that they are unpaid signifies evil speaking. Being solicited to pay bills: Are disliked by your boss. 279

7 Birds—Usually considered to be of an uncertain nature. If you are poor and struggling, birds indicate a coming improvement in your circumstances. But if you are wealthy, you may expect a reverse. It is a good sign if the birds show beautiful plumage and if the birds are singing, it is always fortunate. 187

8 Bird's Egg or Nest—If you see the eggs in the nest, it is a sign of money coming to you; but if the young are visible, it is not a good sign. People destroying bird's eggs: Business loss. Animals eating bird's eggs: Will soon have a change in surroundings. 134

3 Birth—It is a good sign when a woman who is married dreams of giving birth to a child, but for a single woman it foretells trouble in the near future. Divorced woman giving birth to a child: Will inherit a large legacy. Widow giving birth to a child: Will be guilty of foolish actions. Assisting with the birth of a child: Joy and prosperity. Assisting with the birth of a cat or other animals: Death of an enemy. Twins being born: Will have good luck in affairs. 264

6 Birthday—To dream that it is your own birthday is a fortunate sign for money matters or business affairs. To dream that it is the birthday of a friend or relative is a sign that they will benefit shortly, probably in connection with yourself. Sweetheart's birthday: Abundance of money soon coming. Wife's birthday: Good times coming. Husband's birthday: Abundant means. Children's birthday: Approaching money. 231

3 Biscuits—A prosperous journey; sometimes a warning of coming ill health. Giving biscuits away: Are prone to enjoy pleasures too much. 057

6 Bishop or Clergyman—An omen of ill health or some serious disappointments. Talking to a bishop: Business will be satisfactory. 168

9 Bite—To dream that some animal has bitten you is a

sign of trouble over your love affairs. Beware of quarrels. Biting someone else: Will be embarrassed. Biting the tongue: Loss of consideration by other people. Being bitten by a woman: A jealous person is nearby. Being bitten by a man: Beware of quarrels. 351

2 Black—This is an unfortunate color when seen in a dream unless it is in connection with a funeral, when it becomes a dream of contrary meaning. A black dress: Sadness. Purchasing black clothes: Are being deceived. 191

6 Blackberries—Unlike most nature omens, this is bad, owing to the color. Gathering blackberries: Will be unlucky. Buying blackberries: Will be wounded in an accident. Blackberries hanging on bushes: much abundance. A married woman picking blackberries: Will soon be pregnant. 942

1 Blackbird—Another omen that depends upon the color. It is unfortunate. A woman dreaming of hearing blackbirds singing: Will have two husbands. A man dreaming of hearing blackbirds singing: Will have two wives. Unmarried person hearing blackbirds singing: Will soon be engaged. 208

3 Blankets—The importance of this dream depends upon your position in life. If you dream that you are buying or receiving new blankets and you are well to do, it shows that you may expect a loss of money. If you are poor or only moderately off, then expect an improvement in your position. 219

2 Blasphemy—Foretells that a plan of yours will be achieved after great difficulties have been surmounted. Being cursed by others using the name of God: Ambitions will be realized. 416

4 Blot—To dream you make a blot on a clean sheet of paper means a strange bed and a little traveling to come. 292

4 Blunder—This is one of the dreams that go by contraries and means that you will do unexpectedly well in your next undertaking. 823

7 Bleating of Lambs—This is a very fortunate dream and indicates both prosperity in business and happiness at home, but the young lambs must be seen with their

dams, or your dream will show a disappointment at the last moment, just when you expect success. 313

1 Bleeding—An unfortunate omen whatever the details of the dream, a severe disappointment. 208

5 Blind—It does not matter whether you dream of other blind people or that you yourself are blind, it signifies treachery from someone near to you. A young person going blind: False friends are nearby. A baby being born blind: Jealousy and sorrow. Leading a blind person: Strange adventures to come. A woman becoming blind: Some person will appeal to you for help. A man becoming blind: Be cautious in business ventures. 725

8 Blindness—To dream of blind people or that you yourself lose your sight is the sign of an unfortunate love affair. They say that love is blind, and this dream supports the popular view that happiness in love affairs depends upon being blind to the faults of the loved one. 413

3 Blood—To dream of blood in any form is an omen of severe disappointment. The exact significance would depend upon the other details of the dream, but if you yourself are bleeding anywhere it generally indicates an unfortunate love affair or a quarrel with some valued friend. Blood flowing from a wound: Sickness and worry are hovering nearby. Garments stained with blood: Successful career is hampered by enemies. Blood on other people: Severe disappointment. 021

8 Blows—A dream of contrary meaning. If you receive blows in your dream, it shows a reconciliation after a quarrel or some good fortune coming to you from a friend. To give blows to other people is, however, a sign of trouble. Wind blowing: Will have a litigation. Blowing out a fire: Gossip is being spread about you. Blowing in someone's face: Will be tricked by a woman who is cheating. 413

4 Blue—If you see much of this color in your dream, it is a sign of prosperity through other people. The firm for whom you work will thrive and go ahead so that your own financial position will improve at the same time. It may show good fortune in your love affairs and a more

comfortable and happy life owing to your marriage. 526

9 Boar—To chase a wild one: Unsuccessful efforts. To be chased: Separation. Being chased by a boar: Separation from a lover. Killing a boar: Advancement in position. 612

2 Boat or Ship—If you dream that you are sailing and that the water is smooth, it indicates some fortunate business or happiness in married life. If the water is rough, then you will have to face many difficulties. If you fall into the water, then your troubles will prove too much for you. Falling from a boat: Troubles will prove to be too much to handle. A boat sinking: Termination of present love affairs. A boat moving very slowly: Must have patience in life. 389

1 Bones or Skeleton—To dream of ordinary meat bones is a sign of poverty; but if you see a human skeleton, it is a sign of property coming to you under a will. Bones of wild animals: Will have bad business transactions. A few bones of dead people: Will have many troubles. Bones of fish: Illness is near at hand. Animals gnawing on bones: Will fall into complete ruin. 927

8 Books—This is a good sign and indicates future happiness through a quiet way. Reading a book: Will lose a good friend. Reading a mystery book: Will receive a consolation from friends. Reading a religious book: Contentment. Reading schoolbooks: Prosperity. Writing books: Will waste time and money. 737

8 Bookcase—This is a dream of contrary meaning, for if your bookcase is seen almost empty in your dream, then you may expect good fortune through your own endeavors or because of your strong personality. To dream that the bookcase is full is a bad sign. It indicates slovenly, careless work, for which you will surely suffer by loss of employment or by money troubles in business. 143

8 Boots—You can rely upon the faithfulness of your servants or business employees if you dream of new and comfortable boots or shoes, but if they are old or hurt your feet, you will meet with difficulties that are your own fault. 215

1 Borrow—This is a bad dream, for it foretells domestic sorrow, not money loss. If you dream that you repay the loan or that someone repays you then you will sail into smooth waters once again. 217

1 Bosom—To dream that your bosom is inflamed or in pain is a sign of coming illness. Having a beautiful and healthy bosom: Big joy ahead. A woman having hair on her bosom: Her husband will pass away. 109

2 Bottle—This dream depends upon circumstances. If the bottle is full, it shows prosperity. If it is empty, then misfortunes are foretold. If you upset the contents, you may expect domestic worries. A bottle of wine: Will be in a bad humor. A bottle full of liquor: Will be divorced. A full bottle of perfume: Will enjoy much happiness. 128

2 Bound—To imagine yourself bound with ropes is a dream of coming obstacles. Be careful, or trouble will overtake you. Others being bound with ropes: Troubles will overtake you. Binding other people with ropes: Embarrassment and loss of money. 182

2 Bouquet—If you retain the bunch of flowers, you will be all right; but if you throw them away or drop them, it indicates a quarrel or separation from some friend. A withered bouquet: Illness and ensuing death. Preparing a bouquet: Lover is constant. Preparing a bouquet of flowers: Will be married soon. 353

8 Bowls—A fortunate dream, especially if you are taking part in the game, as this denotes further prosperity. 161

7 Bow and Arrows—If you hit the target in your dream, you can rely upon good fortune varying according to the accuracy of your aim. If you miss, then you may expect difficulties resulting from some careless or ill-advised action of your own. Being hit by bows and arrows: Beware of enemies. Having many arrows: money losses. 304

5 Box—This dream also depends upon the circumstances. If you open a box and find something inside, it is fortunate; but if the box is empty, then your plans will be upset. Tying a box: Financial losses. Robbing a strong box: Will lose entire fortune. 176

8 Boxing Match—An astonishing announcement will be

made leading to important events for you. Taking part in a boxing match: Loss of friends. Winning a bet on a boxing match: Accord among friends. Losing a bet on a boxing match: You have one loyal friend. 521

3 Bracelet—This is either a sign of money or of some love affair. Where your affections are concerned, it is a fortunate sign to possess, to wear, or to find a bracelet, expecially if it is gold. Otherwise, you will be lucky in some unexpected financial matter. If you lose or drop your bracelet, then you may expect a monetary loss or a broken love affair. Receiving a bracelet as a gift from a friend: Early and happy marriage. 489

1 Branch—Trees are fortunate, being one of nature's own blessings. 901

7 Branches—If in your dream you see a tree with many fertile branches, it is a most fortunate omen, but be careful if you see any dead or broken branches. Gathering branches together: Will have an operation. Burning branches: Will receive a legacy. Cutting branches from palm trees: Big honors. A tree with withered branches: Recovery from an illness. 421

1 Brandy—Some good news is on the way. Owning a bottle of brandy: Beware of untrue friends. Buying a bottle of brandy: Will receive unexpected good news. Offering a drink of brandy to others: Must control passions. 928

1 Bravery—This warns the dreamer to keep a cool head and act with all courage, as an emergency is at hand which will test his nerve. 352

5 Brass—Observe your associates closely and do not let a false friend make you unhappy. Having something made of brass: A friend will cause unhappiness. Buying brass: Advancement in position. 167

3 Bread—If the bread is new and pleasant to the taste, it is a sign of physical well-being, bodily comfort. But if it is stale and hard, then domestic worries of a commonplace character are indicated. To bake bread is an unfortunate omen. Stale bread: Domestic trouble. Having several loaves of bread: Honor. Buying bread: Big success. 156

1 Break—To damage anything in a dream is a very bad

sign, generally concerning health. Breaking furniture: Quarrels within the home. Breaking a drinking glass: Will have a broken leg. Breaking eyeglasses: Unexpected fortune. Breaking dishes: Failure in own affairs. Breaking bottles: Will have bad health. Breaking a bone in the body: Will receive a legacy. 874

2 Breakfast—An omen of misfortune in a dream. Be careful, or your own ill-considered actions will plunge you into trouble. Preparing a breakfast: misery and illness. Having breakfast in a coffee shop: Will have a new sweetheart. Having breakfast in the home of others: Will take a trip before long. 659

9 Breath—If you dream that you are out of breath or exhausted, that is a warning of coming trouble. 252

2 Breast—If you dream that you are resting on the breast of some person, it is a sign that you have a true and loyal friend. Having a beautiful breast: Much joy ahead. The breast of a woman: Wishes will be gratified. A breast covered with hair: Success in love. A baby sucking at the breast: Will enjoy lasting happiness. Breast being wounded by a gun: Will make plenty of money. 425

7 Breeze—To dream that you are in a strong wind presages a successful speculation. Enjoying a pleasant breeze at night: Will receive a gift from a stranger. 142

4 Briars and Brambles—If they prick you, secret enemies will do you an injury; if they draw blood, expect heavy losses in trade. If you dream you pass through them without harm, you will triumph over enemies and become happy. 706

9 Bribe—A dream of contrary meaning. If you accept money as a bribe in your dream, it is a sign of upright and honorable conduct on your part. Refusing a bribe of money: Will be repaid money unexpectedly. Bribing an official person: Big sorrow. 909

2 Bride—unfortunately, this is a dream of contrary meaning. If you are one, it foretells some great disappointment. Kissing a bride: Will have many friends and much joy. Being kissed by a bride: Will have good health. A bride being pleased with her gown: Will have many

children. A bride being displeased with her gown: Disappointment in love. 263

7 Bridegroom—A bridegroom having a rich bride: Loss of a father. A bridegroom having a beautiful bride: Loss of a mother. A bridegroom having a young bride: Sickness in the family. Bridegroom having an elderly bride: Abundant means. 952

2 Bridesmaid—Being a bridesmaid: great disappointment. Several bridesmaids: Happiness and long life. Not being a bridesmaid: Danger through a secret. Girlfriends being bridesmaids: Unhappiness in love affairs. 607

9 Bridge—To dream that you are crossing a bridge foretells a change of situation or occupation in business or a change in district. This will be a fortunate omen if you cross the stream without too much trouble or delay. If the bridge is damaged or being repaired, then be careful and do not make any fresh plans without due thought. 387

7 Brooch—To dream that you are wearing jewelry depends upon the surroundings for its importance. If you are at home, it is a fortunate omen; but if you wear it at a strange house, then expect trouble. Buying a brooch: Will be deceived. Selling a brooch: Loss of a great deal of money. 970

7 Brook or Running Water—Faithful friends, if the stream is clear. Otherwise, be careful. A brook being near your own home: Will receive an honorable appointment. Brook being nearly dry: Discovery of loss of valuables. 412

9 Broom—Beware of a false friend. Having a new broom: Will make plenty of money. Throwing away an old broom: Good luck to one for whom you care. Hitting something with a broom: Will have a change for the better. 639

9 Broth—To dream that you are taking broth is a fortunate sign. Your affairs will prosper. Boiling broth: Will be married soon. Giving broth to a sick person: Abundance of money. 216

5 Brother—This omen depends upon the sex of the dreamer. If a woman dreams of her brother, it is a sign of much domestic happiness; but if it is a man, then

expect a quarrel. A brother dying: Destruction of enemies. A brother getting married: Family quarrels. 239

9 Brown—Beware of treachery on the part of someone whom you trust. 135

3 Bruises—A warning to all but the most robust that their health is suffering from overstrain. Other people having bruises on the body: Beware of enemies. Other people having bruises on the face: Loss of money. 398

5 Brush—Should you touch or use a brush in your dream, your greatest wish will shortly be granted. Having an old brush: Disappointments. Buying a new brush: Good times are coming. 419

9 Bubbles—A sign of gaiety. Avoid dissipation, or you may lose your sweetheart. Bubbles in a bathtub: Will find a protector. Bubbles from boiling water: Dignity and distinction. 819

9 Buckle—For a woman to dream that the buckle of her belt has come unfastened foretells trouble and difficulty. All mishaps with one's clothes are bad signs. Having a fancy buckle: Will have a change for the better. Buying a buckle: Avoid rivals. A broken buckle: An enemy is seeking your destruction. 540

3 Bugle Calls—This announces success in your efforts. Hearing children playing a bugle: Joy without profit. Soldiers playing a bugle: Danger in love matters. 983

4 Bugs—A warning to act cautiously, as there are unfortunate influences around you. Killing bugs: Will have money. Having bugs in the bedding: Prosperity beyond fondest hopes. 139

6 Building—To dream of building indicates some change in life, and your success otherwise will depend upon their general appearance. If the buildings are small, you will not prove successful. Very tall buildings: Will have much success. 861

2 Bull—The sign of some enemy or rival in love or business. Being chased by a bull: Will receive a present. A furious bull: Will have much success in love. 362

1 Bull Dog—Good news from an absent friend. Owning a bull dog: Advancement in own position. Buying a bull dog: Happiness is assured. Selling the puppies: An enemy is seeking your ruin. 154

2 Bull's-eye—To hit the center of the target is a lucky dream, whereas it is unfortunate to miss it. If you see someone else shooting, be careful about giving him your confidence. Others hitting the bull's-eye: Be careful in giving them your confidence. 812

3 Bunion—Presages the return of a traveler from a great distance. Inflammation leaving a bunion: Will have a new admirer. 273

1 Burden—To carry some burden in a dream shows that you will be dependent upon other people. 190

7 Burglar—Beware of treachery among those you trust. A burglar coming into the house at night: Approaching troubles. Catching a burglar red handed: Will gain good fortune. Burglars having stolen valuable things: Good investments. 628

9 Burial—A dream of contrary meaning, for it denotes a wedding, though this may not be your own. Attending the burial of a friend: Are expecting an inheritance. Attending the burial of a relative: Will be married soon. 153

1 Burning houses—A sign of improved fortune. A house burning: Fortune will improve. A building burning: Losses and worries. Friend's house burning: Triumph over enemies. A big store burning: Loss of money. 019

2 Burns—If you burn yourself in a dream, it is a sign of valuable friendship in your life. 389

2 Bushes—A change is indicated. If you push through them, the change will be for the better. Hiding behind bushes: Opposition and imminent danger. Cutting down bushes: Danger through a secret. 290

5 Butcher—You will meet with someone you have not seen for a long time. Act cautiously, as this is not a lucky dream. A butcher killing an animal: Death of a close friend. A butcher serving you with cut meat: Will live a long life. Arguing with a butcher: Are surrounded by unfortunate influences. 428

3 Butter—This is a good dream, but of a material character such as feasting. It is usually something of a surprise. If you are making butter, some money will reach you unexpectedly. Purchasing butter: Will have a

change for the better. Cooking with butter: Will be fortunate in business. 804

9 Butterfly—A sign of happiness, if you see a gaily colored butterfly in the sunshine; but if it is a moth and seen indoors, then it means some light trouble. Catching a butterfly: Infidelity. Killing a butterfly: Will receive a gift. Chasing a butterfly: Are surrounded by unfortunate influences. 842

3 Buttermilk—To drink it indicates disappointment in love. To the married, trouble, sorrow, and losses. 102

3 Buttons—For a man, this omen shows delay or difficulty in love affairs, but it is fortunate for a woman. 921

3 Buy—To dream that you are buying a lot of articles is a warning of coming troubles; be careful with your money matters. But if in your dream you are carefully considering every shilling you spend, then it is a fortunate sign. 129

C

6 Cab—To dream that you are riding in a cab or taxi shows good fortune, probably in connection with some distant country or through some friend who is living abroad. A man riding in a cab with a woman: Name will be connected with scandal. A woman riding in a cab alone: Will enjoy average success. Riding in a cab in the rain: Correspondence with friends living abroad. Riding in a cab with wife: Will have a long life. Riding in a cab with children: Happiness within the family. 312

2 Cabin—To dream that you are in the cabin of a ship foretells domestic troubles. Being in a cabin at the beach: Love affairs. Being in a cabin with a lover: Death of an enemy. Being in a cabin with friends: Danger with love matters. 113

9 Cabinet—Beware of treachery among those you trust. Buying a cabinet: Great financial gains. Opening a cabinet: Will receive a long awaited letter. 126

8 Cackle—A sign whose meaning varies very much in different localities. It is best to treat it as a warning that care is needed. 341

1 Caddy—You will receive a present which should have arrived sooner. Using services of a caddy: Misfortune is near. 190

7 Cage—To dream that you see birds in a cage is a token of a successful love affair; but if the cage is empty, the engagement will probably be broken off. Wild animals in a cage: Danger of going to prison. 359

2 Cake—Good health is generally denoted by food, provided it is of an enjoyable kind. Baking a cake: Will have a lucky turn of events. Eating a piece of cake: Will lose sweetheart. Buying a cake: Will enjoy the affection of a friend. 182

4 Calendar—To dream that you are worrying about some date is a sign of fortunate marriage, unless you fail to find out what you seek. Buying a calendar: Will receive good news. Tearing off calendar sheets: Will receive an unexpected gift. 976

4 Calf—A good omen for lovers and married people. Owning a calf: Will have a very good future. A calf that belongs to others: Fortune received from parents. 346

9 Calls—To hear your own name called aloud in your dream is fortunate for one in love. It has no money meaning. 414

7 Camel—As with all unusual animals, this foretells difficulties and worries. Many camels: Great financial gain. A camel carrying a load: Inheritance. 673

4 Camera—Looking into one: Someone will deceive you. Owning a camera: Will receive disagreeable news. Buying a camera: Joy without profit. Receiving a camera as a gift: Will have many love troubles. 139

5 Camp—To dream of soldiers in camp is also fortunate for love affairs, for it is a dream of contrary meaning and indicates peace in your domestic affairs. Of camping: Will have good days ahead. 158

9 Can—Good news. To drink out of a can: great joy. 702

4 Canal—This dream follows the rules for all water conditions. If the water is clear, it is a fortunate sign; but if

the water is muddy or covered with weeds, then it is an omen of coming troubles. 913

8 Canary—A certain sign of a cheerful and comfortable home. Owning a canary: Will be deceived by a friend. Buying a canary: Will soon make a trip. A dead canary: Death of a very good friend. 935

3 Candle—This is a good omen provided the candle burns brightly. But if it is extinguished, you may expect trouble. Lighting candles: Will meet with friends. Putting out candles: Will quarrel with a friend. Having colored candles: Will become a widow or a widower. Buying candles: Are inclined to believe enemies. Carrying lighted candles: Death of a friend. 813

2 Candy—Peace and happiness in your home affairs. Making candy: Will reap profit in business. Eating candy: Pleasure in society. Giving a box of candy as a gift: Peace and happiness in the home. Receiving a box of candy as a gift: Are very highly admired. 659

5 Cane—To dream that you have been whipped is a very bad sign. Beware of all business transactions for at least a couple of days. Resting on a cane: Illness in the near future. A woman using a cane: Will have love affairs. 293

4 Canister—Should you enclose anything in a canister, you will soon have a secret to keep. Should you open one, you will discover a friend's secret. 913

3 Cannibals—Disturbing information will vex and hamper you, but you have little to fear. 201

7 Cannon—To dream that you hear the firing of guns or muskets is a certain sign of some vexation and disappointment. A military man firing a cannon: Marriage to a beautiful girl. A man dreaming of hearing a cannon fired: Will have danger in business. A woman dreaming of hearing a cannon fired: Will marry a military man. 241

2 Canoe—A canoe is only intended for one person, and such a dream omen indicates a lack of friends. A canoe overturning: An enemy is seeking your ruin. Being in a canoe with your loved one: Avoid rivals. 326

2 Cap—If you put on your cap or hat in your dream, it

signifies difficulty in your love affairs. If a cap or hat is given to you, then you will marry happily. 182

1 Captain—Advancement, prosperity, and hopes fullfilled after great difficulties have been overcome. Marrying a captain: Will be confronted by a big scandal. Being a captain's sweetheart: Security is forthcoming. 874

4 Captivity—If in your dream, you see yourself a captive or in prison, it is a sign of an unhappy marriage. Other people in captivity: Beware of overstrain. Enemies in captivity: Beware of business losses. Animals in captivity: Dignity and distinction. 301

9 Cards—Playing cards in a dream or watching other people playing cards is an indication of coming quarrels. 153

2 Caress—For a mother to dream that she is caressing her children is a dream of contrary meaning. She will have anxious days on account of illness. A wife caressing her husband: Happy events. A husband caressing his wife: Will have good earnings. Sweethearts caressing each other: Will receive dreadful news. 506

5 Carols—To sing them presages a happy marriage. 194

5 Carpenter—To see workmen busily engaged is a sign that you will overcome your difficulties. Being a carpenter at work: Success in financial matters. Hiring a carpenter: Unexpected good news. 131

8 Carpet—To dream that you are in a room containing carpeting is a fortunate dream. Buying carpet: A mystery will be solved. A carpet burning: Be on guard against spiteful gossip. Laying a carpet: Big catastrophe ahead. 413

8 Carriage or Cart—To dream that you are driving a cart is a sign of a loss of money or position. Making a long trip in a carriage: Will be slow to achieve fortune. An overturned carriage: Misery. 683

2 Carry—To be carried by anyone in your dream is an uncertain omen. If you are carried by a woman or by a poor person, it is a fortunate sign, otherwise, it is not. 317

4 Carrots—This dream signifies profit by inheritance.

2 Carving—This omen's meaning depends upon the circumstances. If you are serving yourself, it shows your

own prosperity, but if you are carving for other people, then someone else will benefit by your actions. 731

9 Cashier—To imagine yourself in charge of other people's money is a bad omen; expect financial worry or even loss. Watching a cashier: Freedom from want. 585

6 Castle—This omen has varying meanings, but it is generally held to indicate a quarrel through your own bad temper. In some places it is said to show a marriage that opens well but drifts into difficulties. Residing in a castle: Good business ventures. A castle on fire: Quarrels because of bad temper. 158

4 Castor oil—Medicines in a dream are omens of contrary meaning. The more unpleasant the dose, the better it will be for the dreamer. Being ordered to take castor oil by a doctor: Short illness. Giving castor oil to children: Will soon take a trip. 202

6 Cat—An unfavorable dream, as is the case if you dream of a dog. It is a dream of contrary meaning and shows unexpected deceit by someone whom you trust. A black cat: Illness is near. Defending yourself from a cat: Will be robbed. Cats playing: Will be visited at home by enemies. A cat with her kittens: Unhappiness in marriage. 429

1 Catechism—Receiving oral instruction from a catechism: Happiness. Reading a catechism manual: Good business activities. Preaching from a catechism: Dignity and disdistiction. 325

8 Caterpillars—An unfortunate omen, trouble from a rival or enemy. 386

9 Cathedral—The important nature of this building has lead to many contrary definitions. It seems best to treat the outside view of a cathedral as showing good fortune, while if you dream of the interior you should take care, or trouble may befall you. 162

7 Cattle—Sign of prosperity in business, if you see yourself driving cattle, it shows that you have to work hard. Fat cattle: Will have a fruitful year. Lean cattle: Will be in want of provisions. Being rich and owning cattle: Disgrace and loss in business. Being poor and owning cattle: Good profits. 934

8 Cauliflower—Like most vegetables, this is an omen of

good health and a comfortable home life. Eating cauliflower: Joy and honor. Buying cauliflower: Will have good health. 215

1 Cavalry—To dream that you see mounted troops is a sign of good fortune in your love affairs. 316

4 Cave—An obstacle dream. If you escape from the cave all will go well, though you must expect trouble at first. But if you fall into a cave or fail to get out, then expect business worries. 247

5 Ceiling—If in your dream anything happens to the room in which you find yourself, it is an omen of trouble through a friend, probably due to severe illness. 312

5 Celery—As with other useful vegetables such a dream means good health and domestic comfort. 419

1 Cellar—An obstacle dream, unless there is plenty of coal in the cellar, when it indicates good business from a distance, perhaps abroad. Going into the cellar: Will be very fortunate. Many things stored in a cellar: Good news. 802

6 Cement—A present is soon to be given you, which will lead to more important events. Working with cement: Will receive unexpected money. 294

9 Certificate—You do not attempt to see things from other people's points of view. Try to be more sympathetic in small ways, and big events will ensue. 297

4 Cemetery—You will conquer all things. Being in a cemetery: Will soon have prosperity. A bride passing a cemetery on way to marriage: She will lose husband. Elderly people putting flowers in a cemetery: Will have no grief. 283

9 Chains—A dream of contrary meaning, showing that you will escape from some difficulty that worries you at the moment. But a gold chain around a woman's neck shows good fortune from some friend or lover. Cutting a chain: Will have worried for a short time. A person wearing chains in jail: Business will be bad. Succeeding in breaking the chains: Will be free of social engagements. Others in chains: Ill fortune for them. 315

3 Chair—To see an empty chair in your dream indicates

news from a long-absent friend. Sitting in a comfortable armchair: Will have prosperity. 201

8 Chalk—To dream of chalk cliffs means disappointment in some cherished hope. Buying chalk: Will have a long life. Handling chalk: Will soon be married. 908

5 Champagne—This is an unfortunate omen for love affairs. 698

8 Champions—To dream that you are successful at sports or games is a sign of poor success in business affairs. Pull yourself together and be more careful. 134

9 Chapel—As with all religious buildings, it is a fortunate dream if you see the outside but not if you find yourself inside. 783

3 Charity—This is a dream of contrary meaning. The more charitable you are in your dream, the less fortune awaits you in your business affairs. Receiving charity: Domestic affliction. Giving clothing to charity: People are laughing at you. Giving foodstuffs to charity: Will have hard work ahead. 102

3 Chastise—This is a dream of contrary meaning. If you find yourself thrashing your children in your dream, it indicates a happy and prosperous home life. But if you yourself are being thrashed, then it shows bad fortune in money matters. 516

4 Cheating—To dream that you have been cheated is a fortunate omen; but take care if you cheat someone else in your dreams. 814

6 Cheering—The bad sound of shouting or cheering in your dreams is an unfortunate omen. Be careful of your actions. 393

9 Cheese—Annoyance and deception from those around you. To eat cheese shows worry through your own hasty action. Foreign cheese: Are prone to liking only the best things. Homemade cheese: Good luck to one for whom you care. 891

5 Chemist—A chemist's shop is not a good subject for a dream: Be warned as to your business dealings. Being a chemist: Business affairs are not good. 923

4 Cherries—To see cherries growing is an omen of coming misfortune: You will be wise to move slowly in your business affairs. A cherry tree without cherries: Will

have good health. Having cherries in the home: Good health. Rotten cherries: Will be disappointed by lover. A man dreaming of picking cherries: Will be deceived by a woman. 814

9 Chest—To dream of a large box concerns your love affairs. If the chest is empty, prepare for a disappointment. Having a small chest: Love affairs will be good. Having a full chest: Family arguments. 190

3 Chestnuts—Domestic affection. Eating chestnuts: Will have some advantages if careful. Buying chestnuts: Will be dissappointed by lover. 804

3 Chew—If you dream you are chewing, you have to overlook another's fault before you will know peace of mind and happiness. 219

9 Chickens—All very young animals show friendships. Of one fine chicken: Will be fortunate in love. Several chickens: Will have many good friends. Chickens laying eggs: Joy and contentment. A chicken sitting on her eggs: Joy and happiness. A chicken with her chicks: Will receive a favor. Killing a chicken: Profit. 351

1 Children—A lucky dream, showing success in business. Several children: Will have abundance in life. Children at play: Good deeds will bear fruit. Adopting children: Own children will dislike those adopted. Children being killed: Misery caused by parents. Children being sick: Obstacles are ahead. 604

5 Chimney—To see a tall chimney predicts fortunate events. Chimney of own house: Will receive good news. A chimney falling down: Joy. 932

8 China—Financial gains from a long distance. Fine china: Good luck in gambling. Buying china: Happiness in your marriage. 359

1 Chips—A business success or wager won. 307

1 Chocolates—To be eating sweets in a dream is a sign of a coming gift. Buying chocolate: A short period of troubles will be followed by prosperity. Drinking chocolate: Will receive a marriage proposal. 325

8 Choir—As the choir is part of the interior of a sacred

building, it is not really a fortunate sign. If the choir-boys are singing, you will hear from an old friend. 494

4 Choking—Strangely enough, it is a fortunate sign to find yourself choking in your dream. Others choking you: Will be abandoned by lover. Children choking: Recovery from an illness. 310

5 Christ—The birth of Christ: Will have peace, joy, and contentment. Christ in the garden: Will have much wealth. Christ in the temple: Efforts will be rewarded. Christ being crucified: Enemies will be defeated. Resurrection of Christ: Will have good hopes in life. Talking to Christ: Will receive much consolation. 275

9 Christening—This dream also has to do with the interior of a sacred building. It is not a fortunate omen. 216

2 Christmas—A good omen, but it refers more particularly to your friends or your family affairs and not to business. Being at a Christmas party: Will have new good friends. Going Christmas caroling: Great financial gains. 092

7 Church—Here again, it is the outside of the building that is fortunate. To dream that you are inside a sacred building is a warning of coming trouble. Talking in a church: Have plenty of envious friends. Praying in church: Consolation and joy. Being in a church during mass: Will receive what you are hoping for. Hearing a dispute in a church: Will have family troubles. Being with a priest in a church: Happy marriage and success. 475

1 Churchyard—Although apparently unpleasant, this is a fortunate dream, as it concerns the outside of a church. 109

4 Churning—To dream that you are churning is a sign of prosperity and plenty. To the single, happy marriage. 391

3 Cider—Gossip about your own private affairs. Act cautiously. 345

2 Cigar—It is a fortunate dream to see yourself smoking. Prosperity awaits you. Having an unlit cigar: Will have misfortune. Having a lighted cigar: May have good hopes. 371

7 Cigarette—To dream you are lighting one signifies new

plans. A half-smoked cigarette held in the hand is a postponement. To smoke it to the end means a successful conclusion to your hopes. 313

7 Circus—A sign of future unhappiness due to your own careless habits. Watching a circus performance: Loss of money. Taking children to a circus: Important and beneficial events to come. 142

3 City—A large city denotes ambition if in the distance. Ambition will be successfully attained should you enter the city in your dream. A city burning: Poverty. Being in a large city: Conclusion of hopes. A city in ruins: Will have illness in the family. Going through a city: Will receive sad news from a friend. 471

6 Climbing—It is a sign of business prosperity to find yourself climbing, unless the effort proves too great for your strength. Still, even then it shows some sort of good fortune, though combined with difficulties. Climbing but failing to reach the summit: Cherished plans will fail. Climbing a ladder to the top: Success in business. A ladder breaking while climbing: Will have unexpected difficulties. Climbing a tree: Will receive a good position. 609

4 Cliffs—A dangerous dream. Do not take any risks, especially of high places from which you might slip, for some time. Going up a cliff: Conclusion of affairs. Descending from a cliff: Don't trust your friends. 103

8 Clock—To dream that you hear a clock strike the hours is a fortunate sign. You will enjoy a comfortable life. Having a wall clock: Will have happiness. Buying a wall clock: Will receive important business news. A clock being stopped: Will be spared from illness. 359

1 Clothes—This is a dream of contrary meaning. If you have plenty of clothes in your dream, it is a warning of coming trouble. If you are partly dressed or naked, then prosperity is coming your way. To put on clothes is a fortunate sign, but if you make any error, you must not correct it or you will spoil your luck. 352

2 Clouds—This depends upon the circumstances. If the sky is stormy and dark, it betokens many sorrows; but if the clouds pass away, then better fortune awaits you.

Downpour of rain from the clouds: Will have hard days ahead. 254

3 Clover—To dream that you are in a clover field is a very fortunate sign, especially to those who are in love. 147

4 Clown—Others think you witless. Being dressed as a clown: Will receive news of a death. Being in the company of a clown: Troubles ahead. A clown making love to a woman: You have many hypocritical friends. 490

2 Club—You will meet with many people whom you have not seen for a long time. Do not let them influence you. Being refused admittance to a club: Will take good care of business. 605

3 Coach—It is not a very good omen when you dream that you are driving in a coach; be careful or you may find yourself in difficulties. 975

4 Coal—This is a warning of danger. If you dream that you are in a coal pit, it is serious and means heavy business losses or a keen disappointment in love. 535

3 Coat—This is a sign of contrary if you are wearing a new coat, beware of business troubles. If your coat is old, or if you tear it in any way, then prosperity is coming to you. Wearing another person's coat: Will be forced to seek a friend's help. Losing a coat: Will soon face financial ruin through speculation. Getting a coat dirty: Will lose a good friend. 912

3 Coat of Arms—To dream of a shield with a Coat of Arms on it is an excellent sign, a powerful friend will protect you. 723

5 Cobweb—To brush one away means a triumph for you over an enemy. 392

5 Cock—Although a cock is a bad omen by itself, it is considered a sign of some unexpected good news if you hear the bird crowing. Cocks fighting: Will have quarrels. A dead cock: Happiness in the family. 194

4 Coffee—This dream also is favorable and signifies great domestic happiness. Buying coffee: Will have the best reputation in business. Pouring coffee: Security is forthcoming. Being in a coffee shop with good people: Highly considered by friends. 913

8 Coffin—Emblematic of the serious illness of some dear friend, perhaps even death if there is much black seen. An elaborate coffin: Death of a partner. A friend in a coffin: Serious illness of a dear friend. Coffin of the head of the family: Must contend with unpleasant matters. 260

6 Coins—To dream of money in the shape of coins is on the whole favorable, but the more important the coin the less fortunate the dream. Copper coins are more favorable than silver, while gold is often considered a bad omen, as is the case with paper money. 159

6 Cold—If you feel cold it is a sign of comfort and friendship. Having a bad cold: Security is forthcoming. Mate having a cold: Abundant means. Children having a cold: Good times are coming. 582

5 College—It is not a fortunate omen to dream that you are at college. 527

4 Colors—If you dream of flags and decorations in many bright colors, it signifies continued prosperity and success in all your undertakings. White is always favorable, especially in matters concerning other people, such as business affairs. Blue and purple represent prosperity through other people, good fortune in your love affairs, and so on. Scarlet or red is a warning of quarrels, the loss of friends; but crimson denotes pleasant news from an unexpected quarter. Yellow and orange are mental tints and show that you need not expect any important change in your affairs for some time. Green indicates a journey or business with people at a distance. 625

9 Collision—A sign of mental strife. You will need all your self-control to overcome the effect of bad tidings. 054

9 Combat—It is not a good sign to be engaged in a fight in a dream; if you are successful, all will come well, but only after difficulty and worry. Helping others in combat: Reconciliation with enemies. 459

1 Companion—To dream that you are with a pleasant companion is a fortunate omen: It shows immediate success. 208

6 Concert—To find yourself at a concert in your dream is

a sign of unexpected news. Singing at a concert: Will receive an inheritance. A sick person dreaming of a concert: Will soon recover. 249

2 Confession—Guard the confidences given to you by others, as you will shortly be strongly tempted to reveal a secret. Going to confession: Will soon be told a secret. 269

8 Congratulations—These signify cause for condolence but better times to follow. Sending congratulations: Joy. Congratulating others: Will have financial gains. 251

2 Confetti—Social disappointments of a trifling nature. Throwing confetti: Will receive a letter with good news. Others throwing confetti at you: Love and happiness. 236

8 Confusion—A dream of confusion presages loneliness and trouble. 269

9 Conscience—It is a dream of contrary meaning if you are being worried by your conscience; all will go well. The more self-satisfied you feel, the less your chance of prosperity. 162

5 Convicted—To be found guilty in a court of justice is a good sign: Prosperity is on the way. 329

9 Consent—If you dream that you consent to the request of someone, it denotes a discovery of lost valuables. Others consenting to your request: Will have good health. Refusing consent: Will have a vigorous mind. 180

3 Convent—An engagement speedily followed by a happy, though not wealthy, wedding. 759

1 Convulsions—To dream you see someone in convulsions means an invitation to a concert. Having convulsions: Prosperous married life. 379

2 Cooking—To dream of cooking, whether by yourself or someone else, is a good sign but only concerns material comforts. Being a cook: Poverty. A young girl being a cook: Will soon become engaged. 506

4 Cord—To knot a cord means the strengthening of a friendship; to unravel it means the breaking of an engagement. 364

3 Corks—If you dream that you are extracting a cork, it

is a sign of some good news of a friend. If you are pushing a cork into a bottle, it shows an unexpected visit to you. 363

7 Corkscrew—It is a sign of illness to use a corkscrew in your dreams. 385

5 Corn—A very fortunate dream, and a sign of money in plenty; according to the state of the growing corn. Eating corn: Success in all your affairs. Harvesting corn: Will hear good news. A field with large ears of corn: Big financial gains. 158

9 Cornet—Family quarrels are foretold when you hear a cornet being played. Playing a cornet: Discovery of lost valuables. 531

6 Corns—To dream that you have corns on your feet is a sign of fortunate business ventures. 240

5 Corpse—An omen of estrangement or separation from friends through your own fault; an unhappy love affair. A corpse in the water: Arguments with your lover. A corpse being lowered into a grave: Separation from a loved one. A corpse at a morgue: Marriage or other happy events. 932

8 Cottage—It is a fortunate sign to find yourself living in a cottage unless you are discontented and endeavor to get away. 593

4 Coughing—This is a dream of contrary meaning and indicates good health, vigor, business prosperity. 526

9 Counterfeit—If you handle counterfeit coins in a dream, you will be asked to help someone who will make you a good friend. 243

5 Court—To dream of going to court means a business loss. Being requested to go to court: High consideration of others. Being punished by a court: Travel and prosperity. Being acquitted by a court: Serious disaster is ahead. 328

6 Courtship—This is also a dream of contrary meaning, for the more fortunate the wooing in your dreams, the worse it will be for your real love affairs. 537

9 Cousin—To dream of your relatives is a sign that you may soon receive unexpected news. 279

5 Cow—Good luck unless you are pursued by the animal, in which case it depends upon what happens. If you

escape the cow, you will survive the evil schemes of some enemy. The greater the number of animals seen, the more serious the warning. 635

6 Crab—As in the case of all unusual creatures, this is a sign of coming difficulties. Many crabs in a fish market: Danger is ahead. Eating crabs: Avoid rivals. 123

7 Cradle—It is not a good sign to dream of an empty cradle; misfortune will come, probably from ill health. A cradle with a baby in it: Avoid rivals. Rocking your own baby in a cradle: Illness in the family. A young woman dreaming of a cradle: Reconsider your present conduct. 682

3 Crawl—An omen of difficulty; your love affairs will not prosper. 534

3 Crew—It is not a good omen if you see sailors on a vessel at work. Expect bad news. 354

9 Cries—These are omens of contrary meaning. If the cries are happy and joyous, then expect bad news. But if they are cries of trouble or distress, then all will go well. 927

4 Crimes—Your undertakings will be crowned with success. 373

7 Cripple—A warning to be kind to those around you. A child being crippled: Will have happiness. Members of family being crippled: Expect too many favors from others. Friends being crippled: Will become a beggar. 241

9 Crochet—A change in your enviroment leading to better times. Your sweetheart crocheting: You are very ambitious. 279

3 Crocodile—Another warning of troubles ahead. Of a crocodile: You are in the grip of a deceitful person. Many crocodiles: Bad catastrophe ahead. 912

2 Cross—An omen of sorrow in the affections. A cross on a grave: You need help. Wearing a cross: You will have the protection of friends. A cross in the church: Big joy. Praying on a cross: Will receive wishes. 794

5 Crow—The sinister color black makes this bird an omen of grief and misfortune. If more than one crow is seen, the matter becomes very serious. A woman dreaming

of a crow: Death of her husband. A man dreaming of a crow: Death of his wife. 518

1 Crowds—Your happiness is assured and will increase. Being in a crowd: Advancement within position. 262

1 Crown—To dream that you have a crown on your head is a sign that you will benefit from people in a better position than yourself. If a cross is seen as well, then you will benefit through a death. Placing a crown on another's head: You are worthy of advancement. Having a crown of flowers: Big success. 190

3 Crucifix—This omen is associated with the interior of a church, so it is not a favorable sign. 597

5 Cruelty—To dream of seeing this means that one near to you is in need of help. 869

7 Crutches—This is an obstacle dream. If you recover and are able to walk without the aid of crutches, all will go well. If not, expect trouble. 232

6 Crystal—You will soon be shown the turning in the long lane that has been worrying you. Buying crystal: Will soon be given nice gifts. Having crystal: Change for the better. 258

4 Cup—An empty cup is a bad omen, but a full one is a sign of prosperity. Drinking from a cup: Good times are coming. Breaking a cup: Death of an enemy. Receiving a cup as a gift: You have faithful friends. 382

8 Cupboard—To dream of an empty cupboard is a bad sign for your business prosperity. If you put things inside it shows that you will recover your losses after some distress. Taking things out of a cupboard: You have many loyal friends. 404

1 Curls—A complete change in your affairs; new environment and better times are in view. 343

3 Curse—To dream of hearing curses and rough language presages a visit of ceremony. Being cursed: Ambitions will be realized. 426

5 Curtain—This is an obstacle dream but refers particularly to bad faith in someone you trust. If you pull the curtain aside, you will be warned in time. Others pulling curtains aside: Warning of trouble. Putting up new curtains: Will entertain a prominent guest. 815

8 Cushions—Signs of comfort in your dreams are not

fortunate. The more comfortable you find yourself, the greater will be your difficulty and business worries. 251

1 Cycling—To dream that you are cycling foretells a visit that you will make at some distance. To see people cycling: Friends from afar will visit you. 208

D

4 Daffodils—All early Spring flowers are fortunate omens. Daffodils particularly concern your love affairs, not your business concerns. A happy future is certain for one who dreams of these beautiful Spring flowers, but for the best results they should be seen out of doors. 184

6 Daggers—Be careful of treachery or you will suffer heavy loss. Being wounded by a dagger: Another person is enjoying what you hoped for. 024

3 Dairy—A fortunate dream. 102

3 Daisies—These simple wild flowers are always a fortunate omen in your dreams. Picking daisies: Great happiness in love. Having them in a vase in a home: Important and very beneficial events. 237

9 Dance—If you dream that you are dancing, it is a sign that money is coming to you or that some cherished plan will meet with success. But if you merely watch others dancing, then you will hear of good fortune coming concerning a friend. 873

4 Danger—This is an omen of contrary meaning. If you face danger in your dreams, you may expect success; but if you avoid it, then trouble will come. 328

1 Darkness—To dream that you are in the dark is a sign of difficulties ahead. If you fall or hurt yourself, then you may expect a change for the worse, but if you succeed in groping your way to the light, then you will face your troubles successfully. 514

8 Darning—To dream you are darning denotes the intro-

duction of a new and kindly friend. To see it is a warning against gossip. 638

2 Daughter—To dream of your children is generally considered a contrary vision. What affects your girls in your dream will concern your boys in real life. 425

4 Dates—You are likely to be admired by some member of the other sex. 202

6 Dawn—This omen depends upon the circumstances. To see the dawn means days of storm and stress lie ahead. 537

5 Dead—This omen depends upon the circumstances, but on the whole it concerns other people, not the dreamer. If you speak to friends or relatives who are dead, it means news of some living friend or relative; if you touch or kiss them, the news will be of a sorrowful nature. To dream of a death means a new birth. 806

1 Deafness—To find yourself suddenly deaf in your dream is a good sign. By some unexpected turn of events, you will escape a great trouble or difficulty. 523

5 Debts—To pay your debts in a dream is a good omen, but if other people repay what they owe you, then expect a loss. 194

8 Decorate—To dream that you are beautifying your room or your house is a dream of contrary meaning. Expect losses in your business affairs. Decorating a grave: Will have very little joy. 386

1 Deeds—Should you dream of signing them, avoid speculation and quarrels with those dear to you, as you are in danger of loss of either money or affection. 901

4 Deer—To dream of wild animals in unnatural captivity is unfavorable and indicates quarrels or disputes. A herd of deer running: Financial distress. Killing a deer: Will receive an inheritance. Having the horns of a deer: Will be cheated by friends. 391

2 Defend—To dream of shielding or defending someone denotes at least one loyal friend. Being unable to defend yourself: Will live a long life. Defending children: Luck and prosperity. 857

7 Deformity—To dream that you are deformed signifies shame and sorrow. Others who are deformed: Beware of

false appearances of others. A young lady dreaming of being deformed: She will break her engagement. 925

1 Delirium—To dream of being delirious signifies danger through a secret. To see someone else in that condition means that a friend is trying to help you secretly. 253

2 Delight—Excessive happiness in your dreams is a bad omen. Expect trouble at home and business worries. 236

9 Deluge—A heavy downpour of rain is an omen of bad luck in your love affairs. Avoid quarrels. 207

1 Dentist—A dream of illness. Being in a dentist's chair: Will have cause to question friends' sincerity. Children in a dentist's chair: Will hear false reports about friends. Friend in a dentist's chair: Misfortune in love affairs. 712

3 Derby—A lucky dream; financial gain will come your way. Attending a derby with loved ones: Approaching good times. 237

8 Desert—To dream that you are traveling across a desert or a wide open area signifies difficulties concerning some cherished plan. It is particularly bad if you encounter bad weather or other troubles. If the sun is shining, the final outcome will be successful. 782

3 Desk—The meaning of this dream depends upon whether the desk is locked or open. If it is locked, then you may expect bad news; but if you are sitting at an open desk, then all will go well. 165

9 Despair—It is an omen of contrary meaning. It shows domestic happiness. 456

8 Dessert—It is always a fortunate omen to dream you are eating ripe fruit. If the fruit, however, is not ripe or has been kept too long, expect business losses. 634

7 Destroy—It is a most unfortunate omen if you break something of value in your dream. Having destroyed something: Warning of troubles. Somebody having destroyed your things: Triumph over enemies. 691

3 Detective—You will hear a confession that will rectify an important mistake in your opinion of someone. Being questioned by a detective: You have one loyal friend. Being blamed by a detective: Financial gains.

7 Devil—It is a very bad omen if you imagine you see Satan, but the outcome will depend upon the circumstances. Whatever happens, however, it means a long struggle. A young girl dreaming of the devil: A happy marriage will occur soon. An elderly sick person dreaming of the devil: Expect trouble. Children dreaming of the devil: Sickness. Having a conversation with the devil: Will be cheated by friends. Fighting with the devil: You are in much danger. 385

4 Devotion—As with most dreams concerning religion, this is a good sign. Wife and husband having devotion for each other: Happiness is assured. Children having devotion for the parents: Important and beneficial events to come. 563

5 Dew—One of nature's blessings. A very fortunate dream if you see dew on grass. 284

7 Diamonds—There is no certainty about this dream, as some authorities call it an omen of misfortune while others declare that it shows some fortunate deal in business or speculation. Probably it depends upon the financial and social position of the dreamer and should be considered a dream of contrary meaning. 124

3 Dice—To dream that you are playing with dice is a sure sign of change in fortune, but which way things will go depends upon the circumstances. 192

1 Dictionary—This denotes quarrels and the loss of a friend. Consulting a dictionary: Triumph over enemies. Buying a dictionary: Change in environment. 523

6 Difficulty—A dream of obstacles. If you succeed in overcoming your difficulty, all will be well. Having personal difficulties: Good times are coming. Having financial difficulties: Will receive money. Sweetheart having difficulties: Will surely be kind and agreeable. Others having difficulty: All will be well. 465

2 Digging—This dream indicates money, not personal affairs. It depends upon the nature of the soil, for it is emblematic. If the soil is good and easily worked, your plans will succeed. 380

1 Dinner—All meals are dreams of contrary meaning. The better the dinner, the greater the difficulties ahead of you. Having relatives over for dinner: Must control

your nerves. Others giving a dinner party: You have one loyal friend. 892

6 Dirt—To dream that your clothes are dirty denotes sorrow. If you yourself are personally unclean or unwashed, it means illness. 735

7 Diploma—To dream that you are being handed a diploma: Own talents are being neglected. You have probably neglected your talents, which, if properly trained, might lead you to success. 502

6 Disasters—These are always dreams of contrary meaning, favorable for business people. 987

4 Disappointment—To dream you are disappointed assures you of success in the very matter dreamed about. Lovers being disapointed: Danger through a secret. 364

1 Discussion—It is a good omen if you have a friendly discussion in your dream, but if you lose your temper it is a warning of trouble. 357

3 Disease—To dream that you are ill is a warning of treachery; it is a very unfavorable dream in the case of lovers. Having a disease: Warning of treachery. Others having a disease: Will make money illegally. Having an unknown disease: Large financial gain. 723

6 Disfigurement—To dream of personal disfigurement presages an unexpected happiness. 312

3 Disgrace—A dream of contrary meaning. It is a fortunate sign if you find yourself in trouble or in disgrace. Others in disgrace: Are surrounded by enemies. Relatives being in disgrace: Hard work awaits. 102

3 Disguise—Fancy costume is not a fortunate sign. It shows trouble, but not of a serious nature. Having disguised yourself: Will take a long trip and change residence. Others being disguised: Triumph over enemies. 219

4 Dish—To break a plate or dish is a bad sign. It shows domestic trouble. 742

3 Dishonesty—An important document will be mislaid. If you are dishonest in your dream, it will be a document affecting your affairs. Other people being dishonest: Are within grip of deceitful people. Family members being dishonest: Temptation will come to you. 309

7 Dislike—This dream depends upon the circumstances.

If you dream that someone does not like you and that you are worried, it is a bad omen. If, however, you do not appear to be upset at all, then your difficulties will be overcome. 421

2 Dismiss—To dream of being dismissed from a business position presages a rise in position. Dismissing an employer: Doomed for disappointment. Others being dismissed: A mystery will be solved. 749

4' Disobedience—To dream of your own disobedience denotes a difficult choice before you, possibly regarding marriage. Children being disobedient: Prompt engagement. 724

5 Disputes—A dream of contrary meaning it signifies success; but there will be obstacles in the way at first. Having a business dispute: Discovery of lost valuables. Others having a dispute: Good times are coming. 365

3 Distance—A dream that you are separated from your friends or family is a bad sign, but if you dream of some person who is separated from you, then you will hear good news. 615

5 Distress—Another of contrary meaning. It is a good sign if you are in distress or in trouble of any sort. Children being in distress: Warning of trouble. Wife or husband being in distress: Will have emotional sorrow. 212

4 Distrust—To dream that you doubt some person is a bad omen. It is just as serious if someone else disturbs you. 706

9 Ditch—All obstacles of a material kind are bad signs. However, beware of unexpected difficulties, especially in money matters. Being pushed into a ditch: Beware of unexpected difficulties. Walking through a ditch: Will be cheated by someone. Digging a ditch: You are going to discover a secret. 531

2 Diving—To dream that you are diving or falling into water is a sign of loss of money. Others diving: Warning of troubles. Children diving: Dignity and distinction. Members of family diving: Business undertaking will be risky. 146

4 Divorce—It is a dream of contrary meaning. If you imagine you are being divorced it is a sign of domestic

happiness. Relatives being divorced: Bad gossip by friends. Children being divorced: Much joy ahead. Friends being divorced: Danger through a secret. 346

3 Doctor—A good dream financially. Going to a doctor: Will have mastery over many things. Calling a doctor for yourself: Will live a long life. Calling a doctor for children: New interests and surroundings. Being a doctor: Joy and profit. Becoming a doctor: Financial gains. 219

9 Dogs—This dream depends upon circumstances. If the dog is friendly, all will be well. If he barks, then beware of quarrels, and if he bites you, expect treachery from someone you trust. Own dog: Will receive favors from a friend. Police dog: Quarrels with a business partner. Unfriendly dog: Will receive help from a good friend. Being bitten by a dog: Will be double-crossed by someone you trust. Dogs playing together: You are in danger. A dog and cat fighting: Arguments with relatives. 378

8 Dolls—To dream of dolls is a sign of domestic happiness. Girls playing with dolls: Will have very good luck. Buying a doll: Prosperity. 134

6 Door—This is almost an obstacle dream. If you are trying to enter a house and the door is not opened, you may expect serious business troubles. If the house or room appears to have many doors, then beware of speculation, for you will lose your money. 271

2 Doves—A fortunate dream, for business and home affairs. A woman dreaming of doves: Fortunate affairs at home. 164

4 Dowry—To receive money in a dream without earning it is always a bad sign. A man giving property to his bride: Expect much uneasiness. Giving a dowry to daughters: Will earn more money. A widow dowry: Will make a good change in your life. 913

5 Dragon—To see one: Great riches. Many dragons: Big disappointment in love. A young girl dreaming of a dragon: Much joy. 356

7 Drawers—To dream of an open drawer is a fortunate omen, but if you cannot open a closed drawer, then beware of trouble ahead. If a woman dreams of her drawers or her underclothing, it is a bad sign. She will

not be faithful to the man who loves her. A married woman dreaming of her drawers: Unfaithful to the man who loves her. A single girl dreaming of her drawers: Will soon be engaged. 925

8 Dreaming—To dream that you consult anyone about your dreams shows that you may expect news from a distance. Dreaming of nice things: You have impossible desires. Dreaming of being rich: Will be disillusioned. Dreaming of being poor: Change in your position. 134

7 Drenched—An unfortunate dream presaging danger of fever for you or someone near to you. Others being drenched: You expect too many favors. Drenching by force: A mystery will be solved. 385

2 Dress—It is always a good sign if you are concerned about your clothes in a dream; you will succeed in your plans. Receiving a beautiful dress: Will be helped by an unknown man. Buying a new dress: Health and happiness. Changing dresses: Will suffer because of own foolishness. Wearing a daring evening dress: Sickness. 524

2 Drink—If you dream that you are thirsty and cannot find water, it shows misfortune. If the water is dirty or muddy, it is a bad sign, as also if it is warm or hot. But to drink clear fresh water is a very good sign. It is also fortunate to drink milk. 218

2 Driving—It is a fortunate dream if someone else is driving you; but if you yourself are the driver, then expect money losses. Loved one driving: Avoid rivals. 398

2 Drown—A most unfortunate dream for business people. But if someone rescues you, then you may expect help from a friend. A businessman drowning: Will go into bankruptcy. Rescuing others from drowning: A friend will reach high position. 524

6 Drugs—A successful speculation, much gossip around you. Having drugs: Infirmity. Taking drugs: Affliction. 924

3 Drums—It is a fortunate omen to hear drums in your dreams. You will have great success. Marching in a parade and playing the drums: Luck and prosperity. Buying a drum: Will have a loss of small importance.

Children playing a drum: Will not have sufficient money. 237

5 Drunk—To dream that you are intoxicated is a warning of financial trouble. If you see someone else who is drunk, then you will lose money through some other person. A woman being drunk: Will commit some bad action. Becoming drunk with good wine: Will make acquaintances of high person. Being drunk and feeling sad: Treachery by relatives. Being sick from drunkenness: Squandering of household money. Husband being drunk constantly: Bad future. 491

4 Ducks—A good sign. If the ducks attack you it means trouble in business affairs. Ducks flying: Marriage and a happy family life. Hunting ducks: Big success. Eating ducks: Honor and fortune. A wild duck dead: Don't forget your friends. Ducks swimming: Beware of great danger. 823

5 Duet—To sing in a duet in your dreams is a good sign for the lover or for the married. It shows much domestic happiness. 176

6 Duel—Trouble from friends and relatives. You have treachery from enemies. 284

4 Dumb—To dream that you cannot speak, or to meet a dumb person in your dream, is a bad dream. Avoid speculation and do not discuss your business affairs. 841

8 Dungeon—This is an obstacle dream. If you cannot escape from the dungeon, expect business losses. If you do escape all will come well, though only after some difficulty. 287

1 Dusk—Darkness is not important in a dream as it would be in real life, as it is your natural surroundings when asleep. It represents some slight difficulty ahead of you, possibly in your love affairs. 415

9 Dust—Dust or dirt is a bad omen and shows struggle against adverse circumstances. To dream that you are dusting a room shows that some improvement will come if you persevere. 135

7 Dwarf—If you see a dwarf in your dream, it is a sign of difficulties in your domestic circle. Ugly dwarfs: Illness and misfortune. 421

8 Dye—To dream that you are dyeing your hair or rouging your cheek is a bad sign: You will suffer through your own folly. 215

5 Dying—If you dream of dying, you will receive empty promises. Relatives dying: Will receive a big inheritance. Children dying: Will receive fortune from abroad. Friends dying: Triumph over enemies. 284

E

3 Eagle—If this noble bird is flying, it signifies good fortune. If it is dead, or wounded, expect a loss of money. If, however, the flying bird threatens the dreamer, then you may expect difficulties. 435

7 Ears—To dream of any trouble with your ears is a bad sign; it shows trouble from some unexpected source. Feeling own ears while dreaming: Will discover a secret. Having ears pierced: Domestic loss. The ears of corn, wheat, rye, or grain: Will have abundant means. 538

8 Earthquake—This is a rare dream, and consequently the meaning varies greatly. People in the East think little of such happenings in real life, so in their dream they attach little importance to it as some small difficulty to be overcome. But for a Westerner, the omen should be treated far more seriously and should be looked upon as a warning. Feeling an earthquake: Death of a relative. A city destroyed by an earthquake: A change in life will soon come. 602

6 Easel—It is a happy omen to dream that you are an artist working at an easel. 916

6 Easter—To dream of this church festival is an omen of coming happiness. Spending Easter with others: Bad days are ahead. Being in an Easter parade: Danger through a secret. 501

2 Eating—An unfortunate omen as a rule and a sign of family quarrels, but if you see other people eating in

your dream, it shows a valuable friendship. To eat
cheese is favorable. Overeating: Discovery of valuables.
Eating with the hands: Danger is ahead. Eating broiled
meat: Good fortune. Eating salads: Advancement within
position. Eating fruits: Happiness is assured. 857

7 Eavesdropping—To dream that you are secretly listening to the conversation of other people is a sign that
some unexpected good fortune is coming to you. Others
eavesdropping on secret conversation: Money is coming
to you. 214

7 Ebony—A voyage to a foreign country. Having ebony
wood: Will meet someone from abroad. Buying ebony
wood: Success in business. Being given things made with
ebony: Will have good earnings. 439

4 Echo—This curious dream is a sign that you will hear
some good fortune, but not concerning yourself. In
some cases the dreamer may even suffer through the
success of some other person. 256

6 Eclipse—This omen is sometimes met in dreams, but it
is rare. It indicates the illnes of someone closely connected with you. 492

5 Eels—When seen in a dream, these indicate difficulties
which you can overcome if you persevere. Holding an
eel: Will be attended by good fortune. Catching a dead
eel: Warning of suffering. Many eels in water: You are
overworking. 536

2 Eggs—A sign of money unless the eggs are rotten or
unpleasant to eat. If the eggshells are broken, it shows
loss of money. Eating eggs: Foretells an early marriage.
Having very fresh egg: Will receive money. White eggs:
Will receive some advantageous news. Having brown
eggs: Will receive bad news. The eggs of a fish: Will
have hard times ahead. 173

5 Elastic—This dream denotes an improvement in your
fortunes. Having something made of elastic: Good times
are coming. Putting elastic bands on bundles of things:
Beware of jealous friends. 689

2 Election—To dream that you are assisting at one means
a speedy success of your own hopes. 352

3 Electricity—Something will happen to surprise you
greatly; guard against small losses. 102

9 Elephant—This friendly beast denotes assistances coming from friends, or outside influences. Feeding an elephant: An important person will befriend you. Getting on the back of an elephant: Good fortune. Giving water to an elephant: Will be of service to an influential person. An elephant in a circus: Danger of death for a relative. An elephant escaping from a circus: Family quarrels. An elephant being free: Will enjoy much independence in life. 279

8 Elevator—Coming down in an elevator: Will be overwhelmed by misfortune. Going up in an elevator: Increase in wealth and advancement in position. Being in an elevator with others: Avoid rivals. Being in an elevator with family: Financial gains. An elevator being out of order: Warning of trouble. Being stuck between floors in an elevator: Will have emotional sorrow. 314

6 Elopement—A dream of contrary meaning. If you are eloping with your lover, it shows quarrels and an unhappy marriage. If you see other people eloping, it is a sign of illness. 348

8 Embankment—Your hopes will not be fulfilled, but someone you have known formerly will shortly return to your life. 125

7 Embrace—This is a dream of contrary meaning, for it is not considered fortunate if anyone embraces you in a dream. But if you see your wife, sweetheart, or friend embracing someone else, then it is a good omen for you. 348

4 Emerald—Various meanings are attached to this beautiful gem. In the East, it is considered the greatest possible good fortune, but in the West it is usually treated as a sign of business with someone at a distance or separation from some loved one. Of an emerald: Will experience difficulty over an inheritance. Selling own emeralds: Separation from a loved one. Buying an emerald: Good business with a person far away. 598

3 Employment—A dream of contrary meaning. It is a sign of prosperity in business if you dream that you are out of work. To dream that you employ others shows interest will clash with you. Being in an employment office seeking a job: A change for the better. 293

8 Enemy—To dream that you meet or are in the company of someone whom you do not like is an omen of contrary meaning and foretells good fortune for you. Fighting with enemies: Will be deceived by friends. Hating an enemy: Loss of your fortune. Killing an enemy: Great joy and pleasures in life. Winning out over an enemy: Will succeed in a lawsuit. 152

1 Engagement—To dream of any engagement, business, social, or matrimonial, is considered a bad sign. A broken engagement: May have to endure disappointments. Engagement of others being broken: Will have emotional sorrow. 361

4 Engagement Ring—To see or wear one means a new attraction; to be engaged, a speedy wedding. Returning an engagement ring: A change in life will soon come. 649

9 Engine—To dream of machinery in motion is not a good omen. you may expect difficulties in the near future. Driving an engine: Change in environment. A steam engine: Money will come easily during entire life. A gas engine: Important and very beneficial event to come. An engine being out of order: Watch out for treachery. An engine stopped: Financial gains. 279

2 Enlistment—To dream of enlisting means a postponed success. 317

5 Entertainment—This dream depends upon the circumstances. It is usually a very fortunate omen unless for any reason you feel uncomfortable. If you leave before the entertainment is over, it is a sign that you will miss some good opportunity through your own carelessness. 482

4 Envelopes—Closed envelopes represent difficulties. If you can open the envelope and remove the contents, then some worry will be smoothed away. Putting a letter into an envelope: Discovery of loss of valuables. Receiving an envelope with many letters: Big disappointment in love. Mailing an envelope: Luck and prosperity. Buying an envelope or envelopes: Change for the better. 319

3 Envy—To dream that other people envy you is a good sign. Envying others: Triumph over enemies. Being

envied by enemies: Are being watched by one with evil intentions. 543

1 Ermine—This signifies a letter from or some association with those of high rank, but to the sick it means a slow recovery. Owning an ermine coat: Will invest in real estate. Buying an ermine coat: Must attempt to save money. 492

1 Eruption—Good luck is coming to you which will make you much envied. 919

6 Errand—This is really an obstacle dream. If you are out on an errand and successfully conclude it, then all will be well. If you cannot conclude it or procure the article you require, then you may expect business trouble. 492

4 Escape—This is a straight dream that depends upon the apparent happenings. If you escape from any difficulty in your dream, it means success in your personal affairs, a triumph over difficulties. If you escape from fire or water, you may expect anxious moments but a successful issue. If from some wild animal, then look for treachery near you. If in your dream you do not escape, then it is a very bad sign. 715

8 Estates—To dream of your own estate denotes a devoted marriage partner. 251

4 Evening—A prosperous time to come later in life. Your earlier worries will be happily ended. 625

9 Evidence—To dream of giving evidence against a criminal in court denotes a friend whose reputation you will be able to save. 360

3 Evil—A very serious omen unless you succeed in driving it away. Be careful in your business. 750

8 Examination—An obstacle dream. If you find that the examination is too difficult, then expect business worries. If, however, you can answer most of the questions and dream that you are doing well, then some unexpected good fortune awaits you. 404

4 Exchange—If you dream that you are exchanging articles with some other people, expect business losses and difficulties. 634

5 Excuse—It is a bad sign if you find yourself making excuses in your dreams. You will suffer loss through your own folly. Others making excuses to you: Will live

a long life. A partner making excuses: Happiness is assured. Children making excuses: Financial gains. 743

1 Excitement—To dream that you are feeling unpleasantly disturbed denotes a successful ending to your plans. 192

8 Execution—The success of your undertakings will be doubtful. Execution of sweetheart: Avoid rivals. Execution of an innocent person: Will be jilted by lover. 125

7 Exercise—This might be called an obstacle dream. If you enjoy the vigorous exercise, all will be well; but if you feel tired, then beware of money losses. 862

8 Exhaustion—In your dream you may not know why you feel exhausted, but it is always a bad sign unless you recover fully in your dream. 359

8 Exile—To dream that you have been sent away signifies that your lot will be cast largely in foreign parts. A woman dreaming of being exiled: Must sacrifice pleasure to take a trip. Being exiled because of guilt: Will have a skin disease for years. 316

4 Expedition—This omen is only fortunate if you carry out your purpose. If you set out to go somewhere or to do something and fail in your purpose, then expect money losses and worry in business. Planning an expedition but not going: Big castastrophe ahead. Failing to reach goal on an expedition: Expect money losses. 742

9 Explosion—Danger to a relative. Of an explosion: Friends will disapprove of your actions. Being injured in an explosion: Must endure vexation. Face being scarred by an explosion: Will be unjustly accused. Being enveloped in flames after an explosion: Friends trespass on rights. Being guilty of causing an explosion: Friends will lose confidence in you. 247

7 Express—If you are traveling in it, beware of offending those over you in business. Mailing an express letter: Danger through a secret. Receiving an express letter: Will be cheated by friends. 925

4 Extravagance—An omen of happy domestic surroundings. Wife being extravagant: Will realize high ambitions. 283

3 Eyeglass—Good news from some friend or sometimes a fortunate business deal. 831

9 Eyes—It is considered fortunate to see strange eyes staring at you in your dream; some important change will soon take place. But if you are worried about your own eyes, then be careful in your actions, for someone is working secretly against you. Having crossed eyes: Will be short of money. Losing your eyesight: Children are in danger of death. Being worried about the eyes: Be careful of your actions. 594

F

7 Faces—The importance of such an omen in a dream depends upon whether the face is smiling or repulsive, for it is a straight dream and anything coarse or ugly means ill fortune. To dream that you are washing your face shows trouble of your own causing. If you see faces are of absolute strangers, it shows a change of residence or occupation. 286

7 Factory—A factory is a sign of some unexpected happening. If the place shows signs of great activity, then the coming change will be all the more important. An idle factory shows that the change will bring worry and loss. Being in a factory: Great riches in the future. Building a factory: Death of a friend. Selling a factory: Sickness is ahead. 835

9 Failure—This is a dream of contrary meaning, since if you fail in any attempt in your dream you will succeed in real life. 351

5 Faint—It is always a bad omen to see signs of collapse or illness in your dream whether you are the sufferer yourself or whether you tend someone who is ill. 392

9 Faithfulness—A dream of contrary meaning. If you dream that you are false to someone, or they are to you, it is a good omen. Having faithful children: Beware of rivals. Having faithful friends: Sickness. 279

7 Falcon—You are surrounded by enemies who envy you. Falcons flying: Will be cheated by friends. 241

4 Fall—To dream that you fall from a height is a sign of misfortune, and the longer the distance you fall the greater will be the coming trouble. Being injured in a fall: Will endure hardship and lose friends. Falling without injury: Will be victorious in your struggles. Falling on the floor: You are menaced by danger. Falling and rising again: Honor. 823

4 Falsehood—Another dream of contrary meaning whether you are the liar or whether you dream that someone is telling lies to you. 634

7 Fame—This is one of the dreams that go by contraries and warn the dreamer against failure. 673

3 Family—To dream of a numerous family is a good sign of prosperous times in store; it is also fortunate to dream of relatives as long as they are friendly. 264

9 Famine—To dream that you have not enough to eat is a contrary dream; you will live in greater comfort. 315

3 Famous—To dream that you have become famous is a bad sign. It shows loss and change for the worse. Children becoming famous: Rapid success of own hopes. 138

3 Fan—Be cautious. This is not actually a bad sign but a warning that you should not be venturesome. A single lady fanning herself: Will soon form profitable acquaintances. A woman losing her fan: A close friend will drift away. A woman buying a fan: She is interested in another man. 732

1 Farewell—It is generally considered a good sign to dream of bidding good-bye to anyone. 361

2 Farm—To dream that you are engaged in farm work is a fortunate omen: It indicates material success, though after some struggle on your part. If you only visit a farm, it indicates good health. A farm burning: Considerable fortune ahead. A vacant farm: Misery. 938

1 Fashions—To dream that you are studying the fashions either in a magazine or in the shop windows is a sign of some small change, either for good or ill. Watching a fashion show: Will have a long life. Fashion models in a store window: Family quarrels. 712

1 Fasting—Times of good cheer are at hand. Members of family fasting with you: Great wealth. 415

9 Fat—To dream that you are growing fat is an unfortunate sign, especially to a woman. 243

4 Father—To dream that you see your father and he speaks to you is a sign of coming happiness. If he is silent or if he appears to be ill or dead, then you may expect trouble. Father being dead: A big catastrophe is ahead. Father being poor: All desires will be accomplished. 418

9 Father-In-Law—To dream you see your father-in-law either dead or alive signifies ill luck, especially if he uses violence or is threatening. 243

6 Fatigue—To dream that you are tired is a contrary omen, for it indicates a coming success in some venture. 105

6 Fault—It is a dream of contrary meaning if you do wrong and are reproved by your friends. Husband being at fault: A false friend. Wife being at fault: A mystery will be solved. Partner being at fault: Will live a long life. Others being at fault: Doomed for disappointment. 357

8 Favor—This is a dream of contrary, for if you dream that someone has done you a favor it shows a loss of money in some business transaction. Receiving a favor from a loyal friend: Change of surroundings. Receiving a favor from a relative: Warning of arguments. 152

3 Fear—This dream has many interpretations, as naturally it varies so greatly in the circumstances. Fear can be felt and shown in so many forms. Roughly speaking, it should be treated as an obstacle dream. If you dream that you overcome your fears or get over your trouble, all will be well; but if the fear persists and you cannot trace the cause, then expect treachery or deceit on the part of someone you trust. 291

9 Feasting—A dream of contrary meaning. Expect difficulties in the near future. Prepare a feast: Another person is enjoying what you desire. 126

1 Feathers—It is wise to put no meaning into feathers in themselves; they should be treated as emblems of color, such as white, black, red, or blue. Collecting feathers:

Will have joy during life. Wearing a tuft of feathers: Great honors will come to you. 271

8 Feeble—To dream that you are tired or worn out is a fortunate omen. Others being feeble: You are looking for money. Children being feeble: Financial gains. 143

5 Feeding—To dream that you are feeding animals is an excellent omen. Your affairs will prosper. It is not, however, a good sign to dream that you yourself are feasting. Others feeding children: You are being deceived. 824

9 Feet—Feet hurting: Likely to have troubles of humiliation. Burning own feet: Failure in own affairs. Having a broken foot: Loss of a relative. Bathing own feet: Will have trouble and be molested. Feet itching: Joy without profit. 198

6 Fence—A dream of a fence, like all dreams concerning obstacles, is a sign of difficulties ahead. The result depends upon the upshot of your dream. 123

9 Fencing—To dream of a fencing match denotes an adventure in which your wits will be your only weapon. 954

8 Ferns—If you are dreaming of ferns in a luxurious growth, it is a very favorable omen. Mother Nature is helping you to succeed. But if it is Autumn or if the foliage is decaying for any reason, then accept it as a warning of coming trouble. If the ferns are in pots instead of growing naturally in the open, then the success will come only after effort and difficulty. 953

9 Ferry—Danger is around you. Try to do nothing you do not wish known, and do not walk by a river unless necessary. Being on a ferry boat alone: Danger is nearby. Being on a ferry boat with family: Good times are coming. 621

4 Festival—This has much the same meaning as feasting. It is not a fortunate omen. Preparing a festival: Another person is enjoying what you desire. 643

2 Fever—This is generally looked upon as an omen of contrary meaning. If you dream that you are ill, you can rest assured that your health is good. Children having a fever: Will get what you desire. Relatives having a fever: Financial gains. 839

9 Fields—Fortunate happenings of a personal character, agreeable and pleasant friends, hospitality, and merry making. A field of grain: Pleasant friends. A field of oats: Prosperity. A field of corn: Good earnings. 324

8 Fighting—Another example of an obstacle dream. The result will depend upon what happens. If you are beaten in a fight, you must expect misfortune or a love reverse. If you are successful in your dream, then you will overcome your difficulties. Others being in a fight: Recovery from an illness. 260

6 Figs—An unexpected and fortunate event. 726

4 Figures—This omen is a difficult one to judge, as the importance of the dream depends upon the magnitude the figures involved, and these again depend upon the circumstances of the dream. As a rough guide, low figures are figures which are fortunate. High figures are bad, while medium figures or in-between figures show difficulties that can be surmounted if you exert yourself. Obviously, high figures for a girl or for a working man would only be low figures for a wealthy individual or prosperous business man and mean little or nothing. 391

5 File—To dream you are using a file presages new work. A nail file: A mystery will be solved. Putting papers in a file: Are confronted with insurmountable obstacles. Taking papers out of a file: An enemy is seeking your ruin. 635

5 Films—A possible journey abroad in the near future, much discussion. Guard against your tongue. 104

9 Finding—This is an omen of contrary meaning. The more valuable the article you find, the greater will be your loss in business. Finding someone naked: Will find new employment. Finding a child: Will have a very complicated lawsuit. Finding gold and silver: Will have many worries. 519

6 Fingers—To cut your finger or otherwise damage it is a sign of quarreling with your friends or family circle. A finger bleeding: Be careful and do not lose money. Having fingernails cut: Loss of friends. Having burned your fingers: Are envied by many people. Breaking the fingers: Will have a good marriage. 519

2 Fire—An omen of warning. If the fire is small and does no mischief, then expect news of some sort, though not of great importance. If the fire burns you, then expect a serious mischance in your affairs. Lots of smoke but no flames: Will be disappointed. Fireman putting out the fire: Will receive good news. Watching a fire being put out: Poverty. Being in a fire: Triumph. Throwing water on a fire: Will lose your temper. 371

6 Fire Engine—It is a dangerous omen to see a fire engine but its importance depends upon whether it is going to the scene of a fire or is returning. This can be judged by the pace and by the clanging of the bell. Being a fireman on a fire engine: Will realize high ambitions. 204

6 Fish—To dream of fish swimming freely is a sign of coming good fortune; but if you catch them or see them dead, as in a shop, then expect trouble. Cooking a fish: Marriage. Eating boiled fish: Joy. Catching a large fish: Joy and profit. Children fishing: Joy and health. 843

9 Flags—There are different interpretations of this omen in various parts of the world, so it is better to ignore it and study instead the other indications in your dream. Some people consider that the generous display of colored bunting is a fortunate omen; but all colors are not propitious, so this point is doubtful. For instance (see Colors) red is generally considered a warning of quarrels with friends, where black is ominous. There should be plenty orange, green, blue, or white if the bunting is to bring good luck. 927

6 Flames—As a rule, this is a bad sign; but if the flames are under control, all will be well. Dark flames: Danger in love matters. Uncontrolled flames: difficulties ahead. 105

1 Flash—To dream of a flash or light, whether from a searchlight or torch, is a sign of important news that will cause your plans to succeed. 397

8 Flattery—This is much the same as falsehood, for all flattery is insincere and unreliable. It is a dream of contrary meaning. If someone is flattering you, then expect trouble or disappointment. Flattering a fiancée:

Must control passions. Flattering friends: Will experience many ups and downs. 143

3 Fleet—Ships at sea always form a bad omen, and it does not really matter what type of vessels they are. Of course, this does not apply to shipwrecks or other maritime disasters. A merchant marine fleet: Will receive a letter from a friend. A naval fleet in a parade: You are being deceived. A foreign naval fleet: Will entertain an unwelcome guest. 012

5 Flirting—On the whole, a prosperous omen, but not if you carry it to a heartless extent or cause tears. Flirting with married woman: Beware of treachery. Flirting with a married man: Suitable time to pursue courtship. Flirting with an unmarried girl: Avoid rivals. Flirting with an unmarried man: You will be deceived. Flirting with a divorced person: Will realize own ambitions. 419

3 Floating—This is a good dream if all goes well. It is really a variation of the obstacle dream. If you sink or find it difficult to keep afloat, then expect trouble ahead. A dead person floating: Will live a long life. A dead fish floating near the beach: Danger through a secret. An empty boat floating: Will have a change of surroundings. 687

6 Floods—This is a good sign for those whose lives bring them in contact with water or the sea, but for others it should be treated as an obstacle dream, and is especially unfortunate for love affairs. Saving yourself from a flood: You have one loyal friend. Floods causing devastation: Worry will be smoothed away. 394

3 Floor—To dream that you are sweeping or washing the floor is a bad omen for business success. You will not be fortunate, though your losses may not amount to a large sum. To sit or lounge on the floor, on the contrary, is a very good dream. 192

5 Flour—It is a bad omen to buy or to use flour in the course of your dream. Making pastries with flour: A happy life is ahead. Dealing with the flour market: Will make risky speculations. 365

8 Flowers—One of the best of nature dreams, this foretells great happiness unless you throw away the blossoms which means you will suffer from your own care-

less actions. A young woman dreaming of receiving flowers: Will have many suitors. Gathering flowers: Will remarry soon. Picking flowers from a plant: Great benefit. Artificial flowers: Misfortune in business. Receiving flowers as a gift: Great joy. 836

1 Flute—It is a very fortunate dream if you see yourself playing the flute, but you may expect difficulties if you see someone else playing. 028

2 Flying—Another obstacle dream, the meaning of which depends on the results. Aviation is of such modern growth, however, that such a dream must indicate ambitious plans, possibly beyond your real power of accomplishing. Being an aviator: Ambitious plans are possibly beyond power to accomplish. Owning a plane: Success in all enterprises. 371

8 Foam—Cheerful scenes will soon surround you. 251

1 Fog—An obstacle dream of great power, especially to those in love. Your prospects of happiness are doubtful. If the fog clears away and the sun shines again, you will get over your disappointment in time. Fog clearing away: Happiness in love. 586

4 Food—It is generally a fortunate sign to eat food in your dream, provided you are soon satisfied. But it is not a good omen to eat like a glutton. Not having enough food: Death of an enemy. People selling food: You will receive some money. Tasting food: Loss of friends. 238

3 Foolish—To dream that you have done some foolish action is a dream of good fortune. Mate being foolish: Financial gains. Lover being foolish: You should mend your ways in life. 732

2 Foot—Beware of treachery if someone trips you up with his foot. Having a broken foot: Loss of a relative. Foot hurting: Likely will have humiliation. Cutting the foot; will have an operation. 326

2 Football—To witness a game of football is a bad sign. You may expect worries, possibly in connection with some friend. It is a good sign to see yourself playing, provided your side wins or you yourself score a goal. 497

8 Footprints—Difficulties which you will soon surmount by your own efforts. Footprints of someone else: A friend is trying to help you secretly. 278

9 Footsteps—You will hear something which will spur you on to greater exertions and success. 819

8 Foreign Country—Your happiness lies at home. Being in a foreign country alone: A change in life will soon come. Being in a foreign country with others: Will have new business ventures. 206

8 Foreigners—To dream of foreigners is usually considered very fortunate for your love affairs. 125

2 Forest—Another variation of the obstacle dream. The meaning will depend on what happens and whether you emerge from the forest. Being alone in a forest: Social activities of a happy nature. Being with others in a forest: Will be cheated by friends. A forest fire: Glad news. A forest with unusually high trees: Good business affairs. 479

4 Forgery—It is a bad omen to dream that you are guilty of forgery; but it is a good sign if someone else forges your signature. 508

5 Fork—To dream of forks is a sign of a quarrel. Receiving a gift of forks: Doomed for disappointment. 167

9 Forsaken—A good omen of the affections of those you dreamed lost. 999

5 Fort—Troubles and losses in store for you. 626

9 Fortune—A dream of contrary meaning. The more fortunate and successful you are in imagination, the greater will your struggles in real life be. Having own fortune told: Great struggle in real life. Being fortunate in business: Gay occasion to come. Being fortunate in love: Will lose plenty of money in gambling. 423

7 Fortune Teller—It is a most unfortunate omen to have your fortune told in a dream, but you will ensure success if you tell the fortune of any other person. Being a fortune teller: Good times are coming. Having own fortune told: Serious disaster is ahead. Hearing a fortune told to others: You have a loyal friend. 214

1 Fountain—A good dream if the water is clear. 352

3 Fowls—To dream of these common domestic birds

shows a commonplace and uneventful life without ups and downs. 534

9 Fox—To see a fox in your dream indicates an enemy or a rival among your acquaintances. If you see the animal killed, you will overcome a threatened trouble. 306

1 Fragrance—It is a good sign to dream of a fragrant perfume, but the results will not be very serious. Some small success is indicated. 253

5 Frantic—To dream of being frantic means a peaceful holiday after strenuous times. 815

5 Fraud—To dream that someone has cheated you is a sign of treachery, but if you dream that you yourself have committed a fraud, it shows coming prosperity. 248

6 French—To dream of speaking and hearing foreign languages is a fortunate sign, especially in love affairs. 312

3 Friends—A good omen, for you will receive unexpected good news unless you dream that your friends are in trouble. Saying good-bye to a friend: Painful experiences ahead. Being separated from a friend: Friends are endeavoring to destroy you. Friends being in trouble: Will receive unexpected good news. A friend being naked: Will have a big fight. Talking with a friend in a room: Joy and consolation. 129

6 Fright—A dream of contrary meaning. The more dreadful your ordeal, the greater your success. Your business affairs will prosper if you preserve your present difficulties. Frightening other people: A change in life will soon come. Being frightened in your sleep: Will discover a secret. 384

2 Frog—Success in business, a good dream. 209

6 Frost—Many troubles ahead of you, be careful what you do in the near future. Frost damaging your plants: Many troubles ahead. 312

2 Fruit—As with colors, the meaning of the fruit in your dreams varies according to its kind. 416

5 Fun—Excessive merriment is a bad sign in a dream and foretells difficulties in business affairs. The more boisterous your amusements, the more serious matters will

be. Quiet homely happiness is a different matter. Having fun with children: Doomed for disappointment. Having fun with friends: Change for the better. Having fun with important people: Honor and happiness. 635

5 Funeral—This dream is associated with the color black, but if you see yourself present at a funeral in black it is appropriate, so no harm need be expected. It is a dream of contrary meaning and indicates a successful love affair. Going to a funeral with family: Loss of friends. Being a pallbearer: Will do something foolish. Attending a funeral of best friend: Long life. A woman attending a funeral in mourning: Unhappy married life. 824

1 Furs—A favorable dream on the whole though it foretells change of some sort. A mink fur: People are being false to you. Being covered with fur: Your lover is faithful to you. 703

6 Furniture—This is generally a good dream, but it depends on the circumstances. Handsome furniture is very fortunate, but naturally this depends upon the person who dreams. What is ordinary furniture for a wealthy woman would be sheer folly for a working class woman, or for a business girl earning her own living. It should be just a little better in quality than what you actually possess. A common person dreaming of nice furniture: Much love. A business girl dreaming of nice furniture: Will earn own living. 789

6 Fury—To dream of a furious person denotes a reconciliation. Of a furious animal: A friend defends your name. 312

1 Future—You may have the chance to make up an old quarrel or mend a wrong. 797

G

9 Gable—Good advice will be given which, if followed, will lead to good fortune. 324

6 Gag—To dream that there is a gag in your mouth is an obstacle dream. If you do not succeed in getting free, then you may expect serious trouble ahead. A young girl dreaming of a gag: Will meet a man who takes her fancy. 654

4 Gain—A sign of contrary meaning. To dream that you have a big income or have pulled off a successful business deal is a bad sign unless you appear to have scored by cheating or by some unfair advantage. 607

7 Gale—Better times to come. Do not take present vexations too seriously, especially quarrels. Being on a ship in a gale: Will realize high ambitions. 214

7 Gallery—Worries will soon pass unless you should dream of falling from a gallery. A gallery of paintings: Big honors and fortune. 628

8 Gallows—This unplesant dream is one that carries a contrary meaning and is generally considered very fortunate in every way. Hanging on the gallows: Dignity and money. Someone you know being on the gallows: Avoid rivals. 287

2 Gambling—Do not act on the ideas of others or you will incur loss. Winning at gambling: Social activities will be of a happy nature. Losing at gambling: Will be relieved of pains. Gambling with dice: Inheritance. Gambling with cards: Loss of prestige. Gambling at roulette: Vain hopes. Gambling at a slot machine: Doomed for disappointment. 920

8 Game—To dream that you are taking part in a game is a mixed omen; for it depends upon the result, for one thing, and it is contrary in its meaning. If you win for yourself or your side, it is an unfortunate sign and means misfortune in business; but to lose indicates that you will be prosperous. 746

6 Gangway—Should you cross it, you have aroused the hostility of a rival. Take care not to lose what is now your own through overconfidence. Coming down the gangway on a ship: Avoid rivals. Other people going up the gangway: Loss of money. 429

4 Garden—A very fortunate dream, nature at its best; but of course it must be a garden that is well kept and not neglected. It concerns money matters. A beautiful gar-

den: Increase in fortune. Walking in a garden: Joy. 391

5 Garlic—This is generally considered a fortunate omen; but there are many people who detest the smell of onions, and in such cases they should be treated as signs of ill success. Cooking with garlic: You are disliked by those working under you. 914

6 Garret—An advancement in position should come speedily. Being in the garret of own house: Happiness is assured. 312

6 Garter—To dream that you have lost your garter indicates coming misfortune. If both garters should be loose and come down, the omen becomes more emphatic. If someone picks it up and returns it to you, it is a sign of a loyal friend that will help you in your difficulties; but if the person retains the garter, then your troubles will be increased by treachery on the part of someone near you. 402

9 Gas—This concerns your love affairs or domestic happiness. If you dream that the light is bad, then your interests will suffer accordingly. If the light goes out suddenly, expect a catastrophe. 279

8 Gems—Jewels are not favorable omens in a dream, nor are any excessive displays of luxury. Selling gems: Misfortune in love. Receiving a gift of a gem: Danger through a secret. Relatives having gems: Sickness within the family. 296

8 Geraniums—Those popular garden plants are often seen in dreams. They can be taken as omens of variety. Buying a geranium plant: Will have plenty of money. Red geraniums: Sickness. 521

6 Ghost—This is unfortunate only if the sight of the apparition appears to cause fright. Then you may expect a troublesome time ahead of you. If you do not fear the ghost, however, you will pull through your difficulties, especially if the spirit disappears. A ghost speaking to you: Beware of enemies. 438

6 Giant—One of the many obstacle omens. It signifies difficulties that can be overcome if met boldly, but the result depends on the circumstances of the dream. Killing a giant: Abundant means. A monstrous giant: Much success. 483

6 Gift—A dream of contrary meaning. Beware of the person from whom you receive a gift under such circumstances. Giving a gift: Bad luck. Receiving a Christmas gift: Treason from friends. Receiving a gift from a woman: Close friendship. Receiving a gift from a man: Change of fortune. 564

3 Gin—To dream of drinking gin denotes short life and many changes. Buying gin: Will have many changes in life. Serving gin: You have false friends. Receiving gin as a gift: Family quarrels. Giving gin as a gift: False favors. Breaking a bottle of gin: Will be visited by a friend. 102

4 Gypsy—An omen of varying meaning. If the gypsies offer any of their wares and you buy, it shows good fortune coming to you, but probably after some change or from a distance. 607

1 Girl—Surprising news; a reply long delayed will reach you at last. A beautiful girl: Increase in business affairs. Kissing several girls: Great success. A girl crying: Will be embarrassed by a friend. 145

4 Glass—This dream depends upon the detail of whether the glass is clear or cloudy. If all is well, it is a fortunate dream, especially in matters of business. Breaking a window glass: Trouble is ahead. Cleaning window glass: Your happiness is in danger. Breaking a drinking glass without water in it: Death of a woman. Spilling a glass of wine: Good news. 427

8 Gloom—A possible change for the better will come your way. Do not hesitate to grasp a chance. 296

8 Gloves—This omen is very similar to that concerning garters, but any good or bad fortune will be short lived. Carrying gloves: Prosperity and pleasure. Buying gloves: A false friend is nearby. Losing own gloves: Will be thrown onto own resources. 935

9 Glue—This portends faithful friendship from one whom you trust. Buying glue: Will realize own ambitions. 891

8 Goats—Many trials, but you will face them bravely. If the animals are black, white, or piebald, then you must take color into consideration as well. 179

8 God—To hear His voice or to dream that He speaks to you: Happiness and joy. Praying to God: Much prosper-

ity. Seeing God face to face: Will have much joy. 917

2 Gold—A dream of contrary meaning as far as the metal itself is concerned, for it signifies loss of money; but if your clothes are of gold cloth or if they are embroidered with gold ornamentation, it is a good sign. Losing gold: Financial distress. Working with gold: Misfortune. Counting gold: You are attempting to deceive friends. 902

8 Goldfish—Trouble in business. Dead goldfish: Disappointments to come. Having goldfish in a bowl in own house: Financial gains. Buying goldfish: Matrimony within the family. 314

4 Golf—To dream that you are spending your time playing games is a warning that your business affairs need attention. Playing on a golf course with others: Unfit to fill your position. 472

5 Gondola—This presages a happy but unromantic life. Being in a gondola with lover: Love will not last very long. 815

7 Gong—An exciting event in the family. Avoid trifling with important matters. 214

5 Good—To dream that you do good signifies jollity and pleasure. To dream that others do good to you means profit and gain. Saying good things about others: Will be embarrassed. People saying good things about you: Will be deceived by friends. 914

9 Gout—Avoid overstrain; you are not too strong at present. Having gout on the feet: Will have misery. Having gout in any other joint: Financial losses because of relatives. 819

7 Government—To dream of a post under government is an omen of a precarious living and much poverty. 583

5 Gown—A dream of contrary meaning. The more handsomely you are dressed, the worse the omen. In fact, the most fortunate dream a woman can have is to imagine herself naked. If, however, your clothes are shabby or torn, it is a fortunate sign, though not so good as nakedness. 329

4 Grain—This is a very fortunate omen, although your success will come to you from hard work and endeavor. Persevere and you will be richly rewarded. Harvesting

grain: Big gains. Grains standing in the field: Will receive plenty of money. Carrying the grain to the barn: Luck and prosperity. Grain catching on fire: A serious disaster is ahead. Sowing grain in a field: Much joy. Selling grain: Financial gains. 841

1 Grandparent—To dream that you are a grandparent or that your grandchildren are present is a very favorable sign. 784

1 Grass—As in the case of a garden, this dream is fortunate if the grass is seen green and flourishing but not otherwise. 127

7 Grasshopper—Loss of harvest. Grasshoppers in your own yard: Bad omen for sick people. Killing grasshoppers: Rivalry by an unexpected person. Others killing grasshoppers: Expect the arrival of a theft. 421

6 Gratitude—Surprising events will happen to you should you dream of being exceedingly grateful to someone; but should you dream of another expressing gratitude to you, the events will happen to someone dear to you. 240.

8 Grave—News from afar. If the grave space is open, news will not be good. A newly prepared grave: Will suffer through the sins of others. Walking on a grave: Unhappy married life. Digging a grave: Big obstacles are ahead. The grave of your father: Inheritance. 125

2 Gravel—To dream that you are walking on a rough gravel path is equivalent to an obstacle dream, but naturally it concerns small affairs. If you complete your journey, all will be well. 794

1 Gray Hair—These signs of advancing age are most fortunate, especially if you are in the company of a gray-haired person in your dream. If you imagine that you yourself are gray, it is still fortunate but indicates difficulties for success. 280

9 Greyhound—You will win more than a race, despite keen rivalry. A greyhound belonging to others: Will win at a lottery. A greyhound racing: Will receive a letter with good news. 324

9 Grief—This indicates joy and merry times. 612

2 Groans—It is not a fortunate dream to hear people groaning unless you assist them. 083

5 Groom—Legal affairs will be made known to you, probably to your advantage. 914

7 Ground—To dream that you are stretched out on the ground signifies a humble status for some time to come. 790

6 Guard—To dream of keeping watch against a peril of some kind is a warning to avoid ill-considered speech which may put you in a difficult position. Being a security guard: Will be saved from a big danger. A guard taking away a prisoner: Will be insulted by friends. 708

1 Guests—Not a fortunate dream. The more visitors to come to you, the greater will be your business difficulties. Others having guests: Beware of illness. Unwelcome guests: Unhappiness in love affairs. 415

1 Guide—To be guiding someone else in a dream signifies a kindly assistance in your own difficulties from good friends. 631

1 Guitar—This is much the same omen as a violin, and it is a fortunate dream if the music pleases you. Any interruptions are a bad sign. Being pleased by guitar music: Love and joy. A young woman dreaming of hearing a guitar: Temptation through flattery. 820.

5 Gum—Someone will stick to you in an emergency. Financial delays are indicated. 516

6 Gun—To hear the report of a gun is an omen of illness concerning some loved one, but it will pass away. If you hear several reports, the illness will last for a longer period. If you yourself fire the gun, you will be the invalid. Shooting a person with a gun: Dishonor. A rifle with a bayonet: Separation of partners. Traveling with a gun: Will soon get married. 915

7 Gunpowder—To a man this dream means a speedy change of residence. To a girl, a wedding with a soldier. 178

1 Gutter—To dream of being in the gutter denotes hard times to come. Should you find anything valuable in a gutter, financial reward will come later for hard work done now. 802

1 Gymnastics—Any violent exercise is a dream of con-

trary meaning. Your plans will fail because you will not be able to put sufficient energy into your work. 937

4 Habit—To dream of putting on or wearing a riding habit indicates a great effort which you will have to make to escape from some unhappy position. Be brave, as you have more friends than you think you have. 841

7 Hag—Gossip and scandal about women friends. 439

3 Hail—This is a bad dream and foretells difficulties and disappointment. 309

9 Hair—To dream about your personal appearance is a sign of continued prosperity if you are satisfied with your image. If your hair is getting thin or falling out, it is a bad sign. If you worry because your hair is turning gray, it shows that difficulties are ahead of you and that your affairs need careful attention. 468

6 Hall—To dream of a great hall in a strange place means important decisions to be made shortly. 249

9 Halo—Present pain will lead to good fortune later. Be brave. Seeing a solar halo: Rapid success of own hopes. Seeing a lunar halo: Change in own environment. 819

4 Ham—A fortunate dream, but it concerns trivial matters. Buying a ham: Will incur debts. Boiling a ham: Big profit. Slicing a ham: Financial gains. Eating ham: Joy and profit. 157

4 Hammer—Unlike hearing the noise of a gun being fired, it is a fortunate sign if you hear the sound of a hammer. It is a good sign for business and love affairs. 913

1 Hammock—This is a sign of a loss and also of a gain of more value than the loss, probably to do with a lover. Children being in a hammock: Misfortune in love affairs. 901

9 Hand—Another dream that concerns your personal appearance. If your hands are dirty, you should be care-

ful over your affairs, for success is doubtful. If your hands should be tied, you will have great difficulty in overcoming your troubles. But to dream that you are shaking hands with some person is fortunate, for some unexpected event will enable you to put things right. 909

1 Handcuffs—This is a dream of contrary meaning. Good fortune awaits you. A dangerous prisoner being handcuffed: Will receive a letter with money. 316

2 Handkerchief—Someone has a gift for you. Losing a handkerchief: Serious troubles. Giving a handkerchief as a gift: Will cry for a long time. Using a handkerchief to blow your nose: Will be loved by people. Buying a handkerchief: Be careful of new ventures. 254

1 Handwriting—It is not a good sign to see written documents in your dream. Be careful of new or untested ventures. 613

6 Hanging—To dream that you are being hanged denotes good to you. To dream that you see a person hanged is an omen of good to him. He will attain wealth and great honor. A criminal hanging: Will make money in a shameful manner. Someone hanging without a cause: You are prone to be stingy. Being freed just before hanging: Will realize own ambitions. 213

3 Happy—Any excessive pleasure or merrymaking in a dream is an omen of contrary meaning. The more boisterious your pleasures, the greater your business difficulties will prove. 246

8 Harbor—Means a happy time to come with one you care for. Falsehood will be exposed. Being alone in a harbor aboard ship: Financial gains. Being with loved one in a harbor aboard a ship: Falsehoods to be exposed. 242

5 Hare—This is not a good sign. Things will be difficult, but a change of residence or occupation will help to put matters right. Shooting hares: Happiness. 248

9 Harem—Truth will out. Things you believe unknown are the subject of much gossip, but you will triumph in the end. 162

3 Harness—A pleasant evening and an introduction which

will lead to a friendship. Buying a horse's harness: Will be tempted by a new love. 903

7 Harp—All pleasant music is a favorable omen in a dream. Playing a harp: Do not trust friends too far. A harp being played at a theater: You have one loyal friend. 313

3 Harvest—To dream that you see the workers busy on the harvest is a most favorable sign; nature favors you. It is very fortunate for those in love. 435

2 Hat—New clothes are generally excellent omens, but shabby things are a warning of trouble. If you lose your hat, beware of false friends. A women's hat: Recovery from an illness. A man's hat: Will have emotional sorrow. Wearing a new hat: Wealth. Wearing a straw hat: You are prone to conceit. 218

8 Hatbox—To dream of opening one denotes a gay occasion unless you find it empty, in which case it means disappointment about a festivity to which you will not be invited. 413

2 Hatchet—You will be in danger soon. Anxiety and trouble. 317

7 Hawk—Birds of prey are omens of coming losses. Be careful about your business ventures and speculations. 097

7 Hay—A very fortunate dream. Nature helps you, and you should be successful both in business and love. 925

9 Head—Pains in your head or dreams about accidents are warnings of difficulties ahead of you. Persevere, but be prudent and do not take any risks. Washing your head: Overwhelming misfortune. A bald head: Will be loved. A head with long flowing hair: Big honor. Having a clean-shaven head: Will be ashamed. Having your head cut off: Pleasure and honor. 549

2 Hearse—Beware of fire and deceit. Save your pennies and trust few people; you are shortly making an important change. 128

7 Heart—Warm affection is felt for you where you least expect it. Having pains in your heart: Long sickness. Being out of breath because of heart trouble: Will surpass friends. 196

7 Heart—You have no reason to worry over your circumstances; but avoid angry thoughts or words. 475

1 Heaven—A dream of heaven is a sign of prosperity and happiness in this life. The heavens being dark: Recovery of money. The heavens without the stars: Will receive bad news. Being in heaven: An immediate marriage. Going to heaven: Prosperity. 208

5 Heirloom—An answer postponed. Do not be dominated by a friend. Putting an heirloom away: You will be humiliated. 329

2 Hell—There are many interpretations concerning this omen in a dream, but it is a sign of disturbed health and not a true dream at all. 091

9 Helmet—Pleasant visitors; avoid extravagance; you will need all your savings. 216

9 Hen—A dream of commonplace affairs. If you see the hen laying eggs you may expect good luck. Chickens, however, are not considered fortunate. 423

7 Herbs—Signs of good fortune in almost any case, as they are favored by nature, but they must be growing vigorously. If flowers are seen, it is a very good sign. 853

2 Hero—A change of heart in someone who has hitherto been cool to you, especially should you dream of some great hero of historic times. 218

7 Herring—Fish are always good omens; you may expect success in business, but you will have to work steadily in order to secure it. 853

2 Hiccup—To dream you have a fit of hiccuping predicts travel. To dream a friend has hiccups means a parting. 308

8 Hide—To dream that you are hiding shows that bad news will soon reach you. 728

6 Hills—These must be looked upon as obstacles. If you succeed in climbing a hill, you will put things right with perseverance. The easier the ascent, the better for your future. 519

8 Hive—Dangerous undertakings which you will bring to a successful conclusion. 107

4 Hoarding—Be on guard against misfortune through de-

ceitful companions. Your affairs will improve before too long. 975

4 Hogs—To dream of hogs if they appear well fed: You have prosperity to come. If they are thin, prepare for bad times. Buying hogs: Joy. Selling hogs: Will be hated by friends. Wild hogs: A friend will try to cause harm. 193

4 Hole—To creep into one or to fall into one: You will come into contact with undesirable people. 328

3 Homicide—Misfortune and heavy loss. 309

9 Holly—A prickly plant. Beware of vexations. 126

5 Home—To dream of your home or school indicates continued prosperity, especially to the lover. Building a home: Honor without joy. Changing homes: Small fortunes. Your home burning: Honor and dignity. Own new home: Prosperity, especially for lovers. 329

4 Honey—If you eat honey, it is a good sign. As the bees are industrious so must you be, and then you will thrive. 319

7 Honeymoon—Changes, journeys, and disappointment. Being on your own honeymoon: You are being deceived. Friends going on their honeymoon: Much disappointment. 304

9 Hoop—To dream of a hoop or anything of a circular nature is a fortunate sign. 207

2 Horns—To dream one has horns on his head signifies dignity, dominion, and grandeur. Blowing a horn: Social activities of a happy nature. Animals with large horns: Expect sorrow. Animals with small horns: Joy and happiness. 218

9 Hornets—A spiteful rival will seek to injure you; be on your guard. 819

2 Horse—These animals are generally good signs but the color must be noted, such as black, white, brown, and so on. This affects the omen. If you are riding a horse and are thrown, it is a bad sign. If someone on horseback comes to visit you, expect news from a distance. It is a very lucky dream to dream of a horse being shod. 470

4 Horseshoe—To find one indicates a legacy; to see one, travel over land and water. 841

462

5 House—It is a most fortunate omen to see a house being built; but take warning if you see one being pulled down. 734

6 Horoscope—To dream of a chart of your starry influences is a sign that a stronger mind than yours will dominate you unless you resist with all your might. Buying a horoscope book: Approaching money. Being told your horoscope: Will be badly tormented. 105

1 Hospital—A warning to alter ways of living which lead to ill health, or a serious misfortune may befall you. 136

6 Hotel—It is not a favorable sign to dream that you are staying in a hotel; any omens of luxury are bad signs. For a wealthy person the dream will carry no particular meaning. It is the sense of luxury that means disaster to your plans. 519

8 Hunchback—A period of many trials and changes to come, to be followed by a happy love affair. 107

1 Hunger—A dream of contrary meaning, for to be hungry in your dream is a sign of prosperity but only through hard work and much effort on your part. 523

3 Hunting—If you are hunting small animals, such as hares, it is a sign of disappointment; but if you hunt a stag, it is an omen of coming prosperity. The dream of hunting a fox shows, however, a risk from clever competition. If you are present at the kill, you will conquer all difficulties. 912

9 Hurry—Danger of fire or accident. Care will avert it. 783

7 Hurricane—A most unfortunate dream both for business and your home life. Be careful of your actions. 673

4 Hurt—A dream of warning. The result depends upon the nature of the accident and whether you recover from it. 526

6 Husband—An omen of contrary meaning in the case of lovers, for if you dream that you are married when you are not, then expect a quarrel with one dear to you. Losing husband by death: Important and very beneficial events to come. Marrying a second husband: Luck and prosperity. A husband divorcing his wife: Quarrels with

one dear to you. Others flirting with your husband: Will
live together all your life. 168

7 Hymns—To dream that you are singing hymns is a
fortunate omen; your plans will be successful. Hearing
others singing hymns: Recovery from illness. 241

9 Hysterics—Be firm and do not allow yourself to be
dominated by others if you would achieve success. 297

I

8 Ice—This is always an unfortunate omen; expect many
difficulties. Breaking through the ice: Anxiety without
cause. 341

4 Iceberg—Every test will be made of your strength;
make a big effort, and you will triumph. 742

6 Icicles—Good luck, happiness, and success in love. 159

3 Idiot—It is a good omen to dream of idiots; some
unexpected good fortune awaits you. 219

6 Idols—Your eyes are about to be opened. Do not show
your feelings too plainly. 483

5 Ignorance—To dream that you are ignorant or cannot
understand some matter is an omen of contrary meaning. Success will crown your efforts. 536

9 Illness—A warning of some great temptation that will
not work out favorably for you, however promising it
appears at first. Having illness: Misfortune in love
affairs. Children having illness: Consolation and happiness. 603

5 Illumination—Great good fortune. To a lover, it is quite
exceptionally fortunate. 671

8 Image—Not a fortunate dream. Postpone important
decisions. The image of a dead person: Expect the death
of a relative. The image of a saint: Failure in business
and in love. The image of your own children: Misfortune in love affairs. The image of dead relatives: Postpone an important decision. 413

6 Incense—It is considered a favorable omen if the

incense is pleasant to your senses, as in the case of all perfumes. But incense is so closely associated with the interior of a church that I am inclined to treat it doubtfully myself and suggest that success will only come after effort and anxiety. 384

5 Income—To dream that you possess a comfortable income is an unfavorable omen. 518

5 Income tax—Financial loss, probably through assisting a friend. Receiving a refund on income tax: Success in own enterprises. Cheating on payment of income tax: Beware of big losses. Having income tax raised: Will be assisted by a friend. 203

1 India—Strange happenings, a message of an unfriendly woman. Going to India: Will have emotional sorrow. Being in India: A big catastrophe is ahead. A native of India: Will have an adventure soon. 361

1 Infant—Children are good omens in a dream, but a helpless baby is generally looked upon as a warning of coming trouble. A beautiful infant: Peace and joy. A newborn infant in diapers: Good events to come. The infant of someone else: Unhappiness in love affairs. 235

7 Injury—To dream that you have been injured by someone shows that you have a rival in business or love who will prove a danger to you. Injury of someone else: Danger is ahead. Children having an injury: Joy without profit. 529

7 Ink—If you spill ink in your dream, expect separation from friends; but to be writing and using ink is a good sign. Buying ink: Financial gains. Writing love letters with ink: Treason. Writing business letters with ink: Loss on business affairs. A young woman dreaming of ink: She will be slandered. 493

6 Inquest—To dream of being at an inquest denotes prosperity. 267

4 Insanity—A dream of contrary meaning. Your plans will prove successful. Relatives being insane: Long life. Friends being insane: Unhappiness. A woman dreaming of being insane: Will be a widow. A man dreaming of being insane: Will divorce his wife. A young girl dreaming of being insane: Will have a happy marriage. A

young single woman dreaming of being insane: Her child will be prominent. 139

8 Insect—The interpretation of a dream concerning insects depends on the circumstances of the dream. If the insects fly or crawl away from you, it is considered that a disappointment awaits the dreamer in his business affairs. Having insects in own home: Be concerned with others. Killing insects outside own home: Financial gains. Killing insects with poison: A mystery will be solved. 926

5 Insult—A dream of difficulty, the result depending upon what happens. If someone insults you and you do not resent it, beware of trouble ahead. There may be a change of residence or of occupation. Insulting friends: Will suffer through own foolishness. Being insulted by enemies: Change of occupation. Being insulted by relatives: Change of residence. 814

6 Intemperance—To indulge to excess either in eating or in drinking foretells trouble. It is equally as bad to see someone else doing this. 735

8 Invalid—This is best treated as an obstacle dream. If you recover from your illness, then all will go well; if not, you must expect to find difficulties in the path of your success. Children being invalid: Expect difficulties on the way to success. Being invalid for the rest of your life: Will soon receive money. 296

6 Invitations—Written or printed documents are not good omens in dreams. Receiving an invitation from a loved one: Financial gains. Sending an invitation to business people: Financial gains. 420

1 Iron—Most metals indicate difficulties when they are prominent in a dream, but the color may be held to affect this. Silver or gold would carry the significance of white or yellow, whereas iron would be similar to black. 712

4 Ironing—A change for the better. Keep yourself free from ties and responsibilities for a time. Help will come to you in an unexpected way. 562

5 Island—Another omen of difficulties ahead, but if you get away from the island you will conquer in the end. 104

4 Itch—Your fears and anxieties are groundless. Having an irritation or rash: Unexpected arrival of friends. Having a sore caused from itching: Trouble from several women. 931

8 Ivory—A very fortunate dream when ivory is concerned. Giving ivory as a present: Money will come easily during life. 539

2 Ivy—Good health awaits you unless the ivy is pulled away from its support. Ivy growing on a house: Wealth. Having ivy in a pot in the house: Happiness is assured. 596

J

4 Jacket—Hard work with little reward. Be patient, but take the first opportunity of a change. Wearing a dark colored jacket: Infirmity. Wearing a sport jacket: Financial gain. Wearing an evening jacket: You will be deceived. 265

2 Jade—To dream of jade ornaments is a fortunate omen, though the color green indicates hard work in front of you if you want to succeed. Wearing jade: Prosperity. Buying Jade: Financial gain. 236

5 Jail—This is generally considered an unfortunate dream unless you are released in due time. Being in jail for a long time: Bad destiny. Being in jail for life: Will receive a big favor. Friends being in jail: Family happiness. A woman dreaming of being in jail: Must endure much suffering. 347

2 Jealous—To dream that you yourself are jealous of some other person is a bad sign; difficulties of your own making are shown. To dream that someone else is jealous of you shows that their attempts to defeat you will turn to your advantage. 452

7 Jeers—To dream that you are being jeered at by companions foretells triumph over enemies. 259

7 Jellyfish—A scheme is on foot to injure you; be on guard. 304

3 Jeopardy—If you dream you are in jeopardy, it will be very fortunate for you. Children being in jeopardy: Financial gains. Sweetheart being in jeopardy: Immediate success in love affairs. 984

2 Jewels—Always a very fortunate dream, especially for lovers. The omen is just as good whether you give the jewels to someone else or receive them yourself. Stealing jewels: Are in danger of committing some disgraceful act. Admiring jewels: Will experience extravagance. Selling jewels: Loss of money. 326

8 Jig—To dream you are dancing a jig portends at least one lover; be careful not to cause jealousy. 917

3 Jingle—To hear the jingle of small bells—either cattle bells, dog bells, or sleigh bells—foretells innocent flirtations and amusements. 354

6 Jockey—If a woman dreams she sees a jockey riding at full speed, she will have an unexpected offer of marriage. A jockey winning a race: Money will come easily during life. A jockey losing a race: Will be cheated by friends. A young girl being fascinated by a jockey: Proposal of marriage. 402

6 Jilted—A dream of contrary meaning. Expect good luck in your wooing and happiness in your married life. A woman jilting a man: Frivolity. A married woman jilting a secret lover: Will have worries over love. An unmarried woman jilting a lover: Unhappiness. 159

9 Journey—A change in your circumstances is shown, but the details of the journey will show the result. If your voyage is a pleasant one, all will be for the best; but if the road is rough or the weather is stormy, then be careful. Taking a journey by steamer: Accord among friends. Taking a journey by plane: Family quarrels. Having stormy weather during journey: Be careful of own affairs. Taking a journey with children: Happiness is assured. 612

5 Joy—A sign of good health when you are happy in your dreams. 428

2 Judge—An obstacle dream. It denotes trouble and difficulty ahead unless the judge takes your side of the case,

in which event you will pull through in time. Being found guilty by a judge: Will have high social standing. Being acquitted by a judge: A big fortune is coming to you. 839

8 Juggler—An advancement in position will come within your grasp. Do not hesitate. 368

9 Jumping—Another of the many obstacle dreams. You will meet difficulties but will overcome them if you persevere. 513

6 Jungle—Financial affairs will cause you anxiety. Economize while there is time. 654

2 Jury—It is considered unfortunate to dream that you are one of a jury, but if you merely dream that you see a jury from the court, then you will overcome your difficulties. 308

K

1 Kangaroo—The hostility of something or someone influential will cause you great anxiety. 532

5 Keg—Filled with liquid: A bad sign in business. With fish: Prosperity. Empty: A change of surroundings. 923

7 Kennel—You will be invited to the house of a man you know well. Do not go alone, and avoid quarrels. 298

1 Kettle—A very happy omen if the kettle is bright and clean. Troubles and losses if the water boils over. 892

9 Keyhole—It is not a good sign to peep through a keyhole in your dream or to see someone else spying in this way. Losses will follow quarrels. 396

6 Keys—To dream that you have lost a key is a bad sign. To give a key to someone shows good fortune in home life. Having a lover's key: You will come out well from present danger. Finding several keys: Peace and happiness in the home. 258

4 Khaki—Anxieties are around you but will be speedily dispersed. Wearing khaki uniforms: You are prone to

frivolity. Buying a khaki uniform: Approaching good times. 907

7 Kick—It is a bad omen to be kicked in your dream, for you will have many powerful adversaries; but it is a good omen if you kick another person. Kicking friends: A friend is trying to help you. 907

2 Kidnapping—Your circumstances are about to improve, and many of your worries are needless. A boy being kidnapped: A catastrophe ahead. 893

2 Killing—Someone wanting to kill you: Will have a long life. Killing a serpent: Separation. Killing a businessman: security. Killing a friend: Will have good health. Killing your parents: A big catastrophe is ahead. Killing a beast: Victory and high position. Killing birds and bees: Damage in business. 704

5 King—To dream of royalty is a very favorable sign unless the royal person shows signs of displeasure. Sending a letter to a king: Danger. Having an interview with a king: Rebellion in own home. 419

4 Kiss—This is a fortunate omen provided you have a right to kiss the person; otherwise, your own ill-judged actions will cause your downfall. Kissing a sweetheart at night: Danger. Kissing a husband or wife: Marital happiness. Kissing a friend: Failure in your affairs. 139

7 Kitchen—News from a distance is generally a good omen unless the kitchen is very bare and untidy. A very neat kitchen: Arrival of a friend. A fire lighted in the kitchen: Will have a change in your help. A coal stove in the kitchen: Misfortune in business. Preparing a meal in the kitchen: Will soon be divorced. 925

7 Kite—This omen depends on the circumstances. If the kite flies easily, you may expect success; and the higher up it goes, the better the omen. 214

7 Kitten—A favorable dream unless you hurt the young creature. Of a newborn kitten: Recovery from an illness. Kittens with their mother: Will have emotional sorrow. 124

4 Knapsack—An obstacle dream unless you feel no strain from carrying it on your shoulder. But at best it means difficulties ahead for a time. 328

8 Knee—Any injury to your knee should be treated as an

obstacle dream. If it is not serious, then you will come
through all right. A broken knee: Poverty. Falling on
the knees: Misfortune in business. The knees of a woman: Good luck. 791

2 Kneel—To dream of praying on your knees to God is
an omen of happiness to come. Kneeling in church or
tabernacle: Desires will be accomplished. 308

9 Knife—Quarrels with friends will lead to much misfortune. A sharp knife: Many worries: A broken knife:
Failure in love. Having many knives: Quarrels. Cutting
yourself with a knife: Must curb your emotions. 108

5 Knitting—Your undertaking will be crowned with success. If you see someone else knitting, you will be
deceived. 419

3 Knocking—Guard your tongue, and you will be well on
the way to happiness. 561

7 Knots—You will meet with much to cause you anxiety.
Tying knots: Will soon meet a true friend. Untying
knots: Will escape from danger. 358.

L

5 Label—Fixing a box with a label or trunk with a label
shows that you may expect a surprise. 275

1 Laboratory—Danger and sickness. People working in a
laboratory: Be cautious in business ventures. 415

8 Laborer—A laborer working; prosperity in own business. Laborers resting: Loss of wealth and mate. Laborers fighting: Will undergo a public crisis. Punishing
laborers: Persecution. Hiring laborers: Profit. Paying
laborers: Will be loved by people. Firing laborers: Beware of actions of neighbors. A laborer tilling the
ground: Profit. 962

8 Ladder—Climbing a ladder is a good sign, but the
reverse is an indication of troubles ahead of you. The
number of rungs should be noted, for this increases the

power of the omen. To feel dizzy when on a ladder is always a bad sign. 125

2 Lake—This is a dream that depends entirely upon the conditions. If the water is smooth, and the sailing or rowing is pleasant, then you may expect comfort in your home life and success in business. If the weather is stormy or unpleasant, then you are faced with difficulties which you may overcome with patience and industry. 902

1 Lamb—A dream of similar importance to that of playing with a kitten: it signifies good fortune unless you spoil your luck by your own action. A lamb particularly concerns your home life. Lambs in a field: Much tranquility. Killing lambs: You will be tormented. Finding a lost lamb: You will win a lawsuit. 361

4 Lame—An omen of business troubles if you find yourself lame or see a lame person in your dream. The result will depend upon what happens, and it can be classed as one more of the obstacle dreams. 609

7 Lamps—This is a fortunate omen, but the result can only be foretold by studying the circumstances of your dream. If the light is dim, you will have to work hard and face the difficulties if you wish to succeed; but if there are many lamps, then your path will be an easy one. If the light goes out, then expect ill health or the failure of your plans. 619

4 Land—A good dream if you possess land and retain it; but if in your dream you move away, then expect a change of occupation, not necessarily for your own good. If the owner of the land orders you away, then expect bitter disappointment. 913

1 Landlady or Landlord—This is not a favorable dream and indicates domestic trouble. 019

3 Lantern—This is usually a fortunate omen, but the light must be good. If it is dim or if it goes out altogether, then expect worries and difficulties. 408

8 Larder—Expect happiness and a joyful time. 125

7 Larks—It is one of the best omens possible to hear a bird singing happily; it is nature in her kindest mood. But if the songster is shut up in a cage, then your own greed will cause the failure of your plans. 142

2 Late—To dream of being late means that your opinions will be asked. Friends being late: You are being deceived. Employees being late: Warning of trouble. 524

7 Laughing—A dream of contrary meaning. It is especially serious if you laugh immoderately or without good cause. Be careful with your love affairs, for laughter in a dream means tears and sorrow in your life. 493

5 Laundry—A sign of a quarrel, parting, or loss. 563

5 Lawn—To dream you see a smooth green lawn portends prosperity and well-being, but should you walk on it the meaning is anxiety. 239

9 Law, Lawsuit, Lawyer—An omen of serious business trouble ahead of you. Do not start upon any fresh or hastily considered plans, for the stars do not foretell your success. Do not lend money, for you will not receive it again; nor should you spend too freely. 315

1 Lazy—To dream of idling denotes trouble to those near you, affecting you indirectly. A legal matter will end in marriage. Children being lazy: Will marry wealthy people. Others being lazy: Warning of trouble. 451

4 Lead—The significance of metals depends largely upon the general color. Lead is not a fortunate dream, so be careful and consider your plans once again before you act. To the married it is a sign of domestic squabbling. 103

6 Leaf—To see trees with full leaves in your dream is a happy omen. Your affairs will prosper. Nature is favorable. It is a very good dream for lovers, especially if a blossom is seen in addition to the leaf. With fruit it is a sign of a happy marriage. But if the leaves are withered or falling, as in Autumn, it shows loss in business, disappointments in domestic affairs, or quarrels with friends. 915

7 Leakage—You are wasting time. Find a wider scope for your activities. 124

2 Leap Year—Frivolity in matters that should be taken seriously. Getting married in leap year: Marriage will not last long. Being born in leap year: Will live a long life. 101

9 Leaping—Another obstacle dream, the full meaning of which depends upon the circumstances. If you surmount the obstacle, your plans will succeed. To those in love it foretells trivial disagreements; or possible rivals, if the obstacle is a serious one. Leaping in the air: Loss of your present position. Leaping into water: Will be persecuted. 315

3 Learning—To dream that you learn something readily is a good sign, but if it proves a difficult task, then you are undertaking more than you can carry through. Learning a foreign language: Unhappiness in love affairs. 705

6 Lease—If you dream that you are taking a house, a shop, or some land on lease, it is a very fortunate omen for both business and love matters. 484

6 Leather—It is an unfortunate omen to dream of leather in any form, whether as a strap or bag, harness, or anything else. Buying leather: Happiness within the family. Giving a gift of leather: Family quarrels. 159

6 Ledger—All written documents or books are unfavorable omens in a dream. This includes keeping or using a ledger or cash book. 213

8 Legacy—It is always a fortunate sign to dream of a legacy or a gift; but naturally the extent of the good fortune will depend entirely upon the nature of the legacy. Receiving a legacy and arguing with relatives about it: Loss of money. Making a legacy to relatives: Will be upset because of difficulties. 413

7 Legs—To dream that you have bruised or injured a leg foretells money difficulties which will last for a short or long period according to the seriousness of the mishap. 394

6 Lemons—They are not fortunate omens unless you see them growing on trees, when it is a sign of an important journey which will affect your affairs seriously. 105

2 Lending—A dream of contrary meaning. If you appear to be lending money or other articles, it foretells that you will want before long; it is an omen of loss and poverty. Lending articles and clothes: An enemy is seeking your ruin and trouble is ahead. Lending your car: Change of environment. Lending household items: Doomed for disappointment. Others lending you money: Failure of affairs. 452

9 Leopards—Difficulties and dangers are ahead of you. It is probable that you will go abroad on business. Hearing a leopard roar: Will suffer grief. Leopards fighting: Sickness. 405

2 Leprosy—This signifies that it is in your power to overcome your worries. 290

4 Lessons—A sign of good fortunes of every kind. 220

9 Letters—To dream that you receive a letter is a sign of unexpected news; but if you post or send a letter, then you will meet some unexpected difficulty that will upset your plans but may not cause any real loss. Letters are a sign of something unexpected. Receiving a letter from a lover: Prompt engagement. Receiving a letter from children: Abundant means. Receiving a business letter: Be cautious in all your affairs. Receiving letters with money: Hopes have been accomplished. 405

5 Lettuce—Difficulties ahead that can be overcome by prompt and vigorous action on your part. 797

4 Libel—A dream of contrary meaning. The more severely you are libeled in your dream, the greater your success in life. 535

4 License—A change of occupation will lead you to better things. Applying for a license: Change of surroundings. Having been refused a license: Important and beneficial event. 625

2 Lice—To dream of lice and that you are killing a great number of them is a good omen. Finding lice in hair: Will be very rich. Finding lice on own clothes: Approaching money. Having lice on own body: Will have money very soon. 803

4 Lie—It is a bad omen to dream that you are telling a lie, as your coming troubles will be due to your own misconduct. 490

1 Lifeboat—This wonderful vessel is an omen of contrary meaning in a dream. If you see it on shore, then expect difficulties. If you watch it at sea saving a life, then all will be peaceful and quiet in your business affairs. 109

2 Light—A good sign unless the light goes out or becomes obscure, when it shows difficulties in store for you. A light in a distance: Safe return from travel. Turning a light on: Success in business. Turning a light out: You

are being cheated by your lover. A light on a ship in a distance: Will take a trip with your sweetheart. Lighting a lamp: Happiness. 704

8 Lighthouse—This is a fortunate dream and is not often encountered. Seeing a lighthouse through a calm sea: Will have a peaceful life. Seeing a lighthouse through a storm: Happiness will come soon. 134

1 Lighting—This is also a favorable dream, though you will have to face worries, as indicated by the dark clouds from which Nature's unexpected light is poured. Persevere, and you are certain of success. 172

7 Lily—Happiness and prosperity await you but only as the result of your own industry. Do not expect help from others; you must depend on your own exertions. If your dream shows the flowers withering or if you throw them away, then your own thoughtless actions will cause your downfall. 304

2 Lilac—Conceit. Do not think too much of appearance, either in yourself or others. 731

5 Limp—This is an obstacle dream. If you are forced to rest and cannot complete your journey, then the signs are more favorable for business ventures or speculations. 392

9 Linen—To dream that you are dressed in clean linen is a favorable sign; you may expect good news before long. If your linen is soiled or stained, it denotes serious loss in business unless you see yourself change the garment, which means you may expect to get over your worst difficulties. The meaning of a dream about linen also depends upon the color of the garment. 909

5 Lion—This dream is not the same in significance as if you see a leopard. The lion signifies some purely personal honor or success not necessarily involving a gain of money; but if you hear the lion roaring as if angry, then expect some misfortune near you through the jealousy of someone. A lion cub is a sign of valuable friendship. Being attached to a lion: Success. Killing a lion: Will have many changes but finally achieve victory. A lion being in a cage: Enemies will fail in their attempt to injure you. Hearing a lion roaring: Will suffer grief. 365

2 Lips—To dream that you have handsome lips is a sign that your friends enjoy their health. To have them dry and chapped means the contrary. 317

3 Liquors—Drinking freely in a dream shows a change of circumstances, and the other surroundings will decide whether this is in your favor or otherwise. 453

7 Lizard—Treachery. Killing a lizard: Will regain lost fortune. Having a lizard in a cage: Will have a good reputation. Having a belt made of lizard: Will have money during your life. Having shoes made of lizard: Will be very healthy. 250

1 Lobster or Crab—Both these are favorable omens for your love affairs or your domestic happiness. 325

6 Locks—This is another obstacle dream, and you will encounter difficulties in the near future. If cabinets or drawers are locked and you cannot find the key, it is a bad sign. You should be very careful in money matters and avoid speculation or risk of any kind. If later you find the keys, you will pull through; but even then it should be taken as a warning. 429

3 Locomotive—To dream of a railway express is a certain sign of travel or the arrival of some friend. This depends upon whether the engine is traveling from you or to you. If you find yourself burdened with luggage, it becomes an obstacle dream. If your luggage is light and easy to handle, then your difficulties will be overcome. 102

9 Locust—Your happiness will be short lived. 612

8 Logs—Logs of wood or the fallen trunks of trees are favorable omens in your dream, but you must not interfere with them or cut them up. 471

2 Lonely—Feeling alone in a dream is a favorable omen, but it shows that you must depend on your own exertions, not on the influences or help of friends or strangers. 731

6 Looking Glass—A woman looking at herself in a looking glass: Friends are cheating you. A man looking at himself in a looking glass: Be careful in business. A lover looking at a mirror: Sweetheart is not faithful. A widow looking in a mirror: Should find out the real underlying motive. A looking glass: Treason. 213

7 Lottery—To dream that you are interested in a lottery or hold a ticket for such a chance is a bad omen. There will be an unhappy attachment or an engagement to some person who will not be worthy of your love. 592

9 Love—This is a dream of contrary meaning as far as sweethearts are concerned. To dream that you do not succeed in love is a sign that you will marry and have a happy life; but to dream that your friends are fond of you is a very fortunate omen and indicates prosperity. To dream that you are in the company of your lover is also fortunate. 972

8 Love Letter—Unpleasant explanations have to be made, and a great deal will rest upon your decision. Remember, frankness is an admirable quality. Reading love letter: Will receive good news. Receiving many love letters: Frankness is an admirable quality. Tearing up love letters: Unhappiness. Saving treasured love letters: You will find out the truth. 305

2 Love Token—A love affair in which you will be greatly interested. Several others know more about it than you think; be circumspect. 290

9 Lucky—This is an omen of contrary meaning, for if you dream that you are lucky in business or in love affairs, it is an unfortunate sign. Be cautious and use your brains; do not trust your affections. 306

6 Luggage—A dream that signifies difficulties in your path though it depends upon the quantity of luggage you have with you and whether you are able to deal with it successfully. For the lover it foretells quarrels slight or important according to circumstances. 690

8 Lumber—Trouble and misfortune. Having plenty of lumber: Unhappiness. Burning lumber: Will receive unexpected money. Piles of lumber: Will face a troublesome task.

8 Lunatic—Surprising news which will lead to different surroundings. Being a lunatic: Warning of troubles. Keeping company with lunatics: Will be guilty of foolish actions. Being in an asylum: Danger in love matters. 512

4 Luxury—Another dream of contrary meaning; for the more your surroundings are luxurious in your vision,

the greater the difficulties you will have to face. You are not likely to be successful in business and will probably lose money through bad debts. In love it foretells a rival, who will probably supplant you. To the married it shows domestic and family quarrels and trouble. 202

4 Lie or Falsehood—It is a bad omen to dream that you are telling lies, as your coming trouble will result your misconduct. Others lying to you: Being cheated by friends. 623

6 Machinery—This dream depends upon whether you feel interested in the machinery. If so, it is a favorable sign, though it means hard work; but if you feel afraid of the machinery, then be careful in your ventures, for you will surely fail to carry out your purpose. 915

3 Madness—To dream that you are mad or in the company of insane people is a good sign. You will prosper in your affairs. It is a good omen for everyone—those in bad health, those in love, businessmen and speculators. 507

4 Magazine—Printed papers are not favorable omens in a dream. Be careful if you would avoid loss. 823

6 Magic—To dream of things happening by supernatural or unknown means is a sign that changes are coming in your affairs through some unexpected source. The ultimate result, fortunate or otherwise, will depend upon the details of your dream, but as a rule the result will be beneficial. The unexpected happening may mean the loss of a friend or some event that appears at the time to be unfortunate. 591

5 Magistrate—To dream that you are being charged with some crime or offense depends upon whether you are convicted or set free. If convicted, fortune is against you. 212

6 Magnet—Personal success and security in business. Be careful not to trust too recklessly. 321

8 Mail—Mailing a package: Will receive a gift. Mailing a letter with a check: Will receive good news. Mailing documents: A false friend is cheating you. Mailing items of value: Will become jealous. 314

1 Man—It is a fortunate omen to dream of a strange man but not of a strange woman. A tall man: Good luck. An armed man: Sorrow. A bald-headed man: Abundance. A fat man: Bad ventures. A naked man: Beware of whom you meet. A man with a beard: Loss of temper. A dead man: Loss of a lawsuit. 325

3 Manicure—A marriage with a much older partner. It will prove a happy one. 768

4 Mansion—All luxury dreams are bad omens. The greater the apparent prosperity, the worse your troubles will be. 823

9 Manure—To dream that you are cultivating the soil is a good sign for those in subordinate situations, but it is not so fortunate for the wealthy. 234

3 Map—To dream that you are studying a map indicates a change of residence and probably also of business or employment. If the map is colored, the omen is a fortunate one. 561

6 Marble—This is really a luxury dream and indicates disappointment and loss. Polishing marble: Will receive an inheritance. Buying marble: Will attend a funeral. 519

1 Marching—To dream of marching predicts advancement and success in business. 307

7 Marijuana—Will be melancholy. Smelling marijuana: Will have protection. Smoking marijuana alone: Will dream of unattainable things. Smoking marijuana with a member of the opposite sex: Security in love. Be arrested for smoking marijuana: You love amusements too much. 312

5 Market—To dream that you are in a market doing business or buying goods is a fortunate sign and shows that your circumstances will be comfortable; but if you are idly looking on, then it is a warning of lost opportu-

nities. If the market is empty and unattended, then it
means you can expect difficulties and troubles. Going to
a fish market: Will have a prominent position. Going to
a meat market: Will receive honors. 419

9 Marriage or Marrying—To dream that you are a witness of marriage is a warning of ill health; but if you
assist at the ceremony, it shows some pleasing news, not
of great importance. To dream that you are being married, either as bride or bridegroom, is a most unfortunate omen. Giving a daughter away in marriage: Good
times ahead. Being a bridesmaid in a marriage: Will be
married soon. 423

6 Marsh or Bog—This is another obstacle dream, and its
meaning depends upon what happens to your troubles
and difficulties. If you find it hard to move along but if
you get out all right onto firm ground, then you will be
able to put most of your misfortunes right. 654

8 Mask—To dream that someone comes to you wearing a
mask or a disguise is a sure sign of treachery. 431

6 Matches—Financial gains are at hand. 591

7 Mattress—A warning of poverty ahead: Guard against
it. Buying a mattress: Will lead an easy life. 475

3 Meat—It is not considered fortunate to eat meat in your
dream, though it is all right if you cook it for other
people. Broiled meat: Good times ahead. Raw meat:
Will receive news of a friend's death. Eating raw meat:
wealth. 102

9 Medals—To dream of wearing them: Merry times are
to come soon. Army and navy personnel wearing
medals: Financial gains. 594

8 Medicine—To dream that you are taking medicine is a
warning that your troubles are not serious, persevere
and you will succeed. Taking bitter medicine: Will attempt to injure one who trusts you. Giving medicine to
children: Hard work awaits. 782

9 Melancholy—A dream of contrary meaning. All will go
well. A young girl being melancholy: Disappointment
from a broken engagement. 504

2 Melody—All pleasant music is a fortunate omen. Per-

severe, and success will attend you. Playing and hearing a melody: Affairs will prosper. 812

3 Mending—To dream of darning clothes portends an inferior and miserable position. 390

9 Mermaid—An unlucky dream, particularly for those in whose lives the ocean plays an important part—seaman, fisherman, etc. 297

3 Mice—An indication of trouble through a friend or a business associate. A cat killing mice: Victory over enemies. Mice being caught in a trap: You will be slandered. A dog catching mice: End of troubles. 516

2 Midwife—This portends news of a birth and the discovery of a secret. 182

9 Milk—To dream that you are drinking milk is a fortunate sign; but it is unfortunate if you sell milk in your dream. To give milk to some other person is a good omen for one in love. It also is a good sign to dream that you are milking a cow, provided that the animal is docile and quiet. 405

9 Miracle—Unexpected events will astonish and occupy you for a little while. 459

8 Mirage—Signifies the loss of one friend in whom you have trusted. 782

1 Mirror—Discouragements. Seeing yourself in a mirror: Illness. Seeing your husband in mirror: Will be unfairly treated. Seeing others in mirror: Unhappy marriage. Seeing a loved one in a mirror: Wealth. A broken mirror: Unexpected death of a relative. A woman seeing herself in a mirror: Friends are cheating you. A man looking into the mirror: Be careful of business. A young girl looking into the mirror: Should change boyfriends. A business executive looking at himself in mirror: Employees are not loyal to you. A widow looking in a mirror: Find out her ulterior motives. 451

1 Miser—An unfortunate dream, for the more you hoard, the more unfortunate you will prove in business. It is a bad sign, particularly for those in love. 208

5 Misfortune—This is a dream of contrary meaning. If you dream that some misfortune happens to you or to someone you love, it shows some fortunate stroke of

business that will result in a far greater success than you expect. 392

9 Mistletoe—Take no chances of any kind. You are not in favor with fortune. 621

7 Missionary—A change to more interesting work and to truer friends. Do not be made unhappy by the desertion of a fickle companion. 817

6 Mistake—Avoid conceit and make sure of your information before acting. Take counsel of those who are willing to guide you. 429

8 Moans—Be on your guard against doubtful friends or dubious actions. 314

4 Monastery—Worldly affairs will prosper. 202

9 Money—To dream that you pay or give money to other people is a fortunate omen; prosperity awaits you. To dream that you receive money also foretells personal success due to hard work. To find money in your dream is not so fortunate, however; there will be some sudden advancement or success, but it will prove disappointing. If you change money it is a sign of difficulties that are your own fault, as if you exchange notes for silver or silver for copper. It is a very bad sign if you dream that you borrow money, either from a friend or from a moneylender. 758

7 Monument—Any handsome monument is a good omen. Success is coming your way as a reward of effort. Monuments in a cemetery: Discovery of lost valuables. 205

3 Moon—This dream depends upon the circumstances. If the moon is bright, shines clearly, and is free from clouds, it foretells success in love and personal happiness. If the moon is clouded over, it shows ill health or some other interruption to your comfort and enjoyment. A new moon is a fortunate sign for business; a full moon, for love affairs. 138

6 Mop—You will need forethought and carefulness to avoid coming trouble. 222

3 Moss—Take care of your correspondence. Write guardedly; seal and post carefully. Someone has an attraction toward you which will soon be expressed. 921

2 Moth—A warning of rivals who will harm you if you

are not careful in your speech and actions. Expect quarrels with your lover, husband, or wife. To those who employ others it is a sign that they are not being faithfully served. 101

7 Mother—To dream that you see your mother and converse with her is a very fortunate omen. Mother being dead: Danger to property and to you personally. Embracing own mother: Expect good fortune. 475

9 Motor—If you are riding in a vehicle powered by one, new surroundings are portended. 837

8 Mountain—Another dream indicating obstacles in your path. The ultimate result depends upon the circumstances. If you climb to the top, all will go well, although it means hard work as unexpected difficulties will confront you. 723

3 Mourning—A dream of contrary meaning. Great prosperity is before you if you are a business man, or married happiness, if you are a lover. 237

5 Mouth—To dream of your own mouth means a hint to guard your tongue. To see a small mouth signifies money to come; A large one, a companion worth more than money. 824

3 Movies—Frivolous invitations. Do not trust fair women. Going to a movie alone: Be cautious in love affairs. Going to the movies with a sweetheart: Great joy. Performing in a movie: A change in life will come soon. Someone you know performing: Warning of troubles. 345

2 Mud—A dream of contrary meaning. Good fortune awaits you. Mud in the street: Advancement within own position. Walking in mud: Family disturbances. Having mud on clothes: Your reputation is being attacked. Others having mud on their clothes: Good fortune awaits you. 839

4 Mummy—Be confident. Success is not far off. 364

7 Murder—Naturally, this dream is even more serious in its warning than manslaughter, for it shows that you have lost control of your difficulties. You cannot expect to succeed so should do your utmost to lessen your liabilities and risks. 412

6 Mushrooms—If you see yourself gathering mushrooms,

your ventures will be fortunate, but if you are eating them, be cautious in your business affairs. 132

2 Music—To dream that you hear pleasant music is a very favorable omen; all your affairs will prosper. It often indicates pleasant news from an absent friend or the renewal of some old friendship; but harsh and unpleasant music is a warning, especially to lovers or married people, for it shows some cunning and underhanded action that will cause you great discomfort and loss. 416

8 Musician—If you dream that you are a musician when this is not the case, it is supposed to show a sudden change in your life. Probably you will move to another area. If you really are a musician, amateur or professional, then the dream is of no importance. 215

1 Mystery—A dream of some happening that puzzles and disturbs you is really an obstacle dream. Solve the mystery, and all will be well. 363

1 Mustard—Danger from free speech. Try to avoid hearing or repeating confidences. 901

3 Mutiny—Your undertakings will lead you into odd company. Keep your promises, but avoid making rash ones. Taking part in a mutiny: You are unhappy in your present position. Being wounded in a mutiny: Infidelity. 363

N

5 Nagging—To dream of being nagged signifies that you will be the recipient of pleasing information. Be careful in whom you confide. 203

8 Naked—It is most fortunate to dream that you are naked or only partially clad. Any troubles will be of your own making, and you will not find it easy to get anyone to help you in your difficulties. It is particularly fortunate for lovers, as it shows reliability. To married people it foretells great happiness. 629

6 Name—If someone calls you by the wrong name in a
dream, it is an unfortunate omen for your love affairs.
123

2 Napkin—Some pleasant news is coming to you soon.
Having an embroidered napkin: Marriage will take
place. Receiving a gift of napkins: Family quarrels. 146

3 Naval Battle—Promotion in the service for a great
friend or relative. 642

8 Navy—Dreams of the navy foretell love troubles. Being
in the navy: Success. Being in the navy and released:
Honor. A wife dreaming of her husband being in the
navy: He commits adultery. High-ranking naval officers:
Troubles in love. 359

9 Necklace—To dream that you are wearing jewelry
around your neck is very fortunate. Your love affairs
are more favored than your business ventures. If the
necklace breaks or falls from the neck, then there will
be quarrels and disappointments in married life. 531

1 Needles—Disappointments in love. It will be very serious if you prick yourself. Threading a needle: Family
burdens. Losing a needle: Disappointment in love.
Pricking yourself with a needle: You are overly affectionate. 991

7 Neighbors—To dream of your neighbors is an omen of
coming misfortune or business loss. Visiting your neighbors: Family quarrels. Being very friendly with neighbors: Loss of money. 619

8 Nervousness—The solution of a puzzle will occur to
you after long thought and bring you great good luck.
305

4 Nest—One of nature's most fortunate omens. Prosperity
and honor are certain to come your way unless the eggs
are broken or the nest contains dead youngsters. A
snake's nest: Dishonor. 328

4 Nets—Omens of prosperous times to come. Using a net:
Success in business. Catching something in a net: Will
receive a surprise. Catching fish in a net: Change of
temperature and much rain. 215

7 News—It is not a good omen to hear news in your
dream unless it is painful or worrying. In fact, it is a

dream of contrary meaning. Hearing bad news: Satisfaction. Giving good news: Great curiosity. Giving bad news: Will learn of the loss of relative. Hearing good news from children: Honor in life. 214

9 Newspapers—If in your dream you are reading a newspaper, it is a sign that a fortunate change will come in your circumstances, but from a distant source. A daily newspaper: Common gossip. A Sunday newspaper: Will have a short life. Throwing a newspaper away: Dishonor. 423

1 New Year—An improvement in circumstances is at hand. You will have an unscrupulous rival; be careful of your confidences. Being drunk at a New Year's Eve party: Love affairs will improve. Proposing on New Year's Eve: Marriage will last forever. Getting married on New Year's Eve: Marriage will not last long. A boy being born on New Year's Eve: Will become a prominent person. A girl being born on New Year's Eve: Will marry a wealthy person. Committing adultery on New Years Eve: Imminent separation. 937

4 Night—To dream that you are suddenly overtaken by night or by an unexplained darkness is a bad sign; misfortune will be your lot. But if you persevere in your dream and once more see the light of day, then you will recover your losses. 652

9 Niece—Mutual affection and assistance between you and a relative. 801

5 Nightmare—To imagine that you are dreaming or have a nightmare, in your dream, is a warning to you of treachery on the part of someone you trust. 869

8 Noise—To hear a loud noise in your dream is a sign of quarrels among your friends or relatives. The louder the noise, the more serious the result. 125

8 Nose—To dream that you are bleeding at the nose is an omen of failing business; be careful in your investments and speculations. It often shows trouble in your home circle. Do not travel, for it will not be fortunate for you; and avoid lending money for the next few weeks. 215

5 Novel—All printed matter is unfortunate in your

dreams. Be careful of your business affairs and speculations. Writing a novel: Unhappiness. Buying a novel: Refrain from speculation in the stock market. 158

5 Noose—Obstacles and competition with which you must hold your own. 896

9 Nosebleed—Not a good omen. Take the utmost care of yourself for a time. 360

2 Numbers—To count the number of persons present in your dream foretells power, satisfied ambition, and dignity. 758

5 Nurse—It is a good sign to dream of a nurse, and your business affairs will prosper. 392

2 Nuts—As a rule, it is a fortunate dream that includes nuts, whether they appear in a dessert or are on a tree; but they refer to the family fortunes rather than to your business affairs, generally. Some important wish will be gratified. 524

O

9 Oak Tree—Any dream that includes a flourishing tree may be looked upon as a fortunate omen. The finer the tree, the better the immediate prospects. If, however, you see healthy young trees, you will not be benefited fully for some years, although it is still a good sign. If the tree is withered or the leaves have fallen, it is a warning of business losses. If the tree has been felled and is lying in your path, it is a very serious omen. 324

7 Oar—It is a good omen in your dream of rowing a small boat. If others are also rowing with you, then expect to face difficulties before success. It is a bad sign if you lose or break an oar. 241

9 Oasis—To dream of wandering in a desert and finding an oasis is a sign of one friend on whose help you can always rely. 126

8 Oath—A comfortable salary and good position will be yours. 593

1 Oats—Success in commerce follows a dream of a growing crop. If the crop is still green or unripe, be careful for a few months or you may make a serious binder. 109

5 Obeying—You have an admirer who is seriously attracted. Do not be depressed by sad tidings from a distance; brighter days are ahead are in store. 923

3 Obituary—To read of a death of someone you know well means news of a marriage. 129

7 Occupation—To dream of doing work you detest means good fortune in every way. 403

6 Oculist—You are being watched; do not be ensnared. Buying glasses from an oculist: Dignity and distinction. Taking children to an oculist: Prosperity. 303

2 Ocean or Sea—The meaning of this dream depends entirely upon the circumstances. If the water is quiet and peaceful, it is a good sign, whether it is the sea, a lake, or a river. But if it is stormy or rough, then beware; for you have a difficult time before you and will need all your courage. 452

8 Odors—Fragrant scents signify contentment; unpleasant odors mean vexations. Pleasing odors: You will excel in everything. Offensive odors: Unreliable servants are in your employ. Smelling odor on hands: Will suffer because of own foolishness. Smelling odor of the body: Will be guilty of foolish actions. 278

9 Offense—To dream that some person has offended you is a warning of family quarrels that will affect your position or your domestic comfort. If you have given cause for offense, then the fault will certainly lie at your own door. 495

5 Offer—It is considered fortunate if someone makes a good offer for your service in your dream. Expect an improvement in your position, but you must work hard. 491

8 Office—To dream that you have lost your situation or that your landlord has turned you out of your office is a warning of trouble in your love affairs or married life.

8 Officer—Guard your speech and letters alike. Important happenings will claim your attention. 413

9 Oil—To dream that you are using oil in any way is an unfortunate omen, except for women, for those who use it normally, such as artists, painters, or contractors. Digging for an oil well: Profit. Taking castor oil: Happiness. Artists and painters using oil: Large earnings. 729

4 Old—To dream that you are very old signifies fame. A dream of old clothes: You should take courage and think more highly of yourself. 247

1 Olives—An omen of peace and happiness in domestic life. 256

4 Onions—A very mixed dream. You will encounter some unexpected good fortune, but it will prove disappointing to you in the end. Pulling onions out of the ground: Revelation of a secret. Eating onions: Quarrels with employees. Cooking onions: Will be visited by a friend. 256

1 Opera—To dream of an opera signifies that success will not be easily obtained. Going to the opera: Family disorder. Being at the opera: Confusion in your business. Hearing grand opera: A long-absent friend will return soon. 235

5 Operation—It is a hospital dream if you imagine that you are undergoing an operation. Success will come to you if no trouble comes in the dream. It is, however, considered a sign of unexpected news if you watch an operation performed on someone else. Neither of these meanings apply in the case of a nurse or medical man. 725

2 Opium—Worries, bad news from the sea, or serious illness of someone dear to you. It is portended by this dream. 128

4 Orchard—To dream that you are in an orchard is always a favorable sign; but the actual extent of your good fortune will depend on the condition of the fruits. If it is ripe and plentiful, you may expect great success; if it is green or scarce, then your fortunes will mend; but it will require time and patience. 589

8 Orchestra—Music is generally considered a fortunate

omen in a dream, but in the case of an orchestra there will be too many difficulties, and failure usually results. 368

1 Organ—This is a fortunate dream unless the music is too loud to be pleasant to you personally. If a funeral march is being played, it is very fortunate for love affairs. Playing an organ: Loss of a relative. 352

9 Orient—To dream of oriental people or countries is an omen of romantic interest which will not prove lasting. Do not be too absorbed in it. Traveling to the orient: Take a little less stock in people's promises. Being among oriental people: Good marriage chance. Bringing back things from the orient: Waste of time. 459

1 Orphans—Whoever dreams of orphans will receive profits or riches by the hand of a stranger. Adopting an orphan: Happiness is assured. 262

2 Ornaments—A dream of contrary meaning. The more ornaments you wear in your dream the greater will be the coming trouble. Giving ornaments to others: Extravagance. Church ornaments: Will have a good spirit. Flower ornaments: Will have pleasure and fortune. 110

2 Ostrich—A slight ailment will worry you; look to your diet. 495

2 Oven—To dream that you are baking or cooking some food in an oven is a sign that your affairs have reached a standstill. If·you burn the food, you will drift to the bad; if the result is a pleasant meal, then in time you will prosper. But in any case you should be very careful for some time and certainly take no risks. 902

5 Overalls—To dream of working in overalls means you will be well paid for some kindness. To tear it means ill luck. 429

9 Overcoat—The more clothes you wear the greater the coming trouble. Taking off an overcoat: Disgrace. Buying one: Will be a person of honor. 315

4 Oxen—To dream that you see a herd of oxen is a very fortunate sign; your affairs will prosper. If they are grazing peacefully, your speculations or investments should be watched, as they should show signs of favorable development. Buy and sell shares carefully. 823

4 Oysters—To dream of eating oysters is a sign that you

have hard work in front of you and that you will need courage, if you are to succeed. But in love affairs it promises happiness if you are patient. Gathering oysters: Will make lots of money. Buying oysters: Someone new will fall in love with you. 283

P

8 Padlock—This is an obstacle dream. Note carefully whether the padlock fastens you inside or whether you use it to fasten some door. 395

2 Pageant—A warning against judging by appearances or paying too much attention to outward things. 181

4 Pain—A dream of contrary meaning. The greater your suffering in your dream, the more successful you will be in real life. To lovers it is extremely fortunate. Having pain in teeth: Unhappiness. Having pain in stomach: Pleasant social activities. Having pains in legs: Will receive good news. 832

9 Painter—Good fortune. 333

7 Painting—Domestic affliction. Painting another's portrait: Friends will be false to you. Painting a landscape: Will make good purchases. 250

2 Palace—It is a good sign for those in lowly circumstances to dream of palaces or showy houses and big estates. It is also favorable for love affairs. Living in a palace: People esteem you highly. 128

1 Palm Trees—Successful speculations and flourishing business ventures. Some unexpected difficulty will be overcome. Young girls dreaming of a palm tree: Will soon be married. A woman dreaming of a palm tree: Will have children. A man dreaming of a palm tree: Will enjoy success and fame. 145

6 Pancake—To dream that you are eating pancakes shows some unexpected success; you will see your way out of

some difficulty perhaps by the assistance of some friend or business associate. If they burn while cooking: Your venture will fail. 249

4 Pantry—To dream that you are in the pantry is not a good omen. You will succeed up to a certain point but will always have obstacles to overcome. 913

2 Paper—To dream of paper is a sign of some trouble. If the paper is clean, you will escape with a light money loss, but if the paper is soiled and dirty, then your own questionable action will prove your undoing. If the paper is folded, it denotes some small disappointments. 875

3 Parachute—Be careful of all extremes and do not overwork or overplay. Yourself coming down in a parachute: Sorrow within the family. Many people coming down in parachutes: Increase in the family. 093

9 Parade—To see a parade of soldiers drilling means that you will quarrel with someone. A union parade: Improvement in family conditions. A parade of protest: Great satisfaction will come to you. 945

1 Paradise—Happy marriage; to the farmer, abundant crops; a good omen to all. Being in paradise: Forgive those who have wronged you. Young girl dreaming of being in paradise: Will have sorrow. Woman being thrown out of paradise: Misery. 415

3 Paralysis—If you dream that you are paralyzed it is a sign of a broken engagement. Having paralysis: Dishonor. Children being paralyzed: A change in life will soon come. 048

5 Parasol—It is considered fortunate if you see yourself with your parasol open. In other words it is a direct indication of favorable weather and sunshine. Borrowing a parasol: Misunderstandings with friends. Lending a parasol: Will be hurt by false friends. A beautifully colored parasol: You will be displeased by your lover. 293

1 Parcel—To dream that you receive a parcel is a very fortunate omen, but if you open it, you may affect your luck. If you are carrying a parcel, expect a change of circumstances. 109

1 Park—This dream of a fine open space is a favorable

one. If you are accompanied by one other person, it shows a happy love affair; but if several people are with you, you can expect difficulties for some time. Children playing in the park: Happiness in love. Sitting in a park alone: Increase in your fortune. Sitting in the park with sweetheart: Enemies will be punished. 397

7 Parrot—Hard work is before you; you will suffer from the idle talk of other people. Children talking to a parrot: You have confidence of friends. A parrot chattering too much: Will be flattered by someone. A young engaged girl dreaming of a parrot: Inquire about fiancé's family. 529

8 Party—It is considered a fortunate omen to dream of being at a party. But it is unfavorable if you yourself give a party, and the smarter the function, the worse the omen. Being at a wild party: Will be a victim of gossip. Someone getting hurt at a party: Will have a long life. 134

3 Passion—It is a warning of trouble, generally domestic, to lose your temper in a dream. A woman being passionate: She will be justified. A man being passionate: A passing love. A wife being passionate: A better future awaiting her. A husband being passionate: Changeable in love. 264

9 Path—This is another obstacle dream, as the meaning depends upon circumstances. If you can walk easily and comfortably, then your affairs will flourish. If you meet obstacles to your progress, then you may be certain that there are difficulties to be faced in the future. 315

6 Pawnbroker—This dream certainly foretells heavy losses and disappointments. Your sweetheart will prove unfaithful; or if you are married, some indiscreet action of your partner will cause great trouble. 762

6 Peach—A dream of personal pleasure, not of business affairs. Of peaches on a tree: Promised attainment of fondest hopes. Many trees loaded with peaches: Earning will be good. Eating peaches with others: Love worries. 249

9 Peacock—A dream of contrary meaning. Your fine plans will fail, and you will be disappointed; but to the

farmer this handsome bird foretells a good harvest after much hard work. A dead peacock: Own good plans will fail. A woman dreaming of a peacock circling: Riches. 531

8 Pearls—A very fortunate dream, but you will have to earn your success by hard work. Be patient, for you will surely succeed. If pearls are given to you in your dream, it is a sign of a very happy and successful marriage. If the string of pearls should break, however, it shows grief and sorrow unless you thread them again in your dream. Buying pearls: Will succeed in your goal. Losing a set of pearls: Will make new friends. Giving a gift of pearls: Are trying to gain favors by a gift. 134

5 Peas—This is a fortunate dream on the whole, but you must exercise patience, particularly if the peas are raw or not cooked sufficiently. It is most favorable when you see peas growing in the garden. Dried peas show money acquired in a doubtful manner. 131

1 Pedlar—To dream of a pedlar signifies deceitful companions. 109

5 Pencil—Take note of the friend who gave it to you in the dream, as a parting from that person is indicated. 212

7 Pendulum—A sudden message will cause you to take a long journey. 304

9 Pens—News about absent friends. 513

6 People—People coming to your house: Will have sorrows and tears. People coming uninvited: Unhappiness. Blind people: Misfortune. People dressed in white: Loss of friendship. People dressed in black: Unhappy events in the near future. People in high office: Honor and dignity. 132

9 Pepper—Talent in your family, particularly if you sniff the pepper until you sneeze. 369

3 Perfume—This is always a favorable dream, both for the man of commerce or the lover. Spilling perfume: Loss of something that brings pleasure. Buying perfume: Will find a new lover. Breaking a bottle of perfume: Disaster to fondest hopes. Receiving a bottle of perfume as a gift: Will be embraced by unknown person. Giving

a gift of perfume: Big profit. Smelling perfume: Frivolity. 642

6 Peril—It is an obstacle omen if you find yourself in peril in your dream. If you come off successfully, then all will go well. 762

7 Perspiration—Great efforts will be required of you and duly rewarded. 826

6 Pest—To dream of house or garden pests is a token of prosperity beyond your hopes. 753

3 Petticoat—A dream of warning against conceit and dissipation. Keep to moderate ways and feelings. Having petticoats: Will soon have a love affair. Buying petticoats: Exercise moderate mode of living. Losing a petticoat: Difficulties in married life. A white petticoat: Will receive a beautiful gift. Colored petticoat: A marriage will soon take place. A torn petticoat: Unhappiness for a long time. 102

3 Photo—It is always fortunate to look at a photo of some other person in a dream, but if it is your own it is a bad omen. 750

5 Physician—This is a very fortunate omen. It is always a good sign to see or speak to a doctor in your dream. Being a physician: Joy and profit. Calling a physician for children: New interests and surroundings. A physician visiting patients: Great wealth. 257

1 Piano—To dream of piano: All of your own affairs will prosper. Owning a piano: Beware of jealous friends. Selling a piano: Loneliness and disappointment. Playing the piano: Disputes. 190

9 Picnic—A doubtful sign concerning your love affairs. The meaning depends upon what happens at the picnic. 342

3 Pictures—To dream of pictures is a bad omen, for it warns you of treachery by one you trust. The more pleasing the pictures appear to you, the more dangerous the omen; it means work without profit. Pictures of naked women: Public disgrace. Pictures of naked men: Unhappiness in love affairs. 651

3 Pie—To dream of cooking one means homely joys; to eat one, dissension in the family. Receiving a pie as a gift: A friend is seeking your ruin. 912

6 Pigs—A very mixed dream, for good and bad luck will both be present in your affairs. Many of your cherished plans will fail, yet others, apparently less important, will succeed and restore the balance. Watch over the members of your household, as trouble may reach you from this source. 897

4 Pigeons—News of importance from afar, but it may not be very favorable and will mean changes in your affairs. Pigeons are favorable for love affairs. It is better to see them flying than walking or settling on ledges. 625

6 Pillow—A clean pillow is a good sign; but if it is soiled and untidy, then expect troubles of your own making. 195

7 Pills—A journey abroad with many pleasures at the end of it. 160

9 Pilot—Cheery scenes and good times ahead, but you will be defeated by a rival in the end. 531

2 Pine Tree—This signifies good news to elderly people but danger to the young. 209

4 Pineapple—Comfortable domestic surroundings, invitations, and pleasure seeking. 580

1 Pipe—A sign of unusual events resulting in good fortune to the smoker. Breaking a pipe: Security. Dirty pipes: Misery. Receiving a pipe as a gift: Advancement in own business. 532

6 Pirate—Exciting times, journeys and financial gains; the deceit of an associate will cause you gain. 420

1 Pistol—To hear the sound of firing foretells misfortune. If you yourself fire a pistol, it is a sign of hard work with very little result therefrom. Carrying a pistol: Will be disliked by people. Other people firing pistols: Will learn of schemes to ruin you. Being an officer and carrying a pistol: Treachery. 514

9 Pit—This is really an obstacle dream. If you descend into a pit or deep hollow, it shows that your business affairs will decline. To a lover it means that he will meet with coldness and indifference. If you fall into a pit, it is a most unfortunate omen, for you will suffer a long time from troubles confronting you. 999

6 Pity—To dream of being pitied means humiliation. Pitying someone else: Small vexations. 124

9 Plank—A sign of a restless state of mind which only travel will satisfy. 126

6 Plaster—False accusations will be made against you if you dream that the plaster is upon you; but if you dream that the plaster is coming off the walls of your house, the trouble is for your family. 348

2 Platform—You will marry when you least expect to; beware of hasty judgments. 371

9 Play—It is more fortunate to watch a play than to dream that you are taking part in one. 216

7 Poison—To dream that you have taken poison is a warning of financial loss through the dishonesty of some person whom you trust. Be careful how you give credit or lend money. Do not speculate or buy shares of stocks. If you recover from the effects of the poison, you can get over your difficulties by exercising care and paying attention to the facts. 241

6 Police—This might be called a dream of contrary meaning, for if you dream of trouble with the police, it shows that some present difficulty will be overcome. Being arrested by police with cause: Misfortune will attend you. Being at a police station for questioning: Happiness. Being with friends at a police station for questioning: Happiness. Being with friends at a police station: Loss of money. 825

9 Portrait—A warning of danger regarding the person whose portrait or photo is envisioned, especially if it is faded or injured. 243

8 Postman—Some unexpected happening. Being a postman: Loss of real estate. Giving a letter to a postman: Listen to the advice of friends. Receiving special delivery letter from a postman: Great love. 512

6 Post office—A change of residence or companions. Mailing a letter at the post office: Will have obstacles in your path. Registering a letter at the post office: Change of companions: Buying a stamp at the post office: Unpleasant things awaiting. Finding the post office closed: Dissension in love affairs. 132

3 Potatoes—Do not try to play Providence for other people, or you may do more harm than good. Planting potatoes: Dearest plans will materialize. Digging potatoes: Big success in own efforts. Boiling potatoes: Will entertain an unwelcome guest. Frying potatoes: Will marry a husky girl. Baking potatoes: Will have arguments with sweetheart. Eating potato salad: Investments will bring profits. 120

1 Poultry—A very fortunate dream. Buying poultry: Consolation. Cleaning poultry: Someone will give you money. 325

4 Poverty—A dream of contrary meaning: Good fortune is coming your way. Other people in poverty: Will give beneficial service to others. Family falling into poverty: Future riches. Friends being in poverty: Health and joy. 139

2 Preacher—The result of your plans will be satisfactory at last although worrying at present. 317

3 Precipice—This is another dream very similar in meaning to that of a pit. It is a warning of trouble ahead, and you should avoid traveling or any change of plans. Take warning and act with prudence. If you fall over the precipice it is a bad sign; but if you walk away from the edge, you will overcome your troubles. 831

7 Pregnant—Being pregnant means that your health will soon improve. A married woman being pregnant: Marital unhappiness. Unmarried woman dreaming of being pregnant: Trouble and injury through scandal. A widow dreaming of being pregnant: She will marry very soon. A young girl dreaming of being pregnant: Won't get married for a long time. 295

6 Priest—To dream of a clergyman is a sign that some quarrel will be cleared up, thus increasing your personal happiness. Confessing sins to a priest: You are dealing in dangerous affairs. A priest being aboard a ship: Bad weather or shipwreck. Family going to see a priest: Family quarrels. 213

1 Prison—This is a dream that indicates much happiness in your home affairs and success in business. To dream that someone is put in prison through your efforts is not a fortunate sign. You are being too venturesome in your

money matters, too eager to secure profit; and it may mean a loss instead of a gain. 109

2 Prize—This is a dream of contrary meaning that forebodes loss through sharp dealing. Be on your guard when offered something cheap. 137

8 Promise—An important decision for you to make. The right answer will lead to happy times for you, so think well. 743

4 Proposal—If you dream of receiving one, be careful not to be drawn into another person's schemes. Should you make one, exciting times are ahead. 319

7 Property—This means you will be disappointed in your hopes. Possessing property: Fortune. Having a large estate of property: Unhappiness. Inheriting property: Will be in mourning. A prospective buyer of property: You are a dreamer. Selling property in the country: Disgrace. 934

1 Prostitute—Being a prostitute: An enemy is seeking your ruin. A prostitute who thinks she is a man: Will give birth to a boy. Embracing a prostitute: Will take a long trip. Receiving a prostitute into your house: Good business ventures. A prostitute dancing: Will go back to your sweetheart. Seeing a prostitute: Good times ahead. 725

4 Puppy—An invitation to a jolly party. Laugh with the people you meet there, but do not become intimate. 526

3 Pump—To pump clear water is a good sign. Your business will prosper. If the water is soiled, however, worries and evil speaking will annoy you. 210

8 Punch—To dream of drinking it is a warning of unpleasant news to come concerning loss of money and, possibly reputation. 269

7 Punishment—To dream of being punished signifies unexpected pleasure. 399

7 Purse—To dream that you find a purse is a good omen if money is inside and a very fortunate omen for lovers; but if you have lost your purse, then expect difficulties or illness as the result of your carelessness. 601

1 Push—To dream of pushing against a door or other heavy object signifies that some overmastering obstacle will be removed from your path. 811

7 Puzzle—An obstacle dream. If you cannot solve the puzzle, then expect heavy losses in business, for trouble is ahead. 394

9 Pyramids—A successful future and a high position in the world are assured to you. 828

Q

7 Quack—To dream that you are under the care of quacks is unfortunate and foretells to the person dreaming that he must beware of these nuisances to society. 124

3 Quarrels—This is one other dream of contrary meaning and foretells prosperity in your business affairs, but there will be opposition for you to face at first. Quarreling with wife or husband: Will be guilty of foolish actions. Quarreling with a sweetheart: Will make up very soon. Quarreling with a friend: Loss of money. 390

8 Queen—A sign of valuable friendship. Going to see a queen: Good fortune. Having an interview with a queen: Rebellion within the home. A queen surrounded by her court: Will be deceived by friends. 548

2 Questions—To dream that someone is asking you questions is an obstacle omen. If you can answer properly, all will go well. 308

7 Quilt—This is a fortunate dream provided it is properly placed on the bed. 124

9 Quicksands—This dream denotes that you are surrounded by many temptations. Do not be imprudent. 216

R

9 Race—One of the ever-recurring obstacle dreams, warning you to persevere if you desire success. Running a

race and winning: Distinction and honor. Running a
race and losing: Will have many competitors in your
affairs. A jockey running a race: A change in life will
soon come. A dog race: Will have mastery over enemies.
135

9 Racecourse—Jolly company but danger of losses
through sharp practices. Friends being at a racecourse:
Death of a loved one. Important personalities at a race
course: Hard work awaits you. 918

2 Racehorse—Seeing a racehorse means you should try
to economize while there is time. To ride one: Do not
speculate; luck is not with you. Your racehorse winning:
You have a lot of enemies. Your racehorse losing: Will
have many competitors. 110

4 Racket—This dream betokens loss of leisure which will,
however, be well repaid later by a new friendship.
Creating a very loud racket: Frivolity. Others making a
racket: Warning of troubles. A tennis racket: Good luck
to one for whom you care. 931

3 Raffle—This dream of risk and chance is a warning to
you that you do not deserve success. Mend your ways
and be more generous in your treatment of others. Taking part in a raffle: Small risks ahead of you. Lovers
holding a raffle ticket: Unhappy association. Losing a
raffle: Engagement will be called off. 624

9 Raft—To dream that you're on a raft means enforced
travel. To see a raft: Varied life for some time. Saving
your life on a raft: Will have mastery of your own
affairs. A very big and long raft: Will travel for a long
time. 126

9 Rags—This is a fortunate dream; any display of wealth
in a dream is generally a bad sign. A woman dreaming
of herself in rags: Unhappiness. A girl dreaming of
herself in rags: Will meet an arrogant man. Washing
rags: Unhappiness. Gathering rags: Big arguments. Buying rags: Will be in the company of happy people. 594

5 Raid—An excellent omen of pleasant times to come. A
police raid: Change of environment. An air raid: A
change of life will come soon. Own home being raided:
Will have emotional sorrow. Other people being raided:
Happiness is assured. 149

6 Railroad—To dream of a railroad means good times ahead. Being on a railroad alone: Rapid rise in business. Being at a railroad with relatives: Abundant means. Being at a railroad with friends: Hard times ahead. Walk on railroad ties: Distress and worry. Being forced to walk the rails: Affairs will bring unmeasured happiness. 312

1 Rainbow—A fortunate dream showing that there will certainly be a change in your affairs for the better before too long. A young girl dreaming of a rainbow: Will have an agreeable sweetheart. Lovers seeing a rainbow together: Happy marriage and riches. A rainbow being over your head: Family inheritance.

6 Rain—An omen that foretells difficulties in the near future. If the downpour is a heavy one, it beomes a serious warning. Getting wet in a downpour of rain: Suffering caused by suspicion of friends. Rain dripping into a room: Beware of false friends. A very bad rain and windstorm: Great joy. Women being out in the rain: Disappointment in love. 321

8 Rake—To rake hay: A wedding to come. To rake leaves: A happy home. 854

4 Rape—To dream of being raped means you will receive a marriage proposal. Raping someone under age: Misfortune. Raping someone over the age of twenty-one: Joy and prosperity. Being raped by a woman: Will receive inheritance. Friends being raped: Will be highly embarrassed. 211

3 Rat—An omen of enemies whom you do not suspect. If you see more than one rat, then the coming trouble will be a serious one and may overwhelm you. To the lover it foretells a fortunate rival. White rats sometimes may be seen. They mean you will get through your trouble successfully. 372

6 Raven—This is really a dream of the color black. Trouble is coming, though you may not deserve it. A raven flying: Your life is in danger. A raven flapping its wings: Death of a friend. Hearing the noise of ravens: Unhappiness. 312

6 Razor—Any sharp cutting instrument is a warning of a coming quarrel. Keep control over yourself. Cutting yourself with a razor: Must control your emotions. Buying a razor: Persecution. 186

4 Reading—It is not a good sign to dream that you are reading; it foretells a dangerous venture, in which you will probably lose money. 814

9 Rebellion—An inferior who has caused you much trouble will soon cease to annoy you. Watching a rebellion: Be cautious with business affairs. Taking part in a rebellion: Much satisfaction. Being wounded in a rebellion: Infidelity. People being killed in a rebellion: Will win at gambling. A foreign rebellion: You are too ambitious. 297

3 Reconciliation—This is a favorable sign in a dream. 309

8 Reflection—To see your own reflection in water means a lonely life; but should you dream of a strange face reflected, it is a sign of meeting and marrying the owner. 305

6 Refreshments—To offer them: A happy marriage. To partake of them: Small vexations. 942

1 Refusal—To dream of a refusal signifies a most certain acceptance. Being refused by relatives: Prospects of better times. Being refused by friends: Jealousy and dissension. Refusing a gift: Will receive another one. Others refusing a gift from you: Will be embarrassed by sweetheart. Refusing to accept a letter: Secret plans. 190

8 Religion—It is generally a bad sign to be troubled by religion in a dream. 287

3 Rent—Unexpected gains will be yours following a dream in which you cannot pay rent or any other debt. 318

8 Rescue—To be rescued is not a good sign, especially if it is from drowning. Avoid travel on the sea. Rescuing others: Will have a good reputation. Rescuing others: Will make big financial gains. Rescuing one who wants to die: Beware of insincere friends. 269

9 Resign—To dream of resigning your work means advancement in the near future and also money gained through legal matters. 179

8 Rest—A contrary dream meaning hard work and good luck in sporting matters. 125

2 Restaurant—To look at others eating in a restaurant signifies ill health; should you be eating also, small enjoyment among new friends. Eating with children at a restaurant: Wealth. Others eating at a restaurant: Will receive money soon. Eating at a restaurant with sweetheart: Bad financial conditions. Husband and wife eating in a restaurant alone: Long happy marriage. 326

6 Return—To dream you see someone who has been away for a long time is a sign of losses soon to be made good, and renewed prosperity. 726

6 Revelry—A contrary dream heralding misfortune unless you dream of looking on at the revelry of others. 240

9 Revolver—To dream of handling a revolver is a sign of danger by water. Try to avoid traveling by sea or river. Firing a revolver: You will be cheated. Killing with a revolver: Will have a long life. Officers with a revolver: Good harvest. 819

4 Revenge—Anxious times, humiliation, and a quarrel; but the latter will soon be made up. Seeking revenge against a man: Humiliation. Seeking revenge against a woman: You are considered to be very vulgar. Seeking revenge against the family: Small arguments solved. 283

6 Reward—Failure of your plans through overconfidence. Remember, there are things money cannot buy. 618

1 Rheumatism—To dream of suffering from this signifies a new lease on life and happiness. 613

7 Rhinoceros—Success in business affairs, but delays and disillusion to those in love. 304

6 Ribbon—A dream of light pleasure and careless spending of money. 276

8 Rice—Be careful of your plans, for they are ill advised. Eating rice with many people: Will make a good marriage. Giving rice to children: Trouble will cease. Eating rice pudding: Money will come easily to you. 350

8 Riches—Unfortunately, this is a dream of contrary meaning. The more flourishing your affairs in your visionary world, the worse they will be in real life. 134

6 Riding—It is a fortunate omen to dream that you are riding a horse unless the animal is out of control or throws you. Riding with others: Plans will turn out

unsatisfactorily. Riding fast in a car: Prosperity may develop. 609

4 Rings—To lose your ring is a warning of trouble coming through a friend or relation. It is a fortunate sign if someone makes you a present of a ring. Having a ring of precious stones: Wealth. An unmarried person dreaming of a ring with precious stones: Matrimony. Married person dreaming of a ring with precious stones: Birth of a child. Losing your ring: Large fortune. A single girl dreaming of losing her ring: She will be left by boyfriend. Giving a gift of rings: Loss of money. Receiving a wedding ring: Will have devoted lover. Having a ring on a chain: Good health. 598

8 Riot—This is a warning of financial failure, especially if you see many rioters fighting. Taking part in a riot: Misfortune in business. Friends taking part in a riot. Persecution by an enemy. Relatives taking part in a riot: Death of a friend. A riot ending: Will receive high honors. 458

8 Rival—This should be treated as an obstacle dream. If you defeat your rival or if he retires, you will prove successful in your business affairs. Being defeated by a rival: Shame and sorrow. A lover dreaming of having a rival: Will be lacking in love affairs. A young woman dreaming of having a rival: Will accept her present lover. 962

9 River—As with all dreams of water, whether of the sea, a lake, or a river, the meaning depends upon the clearness or muddiness of the water. If there are signs of a storm, then be very cautious in your plans, for troubles lies ahead. To fall or jump in shows domestic worries. 243

2 Road—A well-made broad road is a most fortunate omen, but lanes or narrow, winding paths should be treated as obstacles. Traveling on a straight road: Lasting happiness. Traveling on a crooked road: Discovery of a secret. Traveling on a bad road: New undertakings will bring sorrow and losses. 749

7 Roar—The roar of waters means a traveler will return. Of animals: An enemy is watching you. 610

6 Robber—It is considered fortunate to be molested by a

thief in your dream, provided you escape injury. Escaping injury by a robber: Good times ahead. Catching a robber: Triumph over enemies. Killing a robber: Will have a long life. A robber being arrested: Success in business. A robber getting away: Disappointment in love. 591

4 Robin—One of nature's most fortunate omens. 364

7 Rocket—Short-lived success is portended. You must build on firmer foundations next time. 394

1 Rocks—Another obstacle dream, the meaning of which depends upon the circumstances, but it certainly foretells difficulties and hard work. 613

1 Rope—These are obstacle dreams. If you find yourself securely bound by rope, then expect difficult times in your business affairs, for trouble is surely coming. Coming down on a rope: Will overcome all who may seek your downfall. 415

7 Room—This unusual dream signifies success after you have almost given up hope. Of a room: Will discover family secrets. A room that you live in: Financial worries. A hotel room: Death of a friend. A dark room: Loss of money. A bathroom: Sickness. 349

9 Roof—Prosperity and festive garments are soon to be yours. 594

6 Rosary—To dream of telling the beads on your own rosary means a reconciliation with a friend. To see someone else wearing a rosary signifies bereavement. 906

4 Roses—A most fortunate dream for everybody unless the blossoms are withered or fall to pieces in your hands. If the flowers are only slightly faded, it foretells success after some difficulties. 058

3 Rubber—To erase writing with an india rub is a presage of uncertainty of action. Take counsel of older heads than yours. 462

7 Rubbish—You are about to make a valuable discovery. Use it, but try not to hurt a friend by doing so. 232

9 Ruins—It is a fortunate dream in which you are wandering amid building ruins, but it is merely a modern house that has tumbled down, that is a bad sign. Be-

ware of speculation. Marriage being ruined: You are well known for being stingy. A ruined city: Will receive unexpected fortune. A financially ruined family: Will receive money unexpectedly. 216

9 Running—This is generally an obstacle dream. If you succeed in reaching your goal, then all will go well; but if you tire or stop running, then expect business difficulties. A woman running: Will lose her virginity. Running because of being scared: Security. Running because of being afraid: Will go into exile. Running naked: Will be robbed by relatives. Running to catch someone: Good fortune. A woman running naked: Will go crazy. Wanting to run but can't: Will have a serious illness. 835

S

3 Sable—The color betokens tidings of loss; the fur is a warning against extravagance. Others having sable furs: A false friend is nearby. 831

9 Saddle—To dream that you are riding a horse without a saddle foretells ill health through your own carelessness. Revise your plans at once and guard against mistakes. Riding a horse with a new saddle: Joy without profit. Riding a horse without a saddle: Bad health. Others riding horses without saddles: A catastrophe is ahead. Children riding horses without saddles: Reverse your plans. 540

5 Sadness—A good omen for your future; lasting joys. 401

8 Sailing—This is another form of the water dream, and its meaning depends upon whether or not the water is smooth and your voyage pleasant. If not, then you can expect trouble and worry according to the severity of the storm. The smaller the boat, the greater your success in overcoming your misfortune. 314

8 Salmon—Family troubles. Catching salmon: Accord

with friends. Eating salmon: You have a loyal friend. Canned salmon: Approaching money. 809

7 Salt—This is a fortunate dream in every way, but if you spill the salt you can expect some difficulty and hard work before you succeed. Using salt on food: Will have religious arguments. Cooking food with salt: Good days are ahead. Putting too much salt in food: Will squander money. 340

2 Sand—Many small vexations. Working with sand: Years of hard work are ahead. Mixing sand with cement: Success. A sand dune: Will be justified by friends. 947

9 Satin—A fortunate dream for the business man, but the lover should beware of false and flattering words. White satin: Abundant means. Blue satin: Will have damages in own affairs. Red satin: Will be wounded by a bullet. A business man dreaming of satin: Business is secured. A lover dreaming of satin: Beware of false and flattering talk. A beautiful single girl dreaming of satin: Will have an ardent love. A married woman dreaming of satin: Will deceive her husband. 648

1 Sausage—Domestic troubles, often through ill health. Buying sausages: Contentment in life. Eating pork sausages: Will win in gambling. Eating liver sausages: Poverty. 568

1 Savage—Small worries through the dishonesty of another. To dream of many savages signifies rescue by a friend from a trouble of your own making. Being hurt by a savage person: Leading a wild life. Many savages: Rescue by a friend. Fighting with a savage person: Small worries through dishonesty of others. 190

1 Savings—To dream you are accumulating savings foreshadows poverty. 847

7 Saw—It is not a fortunate omen to dream that you are sawing wood. It indicates difficulties to be overcome. 151

3 Scald—A dream of contrary meaning. Good fortune will follow after the first difficulties have been overcome. Children being scalded: Family quarrels. 498

9 School—To dream you begin again and go to school, and cannot say your lessons right, shows you are

about to undertake something which you do not understand. Going to school: Business will be in good standing. Taking children to school: Will set a good example for children. Going to swimming school: Anxiety. Going to dancing school: Your morals make you unfit to fill a position. 270

4 Scissors—A warning of false friends. Beware of giving your confidence too fully. Buying scissors: You are a very precise and proper person. Using manicure scissors: Will live a long life. Lovers handling scissors: Will have a big argument about love matters. 319

1 Scorpion—Will receive damages caused by enemies. Several scorpions: Enemies are talking behind your back. A nest of scorpions: Will overcome your enemies. Scorpions eating lizards: You are an idealist. A scorpion in a cage: You are surrounded by boisterous people. Being bitten by a scorpion: Business will succeed. Killing a scorpion: Will suffer loss through pretended friends. 865

9 Scratched—To dream of being scratched foretells hurt. Scratching own back: Approaching money. Drawing blood from a scratch: Will receive bad news. Being scratched by a woman's nails: Your love is secured. Being scratched by a cat: Sickness. Being scratched by a dog: Will be cheated by friends. 108

5 Scream—It is considered a fortunate sign to find yourself screaming in a dream. Others screaming: An enemy is seeking your ruin. 455

7 Sculptor—Change in present position. Being friendly with a sculptor: Will bring about love but less money. Posing for a sculptor: Social activities of a happy nature. A married woman posing for a sculptor: Will be left by her husband. A virgin posing for a sculptor: Will marry a rich man. A widow posing for a sculptor: Suitable time to pursue her desires. 639

7 Sea—Of the open sea with small waves: Great joy. A blue sea: Business affairs are running smoothly. A dead, calm sea: Will make money from a business transaction. Falling into the sea: Beware of jealous friends. Being thrown by force into the sea: Sickness. Traveling across the smooth sea: Devoted love within the family. Man

and wife traveling on a rough sea: Great and lasting love. A girl dreaming of a stormy sea: Deep anguish because of a double cross. 142

2 Seals—You are pushed on by ambitions but will never attain your goals. A seal coming onto the beach: Will soon become pregnant. A sealskin coat: Approaching money. A small seal in an aquarium: Security in love. 821

7 Secret—To dream of a secret being whispered into your ear means a public indignity is to be bestowed on you. Having a secret: Will have a large fortune. Being told a secret: Must control passions. Telling a secret: Misfortune in love affairs. Couples keeping secrets from each other: Diligence and hard work. Friends telling you a secret: Approaching money. 259

2 Seduce—Will have plenty of money during life. Seducing a very young girl: Business will run as you desire. Seducing a woman by force: Good events will happen to you. Own daughter being seduced: Financial gains. A married person dreaming of being seduced: Will live comfortable life. A widow dreaming of being seduced: Will be robbed. A man being arrested for seducing a woman: Will have many perplexities. A teenager seducing girl of same age: Death in family very soon. 434

1 Separation—To dream that you are separated from those you love foretells the failure of some cherished plan. Husband and wife separated: Gossip by friends. Separation of sweethearts: Idle talk by people around you. Friends being separated: Sickness of children. Sweetheart wanting a separation: Be cautious in business transactions. Separating from a business partner: Success in business. Separating from those you love: Failure of some cherished plan. 154

7 Serpent—Ungrateful people surround you. A serpent with several heads: Will seduce a beautiful girl. Catching a serpent with several heads: Will go fishing. Killing a serpent with several heads: Victory over enemies. Being bitten by a serpent: Enemies are accusing you. 124

9 Servant—For a woman to dream that she is a servant is an obstacle dream. Persevere and stick close to your job. To dream that you employ several servants is an

unfortunate omen. A female servant: Gossip by other people. A male servant: You are disliked by people. Employing several servants: Persevere and stick close to your affairs. Servants at work: Infidelity. Firing a servant: Will sustain heavy losses. Paying a servant: Great joy. 513

3 Sex—A boy of the male sex: Luck and prosperity. A woman of the female sex: Will live a long life. A man having sexual desire: Public disgrace. A woman having sexual desire: Immediate success of hopes. 156

2 Sexual Organs—Sexual organs being in good condition: Will have abundance of money. A man having a disease of the sexual organs: Warning of trouble. A man having a deformed sexual organ: Will be punished for a crime done. A woman having deformed sexual organs: Will have a virtuous son. A man having unusual sexual organs: Will have a death of a son. A woman having unusual sexual organs: Children will have a good reputation. A woman having ovaries removed: Death of a member of the family. Exposing sexual organs: Danger. 614

2 Sew—An obstacle dream. If your sewing is successful and you complete the garment or other article, all will be well. But if you leave off before finishing the work, then look out for troubles. Sewing for the house: Good results in business. Sewing clothes for yourself: Dishonor. A tailor sewing: Will receive news from abroad. 191

3 Shark—This presages a narrow escape from serious trouble or illness. Catching a shark: Affairs are running smoothly. Being killed by a shark: Will overcome obstacles. Being bitten by a shark but not killed: Bad results in business. Others being bitten by sharks: Will escape from serious trouble. 129

1 Shave—To dream that you are shaving or that someone else is shaving you is a warning of difficulty ahead. Be careful in whom you trust and do not lend money, buy shares and stocks. 415

9 Shawl—Deep affection from one you love. Buying a shawl: Will receive a visit from a doctor. Relatives wearing a shawl: Will go to a funeral parlor. Young girls wearing shawls: You are surrounded by fast-talking peo-

ple. A large white shawl: Purity and virtue. A black shawl: Grief. A red shawl: You are too loose with your affections. Giving a shawl as a gift: You will have deep affection from one you love. 315

8 Sheep—A fortunate dream, for it tells of coming success through well-conceived plans. A shepherd leading sheep: Will make much money. Buying sheep: Good earnings in stock speculation. Selling sheep: Death of an enemy. 683

2 Shell—To dream of a shell with the fish alive in it predicts prosperity, but an empty seashell is a bad omen. A clean shell: Will go into bankruptcy. A smooth shell: Will have changes in your life. Gathering shells: Fleeting pleasures. A live shellfish: Prosperity. A dead shellfish: Will receive news of the death of a friend. 767

2 Shepherd—This is considered a bad omen if you see no sheep at the time. If the flock is there also, then the presence of the shepherd increases your difficulties but will not stop your ultimate success. 209

8 Ship—To dream that you are traveling in a ship shows good fortune if you reach your destination safely. A man dreaming of a ship's docking: Unexpected good news. A woman dreaming of a ship's docking: Unexpected bad news. Lovers dreaming of a ship docking: Marriage will not be realized. A ship sinking: Abundance of money. Being on the bridge of a ship: Will take a short trip. A small ship with sails: Will receive unexpected good news. 638

6 Shipwreck—A certain omen of disaster. Losing your life in shipwreck: Arrival of an unexpected friend. Being saved from a shipwreck: Will have emotional sorrow. Being shipwrecked with the one you love: Big catastrophe is ahead. 591

2 Shirt—It is always a fortunate omen when you dream of your shirt or your chemise. Good fortune follows your efforts. An everyday shirt: Prosperous future. A nightshirt: Victory over enemies. Putting on a shirt: Will be neglected. Taking off a shirt: Will be disillusioned in love. Washing a shirt: You will be loved. A dirty shirt: Will contract a contagious disease. 596

9 Shiver—New garments will soon be yours, and they will
be very much to your liking. 450

3 Shoes—This might almost be called a dream of contrary
meaning, for if you see yourself without shoes, then you
may expect success in business. To dream that your
shoes are worn or patched is a certain sign of difficulties, but with care and hard work you will succeed.
New shoes show some fortunate enterprise with unexpected results. Having black shoes: Bad times are ahead.
Having white shoes: Future is completely secure. Having
suede shoes: Will have easy and happy days. Having
high boots: Happiness. Buying new shoes: Will have a
large profit. Being without shoes: Expect success in business. 183

8 Shooting—It is a very bad omen if you kill or shoot
some living creature in your dream. To shoot and miss
shows some success over your difficulties. Shooting with
a shotgun: You are being deceived. Shooting at a target:
Will take a long trip. Shooting enemies: Domestic
troubles. Shooting and killing someone: Disappointments and grief. 125

4 Shop—To dream that you are keeping shop indicates
hard work before you prosper, depending on to what
extent your dream shop does business. A dress shop:
Everything will be wonderful. A food shop: Ruin of
other people. A shop burning: Loss of possessions. 607

8 Showers—A setback in your plans through a deceitful
enemy. 206

4 Shroud—News of a wedding is at hand. 436

7 Signature—Loyal companions will uphold you at all
times. Putting signature on wedding license: Good
health. Putting signature on diploma: Joy. Putting signature on a birth certificate: Riches. Putting signature on
death certificate: Be careful of eyesight. 142

4 Silver—To dream of silver is a sign of some loss. Do not
be hasty in your plans. If the coins are of large value,
you may escape if you are careful. Counting silver: Big
gains. Finding silver money: Prosperity. Changing silver
money: Will be visited by a friend. Buying silver things:
Beware of enemies. Selling silver things: Will receive
money losses. 526

7 Singing—This is a dream of contrary meaning, for it foretells troubles to come; but they will soon pass, so do not despair. To dream that you hear other people singing shows that the difficulties will come through your dealings with other people. Hearing a soprano singing: Good news. Singing operatic songs: Will be afflicted by tears. Watching a singer perform: Small sickness in family. Hearing melancholy songs sung: Illness. Hearing birds singing: Love and joy. Hearing a love song: A happy event to come. 493

1 Sisters—To dream you see your brothers and sisters signifies long life. Arguing with sisters: Family disgrace. A sister arguing with a sister-in-law: Expect small fortune. Two sisters-in-law arguing with a sister: Family shame and sorrow. A sister arguing with a brother-in-law: Good fortune ahead. 271

9 Skating—Generally considered a warning of some coming danger. 315

1 Skeleton—To dream that you see a skeleton is a sign of domestic trouble. 505

8 Skin—Dreaming of your own skin, if it is healthy, means good fortune; if it appears disfigured, kindness from those of whom you least expect it. 521

3 Skull—An engagement is in the near future for you. 354

1 Sky—This is a fortunate dream unless you see heavy clouds. A few clouds probably show difficulties that you will overcome, but watch carefully to see whether the clouds are gathering or disbursing. A red sky: Increase of wealth. Ascending into the sky: Can expect honors to be bestowed. Descending from the sky: Beware of falling. A rainbow in the sky: A peril is near at hand. Stars falling from the sky: Will be unable to have children. 712

3 Sleep—To dream that you sleep foretells evil. A man sleeping with a woman: Enjoyment in life. Sleeping with a little child: Return of love and domestic joy. Sleeping with a person of oppostite sex: Affairs will go well. Sleeping with a handsome young man: Pleasures followed by disgust. Sleeping with a beautiful young girl: Annoyance and worry. Sweethearts sleeping together:

Delightful events to come. Sleeping alone: Beware of temptation. A man sleeping naked with a beautiful woman: Happiness. A woman sleeping naked with a handsome man: Treachery. 498

8 Smuggling—This betokens a plan which will almost succeed but not quite. 035

9 Smoke—Some pleasant success, but you will not really benefit by it. The denser the smoke, the greater will be your disappointment. Smoke coming from a building: A friend is deceiving you. Very thick smoke: A very big disappointment will come. Being overcome by smoke: Beware of flattery. 109

6 Snakes—This dream is a warning of treachery where you least expect it, some unfortunate turn of events that you have not anticipated. Your plans will be wrecked. Killing a snake: Will have conquest over your enemies. Several snakes: Jealous people would like to call your ruin. 690

8 Snow—This is a very good dream, but you may have to work hard, especially if you find yourself walking in a snow storm. Snow falling during the winter: Abundance. Washing yourself with snow: Relief from pain. Eating snow: You have left your place of birth. Driving through snow: Grief. Snow in the mountains: Good profits in the future. Drifts of snow in a city: Will receive good news. 690

6 Soap—An unexpected encounter will result in a solution of matters that have puzzled you. Washing your own body with soap: Will be asked for help by friends. Washing clothes with soap: Will receive money from a rich relative. 834

2 Soldier—Loss of employment, and probably many changes before you settle down once more. Soldiers drilling: Realization of hopes and desires. Wounded soldiers: Loss of sleep. Many soldiers marching: Complete change of life. A young girl dreaming of soldiers: Will have many changes before settling down. Soldiers fighting: The dreamer will be victorious. 209

9 Spade—A new vista of contentment opens before you. Having a spade: Will receive some money. Using a spade: Stay on beaten track when out alone. 198

6 Spear—A good sign of wordly success and renown to come soon. Using a spear to catch fish: Abundance. A spear stabbing a fish: Rapid success of hopes. 762

7 Spending—Be careful to economize for a time; money matters will improve after a long while. Spending money in traveling: Frivolity. Spending money on family: Loss of good friends. Spending money for food: Will have happy days. Spending money foolishly: Be careful and economize for a short time. Spending money for a charity: Affairs will improve after a long while. 250

8 Spider—Good fortune is on the way, especially in your business ventures. Seeing a spider in the morning: Will have a lawsuit. A spider spinning a web: Domestic happiness. Being bitten by a spider: Marital unfaithfulness. 278

2 Spring—To dream of a spring in winter is an omen of a wedding soon to take place. Drinking a glass of spring water: Small disputes. A dry spring: Poverty and sickness. A spring of gushing water: Wealth and honor. 173

6 Spy—Adventure will come your way; but someone will have a protective influence over you, and you will meet with no harm. 915

3 Squirrels—Be content. Hard work is your lot, so stay cheerful, and persevere. A woman dreaming of a squirrel: Will be surprised while doing wrong. A young girl dreaming of a squirrel will be untrue to her boyfriend. Killing a squirrel: Will acquire a few new friends. Being bitten by a squirrel: Will marry for money. 813

4 Stable—A good companion will be yours for life. Racetrack's stables: Will make much money. 875

9 Stain—To dream of stained garments presages scandal to their wearer. Several stains on garments of ladies: Laziness. Stains on children's clothes: Children will grow up healthy. Stains on a tablecloth: Disappointments of own hopes. A stain on a woman's breast: Illness to come. 648

5 Stairs—To decend a staircase means your wish will be granted; to tumble down them means the reverse. Very high stairs: Will be jilted by your lover. 824

7 Stamps—Association with someone in a high official position will cause you some worry but much gain.

Buying stamps: Misery. Collecting stamps: Great joy.
Giving stamps away: Reconciliation with an enemy. 214

4 Star—Shooting stars: Great and good fortune. Seeing
stars at night: Important and very beneficial event to
come. An unusually bright star: Losses in business. A
star shining into a room: Danger of death for head of
family. Stars falling from the sky: Disaster. 157

6 Statues—To dream of seeing statues moving signifies
riches. 645

3 Stealing—A gift of jewelry will be offered you. 192

1 Steeple—An unfortunate dream unless you are climbing
one, which means achievement of your greatest wish.
208

9 Stockings—To see light-colored socks on: Sorrow.
Dark-colored socks: Pleasure. A hole in one: You will
lose something. Woolen socks: Affluence. Silk socks:
Hardships. Torn stockings: Financial losses. Taking off
stockings: Good days ahead. Putting on stockings:
Honor and profit. Knitting stockings: Will meet with
opposition. 297

6 Stones—Angry discussions and new surroundings. Walking on stones: Will have to suffer for a while. Of precious stones: Good business. Buying precious stones:
Good earnings. Admiring precious stones: Sickness.
Wearing precious stones: Abundance. Losing precious
stones: Misfortune. Selling precious stones: Loss of
money. 150

2 Stork—A promise of ill tidings. Two storks together:
Will marry and have good children. Seeing a stork in
the winter: Big disaster ahead. A stork flying in the air:
Robbers are close by. 695

4 Storm—Another obstacle dream. Watching a storm:
Unhappiness in love. Being in a storm: Separation of
loved ones. A storm hitting own house: Discovery of a
secret. A storm demolishing your house: People with
evil intention are nearby. 328

4 Strangers—A dream of contrary meaning. If you dream
of strangers, the more of them you see, the better. It
means the assistance of kind friends who will help you
on in life. 202

4 Strangle—To dream of being strangled: Trouble caused

by the one you dream of. To think you are strangling someone: Your wish will come true. 913

9 Straw—A warning of difficulties. You must work hard in order to overcome your troubles. Several bundles of straw: Joy and honor. Straw in a stable: Happiness in domestic matters. Burning straw: Will attend big festivities. 513

6 String—Strong powers of attraction are yours, which you must use carefully. A voyage is in your near future. 123

1 Struggle—To dream of struggling to escape from something or someone means great improvement in your health and strength. Struggling with a wild animal: Good fortune. Struggling with a woman: Will suffer through own foolish actions. 829

3 Sugar—This means sweet words and a happy future. Cooking with sugar: Will be cheated by friends. Putting sugar on fruit: Will have a happy future. 912

7 Suicide—A sign of an overstraining mind and a warning to change your surroundings for a time. Planning to commit suicide: Troubles were brought on by yourself. Having committed suicide: Unhappiness. Thinking of committing suicide: Must conform yourself to real life. A woman committing suicide: Opposition in love and despair. A husband or wife committing suicide: Permanent change in surroundings. 799

8 Summons—Adverse criticism and scandal will vex you. 323

9 Sun—Success in money matters and love. A beautiful sunset: Will be told false news. A woman dreaming of a beautiful sunset: A child will be born. The sun shining on your bed: Apprehension. The sun peeping through the clouds: Troubles will soon vanish. 702

3 Sunrise—This is a token of ambitions soon to be realized, while to dream of watching the sunset signifies the reverse. 912

1 Surf—You will need all your tact to avoid the attentions of an unwelcome admirer. 631

9 Surgeon—The slight illness of a friend will cause a deeper relationship between you. Being a surgeon: Joy and profit. 270

3 Swan—A good omen, but it only affects your business affairs. A white swan: Riches and good standing in life. A black swan: Domestic troubles and sorrow. Killing a swan: Business affairs need care. 246

6 Swearing—Bad language in a dream is always unfortunate, whether you are yourself to blame or someone else. 249

7 Sweetheart—To dream that your lover is beautiful and pleasing to you is a good omen; but be cautious if you dream he or she is fickle and changeable. 925

8 Swimming—Hard work confronts you; but if you swim to shore or reach your objectives, then you will succeed in the end. Swimming on your back: Will have a bad quarrel. Swimming in a pool: Success. Swimming and reaching your objective: Will be successful in everything. 143

5 Swoon—To dream you see a person swoon is unfortunate to the maid. To the married it is a sign they will become rich and prosperous. 158

8 Swords—All sharp-edged weapons or tools indicate bad news. Being wounded by a sword: Great danger is ahead. A broken sword: Deep discouragement. Wounding another with a sword: Good results in your business. Wounded by an acquaintance's sword: Will receive a service. Blood coming from a sword wound: Will receive a great favor. 953

T

4 Table—It is not fortunate to be seated at a table in your dream; but it is fortunate to see others thus seated. A banquet table: Enjoyment in life. A table with a marble top: Will have a comfortable life. A broken table: Misery and poverty. Breaking a table: Loss of fortune. An empty table: Will fall into poverty. Sitting at a table with sweetheart: Triumph over enemies. 346

3 Tailor—To a girl this dream signifies that she will marry an inferior. A male dreaming about a tailor: Exercise caution in business ventures. Being a tailor: Change of surroundings. Ordering clothes from a tailor: Joy without profit. 309

8 Talk—Talking too much: Will be exposed to some malicious plans. Talking with friends: Will come out of present peril. Talking to parents: Will be granted what you ask for. Talking to a sweetheart: Beware of jealous friends. Talking to your superior: Will become a victim and suffer humiliation. 214

7 Tapestry—Great enjoyment will come to you from small causes. Admiring tapestry: Abuse of confidence. Buying tapestry: Enjoyment will come to you. 142

8 Taxi—Hasty news will be sent to you; be on guard against false information. Riding in a taxi: Will have success in your business. Calling a taxi: New interests and surroundings. Escaping from the path of an oncoming taxi: Avoid rivals. 269

7 Tea—To dream that you are making or drinking tea is a warning of many small difficulties ahead. Persevere and all will go well. Drinking tea: Domestic unhappiness. Tea grounds: Will have many social duties. Tea bags: Will be disappointed in a love affair. 124

6 Teacher—If the dreamer is teaching, an invitation to a solemn occasion is portended; if being taught, anger about a trifling slight will vex him. 501

8 Tears—A sign of contrary meaning. Happiness awaits you. Crying: Will receive a gift. Children shedding tears: Recovery of money due you. Sweethearts shedding tears: Will have consolation. 404

5 Tease—Your secret hopes will be discovered and much discussed, yet you will gain them in the end. Teasing a dog: Will have good earnings. Being teased by friends: Will be offended by enemies. Being teased by sweetheart: You are deeply in love. 491

4 Teeth—It is always unfortunate to dream about your teeth; watch your health. A gold tooth: Corruption and sorrow. Infected teeth: Must give much explanation to other people. Having dirty teeth: Prosperity. Not brushing teeth: Faithful friends. Having teeth pulled: Finan-

cial losses. Teeth falling out: Death. Losing teeth in a fight: Loss of a relative. Having teeth knocked out: Sudden misfortune. Brushing teeth: Misery. 408

9 Telegram—It is more fortunate to receive a telegram than to send one, but neither event is a happy omen. Sending a business telegram: Decline in business. Receiving a business telegram: Will collect money past due you. 135

1 Telephone—Your curiosity will be satisfied. Making a telephone call: Advantages in business. Receiving a telephone call: Postponement of a date. Talking long distance on the telephone: Happiness. Being without a phone: Desires will be realized. 325

1 Telescope—You are apt to exaggerate your troubles. Cares will lessen if they are faced cheerfully. 307

3 Temple—A foreign temple is a portent of curious experiences to be yours before long. Discretion will bring you a big reward. 390

7 Temptation—Obstacles are barring your way to what is rightfully yours; guard your tongue and your good sense will surmount all difficulties. 124

5 Tent—You will find great pleasure in helping the love affairs of some youthful friend of yours. Living in a tent with family: Will undergo great changes in life. Living in a tent with sweetheart: Arguments over love. A military camp of tents: Will take a tiresome trip. 257

5 Theater—To dream that you witness a performance at the theater is a warning of treachery from someone you trust. Be cautious in discussing your plans, otherwise you will lose money. 617

6 Thimble—It is considered very fortunate for a woman to dream that she has lost her thimble. 159

4 Thirst—An obstacle dream: If you satisfy your thirst you will overcome your troubles. 463

2 Thread—To wind thread denotes wealth gained by thrift; to break it, hard times. To unravel knotted thread means a mystery will be solved. 346

9 Thunder—A thunderstorm is a sign of great difficulties in store for you. Like all obstacle dreams, it depends upon what happens in your dream. Lightning following thunder: Death of a friend. Being hit by lightning fol-

lowed by thunder: A woman who is overly sexual. 324

5 Ticket—Good tidings long expected will come at last. 212

6 Tickle—A misunderstanding will be cleared up. If the tickle is in the nose or throat so that you sneeze, you will surely be asked to lend money. 897

5 Tiger—Another obstacle dream. If you are caught by a wild beast, look out for heavy losses. A tiger performing at a circus: Will have helpful friends. A tiger in a cage at the zoo: Death of a prominent person. Hearing a tiger roar: Will suffer grief. 275

7 Tin—A dream signifying that counterfeit friendship will be taken for true. Test your friends before you trust them. 205

3 Toad—Loss and difficulties are shown; but if the creature hops away, hard work may save the situation. Catching toads: A self-inflicted injury will come. Killing toads: A false friend is nearby. Stepping on a toad: Friends will desert you when needed most. 912

5 Tobacco—Your fancied troubles will soon vanish, like smoke. A tobacco shop: A lot of gossip behind your back. Smoking a cigarette: You are squandering money. Women dreaming of smoking cigarettes: Troubles will soon vanish. 716

4 Toboggan—You will soon be involved in someone else's affairs so deeply that it will be difficult for you to extricate yourself. Be careful of every step. 913

9 Tomatoes—A portent of comfortable circumstances, which you will attain by your own efforts. 567

6 Tombs—To dream that you are walking among tombs foretells marriages; to dream that you are ordering your own tomb denotes that you will shortly be married; but to see a tomb fall to ruins denotes sickness and trouble to your family. To dream that you, with another person, are admiring tombs, denotes your future partner to be very suitable for you. To dream you are inspecting the tombs of the illustrious dead denotes your speedy advancement to honor and wealth. 437

5 Toothache—You will have much to be grateful for in a letter from a distant friend. Child having a toothache: Happiness over letter from an old friend. Having a

persisting toothache: Fortune in the future. Receiving relief from a toothache: Love quarrels. 130

1 Torch—This signifies that if you will hold the light of reason to your troubles you will quickly see your way out of them. Woman holding torches: Will fall in love. Holding a flaming torch: A secret will be revealed to you. 136

6 Tornado—A dream warning you against strife in your home or in business. It will surely bring disaster in either. A furious tornado: Loss of friends. A mild tornado: Will have disaster in own affairs. Damages caused by a tornado: Honesty will bring victory for you. 123

3 Torpedo—A presage of love at first sight which will completely alter your life. A torpedo exploding: You are surrounded by envious people. A torpedo hitting a target: Will have joy with children. 831

9 Torture—To dream of being tortured signifies domestic bliss. Torturing animals: Big money losses. Lovers torturing each other: You are unreasonable. 639

3 Towel—You will undergo a brief illness but will recover very quickly. 219

9 Tower—The higher you ascend, the greater your loss will be. It is an obstacle dream. 243

7 Toys—This dream indicates that your family will be very clever and successful. 897

9 Traffic—Many friends and some public dignity are promised. An accident in traffic: Loss of money. Others being hurt in a traffic accident: Will undergo persecution. Being stopped by a traffic officer: You enjoy an active life. 999

8 Trains—Traveling on a train alone: A lawsuit will be ruled in your favor. Traveling on a train with your family: Advantages in life. A cargo train: Will meet a pleasant person. 215

5 Tramp—An absent friend is thinking of you. A letter from that friend is on its way. 302

6 Travel—Difficulties in your business ventures. Success depends upon hard work. Traveling alone: Will avoid unpleasant events. Traveling with loved ones: Delays in personal matters. Traveling in a carriage: Will enjoy a

large fortune. Traveling in a car: Happiness and family love. Traveling on a horse: Will have dealings with obstinate people. Traveling to foreign countries: Consider the results before acting. 915

8 Treasure—It is a most unfortunate omen to dream that you have discovered a treasure. Beware of treachery among those you trust. Finding a hidden treasure: Danger. Finding a treasure chest: Inheritance. Digging for a treasure: Disgrace. Stealing a treasure: Beware of double cross from those you now trust. 854

4 Trees—If you dream of trees in full leaf, it is a very fortunate omen, for nature is kind to you. If you see a tree cut down, then expect loss in business. To dream of climbing trees is a certain omen of hard work and little luck, whatever else happens in your dream. Falling out of a tree: Loss of employment. A barren tree: Someone is cheating you. Heavily ladened fruit trees: Riches and fortune in business. Blossoming trees: Joys and sweet satisfaction. A Christmas tree: Joy and happiness. Escaping from a forest fire: Will have an unusual accident. 832

6 Trial—You have an admirer whose merits you have not hitherto valued. You would be wise to study and develop this friendship. Being on trial: Will enjoy lifelong security. Being unjustly accused on trial: You are enjoying much passion. Being on trial for wrongdoings against a woman: Will receive bad news. Being on trial for wrongdoings against a man: Hard days ahead. 636

3 Trunk—A traveler will return from abroad. A wish will be granted in connection with the home. 264

3 Trouble—If you find yourself in trouble in your dream, it is a sign of change in residence. A married person being in trouble: Disaster is ahead for you. A single person being in trouble: Shame and sorrow. A girl being in trouble: Will have many sweethearts. A widow being in trouble: She will be pregnant. Facing trouble: Will have success. Avoiding trouble: Troubles will come to you. 435

8 Trousers—This dream signifies flirtations to the married and quarrels to the single dreamer. Having a hole in trousers: Flirtations with a married woman. A single girl

dreaming of a man's trousers: Will have quarrels. 242

3 Tug—Merry company and a wedding between middle-aged lovers. 102

5 Tunnel—Another obstacle dream. If you escape from the tunnel, all will go well. Driving a car through the tunnel: Unsatisfactory business undertaking. Going through a tunnel on a train: You have many false friends. 284

1 Turkey—Trouble with your friends, with your husband or wife, and your business customers or associates. Visiting the country of Turkey: Loss of all possessions. Killing a turkey: Infidelity. Eating turkey: Great joy. Carving a turkey: Quarrels with business partners. 730

6 Turtle—These creatures are omens of unfulfilled wishes or ambitions. With hard work you may succeed. Catching a sea turtle: A mystery will be solved. Eating a sea turtle: You have secret enemies. Drinking bouillon made from a sea turtle: Long life and success. 204

4 Twins—Babies are not considered fortunate omens in a dream, though young children are favorable. Twin babies make the omen more dangerous. 931

7 Ugliness—It is a fortunate omen to dream of an ugly person. 403

9 Undertaker—This is one of the contrary dreams and denotes a wedding. An undertaker removing a body from the house: Happiness. Going to an undertaker's parlor: Will live a long life. 639

1 Undress—If you dream of being in public not fully dressed, be cautious of word and act; gossip will distress you. Undressing in privacy: A guarded secret will be discovered. Undressing before others: People are talking badly behind your back. Undressing in a hotel room:

Satisfactory love life. Husband and wife undressing in same room: Business affairs will go badly. Undressing in public: Disaster and worry will come to you. 856

1 Unfaithful—A dream of contrary meaning. All will go well with your future. If you dream that your husband, wife, or lover is unfaithful, there is a lot of good fortune in store for you. 982

4 Unhappy—A dream of contrary meaning. The more miserable you are in your dream, the better for you in real life. A woman being unhappy with her husband: Receive invitation by prominent person. Sweethearts being unhappy with each other: Doubt and distrust without reason. 409

7 Uniform—This dream signifies a change for the better, a promotion which will bring you good fortune in love as well as a better position. A member of own family in uniform: Glory and dignity. Wearing a uniform: Valor and prominence. Woman wearing uniforms for her business: You are too arrogant. 304

9 University—A sign that you are fortunate in your talents and in your friends. 153

4 Unmarried—For married people to dream of being single again is a sign of danger from jealousy and gossip. Be sure and trust each other, and all will be well. A single person desiring to get married: Will receive good news. An old bachelor wanting to get married: Will marry a healthy woman. An old maid wanting to get married: She will marry a young man. 805

1 Uproar—To dream of scenes and confusion and uproar signifies a decision which will be arrived at soon after long delay; it will be as you wish. 109

3 Vaccination—You are in danger of giving more affection than its recipient is worth; keep a guard on your

heart and obey your head. Children being vaccinated: Beware of squandering money. Being vaccinated by a nurse: Will have opposition in life. Others being vaccinated: Enemies will occupy your time. 102

3 Valentine—This predicts news of an old sweetheart who still thinks much of you. Sending valentines: Will lose an opportunity to make money. Receiving a valentine: Will take advantage of available opportunities. A sweetheart receiving a valentine: Victory over enemies. A sweetheart sending a valentine: Contradiction. 534

5 Valley—To dream that you are in a valley is a warning of ill health. Do not overtax yourself or your powers. A beautiful valley: Be cautious in all your affairs. Crossing a green valley: Contentment and ease. A barren valley: Dissatisfaction and want. 248

3 Vampire—A bad omen. You will marry for money and find it a bad bargain. Fighting with a vampire: Will receive good news. 525

2 Vase—You are apt to give too much thought to appearances; try to value useful qualities in one who loves you. 362

4 Vault—To dream that you are in a vault is a sign of difficulties in your path. If eventually you escape, all will be well once more; but be careful of undertaking new ventures. 832

8 Vegetables—Hard work for little result will surely follow a dream of these green offerings of nature. Persevere, and do not lose heart. 152

3 Veil—To dream that you are wearing a veil is a bad omen, even if it is a bridal veil, unless you remove it before the dream is concluded. Opening a veil or folding it: Favorable circumstances. 453

5 Velvet—A fortunate dream, but it will depend largely upon the color. Sewing with velvet: Will receive assistance from a friend. 329

9 Vermin—Nearly all unpleasant dreams of this sort go by contraries and mean good luck. 612

5 Village—This dream promises an offer of a change which will prove most important to your future. A village burning: Will make a pilgrimage. The village where you live: Improved conditions in the future. 392

7 Villain—To dream of a ruffian or villain denotes a letter or present from one you love. 313

4 Vinegar—Useless toil. Fresh vinegar: Sickness. Cooking with vinegar: Disaster in your industry. Making vinegar sauce for a salad: Will participate in an orgy. Eating foods made with vinegar: Poverty. Buying vinegar: Abundance. 193

5 Vine—One of the most fortunate dreams, especially if the vine is in full leaf. You may have to work hard, but success is certain to come. 140

3 Violets—Very fortunate for the lover. Picking violets: Will have a happy marriage. Buying violets: Will have a lawsuit. 399

4 Violence—If you are violently attacked, it portends better times for you; to see violence to others means festivities and cheerful friends. 580

9 Violin—To hear sweet music is a sign of social and domestic happiness, but beware if one of the strings should break, for it foretells a quarrel. Playing a violin: Bliss between husband and wife. Playing a violin in solitude: Will attend a funeral. 594

3 Virgin—To dream of an effigy of the virgin is a warning of threatened trouble; be reserved and on guard with all but trusted friends. Being introduced to a virgin: Pleasures without secrecy. Realizing a person is not a virgin: Much personal grief. Knowing a virgin with many boyfriends: Be on guard and don't trust friends. A sick person dreaming of a virgin saint: Will recover completely. 102

8 Visit—To pay a visit means obstacles to your plans; to receive a visit from a friend signifies travel for pleasure. A doctor visiting you: Will have advantages over others. Visiting your friends: Your situation is not good. Receiving business visits: Will have sorrow that will cause tears. 376

5 Visitors—It is not a good omen to dream of visitors; the more people there are around you, the greater will your business difficulties be. 104

9 Voice—To hear people speaking is a dream of contrary meaning. If they appear to be happy and merry, then expect reverses in business and many worries. 234

1 Volcano—To dream of a volcano foretells great disagreements, family jars, and lover's quarrels. To a man of commerce it portends dishonest servants and a robbery of some sad convulsion. To lovers it is a sign that all deceit, intrigue, and base designs on one side or the other will be exploded; and the designer will be branded with the contempt and execration so justly deserved. 901

7 Vomit—To dream of vomiting, whether of blood, meat, or phlegm, signifies to the poor, profit, and to the rich, hurt. Vomiting wine: Will lose in real estate dealings. Vomiting after drinking liquor: Will easily spend money won in gambling. 358

8 Voting—You must be more confident if you wish to fulfill your hopes; you are favored but too difficult. 492

3 Voyage—A message from a distance is soon to be received. Taking a voyage to a foreign country with relatives: Fortune. Taking a voyage alone: Good times ahead. 901

2 Vulture—Dangerous enemies. To kill a vulture indicates conquest of misfortune; To see one devouring its prey—your troubles will cease and fortune smile upon you. 839

6 Wade—It is considered a good sign for lovers if they dream of wading in clear water, if the water is muddy or rough, disillusion will soon come. 564

9 Wager—This portends losses. Act cautiously. Accepting a wager: You are very confused in your thinking. Losing a wager: Will acquire wealth dishonorably. 819

1 Wages—To receive them, danger of loss; to pay them, money from legacy. Being refused payment of wages:

Will have lawsuit. Receiving your own wages: Loss. 280

3 Wailing—To dream you hear wailing and weeping from unseen voices is a bad sign of loss of someone dear to you. 903

4 Waiter—To dream of being at a table where you are waited upon is a sign of an invalid whom you will have to nurse shortly. 328

1 Wallet—This portends important news from an unexpected source. An empty wallet: Fortune. A full wallet: Discovery of a secret. Finding a woman's wallet: Will receive a small amount of money. 217

5 Walking—Small worries that will vanish if you tackle them bravely. Walking forward: Will have a change in fortune that will bring profit. Walking backward: Loss of money. Walking at night: Annoyance. Walking along muddy streets: Will be molested. Walking on crutches: Losses in gambling. Walking in water: Triumph and success. 203

4 Walls—These are obstacles and, if you climb over them, all will be well for you. But you will have to face hard work. A wall falling down: Personal and business losses. Climbing a wall with a ladder: Joy. 562

1 Waltz—An admirer is concealing his affection from you. Be kind. Dancing a waltz: Good humor and happiness. Waltzing with husband or wife: Sickness. Waltzing with lover or sweetheart: An admirer is concealing his affections. 208

6 War—To dream of war and affairs of war signifies trouble and danger. Watching a war: Misfortune. Being in a war: Danger of illness. 735

9 Warts—To see warts on your hands in a dream indicates that as many sums of money as you can see warts will come to you; on the hands of others, warts signify rich friends. 612

5 Wasps—Enemies among those whom you trust. 923

1 Watch—A journey by land. Watching someone you don't care for: The moon will bring rain. Watching from a high window: People are spying on you. Wearing a wristwatch: Loss in business. A young girl receiving a

gift of a wristwatch: Will receive marriage proposal. Buying a wristwatch: Joy and tranquility. 154

4 Water—Drawing water from a well: Will be tormented by wife. Bathing in clear water: Good health. Bathing in dirty water: Sickness. Drinking water from a glass of water: Prompt matrimony. Drinking ice water: Prosperity and triumph over enemies. Breaking a glass of ice water: Death of mother and health for children. Falling in to water and waking immediately: Entire life ruined by woman you marry. Water flooding house and ruining furniture: Will quarrel with enemies. A river flooding: Will receive good news concerning pending lawsuits. Falling into rough water from a boat: Loss of fortune. Pouring water on fire: Will lose lawsuit. Water on your head: Profit. Swimming pool water: Fortune. 526

8 Waterfall—An invitation to a place of amusement. You are observed and gossiped about. 583

3 Web—Travel and gratified wishes. A sign of wealth. 534

3 Wedding—A dream of contrary: Expect trouble in your family circle. Attending a sister's wedding: Big danger. Attending a brother's wedding: Will make money. Attending the wedding of a son: Approaching money. Attending the wedding of a daughter: Wealth. Attending the wedding of a widow: Will make abundant money. 183

6 Wedding ring—A parting. To take it off in a dream means the parting you see will be final. 492

7 Weeping—To dream one weeps is joy and mirth. Weeping along with grief: Will enjoy pleasures. 340

7 Well—To draw water means success and profit; to fall in; danger that can scarcely be avoided. A well full of clear water: Luck and prosperity. An overflowing well: Death of children and losses in business. A dry well: Will have some damages in own affairs. Throwing someone in a well of water: Death for the dreamer. 529

1 Whale—Misunderstandings that will be cleared up in time. A delayed wedding is indicated. 121

9 Wheels—Property will be left to you. A broken wheel: New interest and surroundings. The wheel of a mill: You are faced with great danger. The wheel of a car:

Unhappiness, in married life. A gambling wheel: Will suffer much embarrassment. 324

2 Whip—An affectionate message. Good tidings will come shortly. 101

2 Whirland—Beware of dangerous reports. 506

6 Whirlpool—Advice will be given to you well worth following. An inheritance in the future. 924

8 Whispering—A rumor will be confirmed. Financial gains are at hand. 395

6 Whistle—To hear scandal is being spread about you; to dream that you are whistling merrily indicates sad news coming. 591

1 Whiskey—This is a foreboding of ill; it signifies debts and difficulties. Offering whiskey to relatives: Be on the lookout for a double cross. Offering whiskey to mate: Realization of high ambitions. Offering whiskey to a lover: Temptation will come to you. Being offered a drink of whiskey: A mystery will be solved. 406

7 Wife—Of your own wife: Must control your passions. Taking a wife: Accomplishment of desires. Arguing with your wife: Will have a quarrel lasting several days. Wife being beautifully dressed: Warning of trouble. Own wife undressing: You must mend your ways of life. Own wife being naked: She is unfaithful to you. Wife being in a bathtub: Misfortune in love affairs. A wife dreaming of being married to another man: Sudden separation, or death, of husband. 574

3 Wig—Two proposals to come. The darker man loves you best. A woman wearing a blond wig: Will have many admirers. A man wearing a light colored wig: Will be refused by several women. A man wearing a dark colored wig: Will be loved best by one woman. A woman wearing a white wig: Will marry a rich man. A woman wearing a dark wig: Should mend her ways in life. A woman wearing a brunette wig: Will marry a poor man. 183

2 Widow—To dream that you are conversing with a widow foreshadows that you will lose your wife by death. For a woman to dream that she is a widow portends the infidelity of her husband. For a young woman

to dream of being a married widow: Prognosticates that
her lover will abandon her. 353

7 Widower—To dream that you are one denotes the
sickness of your wife. For a young woman to dream she
is married to a widower denotes much trouble with false
lovers, but she will be happily married at last to a man
of good sense and good conduct. 349

5 Wind—Good news is coming; the stronger the gale of
wind, the sooner you may expect good fortune. Battling
with the wind: Attending success and untrying energy.
The wind blowing own hat away: Future conditions will
improve. The wind turning umbrella inside out: Joy. A
ship battling against the wind: Will discover a secret. A
wind blowing away a boat sail: Approaching troubles.
The wind sinking or destroying a vessel. Money will
come easily. 923

5 Windmill—Some gain but only of small character.
Windmill stopped: Will receive inheritance from a rich
relative. 428

7 Window—An open one: Success will attend you. A
closed one: You will suffer desertion by your friends. A
broken window: Be suspicious of robbery by friends.
Jumping from a window: Will have a lawsuit. Climbing
from a window on ladder: Will become bankrupt. A very
big window: Very good success in business. Seeing people kissing in front of a window: Death of a pet bird.
Viewing something from a window: Victory over enemies. Throwing things from a window: Advancement
within own position. 943

6 Wine—A sign of comfortable home life, it does not
refer to business and love matters. Drinking wine: Will
receive many good things. Spilling wine: Someone will
be injured and lose much blood. Buying wine: New
employment. Receiving wine as a gift: Doomed for disappointment. Making wine: Good results in all affairs.
Getting drunk on wine: Big success. 195

8 Winter—To dream of a wintry scene with snow on the
ground is an omen of prosperity but to dream of summer in winter is the reverse. Being sick during the
winter: Relatives are envious of you. Living through a
severe winter: Will receive a gift. 215

1 Witness—To dream of being a witness in court is a warning to be on your guard against false accusations that will be made against you. Witnesses testifying on your behalf: Good results in business affairs. Being a witness for someone else: A big catastrophe is ahead. 910

9 Witch—An ill omen in every way. Being scared by a witch: Abuse of confidence. Becoming nervous because of a witch: Damages to your health. 360

2 Wolf—Enmity. To kill one, success. To pursue one, dangers overcome. Pursued by one, danger. A wolf running: Will have dealing with smart and treacherous enemies. 794

3 Woman—To see many women is a dream of wealth and renown; a beautiful woman, a happy marriage; an ugly woman, worry and vexation, a woman's voice changes in position. A woman lying on a bed: Security. A beautiful naked woman: Big unhappiness. A woman making advances to a man: Jealousy. A man dreaming of a woman of ill repute: Serious disaster ahead. Being a woman of ill repute: Will suffer humiliation. A woman dreaming of being a man: Birth of a son who brings honor to family. A woman with white hair: Dignity and distinction. A woman with long beautiful blond hair: Will enjoy a happy life. A married woman dreaming of being pregnant: Will receive happy news. 912

7 Worms—Danger of infectious diseases. Destroying worms: Will have money. Worms being on plants: Will receive unexpected money. Worms being on own body: Big riches. 169

6 Wounds—To dream that you are wounded is a favorable dream. 303

6 Wreck—Threatened trouble to health and business. Broken pieces of a ship after a wreck: Peril of death. People in a raft after a wreck: Must endure trouble before realizing desires. People being saved from a wreck: Danger in business affairs. An automobile wreck: Dishonor. Being killed in an automobile wreck: Unhappiness in family. Being injured in an automobile wreck: Joy and profit. Family being killed in automobile wreck: Will require welfare aid. Friends being in an automobile wreck: Will suffer humiliation. 627

9 Wrestling—An unfortunate dream for it means loss of money through ill-health. 243

3 Wrinkles—Compliments and social pleasures. Having wrinkles in own face: Long life after a sickness. An elderly person without wrinkles: Compliments and social pleasures. Being wrinkled at middle age. You are very gullible. 715

1 Writing—Written or printed matter is always an unfavorable omen. If you dream that you are writing, you are creating difficulties by your own actions. 316

8 Yacht—To see one means good luck if the sea is smooth; to be in one, ambition is realized unless the sea be rough which means disappointment. 152

2 Yard—News of an engagement among your friends. The wedding will bring you a new admirer. Working in a yard: An admirer will soon be married. Having a well-kept yard: Family arguments. A ship yard: Fortune. A lumber yard: Riches. Planting things in a yard: Joy. Picking flowers from a yard: Death. 281

4 Yarn—You will receive a fine present from an unexpected quarter. A man dreaming of yarn: Will attain business success. A woman dreaming of yarn: Will have plenty of money. 724

3 Yawning—An obstacle dream but not of serious importance. 309

9 Yearning—To dream of a strong feeling of longing means that you will be confidently indifferent where you would like to be kind. 394

9 Yell—To dream of hideous yells and noises is a sign of peace after strife. An introduction will alter your plans.

Yelling yourself: Family quarrels. Hearing others yelling: Will have strife followed by peace. 819

1 Yield—To dream of yielding to persuasive words is a warning against pride; do not believe flatterers. Yielding to persuasive words: False friend is near by. Lovers yielding to persuasive stories: Danger in love affairs. 415

7 Young—To dream that you have become young again is a favorable omen. But the change for the better will not last long. 340

7 Zebra—Disagreement with friends. A zebra being attacked by wild animals: Your honor is in danger. A zebra being fed at a zoo: Ingratitude. 412

4 Zeppelin—A dream signifying an ambition far beyond your reach. Being in a zeppelin: Will be molested. Coming down in a zeppelin: Will receive good news. Watching a zeppelin moving slowly: People are meddling in your affairs. 346

2 Zoo—Although wild animals in captivity are not generally good omens in themselves, it is considered fortunate to visit a zoological gardens. Going to the zoo alone: Will be molested. Going to zoo with family and children: Good hopes for the future. Going to the zoo with sweetheart: Danger of misfortune. 524

LUCKY DAYS

In every human mind is a spark of the gambling instinct—a desire to take chances that afford the thrill of gaining or losing in such a venture. Life itself is a speculation: a child is born—perhaps it will live, perhaps it will not; a merchant opens a business—perhaps he will succeed, perhaps he won't; an aviator takes a long flight—perhaps he will make a safe landing, perhaps he will not. The desire to take chances is innate in all humanity, primitive or civilized.

Emerson said, "Astrology is Astronomy brought to earth and applied to the affairs of men." Astrology, the oldest science in the world, has outlined the proper courses for people to follow for many thousands of years. "There is a time and a place for all things," and no more practical science in the world can be applied to mankind's daily affairs than the sciences of astrology and numerology.

Ptolemy, a great astrologer and philosopher of ancient times, has said, "Judgment must be regulated by thyself, as well as by the science—it is advantageous to make choice of days and hours at a time constituted by the nativity."

Although the author of this book does not recommend or encourage promiscuous gambling in any form, he is mindful that so long as human beings remain constituted as they are, they are going to indulge in some form of speculation, whether for pleasure and amusement; starting businesses; taking trips; buying and selling stocks, real estate, commodities; and so on. Hence, if people MUST speculate, this book will be of value to anyone by showing how to combine the laws that rule and regulate the universe with one's own judgment. You will remember that accurate judgment is also necessary for the success of any enterprise, yet by combining this with the fundamental laws of cause and effect outlined by the science of the universe herein treated, a greater measure of success may be attained than by attempting things at a time that might prove to be very inopportune.

We present this information for what it may be worth. It may appeal to you as a pastime flavored with the thrill of sport, or a test of skill tempered by your judgment. We would have all readers pleased and interested, but none enslaved by it.

For those who have read the contents of this book with interest and wish to test it out for results, we suggest that you keep tabs on the schedule outlined; it will save you considerable money and will bring excellent results.

YOUR FORTUNATE NUMBERS

These methods, based on the science of numerology, are different for every person. The author has spent many years studying the occult meaning of numbers, and although results cannot be guaranteed, many use them with great success.

What You Must Know

FIRST; Learn how to tell magic time, as follows:

Magic Time

A.M.   1-2-3-4-5-6-7-8-9-10-11-12
P.M.   13-14-15-16-17-18-19-20-21-22-23-24

SECOND: Note the day of the week. Monday is 1; Tuesday is 2; Wednesday is 3; Thursday is 4; Friday is 5; Saturday is 6; Sunday is 7.

THIRD: Count the number of letters in your name. *Example:* Jack Brown has four letters in his first name and five in his second name. 4 plus 5 equals 9. This number is always lucky for Jack Brown.

FOURTH: A lucky number is found by combining the values of the day and month in which you were born. *Example:* If you were born on June 25 (June is the sixth month), combine 6 and 25 to get 625 or 67. Add these figures: 6 plus 2 plus 5 equals 13. Add again, 1 plus 3 equals 4. This gives four magic numbers, all with the same strength: 625, 67, 13, 4. Use the one that suits you best. January equals 1; February 2; March 3; April 4; May 5; June 6; July 7; August 8; September 9; October 10; November 11 (or 2); December 12 (or 3).

Four Methods for Using Your Fortunate Numbers

1. THE MAGIC HOUR: Use the number of the day of the week and the number of the hour at which you play or bet. *Example:* Suppose it is 4 P.M. on Friday. See the clock: 4 P.M. is 16 o'clock. Friday is 5. Combine these to make 165 or 75. Then add 1 plus 6 plus 5 equals 12. Add again, 1 plus 2 equals 3. This gives four magic numbers: 165, 75, 12, 3 with the same strength. Use the one that suits you best.

2. STRIKE THE KEYNOTE: Use the number of letters in your name and the hour of play. *Example:* Suppose Jack Brown (9) wants a lucky number at 8 P.M. Combine 9 and 20 to make 920. Add these: 9 plus 2 plus 0 equals 11. Add again, 1 plus 1 equals 2. This gives four magic numbers: 920, 29, 11, 2. Use the one that suits you best.

3. YOUR PINNACLE OF SUCCESS: Use the number of the day on which you were born and the number of the month. *Example:* Suppose you were born on August 24. Combine 24 and 8. This gives 248 or 68. Add 2 plus 4 plus 8 equals 14. Add again, 1 plus 4 equals 5. This gives you four lucky numbers of the same magic power: 248, 68, 14, 5.

4. LADY LUCK METHOD: Count the number of letters in your sweetheart's name and combine with the number of letters in your own name. *Example:* Maybelle Jones (13 letters) and Jack Brown (9 letters) makes 139 or 49. Add these: 1 plus 3 plus 9 equals 13. Add again, 1 plus 3 equals 4. This gives you four lady luck num-

bers: 139, 49, 13, 4. Use the one that suits the occasion best.

NOTE: If you want more than one lucky number in a day, combine your lady luck number with the hour. *Example:*At 20 o'clock (8 P.M.), combine Maybelle Jones (13) with Jack Brown (9): 20, 139. Add these to suit your convenience. ALWAYS NOTE THE HOUR. The time figure changes only when the hour changes. Adding, transposing, or combining a magic number does not alter its strength. *Example:* 165, 75, 12 or 3. Also, a zero in a number can be used or not—200, 20, 2.

Astrology indicates the exact periods when you should speculate and when you should not do so. The earth going through the twelve signs of the zodiac forms certain configurations which indicate your prospects in any game of chance. Thus, there are regular periods every year when you may win or lose. It is up to you to make use of this information. For the most accurate reading, your sign has been divided into three sections. This division, by decanate, gives you about ten days, which are influenced by the sun's transits.

LUCKY DAYS — ARIES

*For All Those Born Between March 21
and April 20, Any Year*

If you were born on March 21, 22, 23, 24, 25, 26, 27, 28, 29, and 30. You may speculate during the following periods, and may expect to win:

January	21	to	31
May	21	to	31
July	23	to	August 3
November	23	to	December 3

From March 21 to 31, you will be tempted to speculate, but you must determine for yourself whether or not this period is fortunate. Do not speculate from June 22 to July 2, September 23 to October 4, and December 22 to January 3 of any year.

If you were born on April 1, 2, 3, 4, 5, 6, 7, 8, 9, and 10. You may speculate during the following periods of any year, and may expect to win:

February	1	to	11
June	1	to	12
August	3	to	14
December	2	to	13

From April 1 to 12, you will also be tempted to speculate, but you must find out for yourself whether or not you can win. Do not speculate from January 2 to 13, July 2 to 14, and October 3 to 15.

If you were born on April 11, 12, 13, 14, 15, 16, 17, 18, 19, and 20. You may speculate during the following periods of any year, and may expect to win:

February	9	to	20
June	10	to	21
August	12	to	23
December	11	to	13

From April 10 to 20, you will also be tempted to speculate, but you must find out for yourself whether or not you can win. Do not speculate from January 12 to 19, from July 13 to 23, and October 14 to 23.

All Aries-born are inclined to take chances between July 22 and August 23. When you speculate in cooperation with others, it would be advisable to have a partner born under one of the following signs:

Aquarius—January 21 to February 19
Gemini—May 22 to June 21
Leo—July 24 to August 23
Sagittarius—November 23 to December 22
Libra—September 24 to October 23

Miscellaneous Things to Observe

Those born between March 21 and March 28 will have better chances in speculation during the new moon.

Those born between March 29 and April 5 will have better chances in speculation during the second quarter of the moon.

Those born between April 6 and April 13 will have better chances in speculation during the full moon.

Those born between April 14 and April 20 will have better chances in speculation during the fourth quarter of the moon.

Nearly all calendars give the four quarters of the moon.

Numerology

According to the science of numerology, the celestial number of Aries is 7. Mars, the ruling planet of this sign, has the number 6 for its numerical value. Combining these two numbers we have 7 plus 6, which equals 13. This number must now be reduced to a single digit. Therefore, 1 plus 3 equals 4. The number 4 is then the key number for all persons born in Aries. Bear this in mind on all occasions. When you buy a ticket of any sort, make sure that the serial number has 4 as the predominating number. Room number 4 in a hotel, a street number containing a 4 or several 4's, horse number 4 in a race, player number 4 in a sport game, a card that totals 4 in a card game, a 4 rolled with dice, 4 on a spin wheel, and so on, are considered fortunate for you.

Illustration: Suppose you have two cards in your hand: a 10-spot and a 3-spot. 10 plus 3 equals 13, and 1 plus 3 equals 4. Therefore, such a hand of cards or any other combination that could be reduced to 4, would be fortunate for you. If you have a combination that totals 31, that would also reduce to 4, because 3 plus 1 equals 4, and so on. Use the same method of reduction to a single digit with other combinations.

To Find Your Best Days for Speculation

Any day of any month that totals 4 is considered fortunate for you. Thus, the 13th, the 22nd, and the 31st of a month are fortunate for you because any of these dates reduced to a single digit make 4. The days of the month that are best for speculation are the 4th, 13th, 22nd, and 31st. However, you should engage in speculation only in your proper months or periods, as explained below.

Proper Hours for Speculation

The proper hour for speculation is when your ruling planet is governing. Refer to your daily paper, almanac, or calendar to find the time of sunrise. Then, count the hours after sunrise. These hours are the same every week, month, and year. Only the time of sunrise changes.

Hours for Speculation: Sunday: 7th, 14th, 21st hour after sunrise. Monday: 4th, 11th, 18th hour after sunrise. Tuesday: 1st, 8th, 15th, 22nd hour after sunrise. Wednesday: 5th, 12th, 19th hour after sunrise. Thursday: 2nd, 9th, 16th, 23rd hour after sunrise. Friday: 6th, 13th, 20th hour after sunrise. Saturday: 3rd, 10th, 17th, 24th hour after sunrise.

LUCKY DAYS — TAURUS

*For All Those Born Between April 21 and
May 21, Any Year*

If you were born on April 21, 22, 23, 24, 25, 26, 27, 28, 29, and 30, and May 1. You may speculate during the following periods, and may expect to win:

February	20	to	March 1
June	22	to	July 3
August	24	to	September 4
December	23	to	January 3

From April 21 to May 2, you will also be tempted to speculate, but you must determine for yourself whether or not you can win. Do not speculate from January 21 to February 2, from July 24 to August 4, and from October 24 to November 3.

If you were born on May 2, 3, 4, 5, 6, 7, 8, 9, 10, and 11. You may speculate during the following periods, and may expect to win:

January	2	to	12
March	1	to	11
July	2	to	13
September	2	to	14

From May 1 to 12, you will also be tempted to speculate, but you must determine for yourself whether or not you can win. Do not speculate from February 1 to 11, from August 2 to 14, and from November 2 to 13.

If you were born on May 12, 13, 14, 15, 16, 17, 18, 19, 20, and 21. You may speculate during the following periods, and may expect to win:

January	10	to	20
March	11	to	20
July	12	to	23
September	12	to	23

From May 10 to 21, you will also be tempted to speculate, but you must determine for yourself whether or not you can win. Do not speculate from February 9 to 19, from August 10 to 23, and from November 11 to 23.

All Taurus-born are inclined to take chances between August 24 and September 23. When you speculate in cooperation with others, it would be advisable to have a partner born under one of the following signs:

Pisces—February 20 to March 20
Taurus—April 21 to May 21
Cancer—June 22 to July 23
Virgo—August 24 to September 23
Scorpio—October 24 to November 22
Capricorn—December 23 to January 20

Miscellaneous Things to Observe

Those born between April 21 and April 28 will have better chances in speculation during the new moon.

Those born between April 29 and May 5 will have better chances in speculation during the second quarter of the new moon.

Those born between May 6 and May 14 will have better chances in speculation during the full moon.

Those born between May 15 and May 21 will have better chances in speculation during the fourth quarter of the moon.

Nearly all calendars give the four quarters of the moon.

Numerology

According to the science of numerology, the celestial number of Taurus is 9. Venus, the ruling planet of this sign also has the number 9. Combining these two numbers we have: 9 plus 9 which equals 18. This number must now be reduced to a single digit. Therefore, 1 plus 8 equals 9. The number 9 is the key number for all persons born in Taurus. Bear this in mind on all occasions. When you buy a ticket of any sort, make sure that the serial number has 9 as the predominating number: room number 9 in a hotel, a street number containing a 9 or several 9's, horse number 9 in a race. Player number 9 in a sport game, cards that total 9 in a card game, a 9 rolled with dice, 9 on a spin wheel, and so on, are considered fortunate for you.

Illustration: Suppose you have two cards in your hand: a 4-spot and a 5-spot. Since 4 plus 5 equals 9, such a hand of cards or any other combination that could be reduced to 9 would be fortunate for you. If you should have a combination that totals 36, that would also reduce to 9, and so on. Use the same method of reduction to a single digit with other combinations.

To Find Your Best Days for Speculation

Any day of the month that totals 9 is considered fortunate for you. Thus, the 18th and the 27th are fortunate because these dates reduce to a single digit making 9. The days of the month that are best for speculation are the 9th, 18th, and 27th. However, you should engage in speculation only in your proper months or periods as explained below.

Proper Hours for Speculation

The proper hour for speculation is when your ruling planet is governing. Refer to your daily paper, almanac, or calendar to find the time of sunrise. Then count the hours after sunrise. These hours are the same every week, month, and year, only the time of sunrise changes.

Hours for speculation: Sunday: 2nd, 10th, 16th hour after sunrise. Monday: 6th, 13th, 20th hour after sunrise. Tuesday: 3rd, 8th, 15th, 24th hour after sunrise. Wednesday: 7th, 14th, 21st hour after sunrise. Thursday: 4th, 11th, 18th hour after sunrise. Friday: 1st, 8th, 15th, 22nd hour after sunrise. Saturday: 5th, 12th, 19th hour after sunrise.

LUCKY DAYS — GEMINI

For All Those Born Between May 22 and June 21

If you were born on May 22, 23, 24, 25, 26, 27, 28, 29, 30, and 31, and June 1. You may speculate during the following periods, and may expect to win:

January	21	to	30
March	21	to	31
July	24	to	August 3
September	23	to	October 3

From May 22 to June 1, you will also be tempted to speculate, yet must determine for yourself whether or not you can win. Do not speculate from February 20 to 29, August 24 to September 3, and November 23 to December 2.

If you were born on June 2, 3, 4, 5, 6, 7, 8, 9, 10, and 11. You may speculate during the following periods, and may expect to win:

January	31	to	February 9
April	1	to	10
August	4	to	13
October	4	to	13

From June 2 to 11, you will also be tempted to speculate, yet must determine for yourself whether or not you can win. Do not speculate from March 1 to 10, September 4 to 13, and December 3 to 12.

If you were born on June 12, 13, 14, 15, 16, 17, 18, 19, 20, and 21. You may speculate during the following periods, and may expect to win:

February	10	to	19
April	11	to	20
August	13	to	23
October	14	to	23

From June 12 to 21, you will also be tempted to speculate, yet you must determine for yourself whether or not you can win. Do not speculate from March 11 to 20, September 13 to 23, and December 13 to 22.

All Gemini-born are inclined to take chances between September 24 and October 23. When you speculate in

548

cooperation with others, it would be advisable to have a partner born under one of the following signs:

Aquarius—January 21 to February 19
Aries—March 21 to April 20
Gemini—May 22 to June 21
Leo—July 24 to August 23
Libra—September 24 to October 23
Sagittarius—November 23 to December 22

Miscellaneous Things to Observe

Those born between May 22 and May 29 will have a better chance in speculation during the new moon.

Those born between May 30 and June 6 will have a better chance in speculation during the second quarter of the moon.

Those born between June 7 and June 14 will have a better chance in speculation during the full moon.

Those born between June 15 and June 21 will have a better chance in speculation during the fourth quarter of the moon.

Nearly all calendars give the four quarters of the moon.

Numerology

According to the science of numerology, the celestial number of Gemini is 3. Mercury, the ruling planet of this sign, has the numerical value 4. Combining these two numbers we have 3 plus 4 which equals 7. The number 7 is the key number for all persons born in Gemini. Bear this in mind on all occasions. When you buy a ticket of any sort, make sure that the serial number has 7 as the predominating number. Room number 7 in a hotel, a street number containing a 7 or several 7's, horse number 7 in a race, player number 7 in a sport game, cards that total 7 in a card game, a 7 rolled with dice, 7 on a spin wheel, and so on, are considered fortunate for you.

Illustration: Suppose you have two cards in your hand: a 3-spot and a 4-spot. Since 3 plus 4 equals 7, such a hand of cards or any other combination that could be reduced to 7, would be fortunate for you. If you should have a combination that totals 52, that will also reduce to 7. Use the same method of reduction to a single digit with other combinations.

To Find Your Best Days for Speculation

Any day of any month that totals 7 is considered fortunate for you. Thus, the 16th, and the 25th are fortunate because these dates reduced to a single digit total 7. The days of the month that are best for speculation are the 7th, 16th, and 25th, however, you should engage in speculation only in your proper months or periods as explained below.

Proper Hours for Speculation

The proper hour for speculation is when your ruling planet is governing. Refer to your daily paper, almanac, or calendar to find the time of sunrise, then count the hours after sunrise. These hours are the same every week, month, and year. Only the time of sunrise changes.

Hours for speculation: Sunday: 3rd, 10th, 17th, 24th hour after sunrise. Monday: 7th, 14th, 21st hour after sunrise. Tuesday: 4th, 11th, 18th hour after sunrise. Wednesday: 1st, 8th, 15th, 22nd hour after sunrise. Thursday: 5th, 12th, 19th hour after sunrise. Friday: 2nd, 9th, 16th, 23rd hour after sunrise. Saturday: 6th, 13th, 20th hour after sunrise.

LUCKY DAYS — CANCER

For All Those Born Between June 22 and July 23

If you were born on June 22, 23, 24, 25, 26, 27, 28, 29, 30, and July 1, and 2. You may speculate during the following periods and may expect to win:

February	20	to	29
April	21	to	May 1

August	24	to	September 3
October	24	to	November 2

From June 22 to July 2, you will also be tempted to speculate, but you must determine for yourself whether or not you can win. Do not speculate from March 21 to 31, September 24 to October 3, and December 22 to 31.

If you were born on July 3, 4, 5, 6, 7, 8, 9, 10, 11, 12, and 13. You may speculate during the following periods and may expect to win:

March	1	to	10
May	2	to	12
September	4	to	13
November	3	to	12

From July 3 to 13, you will also be tempted to speculate, but you must determine for yourself whether or not you can win. Do not speculate from April 1 to 10, October 4 to 13, and January 1 to 12.

If you were born on July 14, 15, 16, 17, 18, 19, 20, 21, 22, and 23. You may speculate during the following periods, and may expect to win:

March	11	to	20
May	12	to	21
September	14	to	23
November	13	to	22

From July 14 to 23, you will also be tempted to speculate, but you must determine for yourself whether or not you can win. Do not speculate from April 11 to 20, October 13 to 23, and January 10 to 20.

All Cancer-born are inclined to take chances between October 24 and November 22. When you speculate in cooperation with others, it would be advisable to have a partner born under one of the following signs:

Pisces—February 20 to March 20
Taurus—April 21 to May 21
Cancer—June 22 to July 23

Virgo—August 24 to September 23
Scorpio—October 24 to November 22
Capricorn—December 23 to January 20

Miscellaneous Things to Observe

Those born between June 22 and June 29 will have better chances in speculation during the new moon.

Those born between June 30 and July 7 will have better chances in speculation during the second quarter of the moon.

Those born between July 8 and July 17 will have better chances in speculation during the full moon.

Those born between July 18 and July 23 will have better chances in speculation during the fourth quarter of the moon.

Nearly all calendars give the four quarters of the moon.

Numerology

According to the science of numerology, the celestial number of Cancer is 8. The moon, the ruling planet of this sign, has the numerical value of 3. Combining these two numbers we have 8 plus 3, which equals 11. This must be reduced to a single digit, therefore, 1 plus 1 equals 2. The number 2 is the key number for all persons born in Cancer. Bear this in mind on all occasions. When you buy a ticket of any sort, make sure that the serial number has the predominating number 2 in it. Room number 2 in a hotel, a street number containing a 2 or several 2's, horse number 2 in a race, player number 2 in a sport game, cards that total 2 in a card game, a 2 rolled in dice, 2 on a spin wheel, and so on, are considered fortunate for you.

Illustration: Suppose you have two cards in your hand; a 9-spot and a 2-spot. 9 plus 2 equals 11, and 11 added (1 plus 1) equals 2. Therefore, such a hand, or any other combination of cards that could be added and reduced to 2, would be fortunate for you. If you have a combination that totals 45, it would reduce to 2. Use the same method with other combinations and totals.

To Find Your Best Days for Speculation

Any day of the month that totals 2 is considered fortunate for you. Thus, the 11th, 20th, 29th are fortunate because these dates reduce to a single digit 2. Therefore, the days of the month that are best for speculation are the 2nd, 11th, 20th, and 29th. However, you should engage in speculation only in your proper months or periods as explained below.

Proper Hours for Speculation

The proper hour for speculation is when your ruling planet is governing. Refer to your daily paper, almanac, or calendar to find the time of sunrise; then count the hours after sunrise. These hours are the same every week, month, and year. Only the time of sunrise changes.

Hours for speculation: Sunday: 4th, 11th, 18th hour after sunrise. Monday: 1st, 8th, 15th, 22nd hour after sunrise. Tuesday: 5th, 12th, 19th hour after sunrise. Wednesday: 2nd, 9th, 16th, 23rd hour after sunrise. Thursday: 6th, 13th, 20th hour after sunrise. Friday: 3rd, 10th, 17th hour after sunrise, also the 24th. Saturday: 7th, 14th, 21st hour after sunrise.

LUCKY DAYS — LEO

For All Those Born Between July 24 and August 23

If you were born on July 24, 25, 26, 27, 28, 29, 30, and 31, and August 1, 2, and 3. You may speculate during the following periods, and may expect to win:

March	21	to	31
May	22	to	June 1
September	24	to	October 3
November	23	to	December 2

From July 24 to August 5, you will also be tempted to

speculate, but you must determine for yourself whether or not you can win. Do not speculate from January 21 to 30, April 21 to May 2, and October 23 to November 3.

If you were born on August 4, 5, 6, 7, 8, 9, 10, 11, 12, and 13. You may speculate during the following periods and may expect to win:

April	1	to	11
June	2	to	12
October	3	to	13
December	3	to	12

From August 2 to 14, you will also be tempted to speculate, but you must determine for yourself whether or not you can win. Do not speculate from January 31 to February 10, May 2 to 12, and November 2 to 13.

If you were born on August 14, 15, 16, 17, 18, 19, 20, 21, 22, and 23. You may speculate during the following periods and may expect to win:

April	10	to	20
June	12	to	21
October	13	to	23
December	12	to	22

From August 12 to 23, you will also be tempted to speculate, yet must determine for yourself whether or not you can win. Do not speculate from February 12 to 19, May 11 to 21, and November 12 to 22.

All Leo-born are inclined to take chances between November 23 and December 22. When you speculate in cooperation with others, it would be advisable to have a partner born under one of the following signs:

Aquarius—January 21 to February 19
Aries—March 21 to April 20
Gemini—May 22 to June 21
Leo—July 24 to August 23
Libra—September 24 to October 23
Sagittarius—November 23 to December 22

Miscellaneous Things to Observe

Those born between July 24 and July 31 will have better chances in speculation during the new moon.

Those born between August 1 and August 7 will have better chances in speculation during the second quarter of the moon.

Those born between August 8 and August 16 will have better chances in speculation during the full moon.

Those born between August 17 and August 23 will have better chances in speculation during the fourth quarter of the moon.

Nearly all calendars give the four quarters of the moon.

Numerology

According to the science of numerology, the celestial number of Leo is 5. The sun, the ruling planet of this sign, has 9 as its numerical value. Combining these two numbers we have 5 plus 9, which equals 14. This must be reduced to a single digit. Therefore, 1 plus 4 equals 5. The number 5 is the key number for all persons born in Leo. Bear this in mind on all occasions. When you buy a ticket of any sort, make sure that 5 is the predominating number. Room number 5 in a hotel, a street number containing a 5 or several 5's, horse number 5 in a race, player number 5 in a sport game, cards that total 5 in a card game, a 5 rolled with dice, 5 on a spin wheel, and so on, are considered fortunate for you.

Illustration: Suppose you have two cards in your hand: a 2-spot and a 3-spot. Since 2 plus 3 equals 5, such a hand, or any other combination of cards that could be added and reduced to 5, would be fortunate for you. If you have a combination that totals 41, it would also reduce to 5; 4 plus 1 equals 5. Use the same method with other combinations and totals.

To Find Your Best Days for Speculation

Any day of the month that totals 5 is considered fortunte for you. Thus, the 14th or 23rd are fortunate because these dates reduce to a single digit 5. Therefore, the days of the month that are best for speculation for you are the 5th, 14th, and 23rd. However, you should engage in speculation only in your proper periods as explained below.

Proper Hours for Speculation

The proper hour for speculation is when your ruling planet is governing. Refer to your daily paper, almanac, or calendar to find the time of sunrise; then count the hours after sunrise. These hours are the same every week, month, and year. Only the time of sunrise changes.

Hours for speculation: Sunday: 1st, 8th, 15th, 22nd hour after sunrise. Monday: 5th, 12th, 19th hour after sunrise. Tuesday: 2nd, 9th, 16th, 23rd hour after sunrise. Wednesday: 6th, 13th, 20th hour after sunrise. Thursday: 3rd, 10th, 17th, 24th hour after sunrise. Friday: 7th, 14th, 21st hour after sunrise. Saturday: 4th, 11th, 18th hour after sunrise.

LUCKY DAYS — VIRGO

For All Those Born Between August 24 and September 23

If you were born on August 24, 25, 26, 27, 28, 29, 30, and 31, and September 1, 2, and 3. You may speculate during the following periods, and may expect to win:

April	21	to	May 1
June	22	to	July 2
October	24	to	November 3
December	22	to	December 31

From August 23 to September 3, you will also be tempted to speculate, yet must determine for yourself whether or not you can win. Do not speculate from February 20 to 29, May 22 to June 1, and November 23 to December 3.

556

If you were born on September 4, 5, 6, 7, 8, 9, 10, 11, 12, and 13. You may speculate during the following periods, and may expect to win:

January	1	to	11
May	2	to	12
July	3	to	13
November	2	to	12

From September 3 to 14 you will be tempted to speculate, yet must determine for yourself whether or not you can win. Do not speculate from March 1 to 11, June 2 to 12, and December 2 to 13.

If you were born on September 14, 15, 16, 17, 18, 19, 20, 21, and 22. You may speculate during the following periods and may expect to win:

January	11	to	21
May	11	to	21
July	12	to	23
November	12	to	22

From September 12 to 23, you will be tempted to speculate, but you must determine for yourself whether or not you can win. Do not speculate from March 9 to 20, June 11 to 21, and December 12 to 22.

All Virgo-born are inclined to take chances from December 23 to January 20. When you speculate in cooperation with others, it would be advisable to have a partner born under one of the following signs:

Pisces—February 20 to March 20
Taurus—April 21 to May 21
Cancer—June 22 to July 23
Virgo—August 24 to September 23
Scorpio—October 24 to November 22
Capricorn—December 23 to January 20

Miscellaneous Things to Observe

Those born between August 24 and August 31 will have better chances in speculation during the new moon.

Those born between September 1 and September 7 will have better chances of speculation during the second quarter of the moon.

Those born between September 8 and September 17 will have better chances of speculation during the full moon.

Those born between September 18 and September 23 will have better chances in speculation during the fourth quarter of the moon.

Nearly all calendars give the four quarters of the moon.

Numerology

According to the science of numerology, the celestial number of Virgo is 8. Mercury, the ruling planet of this sign, has the numerical value of 4. Combining these 2 numbers, we have 8 plus 4, which equals 12. This number must be reduced to a single digit. Therefore, 1 plus 2 equals 3. Number 3 is the key number for all people born in Virgo. Bear this in mind on all occasions. When you buy a ticket of any sort, make sure that 3 is the predominating number, if it contains a serial number. Room number 3 in a hotel, a street number containing a 3 or several 3's, horse number 3 in a race, player number 3 in a sports game, cards that total 3 in a card game, a 3 rolled with dice, 3 on a spin wheel, and so on, are considered fortunate for you.

Illustration: Suppose you have two cards in your hand: a 10-spot and a 2-spot. Now, 10 plus 2 equals 12 and reducing to a single digit, 1 plus 2 equals 3. Therefore, such a hand would be fortunate for you. Any other combination of cards that could be added and reduced to 3 can also be used. If you have a combination that equals 21, it would reduce to 3, and so on. Use the same method with other combinations or totals.

To Find Your Best Days for Speculation

Any day of any month that totals 3 is considered fortunate for you. Thus, the 12th, 21st, 30th, would be fortunate because these dates reduce to the single digit 3.

Therefore, the days of the month that are best for speculation for you are the 3rd, 12th, 21st, 30th. However, you should engage in speculation only in your proper periods as explained below.

Proper Hours for Speculation

The proper hour for speculation is when your ruling planet is governing. Refer to your daily paper, almanac, or calendar to find the time of sunrise, then count the hours after sunrise. These hours are the same every week, month, and year. Only the time of sunrise changes.

Hours for speculation: Sunday: 3rd, 10th, 17th, 24th hour after sunrise. Monday: 7th, 14th, 21st hour after sunrise. Tuesday: 4th, 11th, 18th hour after sunrise. Wednesday: 1st, 8th, 15th, 22nd hour after sunrise. Thursday: 5th, 12th, 19th hour after sunrise. Friday: 2nd, 9th, 16th, 23rd hour after sunrise. Saturday: 6th, 13th, 20th hour after sunrise.

LUCKY DAYS — LIBRA

For All Those Born Between
September 24 and October 23

If you were born on September 24, 25, 26, 27, 28, 29, and 30, and October 1, 2, and 3. You may speculate during the following periods and may expect to win:

January	21	to	30
May	22	to	June 1
July	24	to	August 3
November	23	to	December 3

From September 23 to October 5, you will also be tempted to speculate, yet must determine for yourself whether or not you can win. Do not speculate from March 21 to 31, June 22 to July 3, and December 22 to 31.

If you were born on October 4, 5, 6, 7, 8, 9, 10, 11, 12, and 13. You may speculate during the following periods and may expect to win:

January	31	to	February 9
June	1	to	12
August	3	to	14
December	2	to	12

From October 2 to 14 you will also be tempted to speculate, but you must determine for yourself whether or not you can win. Do not speculate from January 1 to 12, April 1 to 11, and July 2 to 15.

If you were born on October 14, 15, 16, 17, 18, 19, 20, 21, 22, and 23. You may speculate during the following periods and may expect to win:

February	9	to	19
June	11	to	21
August	12	to	23
December	11	to	22

From October 10 to 23, you will also be tempted to speculate, but you must determine for yourself whether or not you can win. Do not speculate from January 9 to 20, April 10 to 20, and July 12 to 23.

All Libra-born are inclined to take chances between January 21 and February 19. When you speculate in co-operation with others, it would be advisable to have a partner born under one of the following signs:

Aquarius—January 21 to February 19
Aries—March 21 to April 20
Gemini—May 22 to June 21
Leo—July 24 to August 23
Libra—September 24 to October 23
Sagittarius—November 23 to December 22

Miscellaneous Things to Observe

Those born between September 24 and September 30

will have better chances in speculation during the new moon.

Those born between October 1 and October 7 will have better chances in speculation during the second quarter of the moon.

Those born between October 8 and October 17 will have better chances in speculation during the full moon.

Those born between October 18 and October 23 will have better chances in speculation during the fourth quarter of the moon.

Nearly all calendars give the four quarters of the moon.

Numerology

According to the science of numerology, the celestial number of Libra is 6. Venus, the ruling planet of this sign, has a numerical value of 9. Combining these two numbers we have: 6 plus 9, which equals 15. This number must be reduced to a single digit. Therefore, 1 plus 5 equals 6. The number 6 is the key number of all persons born under Libra. Bear this in mind at all times. When you buy a ticket of any sort, make sure that the serial number has 6 as the predominating number. Room number 6 in a hotel, a street number containing a 6 or several 6's, horse number 6 in a race, player number 6 in a sport game, cards that total 6 in a card game, a 6 rolled with dice, 6 on a spin wheel, and so on, are considered fortunate for you.

Illustration: Suppose you have two cards in your hand: a 4-spot and a 2-spot. Since 4 plus 2 equals 6, such a hand, or any other combination that totals and reduces to 6, would be fortunate for you. If you have a combination that totals 51, it would reduce to 6, and so on. Use the same method with other combinations and totals.

To Find Your Best Days for Speculation

Any day of the month that totals 6 is considered fortunate for you. Thus, the 15th and 24th are fortunate because these dates reduce to the single digit 6. Therefore, the days of the month that are best for speculation for you are the 6th, 15th, and 24th. However, you should engage in speculation only in your proper periods as explained below.

Proper Hours for Speculation

The proper hour for speculation is when your ruling planet is governing. Refer to your daily paper, almanac, or calendar to find the time of sunrise, then count the hours after sunrise. These hours are the same every week, month, and year. Only the time of sunrise changes.

Hours for speculation: Sunday: 2nd, 9th, 16th, 23rd hour after sunrise. Monday: 6th, 13th, 20th hour after sunrise. Tuesday: 3rd, 8th, 15th, 24th hour after sunrise. Wednesday: 7th, 14th, 21st hour after sunrise. Thursday: 4th, 11th, 18th hour after sunrise. Friday: 1st, 8th, 15th, 22nd hour after sunrise. Saturday: 5th, 12th, 19th hour after sunrise.

LUCKY DAYS — SCORPIO

For All Those Born Between October 23 and November 22

If you were born on October 24, 25, 26, 27, 28, 29, 30, and 31 and November 1 and 2. You may speculate during the following periods and may expect to win:

February	20	to	29
June	22	to	July 2
August	24	to	September 3
December	21	to	31

From October 23 to November 3, you will also be tempted to speculate, but you must determine for yourself whether you can win. Do not speculate from January 20 to 31, April 21 to May 2, and July 23 to August 4.

If you were born on November 3, 4, 5, 6, 7, 8, 9, 10, 11,

and 12. You may speculate during the following periods and may expect to win:

January	1	to	11
March	1	to	10
July	2	to	13
September	3	to	14

From November 1 to 13, you will also be tempted to speculate, but you must determine for yourself whether you can win. Do not speculate from February 1 to 12, May 1 to 12, and August 2 to 15.

If you were born on November 13, 14, 15, 16, 17, 18, 19, 20, 21, and 22. You may speculate during the following periods and may expect to win:

January	11	to	20
March	10	to	20
July	12	to	23
September	13	to	23

From November 10 to 23, you will also be tempted to speculate, but you must determine for yourself whether you can win. Do not speculate from February 8 to 20, May 11 to 21, and August 13 to 23.

All Scorpio-born are inclined to take chances from February 20 to March 20. When you speculate in co-operation with others, it would be advisable that your partner is born under one of the following signs:

Capricorn—December 23 to January 20
Pisces—February 20 to March 20
Taurus—April 21 to May 21
Cancer—June 22 to July 23
Virgo—August 24 to September 23
Scorpio—October 24 to November 22

Miscellaneous Things to Observe

Those born between October 24 and October 30 will have better chances in speculation during the new moon.
Those born between October 31 and November 8 will

have better chances in speculation during the second quarter of the moon.

Those born between November 9 and November 16 will have better chances in speculation during the full moon.

Those born between November 17 and November 22 will have better chances in speculation during the fourth quarter of the moon.

Nearly all calendars give the four quarters of the moon.

Numerology

According to the science of numerology, the celestial number of Scorpio is 5. Pluto, the ruling planet of this sign, has the numerical value of 3. Combining these two numbers we have: 5 plus 3 equals 8. Number 8 is the key number for all persons born in Scorpio. Bear this in mind on all occasions. When you buy a ticket of any sort, make sure that the serial number has 8 as the predominating number. Room number 8 in a hotel, a street number containing an 8 or several 8's, horse number 8 in a race, player number 8 in a sport game, cards that total 8 in a card game, an 8 rolled with dice, 8 on a spin wheel, and so on, are considered fortunate for you.

Illustration: Suppose you have two cards in your hand: a 4-spot and another 4-spot. Since 4 plus 4 equals 8, such a hand or any other combination of cards that would total 8 would be fortunate for you. If you have a combination that totals 26 or 53, that would also reduce to 8. Use the same methods with other combinations and totals.

To Find Your Best Days for Speculation

Any day of any month that totals 8 is considered fortunate for you. Thus, the 17th and 26th are fortunate because these days reduce to the single digit 8. Therefore, the best days for speculation for you are: the 8th, 17th, and 26th. However, you should engage in speculation only in your proper periods as explained below.

564

Proper Hours for Speculation

The proper hour for speculation is when your ruling planet is governing. Refer to your daily paper, almanac, or calendar to find the time of sunrise; then count the hours after sunrise. These hours are the same every week, month, and year. Only the time of sunrise changes.

Hours for speculation: Sunday: 7th, 14th, 21st hour after sunrise. Monday: 4th, 11th, 18th hour after sunrise. Tuesday: 1st, 8th, 11th, 22nd hour after sunrise. Wednesday: 5th, 12th, 19th hour after sunrise. Thursday: 2nd, 9th, 16th, 23rd hour after sunrise. Friday: 6th, 13th, 20th hour after sunrise. Saturday: 3rd, 10th, 17th, 24th hour after sunrise.

LUCKY DAYS — SAGITTARIUS

For All Those Born Between November 23 and December 22

If you were born on November 23, 24, 25, 26, 27, 28, 29, and 30 and December 1 and 2. You may speculate during the following periods and may expect to win:

January	21	to	30
March	21	to	31
July	23	to	August 3
September	23	to	October 4

From November 22 to December 3, you will also be tempted to speculate, but you must determine for yourself whether or not you can win. Do not speculate from February 19 to 29, May 21 to June 3, and August 22 to December 4.

If you were born on December 3, 4, 5, 6, 7, 8, 9, 10, 11, and 12. You may speculate during the following periods and may expect to win:

January	31	to	February 9
April	1	to	11

August	12	to	23
October	3	to	14

From December 1 to 14, you will also be tempted to speculate, but you must determine for yourself whether or not you can win. Do not speculate from March 1 to 13, June 1 to 12, and September 2 to 14.

If you were born on December 13, 14, 15, 16, 17, 18, 19, 20, 21, and 22. You may speculate during the following periods and may expect to win:

February	9	to	20
April	10	to	20
August	13	to	23
October	12	to	23

From December 10 to 22, you will also be tempted to speculate, but you must determine for yourself whether or not you can win. Do not speculate from March 10 to 21, June 11 to 21, and September 12 to 23.

All Sagittarius-born are inclined to take chances between March 21 and April 20. When you speculate in cooperation with others, it would be advisable to have a partner born under one of the following signs:

Aquarius—January 21 to February 19
Aries—March 21 to April 20
Gemini—May 22 to June 21
Leo—July 24 to August 23
Libra—September 24 to October 23
Sagittarius—November 23 to December 22

Miscellaneous Things to Observe

Those born between November 23 and November 29 will have better chances in speculation during the new moon.

Those born between November 30 and December 7 will have better chances in speculation during the second quarter of the moon.

Those born between December 8 and December 16 will have better chances in speculation during the full moon.

Those born between December 17 and December 22 will have better chances in speculation during the fourth quarter of the moon.

Nearly all calendars give the four quarters of the moon.

Numerology

According to the science of numerology, the celestial number of Sagittarius is 8. Jupiter, the ruling planet of this sign, has the numerical value of 9. Combining these two numbers we have 8 plus 9 equals 17. Now this must be reduced to a single digit. Thus, 1 plus 7 equals 8. The key number for all persons born in Sagittarius is 8, the same as for Scorpio. Since there are only 9 digits, and there are 12 signs, some Zodiacal signs have duplicate numbers. Bear in mind at all times that 8 is your celestial number. When you buy a ticket of any sort, make sure that the serial number has a predominance of 8 in it. Room number 8 in a hotel, player number 8 in a sport game, horse number 8 in a race, a street number with an 8 or several 8's, cards that total 8 in a card game, an 8 rolled with dice, 8 on a spin wheel, and so on, are considered fortunate for you.

Illustration: Suppose you have two cards in your hand: a 6-spot and a 2-spot. Since 6 plus 2 equals 8, such a hand or any combination of cards that would total 8, would be fortunate for you. If you have a combination that totals 35 or 53, that would also reduce to 8. Use this same method for other combinations.

To Find Your Best Days for Speculation

Any day of any month that totals 8 is considered fortunate for you. Thus the 17th and the 26th are fortunate because these dates reduce to a single digit 8. Therefore, the best days for speculation for you are the 8th, 17th, and 26th. However, you should speculate only in your proper periods as explained below.

Proper Hours for Speculation

The proper hour for speculation is when your ruling

planet is governing. Refer to your daily paper, almanac, or calendar to find the time of sunrise, then count the hours after sunrise. These hours are the same every week, month, and year. Only the time of sunrise changes.

Hours for speculation: Sunday: 6th, 13th, 20th hour after sunrise. Monday: 3rd, 10th, 17th, 24th hour after sunrise. Tuesday: 7th, 14th, 21st hour after sunrise. Wednesday: 4th, 11th, 18th hour after sunrise. Thursday: 1st, 8th, 15th, 22nd hour after sunrise. Friday: 5th, 12th, 19th hour after sunrise. Saturday: 2nd, 9th, 16th, 23rd hour after sunrise.

LUCKY DAYS — CAPRICORN

For All Those Born Between December 23 and January 20

If you were born on December 22, 23, 24, 25, 26, 27, 28, 29, 30, and 31. You may speculate during the following periods and may expect to win:

February	20	to	29
April	21	to	May 2
August	23	to	September 3
October	22	to	November 2

From December 20 to 31, you will also be tempted to speculate, but you must determine for yourself whether you can win. Do not speculate from March 21 to 31, June 22 to July 3, and September 24 to October 4.

If you were born on January 1st, 2nd, 3rd, 4th, 5th, 6th, 7th, 8th, 9th, and 10th. You may speculate during the following periods and may expect to win:

March	1	to	10
May	2	to	12
September	4	to	14
November	2	to	12

From January 1 to 12 you will also be tempted to speculate, but you must determine for yourself whether or not you can win. Do not speculate from April 1 to 11, July 2 to 13, and October 3 to 14.

If you were born on January 11, 12, 13, 14, 15, 16, 17, 18, 19, and 20. You may speculate during the following periods and may expect to win:

March	10 to	20
May	11 to	21
September	13 to	24
November	13 to	22

From January 9 to 21, you will also be tempted to speculate, but you must determine for yourself whether or not you can win. Do not speculate from April 10 to 20, July 13 to 23, and October 12 to 23.

All Capricorn-born are inclined to take chances between April 21 to May 21. When you speculate in cooperation with others, it would be advisable to have a partner born under one of the following signs:

Capricorn—December 23 to January 20
Pisces—February 20 to March 20
Taurus—April 21 to May 21
Cancer—June 22 to July 23
Virgo—August 24 to September 23
Scorpio—October 24 to November 22

Miscellaneous Things to Observe

Those born between December 23 and December 30 will have better chances in speculation during the new moon.

Those born between December 31 and January 6 will have better chances in speculation during the second quarter of the moon.

Those born between January 7 and January 14 will have better chances in speculation during the full moon.

Those born between January 15 and January 20 will have better chances in speculation during the fourth quarter of the moon.

Nearly all calendars give the four quarters of the moon.

Numerology

According to the science of numerology, the celestial number of Capricorn is 8. Saturn, the ruling planet of this sign, has the numerical value of 3. Combining those numbers we have 8 plus 3, which equals 11. This must be reduced to a single digit. Thus, 1 plus 1 equals 2. The key number for all persons born in Capricorn is 2, the same as for those born in Cancer. There are only nine digits, but there are twelve signs, therefore some signs have duplicate numbers. Bear in mind at all times that 2 is your celestial number. When you buy a ticket of any sort, see that the serial number has 2 predominating, room number 2 in a hotel, player number 2 in a sport game, horse number 2 in a race, a street number with 2 or several 2's in it, cards that total 2 in a card game, a 2 rolled with dice, 2 on a spin wheel, and so on, are considered fortunate for you.

Illustration: Suppose you have two cards in your hand: a 10-spot and an ace. Now 10 plus 1 equals 11 and that reduced to a single digit equals 2, therefore, such a hand would be fortunate for you, or any other combination of cards that total 2. If you have a combination that totals 20, that would also reduce to 2. Use this same method for other combinations.

To Find Your Best Days for Speculation

Any day of any month that totals 2 is considered fortunate for you. Thus, the 11th, 29th, and so on, because these reduce to the single digit 2. Therefore, the best days for speculation for you are the 2nd, 11th, and 29th. However, you should speculate only in your proper periods as explained below.

Proper Hours for Speculation

The proper hour for speculation is when your ruling planet is governing. Refer to your daily paper, almanac, or calendar to find the time of sunrise, then count the hours after sunrise. These hours are the same every week, month, and year. Only the time of sunrise changes.

Hours for speculation: Sunday: 5th, 12th, 19th hour after sunrise. Monday: 2nd, 9th, 23rd hour after sunrise. Tuesday: 6th, 13th, 20th hour after sunrise. Wednesday: 3rd, 8th, 15th, 24th hour after sunrise. Thursday: 7th, 14th, 21st hour after sunrise. Friday: 4th, 11th, 18th hour after sunrise. Saturday: 1st, 10th, 17th, 22nd hour after sunrise.

LUCKY DAYS — AQUARIUS

For All Those Born Between January 21 and February 19

If you were born on January 21, 22, 23, 24, 25, 26, 27, 28, 29, and 30. You may speculate during the following periods and may expect to win:

March	21	to	31
May	22	to	June 2

From January 20 to 31, you will also be tempted to speculate, yet must determine for yourself whether or not you can win. Do not speculate from April 21 to May 2, July 23 to August 3, and October 24 to November 3.

If you were born on January 31 and February 1, 2, 3, 4, 5, 6, 7, 8, and 9. You may speculate during the following periods and may expect to win:

April	1	to	12
June	1	to	11
October	3	to	13
December	3	to	13

From January 30 to February 10 you will also be tempted to speculate, yet you must determine for yourself whether or not you can win. Do not speculate from May 2 to 12, August 2 to 14, and November 1 to 12.

If you were born on February 10, 11, 12, 13, 14, 15, 16,

17, 18, and 19. You may speculate during the following periods and may expect to win:

April	11	to	20
June	11	to	21
October	13	to	23
December	11	to	22

From February 9 to 20 you will also be tempted to speculate, yet must determine for yourself whether or not you can win. Do not speculate from May 10 to 22, August 13 to 23, and November 11 to 22.

All Aquarius-born are inclined to take chances between May 22 and June 21. When you speculate in co-operation with others, it would be advisable that your partner is born under one of the following signs:

Aries—March 21 to April 20
Gemini—May 22 to June 21
Aquarius—January 21 to February 19
Leo—July 24 to August 23
Libra—September 24 to October 23
Sagittarius—November 23 to December 22

Miscellaneous Things to Observe

Those born between January 21 and January 28 will have better chances in speculation during the new moon.

Those born between January 29 and February 6 will have better chances in speculation during the second quarter of the moon.

Those born between February 7 and February 14 will have better chances in speculation during the full moon.

Those born between February 15 and February 19 will have better chances in speculation during the fourth quarter of the moon.

Nearly all calendars give the four quarters of the moon.

Numerology

According to the science of numerology, the celestial number of Aquarius is 8. Uranus, the ruling planet of this sign, has the numerical value of 4. Combining these two numbers we have, 8 plus 4, which equals 12. This must be reduced to a single digit. Thus, 1 plus 2 equals 3. The key number for all persons born in Aquarius is 3, the same as Virgo. There are only 9 digits, but there are 12 signs, therefore some signs must have duplicate numbers. Bear in mind at all times that 3 is your celestial number. When you buy a ticket of any sort make sure that the serial number has 3 or several 3's. Room number 3 in a hotel, a street number containing 3 or several 3's, horse number 3 in a race, player number 3 in a sport game, cards that total 3 in a card game, a 3 rolled with dice, 3 on a spin wheel, and so on, are considered fortunate for you.

Illustration: Suppose you have two cards in your hand: a 9-spot and a 3-spot. Since 9 plus 3 equals 12 and that reduced to a single digit equals 3, such a hand or any other combination of cards that would total 3, would be fortunate for you. If you have a combination that totals 48 or 66, that would total 12 and this reduced gives 3. Use the same method with other combinations and totals.

To Find Your Best Days for Speculation

Any day of any month that totals 3 is considered fortunate for you. Thus, the 12th, 21st, and 30th are fortunate because these reduce to the single digit 3. Therefore, the best days for speculation for you are the 3rd, 12th, 21st, and 30th. However, you should speculate only in your proper periods, as explained below.

Proper Hours for Speculation

The proper hour for speculation is when your ruling planet is governing. Refer to your daily paper, almanac, or calendar to find the time of sunrise, then count the hours after sunrise. These hours are the same every week, month, and year. Only the time of sunrise changes.

Hours for speculation: Sunday: 3rd, 10th, 17th, 24th

hour after sunrise. Monday: 7th, 14th, 21st hour after sunrise. Tuesday: 4th, 11th, 18th hour after sunrise. Wednesday: 5th, 12th, 19th hour after sunrise. Thursday: 2nd, 9th, 16th, 23rd hour after sunrise. Friday: 6th, 13th, 20th hour after sunrise. Saturday: 1st, 8th, 15th, 22nd hour after sunrise.

LUCKY DAYS — PISCES

For All Those Born Between February 20 and March 20

If you were born on February 20, 21, 22, 23, 24, 25, 26, 27, 28, and 29. You may speculate during the following periods and may expect to win:

April	21	to	May 2
June	22	to	July 3
October	23	to	November 2
December	22	to	31

From February 19 to 29 you will also be tempted to speculate, yet must determine for yourself whether or not you can win. Do not speculate from May 21 to June 2, August 23 to September 4, and November 21 to December 4.

If you were born on March 1, 2, 3, 4, 5, 6, 7, 8, 9, and 10. You may speculate during the following periods and may expect to win:

January	1	to	10
May	1	to	12
July	2	to	13
November	1	to	12

From March 1 to 12 you will also be tempted to speculate, yet must determine for yourself whether or not you can win. Do not speculate from June 1 to 13, September 2 to 13, and December 1 to 12.

If you were born on March 11, 12, 13, 14, 15, 16, 17,

18, 19, and 20. You may speculate during the following periods and may expect to win:

January	10 to 20
May	11 to 21
July	13 to 23
November	11 to 22

From March 9 to 21 you will also be tempted to speculate, yet must determine for yourself whether or not you can win. Do not speculate from June 10 to 22, September 12 to 23, and December 10 to 22.

All Pisces-born are inclined to take chances between June 22 and July 23. When you speculate in cooperation with others, it would be advisable to have a partner born under one of the following signs:

Capricorn—December 23 to January 20
Pisces—February 20 to March 20
Taurus—April 21 to May 21
Cancer—June 22 to July 23
Virgo—August 24 to September 23
Scorpio—October 24 to November 22

Miscellaneous Things to Observe

Those born between February 20 and February 26 will have better chances in speculation during the new moon.

Those born between February 27 and March 5 will have better chances in speculation during the second quarter of the moon.

Those born between March 6 and March 13 will have better chances in speculation during the full moon.

Those born between March 14 and March 20 will have better chances for speculation during the fourth quarter of the moon.

Nearly all calendars give the four quarters of the moon.

Numerology

According to the science of numerology, the celestial number of Pisces is 8. Neptune, the ruling planet of this sign, has the numerical value of 5. Combining these two numbers we have 8 plus 5 equals 13. This must be reduced to a single digit. Thus, 1 plus 3 equals 4. Number 4 is the key number for all persons born in Pisces, the same as for those born in Aries. There are only 9 digits. Since there are 12 signs, some signs will have duplicate numbers. Bear in mind that your key number is 4. When you buy a ticket of any sort, make sure that the serial number 4 is the predominating number. Room number 4 in a hotel, a street number containing 4 or several 4's, horse number 4 in a race, player number 4 in a sport game, cards that total 4 in a card game, a 4 rolled with dice, 4 on a spin wheel, and so on, are considered fortunate for you.

Illustration: Suppose you have two cards in your hand: a 9-spot and a 4-spot. Since 9 plus 4 equals 13, and this reduced equals 4, so this or any other combination that could be reduced to 4, would be a fortunate hand for you. Use the same method with other combinations, such as 31 or 67, which reduce to 4.

To Find Your Best Days for Speculation

Any day of the month that totals 4 is considered fortunate for you. Thus, the 13th, 22nd, and 31st of a month would be fortunate for you, because these days reduce to a single digit, making 4. The days of the month that are best for speculation are the 4th, 13th, 22nd, and 31st. However, you should engage in speculation only in your proper periods as explained below.

Proper Hours for Speculation

The proper hour for speculation is when your ruling planet is governing. Refer to your daily paper, almanac, or calendar to find the time of sunrise, then count the hours after sunrise. These hours are the same every week, month, and year. Only the time of sunrise changes.

Hours for speculation: Sunday: 2nd, 9th, 16th, 23rd hour after sunrise. Monday: 5th, 12th, 19th hour after sunrise. Tuesday: 6th, 13th, 20th hour after sunrise. Wednesday: 3rd, 10th, 17th, 24th hour after sunrise. Thursday: 7th, 14th, 21st hour after sunrise. Friday: 1st, 8th, 15th, 22nd hour after sunrise. Saturday: 4th, 11th, 18th hour after sunrise.

FORTUNATE AND ADVERSE CYCLES

Jupiter, the largest planet in our solar system, plays an important part in human life. In size alone, Jupiter is three times as big as all the rest of the planets put together. It takes twelve years for this planet to go through the twelve signs of the Zodiac and during this period it influences all human beings. Just as its power is great enough to change the course of comets, so it changes the destiny of empires and men. Its cycle means that every twelve years, this planet is at the same place in the Heavens as at your birth, marking the beginning of a new cycle for you. This law holds true for every man and woman. Thus, it is possible to calculate, for each one of us, the fortunate years as well as those years when we are wasteful, extravagant, and careless, and face losses. The following interpretation of the Jupiter cycle is the same for all of us, but this does not mean that it is general; this planet takes one year to go through one sign and therefore it is easy to calculate its exact position for every year of your life.

King Solomon said: "To everything there is a season, and a time for every purpose under the Heaven." This means that human life should be planned in accordance with the planetary influences operating at one's birth and those influencing each of us now. But everyone is given the freedom to work in harmony with those great natural Laws or to act contrary to them. It is up to us to plan our lives in such a way that we expand under favorable influences and to hold back when the planets are at critical angles. Those that do not understand those laws go blindly ahead and blame destiny for their ill-luck. All of us, regardless of when born, have periods when we are fortunate and success smiles upon us, but from time to time, we are under a cycle when our affairs go wrong and opportunities are few. Luckily, those cycles come at regular intervals and it is possible to indicate exactly the cycle you are under at a certain age of your life.

Regardless of other planetary influences operating in your life, the following cycles are fortunate for you and it is up to you to make use of them.

Fortunate cycles: At the ages of 16, 20, 22, 26, 28, 32, 34, 38, 40, 44, 46, 50, 56, 58, 62, 64, 68, 70, 74, 76, and 80. Of course, you may have some difficulties those years but some good fortune will come your way, somebody will help you, an opportunity will present itself, and chances for making money are good. To those out of work, it means that they will be able to find employment, even if it is not what they would like to have. Changes made will prove profitable and business will increase. It marks a fortunate time for expanding in business, to take long journeys, for legal affairs or to establish yourself securely. It is a time when things come our way, when we receive many gifts, when we win at games of chance or when the opposite sex favors us. Your fortunate cycles last about nine months and start about four months before your birth month to four months afterwards. For many of us, those are the years of prosperity.

Next to consider are the adverse cycles, also called cycles of restrictions. They mark periods in your life when you will not feel well, when your blood will be impure, and when you will be careless and extravagant. It is an adverse time to speculate or gamble and those in business should not expand and should beware of wild schemes that will end in lawsuits. Others will refuse to cooperate, and some of us may even lose our jobs. Do not take foolish chances. Thus, you will protect yourself against illusion and disappointments.

Cycles of restriction also operate for nine months. You will feel them about four months before your birth month and the fourth month afterwards.

Adverse cycles: At the ages of 15, 18, 21, 27, 30, 33,

39, 42, 45, 51, 54, 57, 63, 66, 69, 75, 78, 81. A new cycle starts about every twelve years of your life and marks a complete change in your affairs. No doubt you know that the world conditions are influenced by the sun spots, whose cycle is about eleven and a half years, similar to your own cycle. Without consulting the planets on the day and year you were born, it is not possible to tell you whether you will have success or misfortune when such a cycle begins. Perhaps if you go back in your life and go over the events that took place at the age of 12 and 24, you can tell if the beginning of a new cycle is good or bad for you. New cycles start for everybody at the ages of 12, 24, 36, 48, 60, 72, 84, 96.

History records many amazing predictions about the destiny of nations, rulers, and individuals, all based on cycles—this was the secret of the Egyptians and all past civilizations. It is up to every one of us to make use of those cycles in our affairs. Before anyone makes a plan for the future, he should see if he is under a fortunate cycle or an adverse cycle. If it is a fortunate cycle, then he can go ahead with his plans, expand, take chances, and make radical changes in his affairs. If the cycle is adverse, it means that he must wait for at least one more year before launching new ventures or making any radical changes.

There are, of course, other cycles yet we cannot go into them any further until you have learned to apply what you just have read. It would be very interesting for you to look back into your past and see how many fortunate happenings you can trace to the fortunate cycles and how many losses or sorrows you can show for the adverse cycles. Thus, you will learn one of the fundamental laws of life.

It is hoped that with this information, you will be more successful and find greater happiness, also protected and warned against pitfalls and losses. Nothing can be more valuable than to know whether you are lucky now or whether you must be on your guard. Realize how many times fate has been kind to you and you did not take the opportunity. When your affairs are going smoothly and success is yours and you know that it is part of a fortunate cycle, you can time its end and thus not expect your luck to last longer than it really will. You may be successful now but in a few months you may come under a critical cycle. Prepare yourself for it and do not live or act as if your good fortune will keep on going on for many more months. Establish yourself and enjoy the good things that come your way. But if fate is unkind to you, when every hope is gone, you will want to know just when luck, success, and happiness will be yours again. Consult these pages and see when your next favorable cycles will come and prepare yourself for your ship to come in. Perhaps it would be well for you to ponder the words of Dryden:

The lucky have whole days, and those they choose.
The unlucky have but hours, and those they lose.

PUBLISHERS CLEARING HOUSE has a wide variety of unbeatable magazine values available by subscription. Among the titles are TV GUIDE, U.S. NEWS, LADIES HOME JOURNAL, PREVENTION and many more. To order please write to:

PUBLISHERS CLEARING HOUSE
101 WINNERS CIRCLE • PORT WASHINGTON, NEW YORK 11050